L
D
M

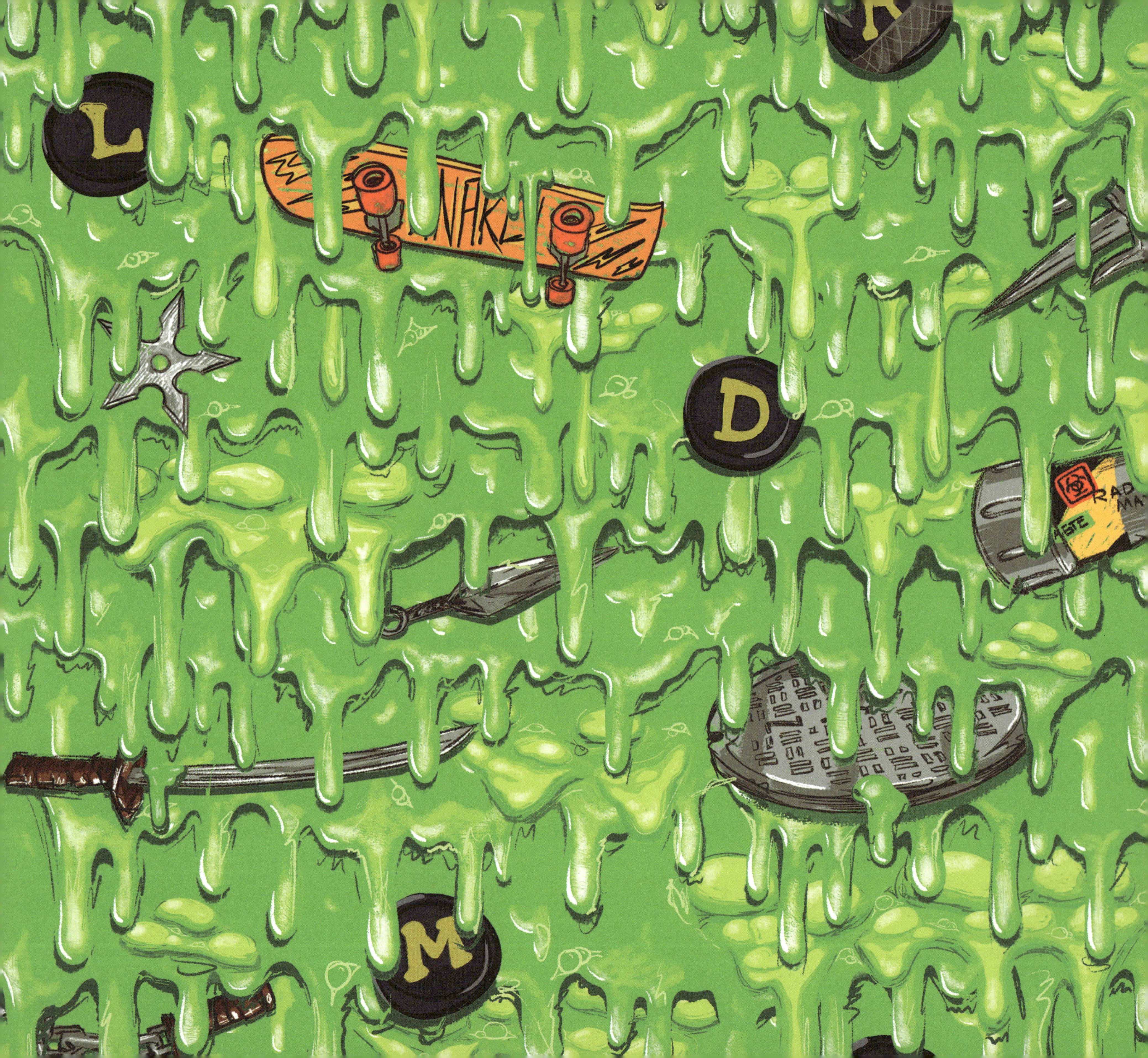
L
D
M

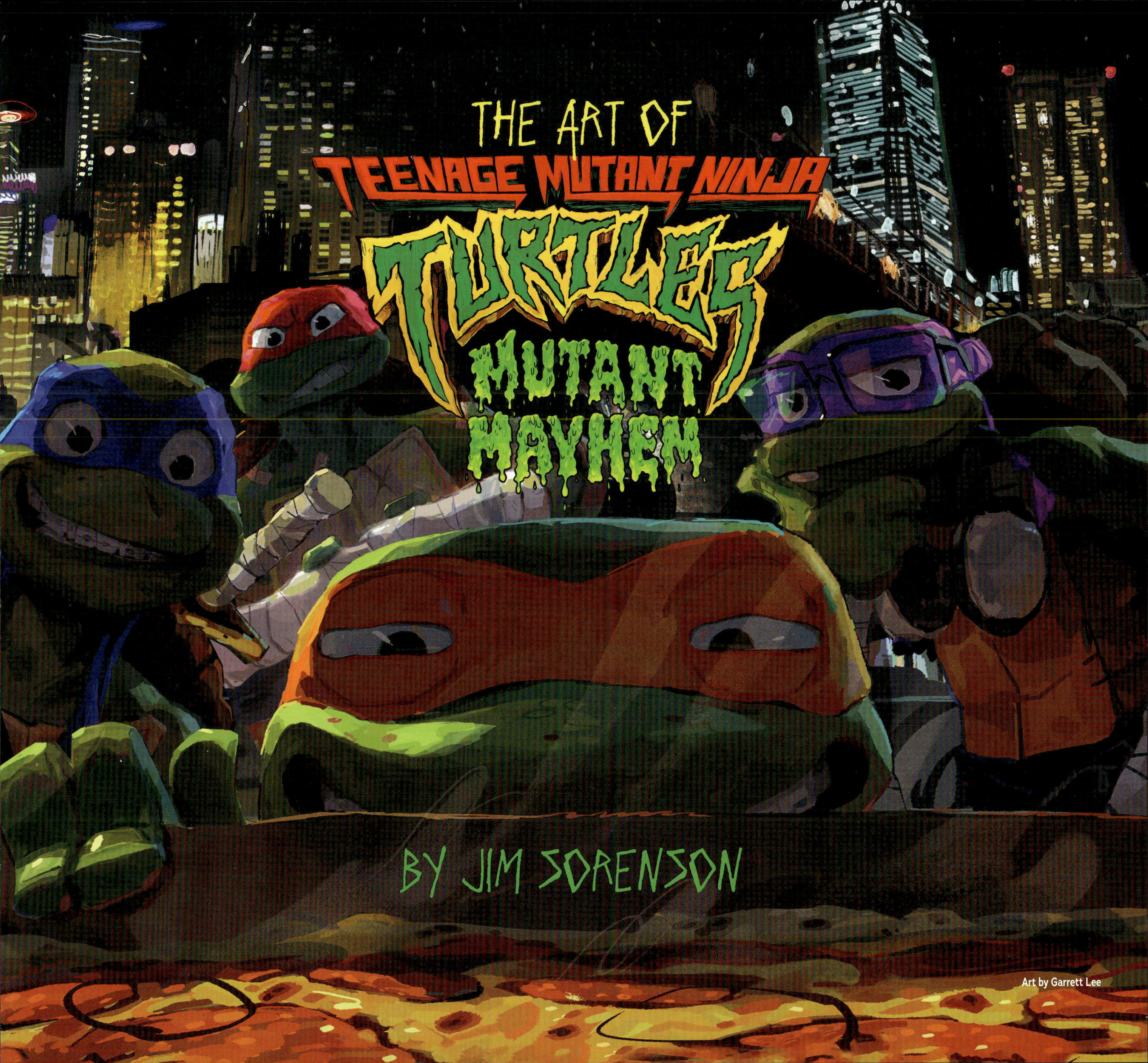

Art by Garrett Lee

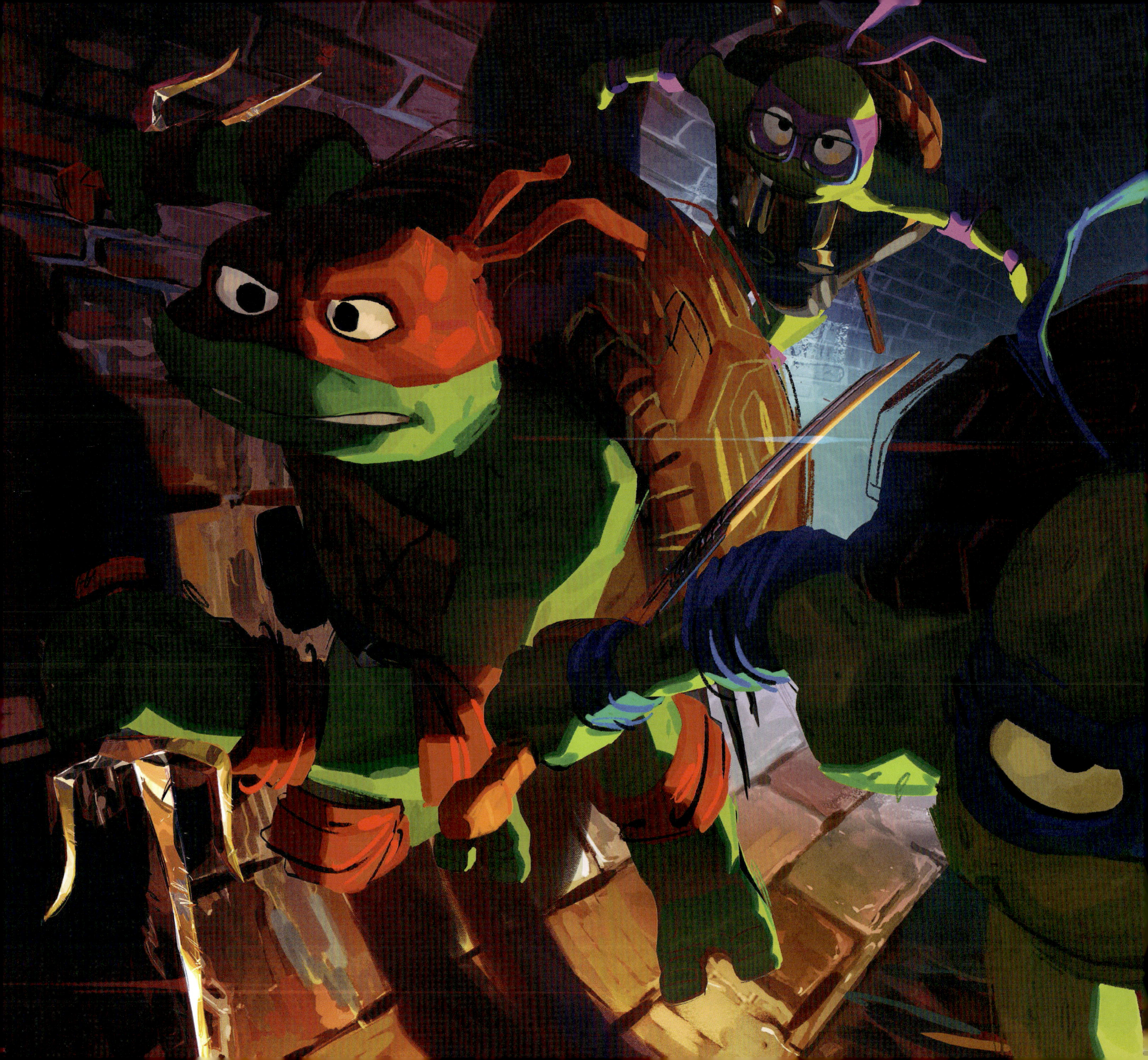

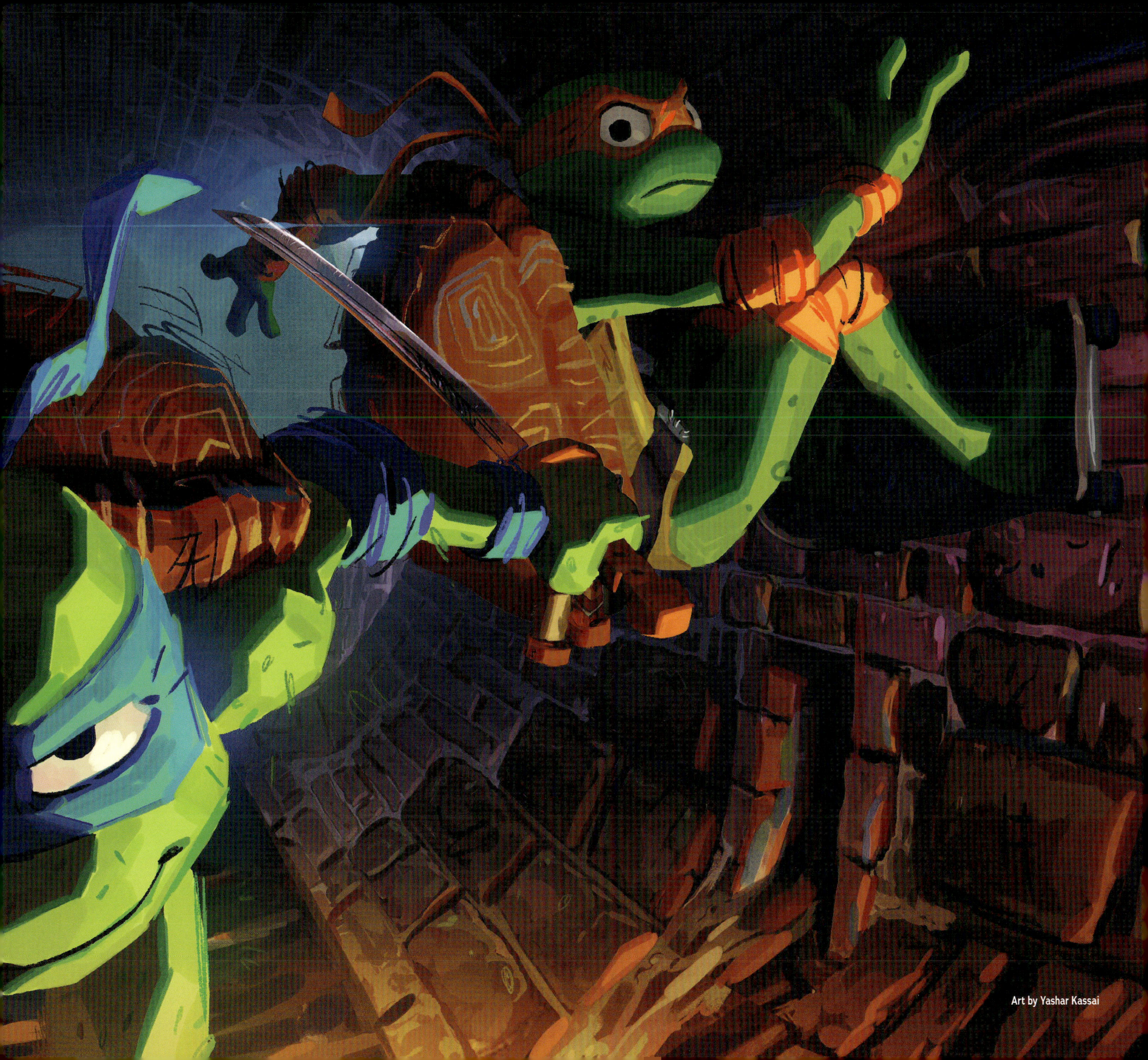

Art by Yashar Kassai

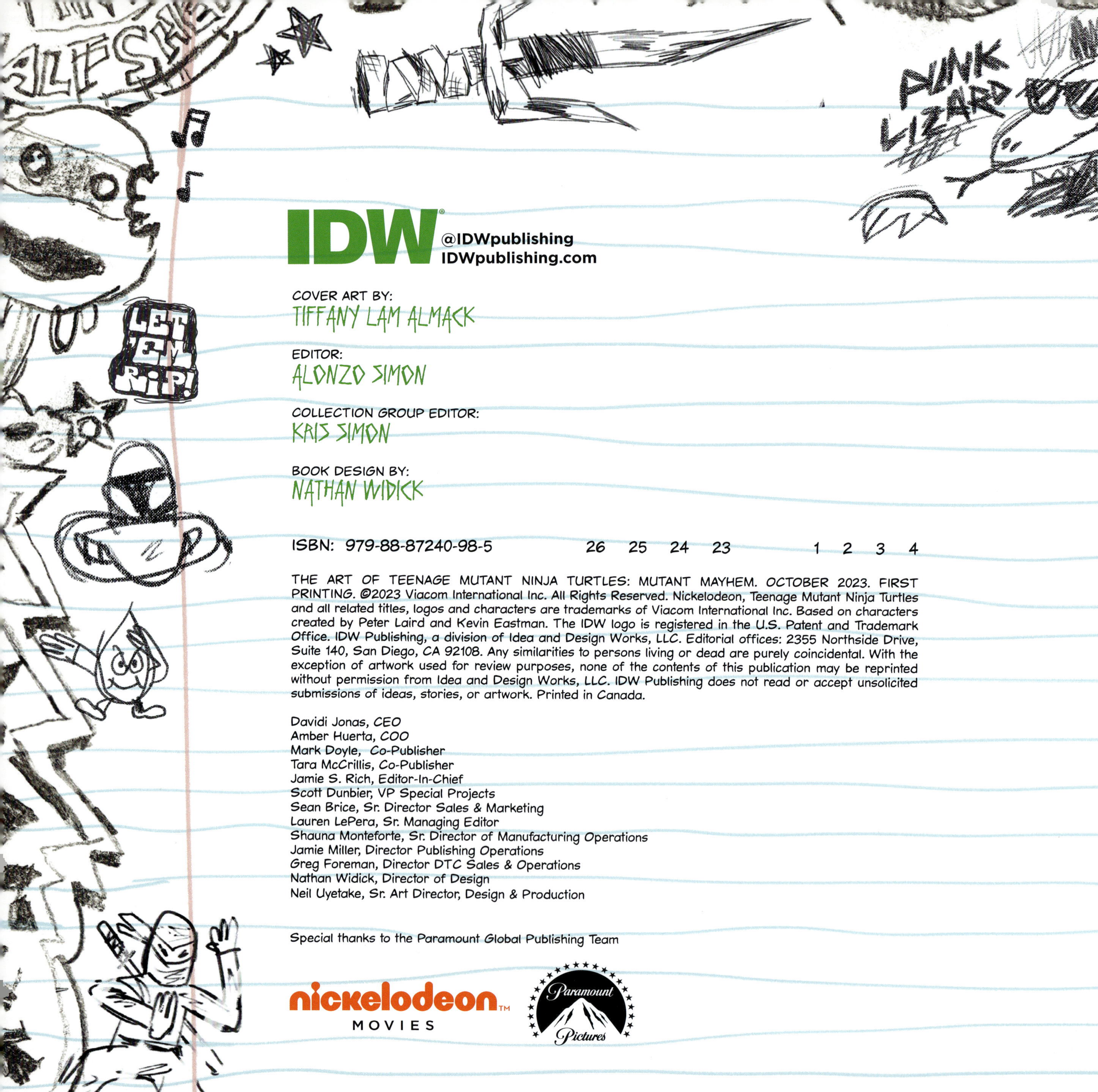

IDW @IDWpublishing
IDWpublishing.com

COVER ART BY:
TIFFANY LAM ALMACK

EDITOR:
ALONZO SIMON

COLLECTION GROUP EDITOR:
KRIS SIMON

BOOK DESIGN BY:
NATHAN WIDICK

ISBN: 979-88-87240-98-5 26 25 24 23 1 2 3 4

THE ART OF TEENAGE MUTANT NINJA TURTLES: MUTANT MAYHEM. OCTOBER 2023. FIRST PRINTING.

Special thanks to the Paramount Global Publishing Team

nickelodeon MOVIES

Paramount Pictures

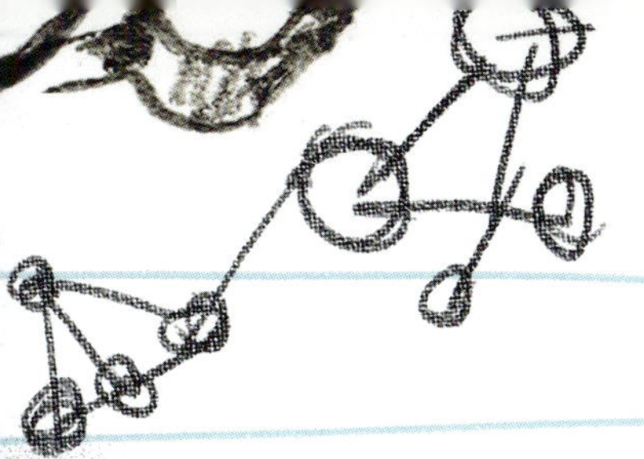

TABLE OF CONTENTS

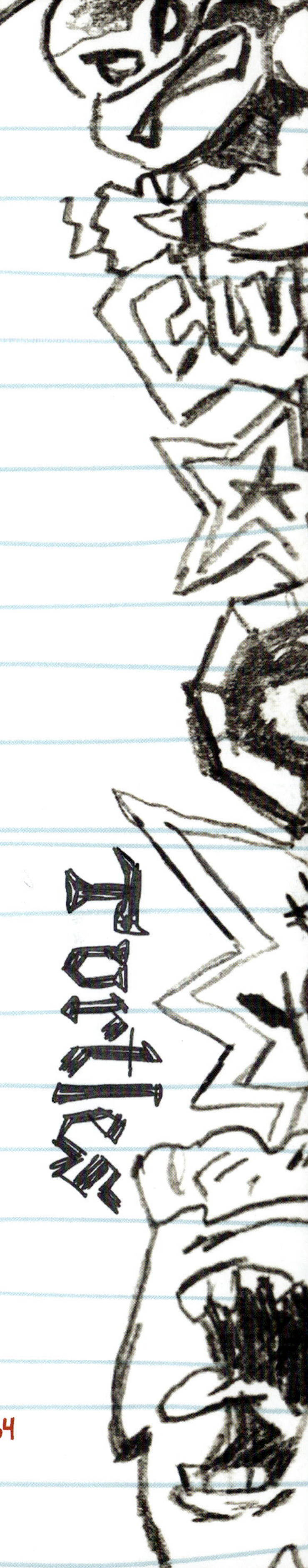

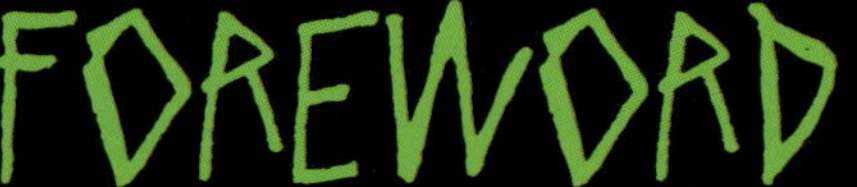

FOREWORD

It's an age-old story: the hero's journey. The known and unknown. Trials and tribulations. Risk, reward, and redemption...All provoked by a deep cry from the soul: Who am I? What am I? Will I be accepted? Am I really...a turtle? Like, really? Okay, maybe it's not an age-old story.

Teenage Mutant Ninja Turtles is the story of four unlikely words, strung together nearly 40 years ago by creators Kevin Eastman and Peter Laird, to describe an unlikely band of four brothers brought together by fate, destiny, and OOoooooze.

From their very first Turtles drawing, which I believe was on a napkin, Kevin and Peter set out on a journey to bring their concept and characters to life. And they did it, to great effect, through what has turned out to be generations of comic books, TV shows, movies, video games, toys, books, and on and on and on...with fans around the globe and back again.

The story they came up with has become our story. Their Turtles are now our Turtles. And these Turtles, the ones depicted in *Mutant Mayhem* were nurtured, raised, and let loose by Master Storytellers Jeff Rowe, Seth Rogen, Evan Goldberg, James Weaver, and their team. They expanded the characters' original mythology, hewing closely to what made them so loved to begin with, while bringing them into the modern world with a heartfelt, teenage coming-of-age story. It's a super fun mash-up of sci-fi, stylish realism, comedy, action/adventure, and truth.

Mutant Mayhem pushes the Turtles' origin story even further into new territory, while pushing the envelope visually to where the film's "comic book realism" segues into something magical, with a feeling we're watching something we know well and yet have never seen before. There is love, sweat, and tears embedded in the artists' fingerprints all over this film. It lives and breathes. It has something to say.

Describing this movie as an achievement isn't quite enough, because we made this film for the devoted fans, and that is an enormous point of pride and joy for Paramount Pictures, Nickelodeon Animation, Jeff, Seth, and everyone at Point Grey. We want to thank all of you who have been patiently waiting to get back together with your favorite Heroes in a Half-Shell, to let you know, in the spirit of the Turtles themselves, that we honor and accept you.

Ramsey Naito

Nickelodeon & Paramount Animation President

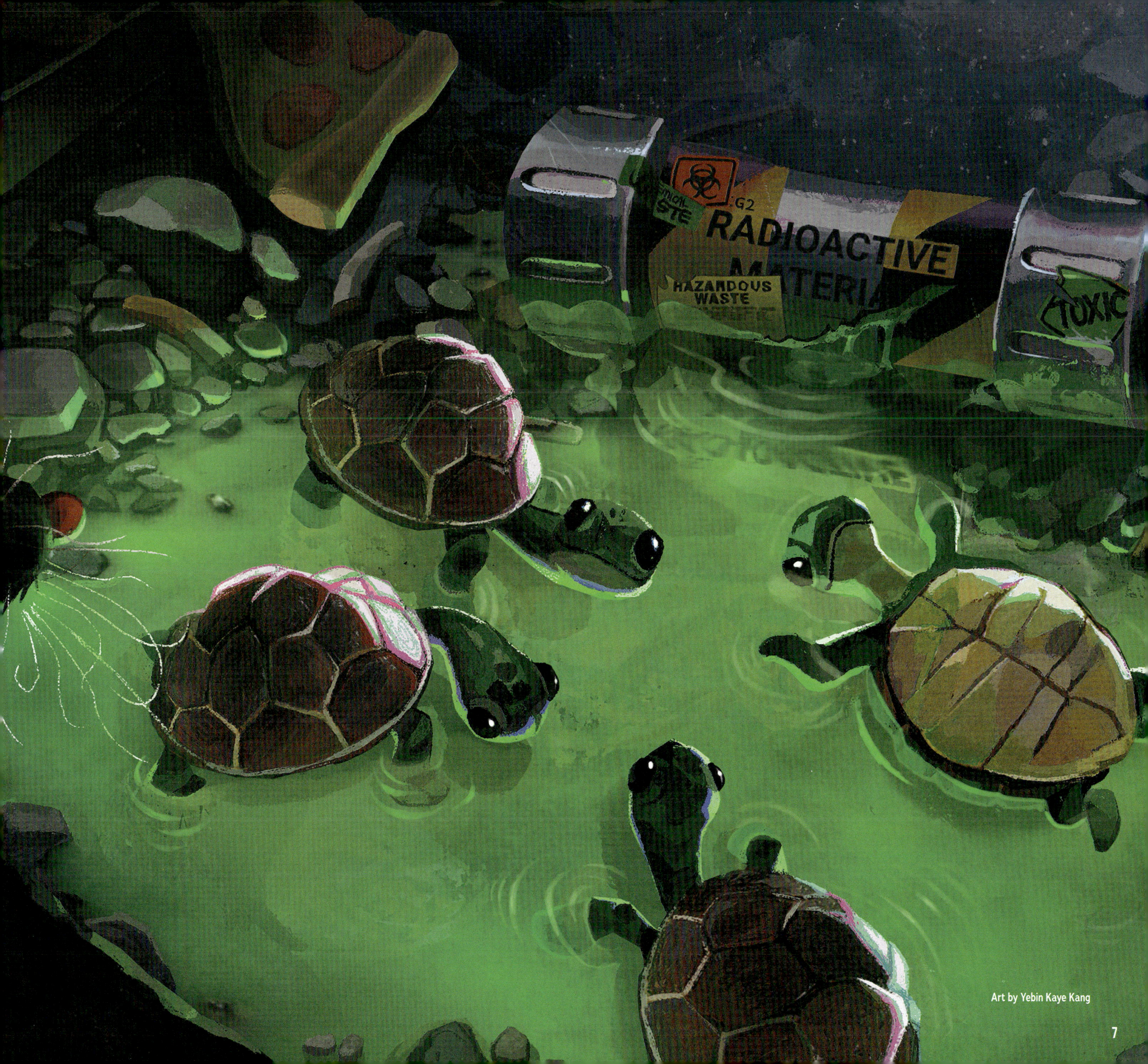

Art by Yebin Kaye Kang

INTRODUCTION

Oh man, you goofed up! You bought a book of beautiful pictures and you stopped to read the introduction. You fool! I'm kidding. Thank you for buying this book. Or pretending to read it in a Barnes & Noble so you can use the customers-only restroom.

I've done the same thing many times. I hope we can both outgrow our childhood trauma and one day learn how not to feel shame for going potty. But until that day, let's talk Teenage Mutant Ninja Turtles. Howsoever this book may've found its way into your hands, dear stranger, I'm grateful. These pages represent the tireless work of some of the greatest artistic minds that I've had the privilege of knowing. For two years they've toiled away generating these images. First during COVID-19, working from their apartments around the world. Then eventually from a dingy, poorly lit office in the Mae West building at Paramount Studios. At one point, we even put up Christmas lights. They somehow made things sadder. But despite the breakneck pace of production, abysmal office, and near constant story changes that required us to throw months of design work in the trash, they continued to pour their entire souls into every Wacom tablet stroke.

Time and time again. Without fail. As a director, my asks of them always boiled down to one simple thing: whatever you're supposed to do, do the opposite. If you've seen it before, throw it away. Break convention. Draw like a child. Can you make this uglier? "The only rule is there ARE NO RULES, MANNNN!" And boy, did they listen. They broke rules. They made mistakes. They pushed boundaries. They took their inspiration from influences as diverse as the street photography of Alex Webb, Japanese Bosozoku cars, the early '90s plastic molded Technodrome toy, and the films of Peter Greenaway. Their impeccable taste was channeled through art designed to look deliberately childlike. Never have I seen a team so technically proficient throw themselves outside their comfort zones so wantonly.

They were concert pianists. I asked them to hit electric guitar strings with sledgehammers. They ran with it, and in doing so, they made the strangest, most beautiful, most ugly, most visually wild 3D, CG-animated film I've ever seen. It's high art. It's low-brow. It's a moving painting. It's an '80s toy commercial fever dream. And hopefully in the middle of all that is something that really feels like being a teenager. If you like the way this movie looks, it's because of Yashar and Arthur and Tiffany and Woodrow and Kellan and Garrett and Jules and Tom and Chalky and Dustin and Alger and Paulette and Nikita and Sean and James and JJ and Kaye and Adel and Lauren and Dave and Jeffrey and Lily. And hundreds more people at Mikros Paris and Montreal and Cinesite Vancouver. They are the world's most fearsome fighting team. They are my heroes. My job began and ended the day I hired them.

Jeff Rowe
Director, *Teenage Mutant Ninja Turtles: Mutant Mayhem*

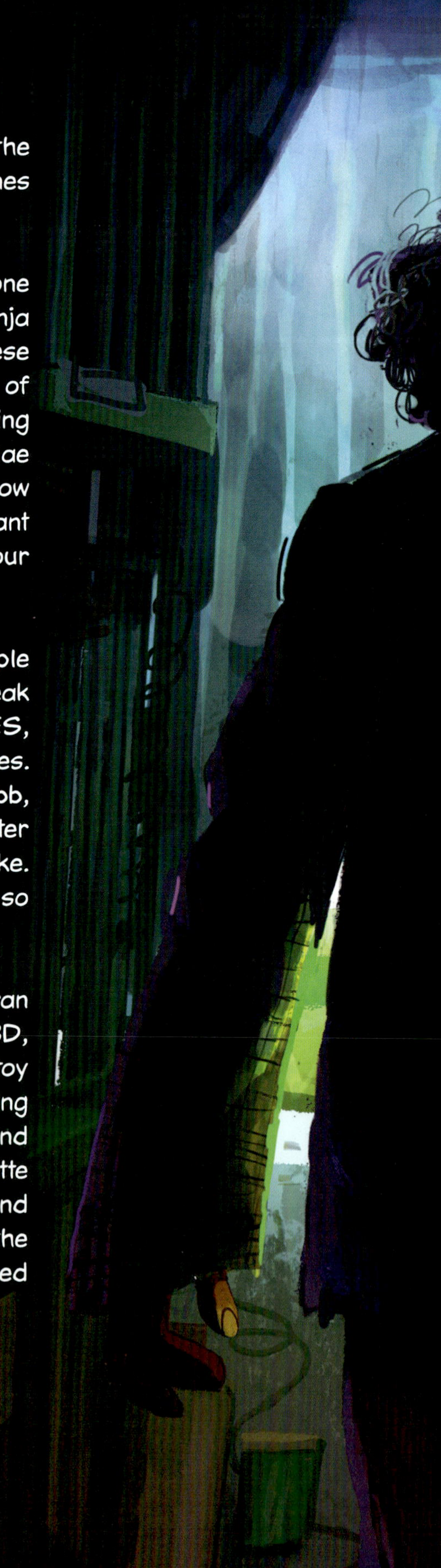

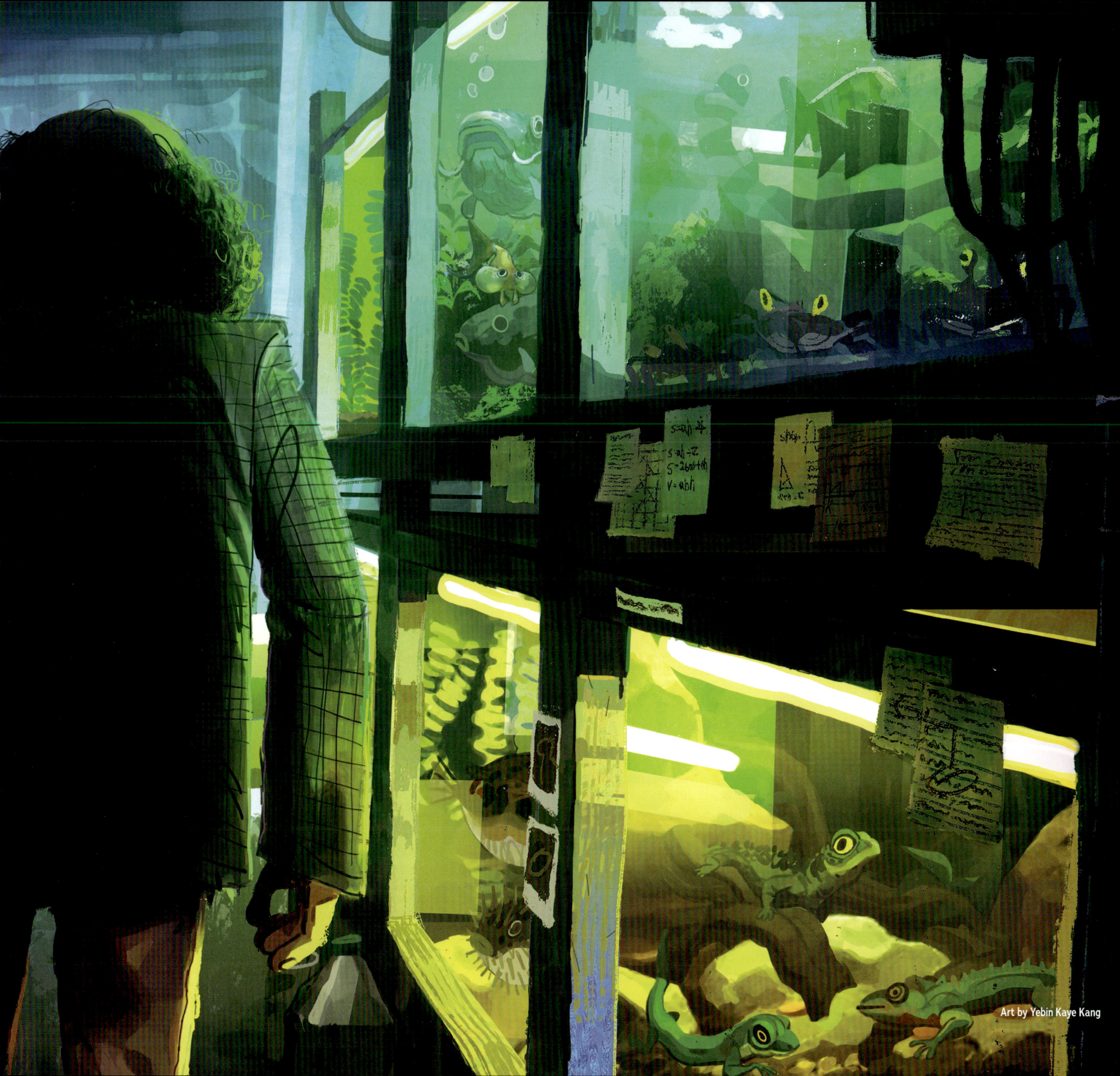

Art by Yebin Kaye Kang

A Brief History of the

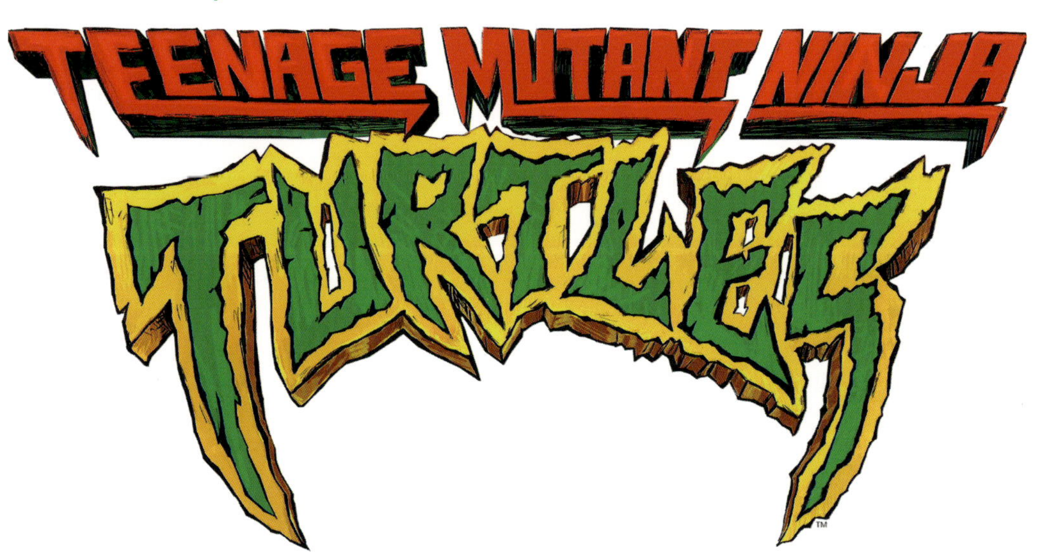

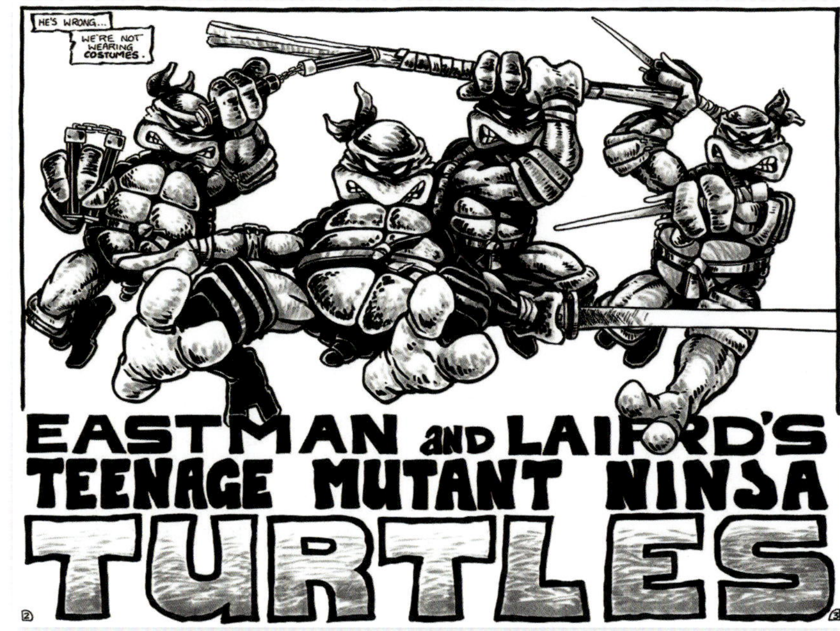

Teenage Mutant Ninja Turtles issue #1, pages 2–3. Art by Kevin Eastman & Peter Laird.

In 1984, Kevin Eastman and Peter Laird self-published a 40-page, oversized, black-and-white comic called *Teenage Mutant Ninja Turtles.* A pastiche of what was hot in the comics world of the early 1980s, it featured mutants, anthropomorphic animals, teenagers, and, of course, ninja. Frank Miller's *Daredevil* was an especially prominent influence, with elements such as the Hand Clan becoming the Foot, and Daredevil's mentor, Stick, becoming wise, old Splinter. With a limited print run of about 3,000, the comic was soon forgotten and Eastman and Laird moved on to other things.

Sike! We'd hardly be here today, reading—or, in my case, writing—the history of *Teenage Mutant Ninja Turtles* if it ended there. Against all odds, *Teenage Mutant Ninja Turtles* became a meteoric success, the hottest property in comics. Mirage Studios—so named because, in Eastman's words, "There wasn't an actual studio, only kitchen tables and couches with lapboards"—was a mirage no longer. After they spent two years kicking butt in the comics world, their agent, Mark Freedman, approached the then obscure company, Playmates Toys. Playmates was intrigued but wanted more recognition among their target audience, and that meant a cartoon. Syndication was taking off, and so Playmates funded a five-episode miniseries, produced in partnership with Fred Wolf Films. Written primarily by veteran animation writer David Wise and animated by the legendary Japanese studio Toei, the miniseries aired in December 1987. It was a bona fide hit. In one fell swoop, *Teenage Mutant Ninja Turtles* had jumped from comics to both television and toy shelves.

The original cartoon would go on to air for a total of ten seasons, from 1987 to 1996, and a whopping 193 episodes. Running in parallel was the hugely popular toy line, which released hundreds of different figures from 1988 through 1997, not to mention numerous play sets and vehicles. Scores of new characters were introduced, including the breakout favorites Bebop and Rocksteady, and many existing characters were reinterpreted. Notably, the Turtles were given different-colored masks to help differentiate them from one another—in the Mirage comics they all wore red—and April O'Neil became a redheaded reporter for Channel 6 News. In the original comic, she was Baxter Stockman's lab assistant.

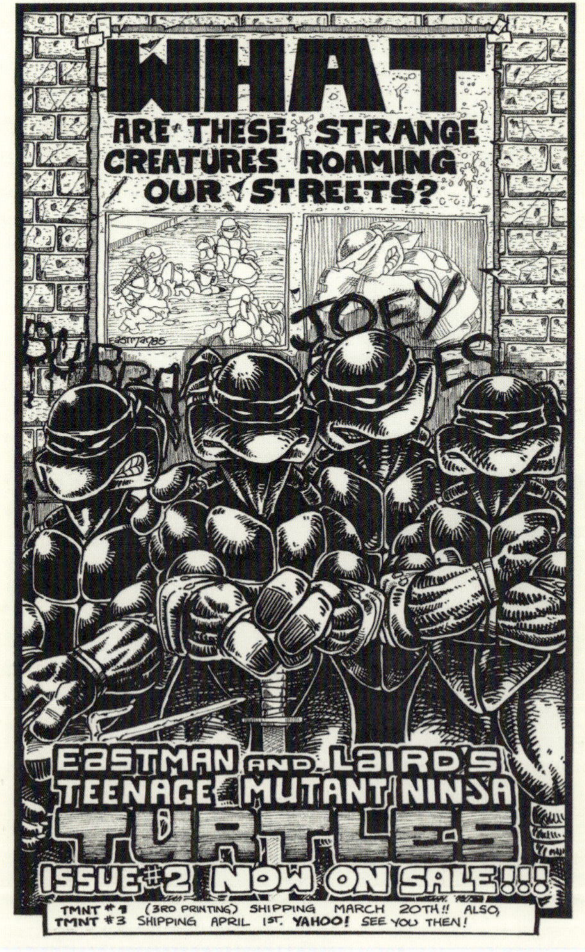

Ad for *TMNT* issue #2 by Kevin Eastman.

But the franchise wasn't done steamrolling everything in its path yet; there were new frontiers to conquer. And perhaps no arena is quite so fraught as the world of live-action cinema. The late '80s were a tough time to be shopping around a franchise like TMNT. Though king of the B-movies Roger Corman had expressed an interest in a more comedic take on the property, that wasn't what Laird and Eastman had in mind. For a time, it seemed that the world wasn't quite ready for a Turtles adventure on the silver screen. CG was barely a thing, and according to Eastman, "We just had horrific grimaces thinking of movies that had somebody in a rubber suit." It had been only a few years since the disappointing box office returns of comparable properties like *Howard the Duck* or *Masters of the Universe,* so no one in Hollywood wanted to invest heavily in the property, despite its popularity in other mediums.

Eventually, Hong Kong-based Golden Harvest agreed to finance, albeit on a shoestring. Fortunately for all involved, Jim Henson's Creature Shop developed the cutting-edge animatronics that brought the Turtles to life. It was one of the last projects Jim Henson himself ever had worked on. New Line Cinema agreed to distribute, at least partially because the President of Production, Sara Risher, had a five-year-old who loved the toys and the cartoon. The budget kept growing, ballooning from three million dollars to six to eight to, ultimately, 13 million dollars. The movie was shot mostly in North Carolina to save money, and the suits were incredibly uncomfortable in the heat and prone to malfunctions. But despite all the challenges, the film was a surprise hit, both financially and creatively. Kids loved the humor, and director Steve Barron managed to wring some true emotional stakes from the source material, especially the comic. The film managed to gross over 25 million dollars in its opening weekend in March 1990 and went on to rake in over 200 million dollars in its theatrical run. Truly, Turtles were a part of the cultural landscape.

And the party just doesn't stop! There would be two more live-action sequels released in the 1990s, *Teenage Mutant Ninja Turtles II: The Secret of the Ooze* in 1991 and *Teenage Mutant Ninja Turtles III* in 1993. There was also a live-action television show from Saban Entertainment that ran for one season in 1997–1998. *Ninja Turtles: The Next Mutation* was notable for introducing a fifth Turtle, Venus de Milo, the first female Turtle. Despite strong ratings, the show would be canceled amid budgetary and production concerns on the part of Saban.

Meanwhile, *Turtles* continued to be a force in comics, with a more youth-oriented book published by Archie Comics from 1988 to 1995 while Mirage Studios continued to produce issues all the way through 2014. IDW Publishing would release their own interpretation of the Turtles beginning in 2011, and indeed, they've produced the very book you're holding in your hands—or possibly reading on some kind of device. I don't judge. Naturally, TMNT also entered the realm of video games, with more game releases that I can comfortably count. Perhaps the most notable was the *Turtles in Time* stand-up arcade game from 1991, later ported over to the SNES and remade in 2009 for Xbox and Playstation 3.

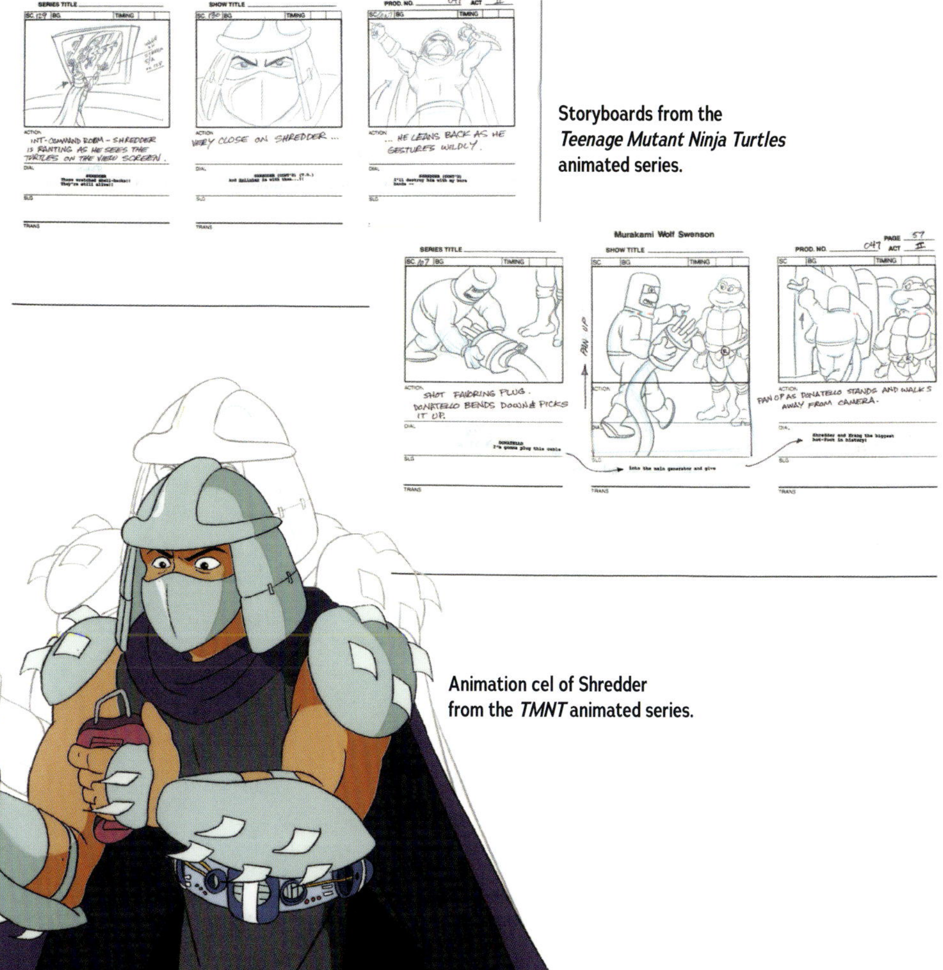

Storyboards from the *Teenage Mutant Ninja Turtles* animated series.

Animation cel of Shredder from the *TMNT* animated series.

Promotional photo for the live-action *Teenage Mutant Ninja Turtles* movie.

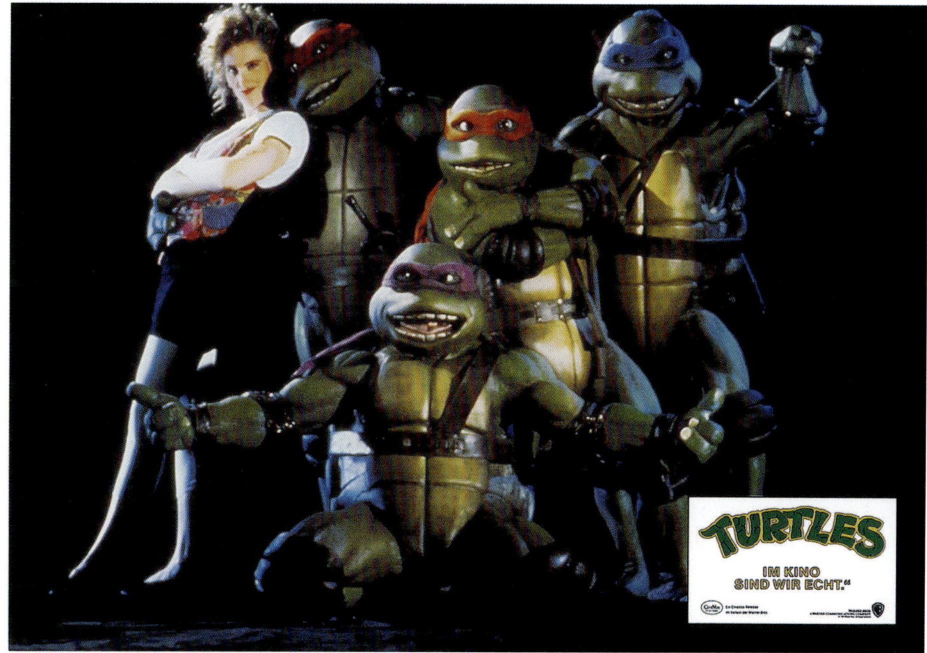

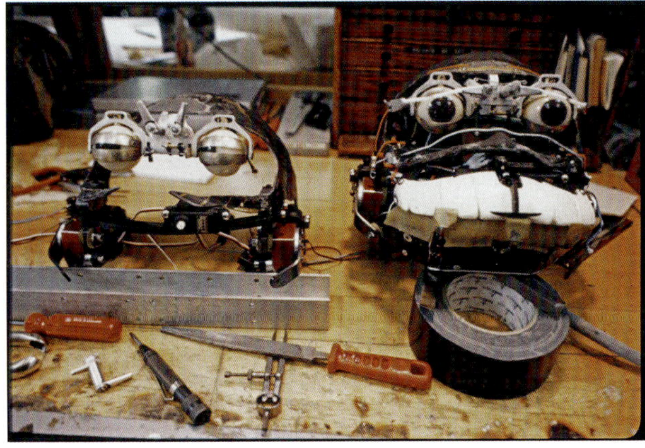

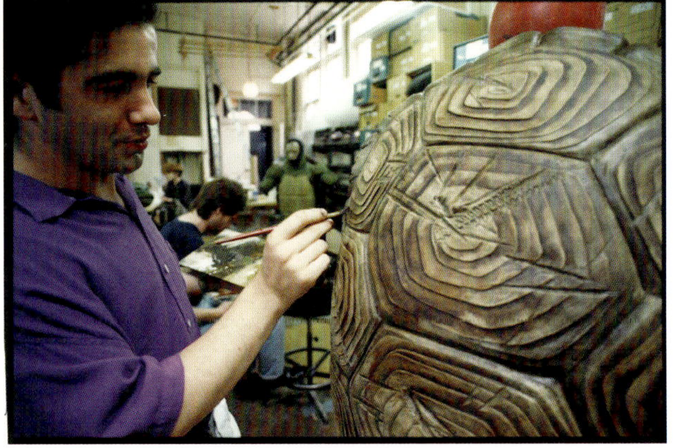

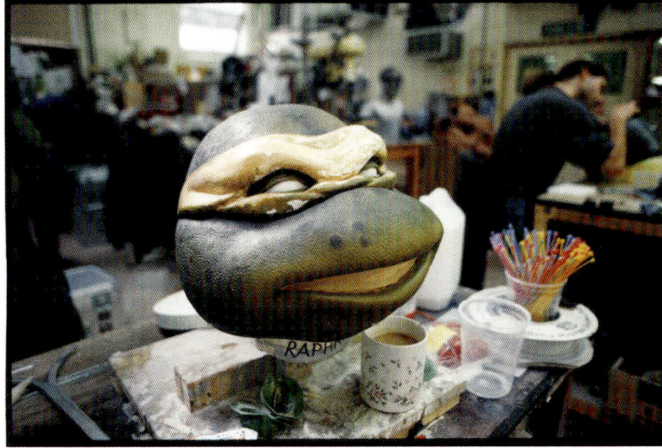

Photos of the animatronics from Jim Henson's Creature Shop for the live-action movie.

In the 21st century, the Turtles would continue to be a force in television animation. In 2003, 4Kids Entertainment released the first season of a new traditionally animated Turtles reboot, one that would ultimately air for 155 episodes across seven seasons. They would also air a number of shorts, alongside a finale movie event in 2009 featuring a crossover with the 1987 animated Turtles and even a side trip to the original Mirage Studios continuity. The only Turtles series written and voiced in New York City, it drew more heavily from the comics than its 1987 counterpart, especially in early episodes. The Turtles would return in 2012 on Nickelodeon, this time as a CG series. The five-season run aired 124 episodes through 2017. It borrowed liberally from both the comic interpretation and the 1987 animated series, while still forging its own identity. Most recently, the two-season *Rise of the Teenage Mutant Ninja Turtles* aired on Nickelodeon from 2018 to 2020, a 39-episode run with a film-length finale that aired on Netflix in 2022. *Rise* introduced the notion that each Turtle was a separate species of turtle and featured a more magical environment than most previous interpretations.

Of course, the Turtles weren't done on the big screen, not by a long shot. A CG-animated film was released by Warner Bros. in 2007, titled *TMNT*. It was somewhat ambiguous whether it took place in its own continuity, as Laird stated, or it was a continuation of the original live-action trilogy as director Kevin Munroe asserts. More notably, in 2014, Paramount released a live-action reboot produced by Michael Bay, along with a 2016 sequel subtitled *Out of the Shadows*. These more bombastic interpretations featured a mix of on-set actors and CGI elements, especially the motion capture Turtles themselves. Combined, the six theatrical releases from 1990 to 2016 have earned well over a billion dollars at the box office.

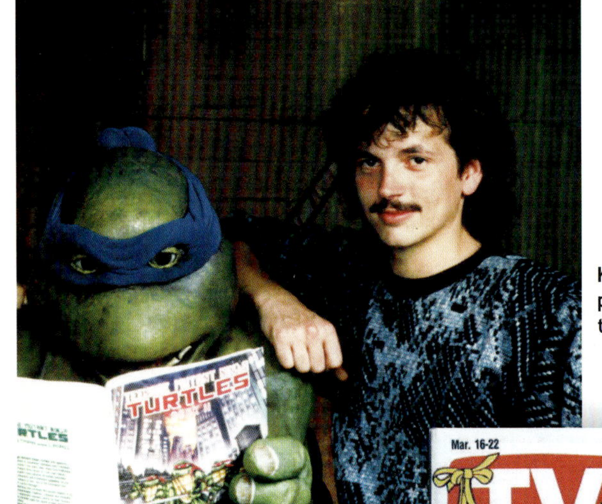

Kevin Eastman posing with one of the stunt actors.

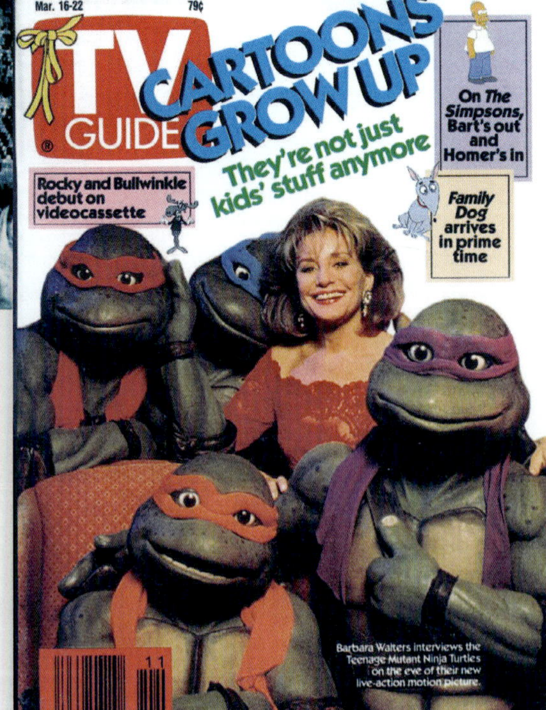

The Turtles on the cover of *TV Guide*, March 16, 1990.

With over 500 television episodes and half a dozen theatrical films, it wouldn't be unfair to characterize *Teenage Mutant Ninja Turtles* as a juggernaut. (And, naturally, every movie and television release was accompanied by a tie-in toy line from Playmates.) Which brings us to the latest iteration of the property: *Teenage Mutant Ninja Turtles: Mutant Mayhem,* from the year this book is being written, 2023. It's the seventh TMNT theatrical release, the second animated feature film. And yet, it's also something completely new and fresh. I hope you can appreciate just how unique an interpretation *Teenage Mutant Ninja Turtles: Mutant Mayhem* is as you peruse the pages before you.

–Jim Sorenson

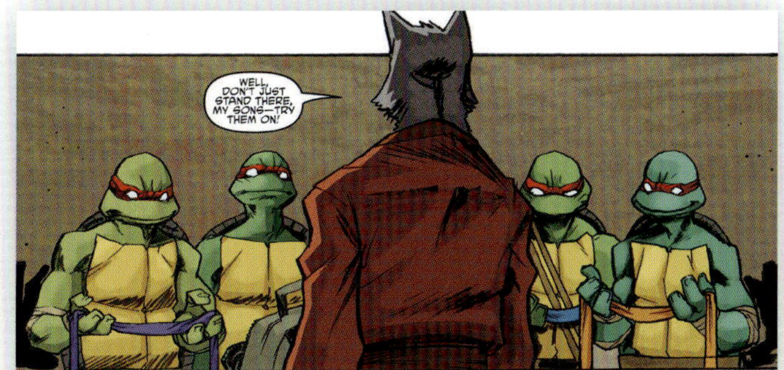

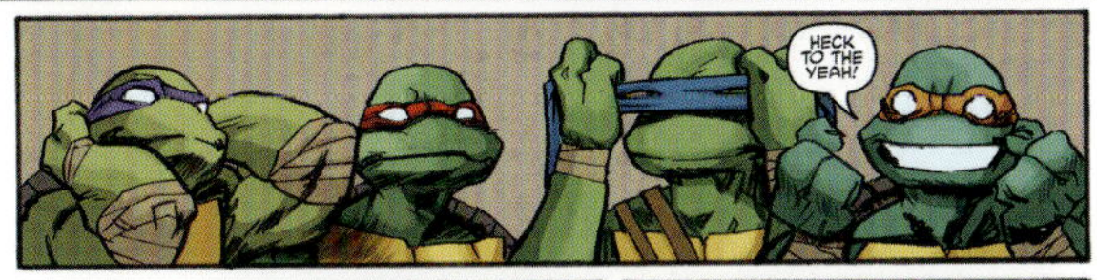

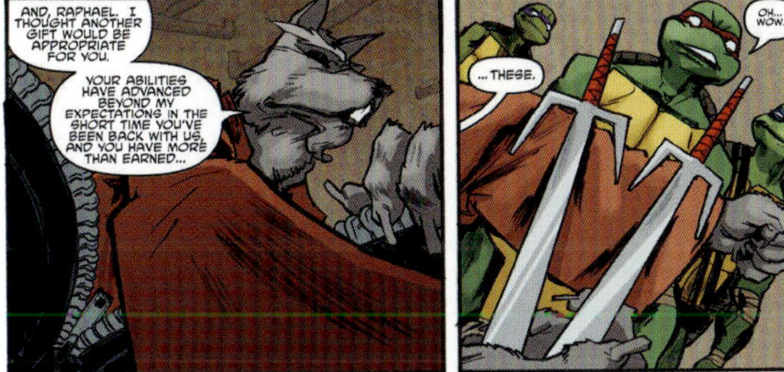

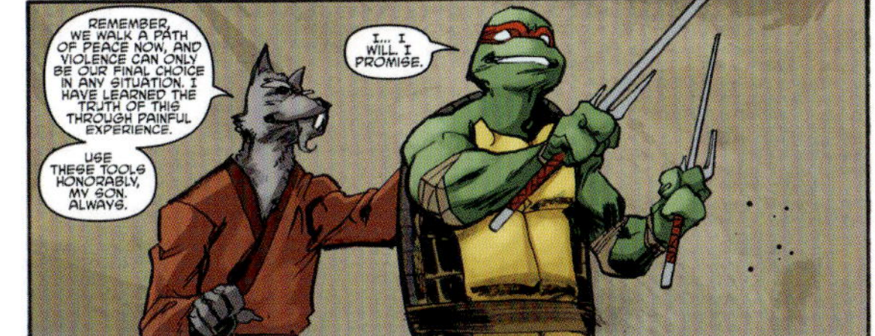

Art from IDW's comic series, *Teenage Mutant Ninja Turtles* issue #5, page 20. Art by Dan Duncan with colors by Ronda Pattison and lettering by Shawn Lee. Published by IDW Publishing.

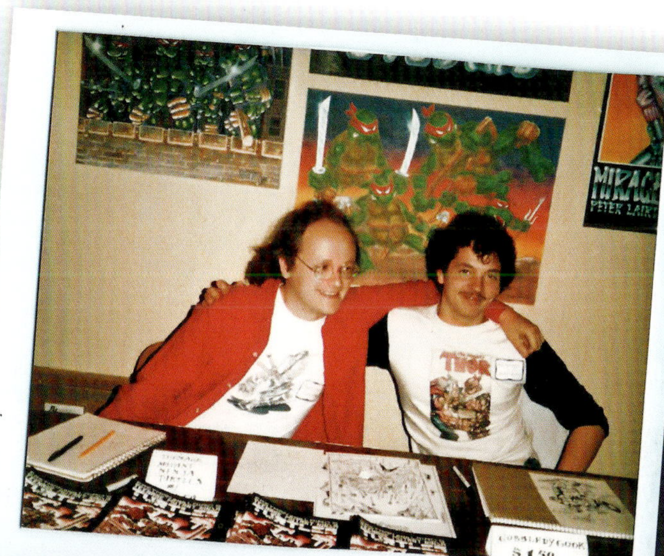

Peter Laird and Kevin Eastman at the official release of *Teenage Mutant Ninja Turtles* issue #1. Portsmouth, NH, May 5, 1984.

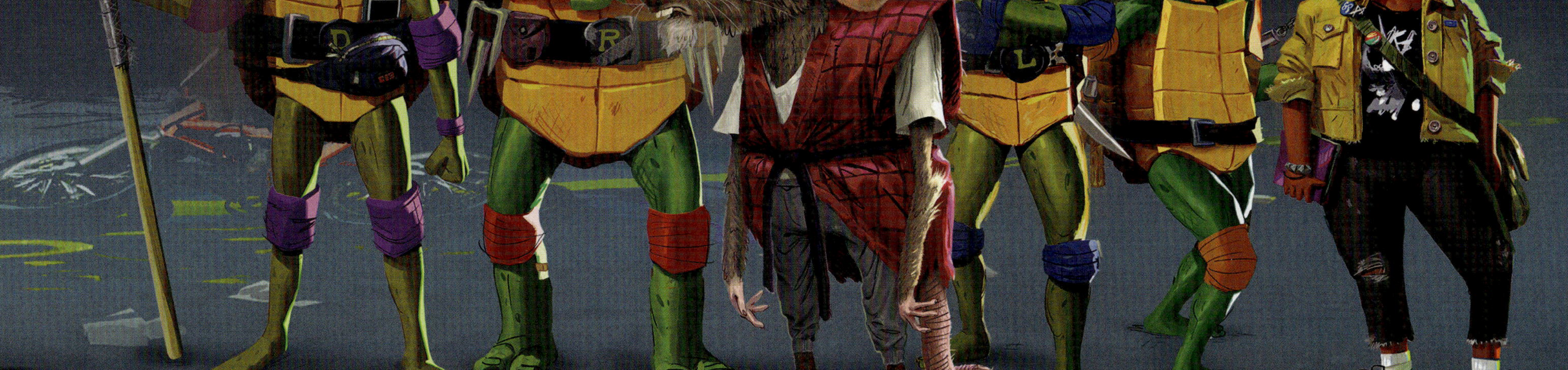

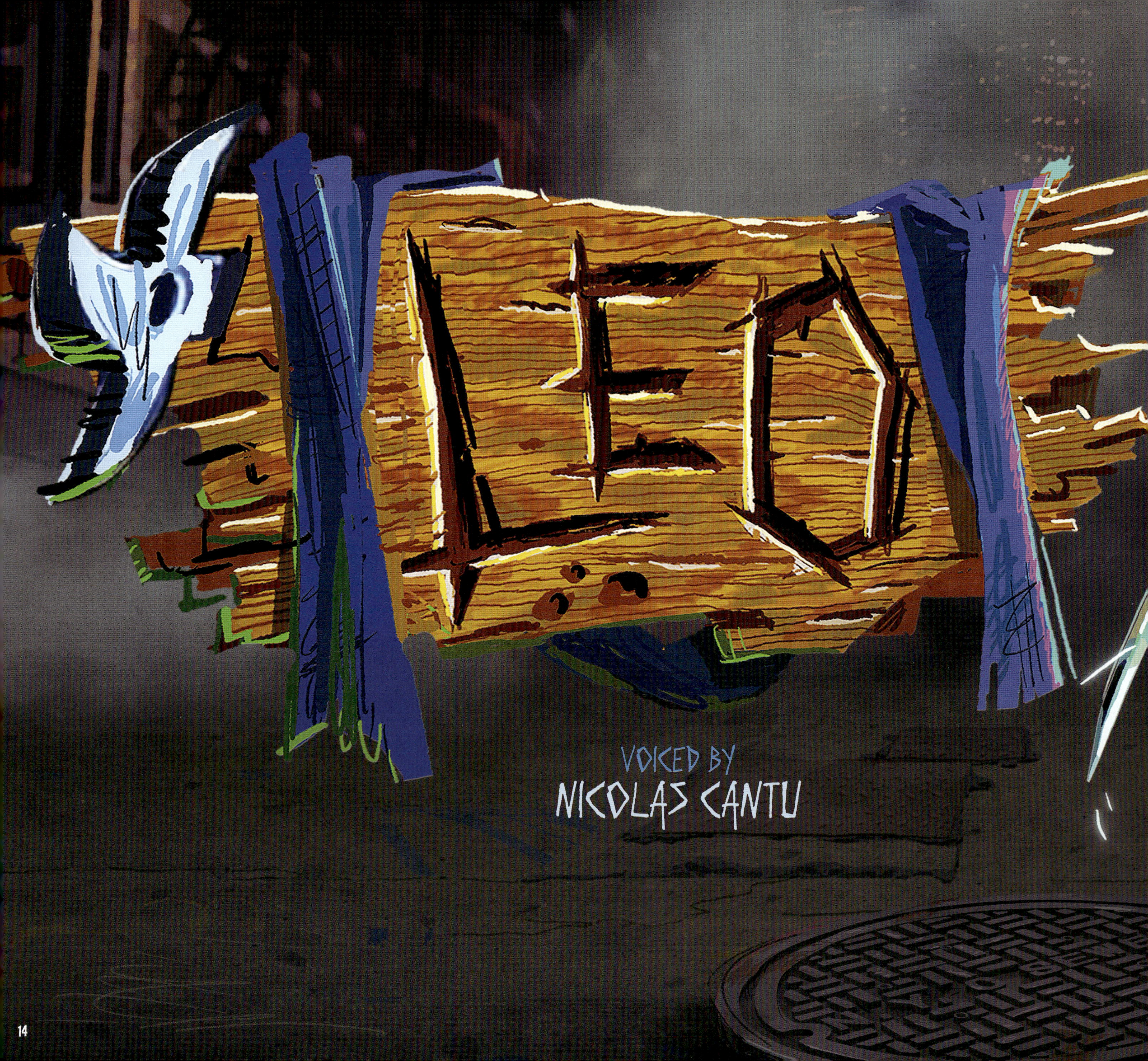
LEO
VOICED BY
NICOLAS CANTU

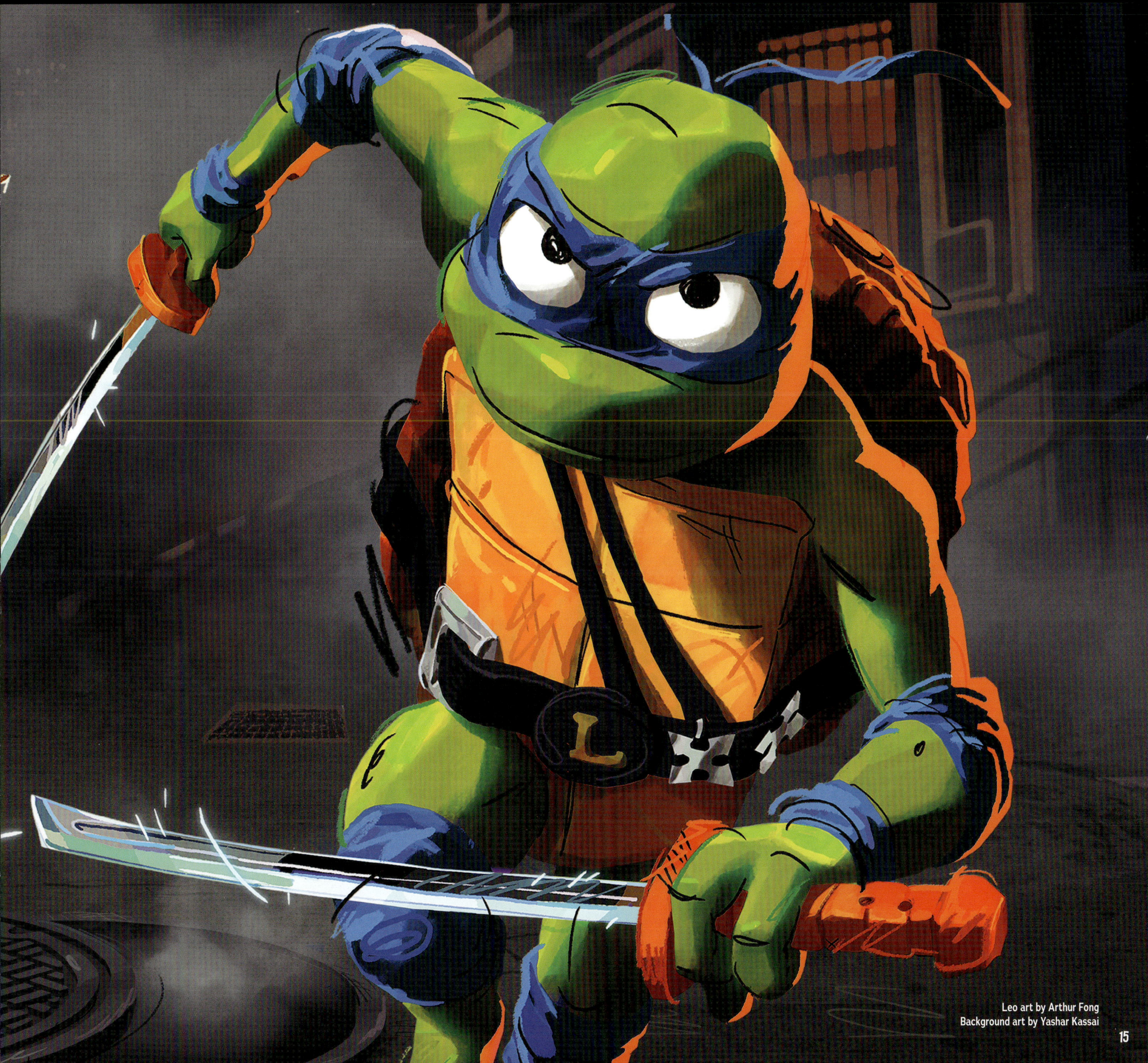

Leo art by Arthur Fong
Background art by Yashar Kassai

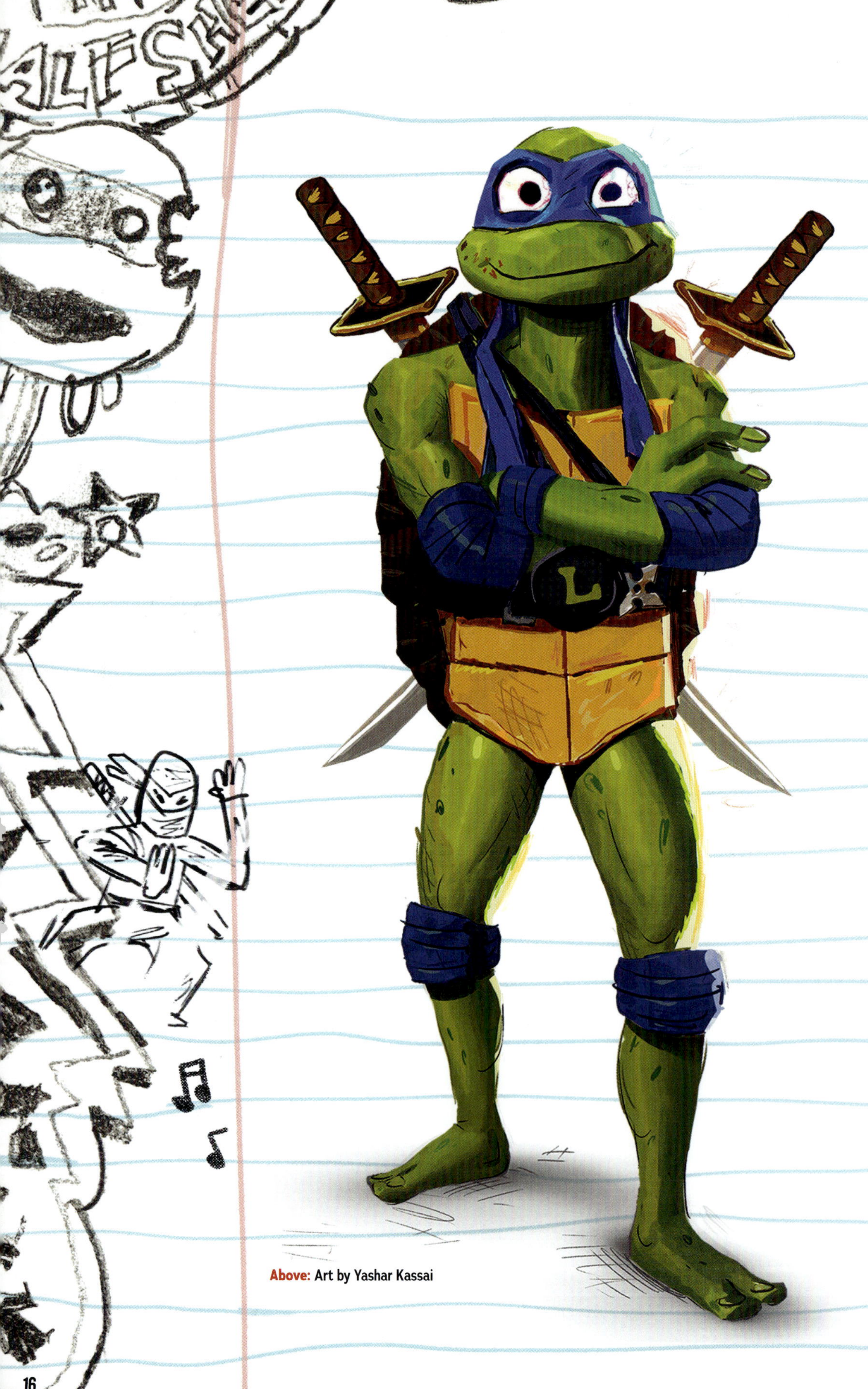

Above: Art by Yashar Kassai

"Leo is painfully unaware of how uncool he is."

—Director
Jeff Rowe

"Leonardo is the all-arounder, desperate to be a leader, so he's constantly training, in decent shape. We basically defaulted to a pretty standard Turtle design that comes from probably our favorite iteration, the 1987 animated series, the one that started everything when it comes to the animated Turtles world. We drew on that, harnessed the design aesthetic of those characters for Leonardo. We wanted one foot steeped in that classic version of the characters. The rest of the Turtles we took more liberties with and tried to differentiate them in distinct ways."

—Production Designer
Yashar Kassai

"I would say my favorite teenage turtle is Leonardo. I don't know the entire truth on why I chose Leo when I was three years old, but seeing how my life is now, it must be because I was drawn to being a leader, someone who believes in the necessity of rules, someone who is mature for his age (in certain parts of my life), and someone who is a bit of a romantic. There's truly a turtle for everyone and to me that is what makes TMNT so special."

–Art Director
Arthur Fong

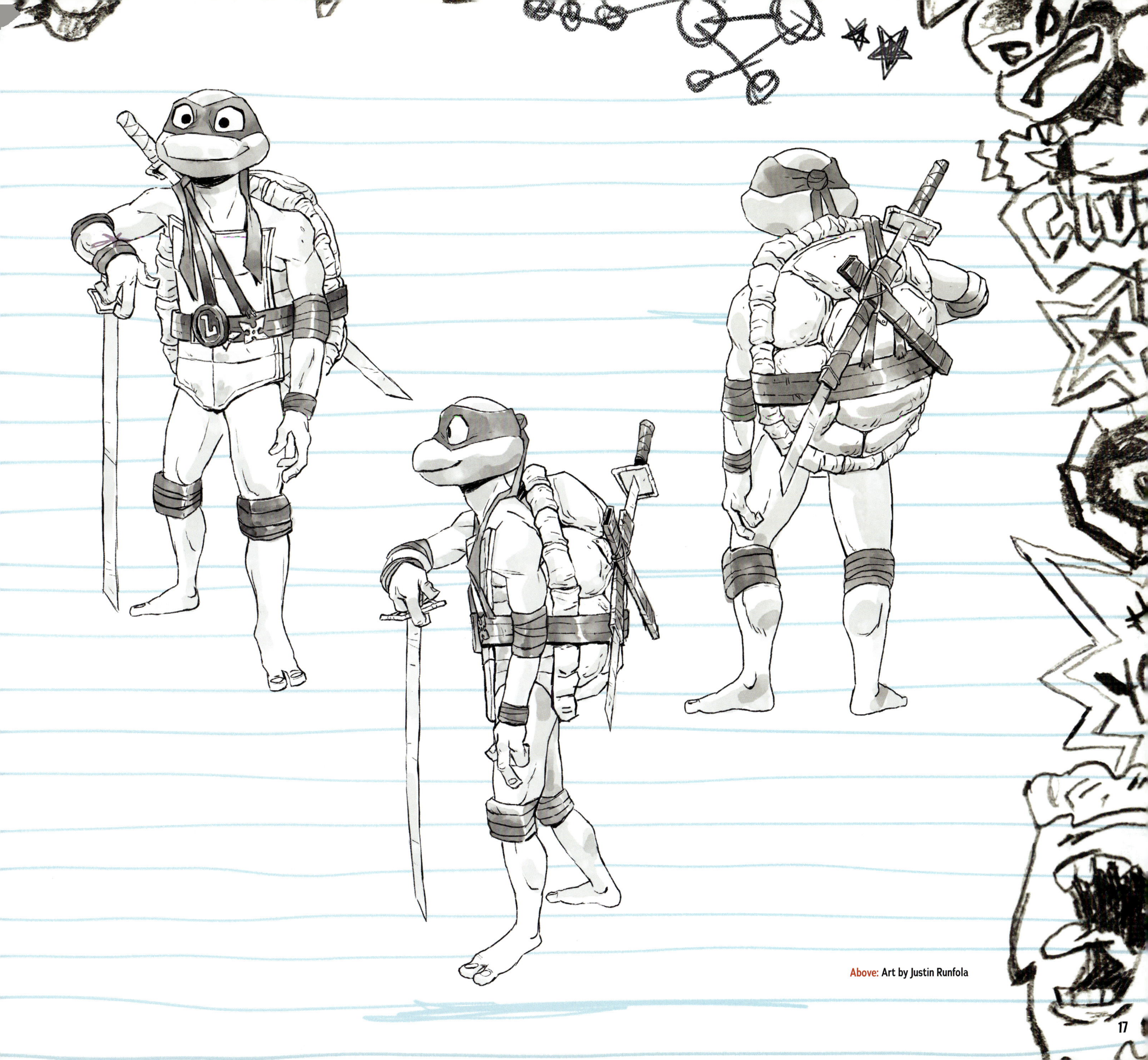

Above: Art by Justin Runfola

Turtles

SQUASH

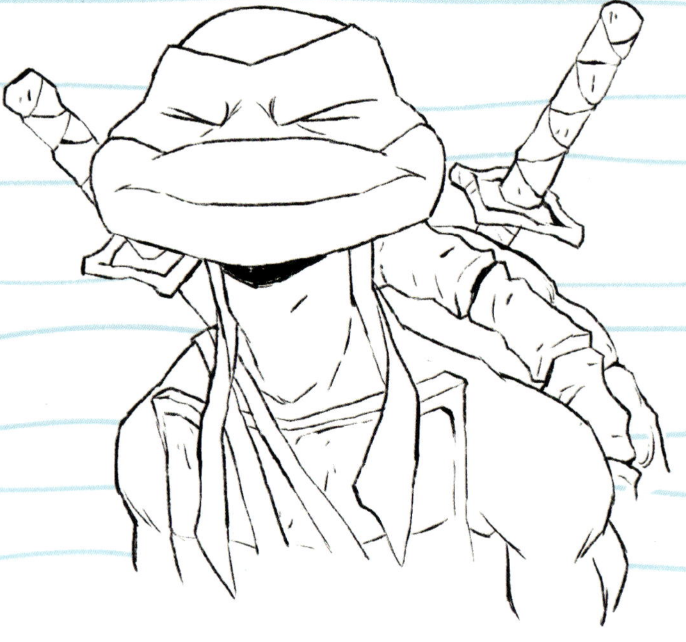

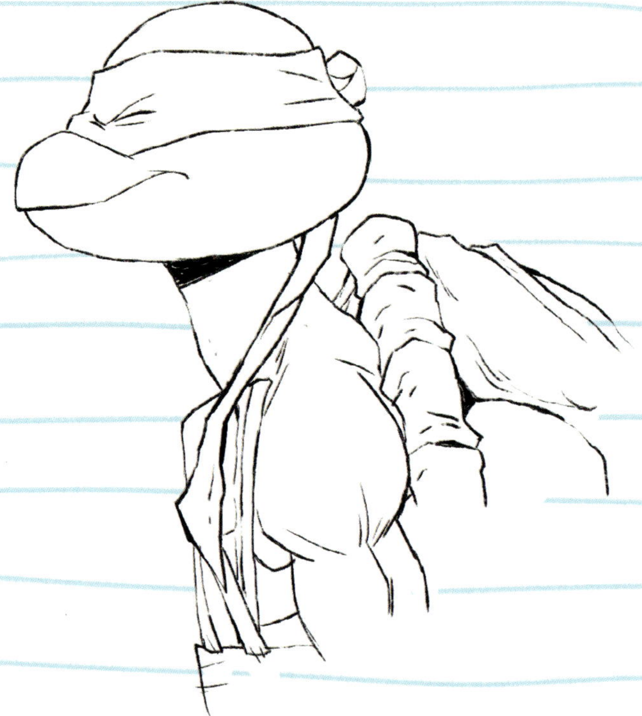

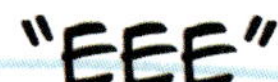

"OOO"

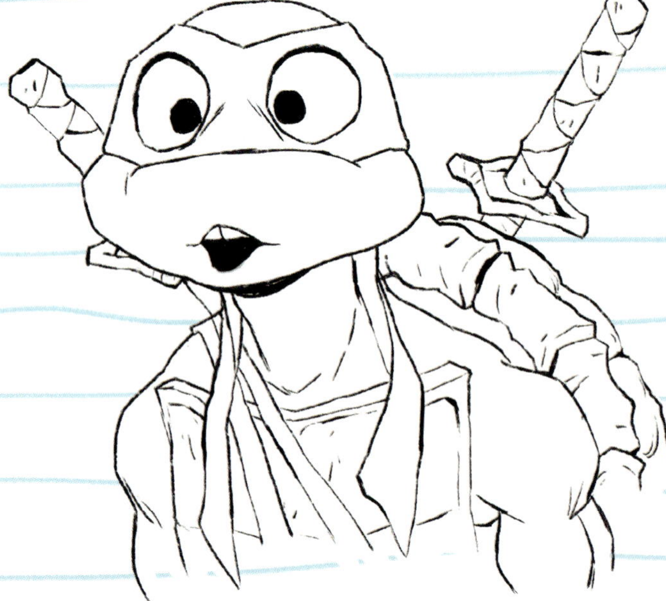

"EEE"

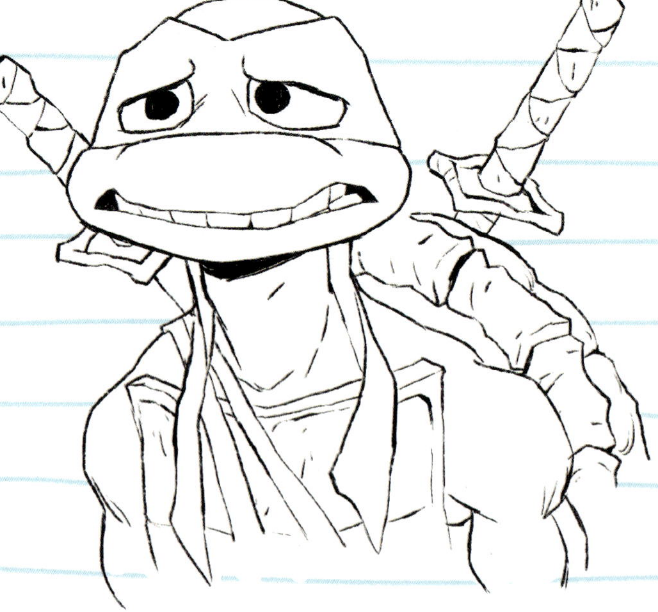

Above and Opposite: Character expressions by Justin Runfola

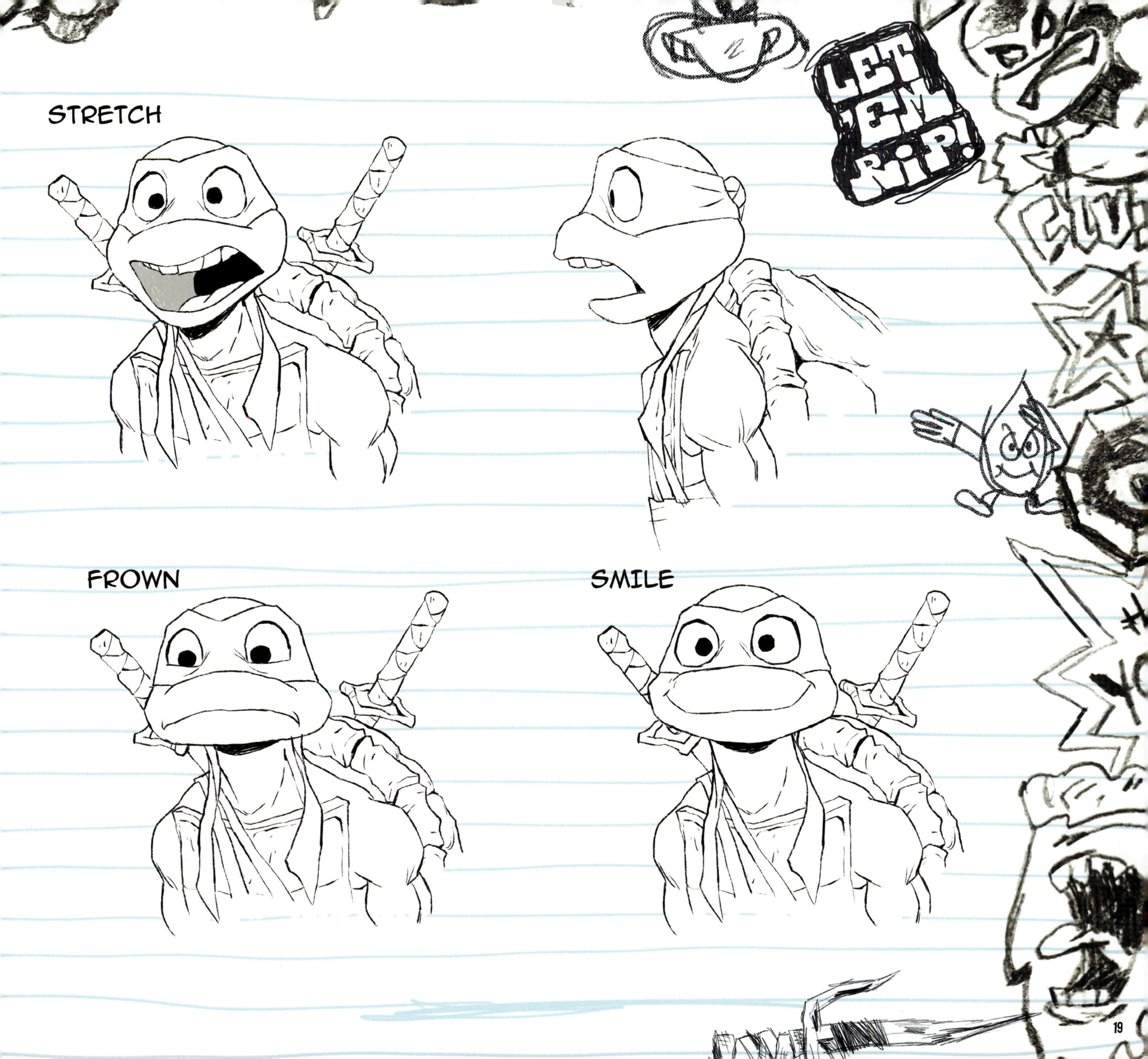
STRETCH
FROWN
SMILE
LET 'EM RIP!

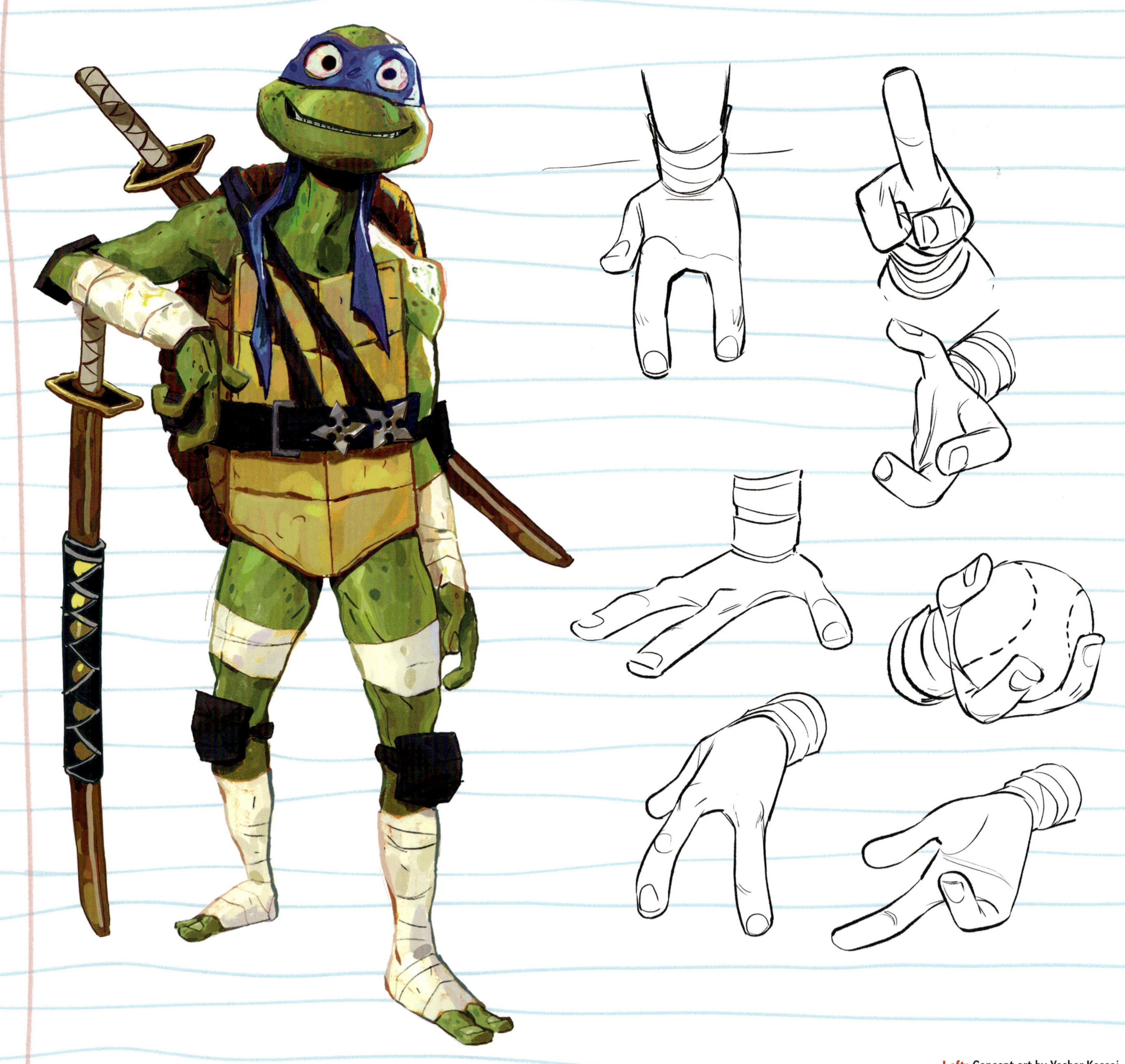

Left: Concept art by Yashar Kassai
Right: Hand design art by James A. Castillo

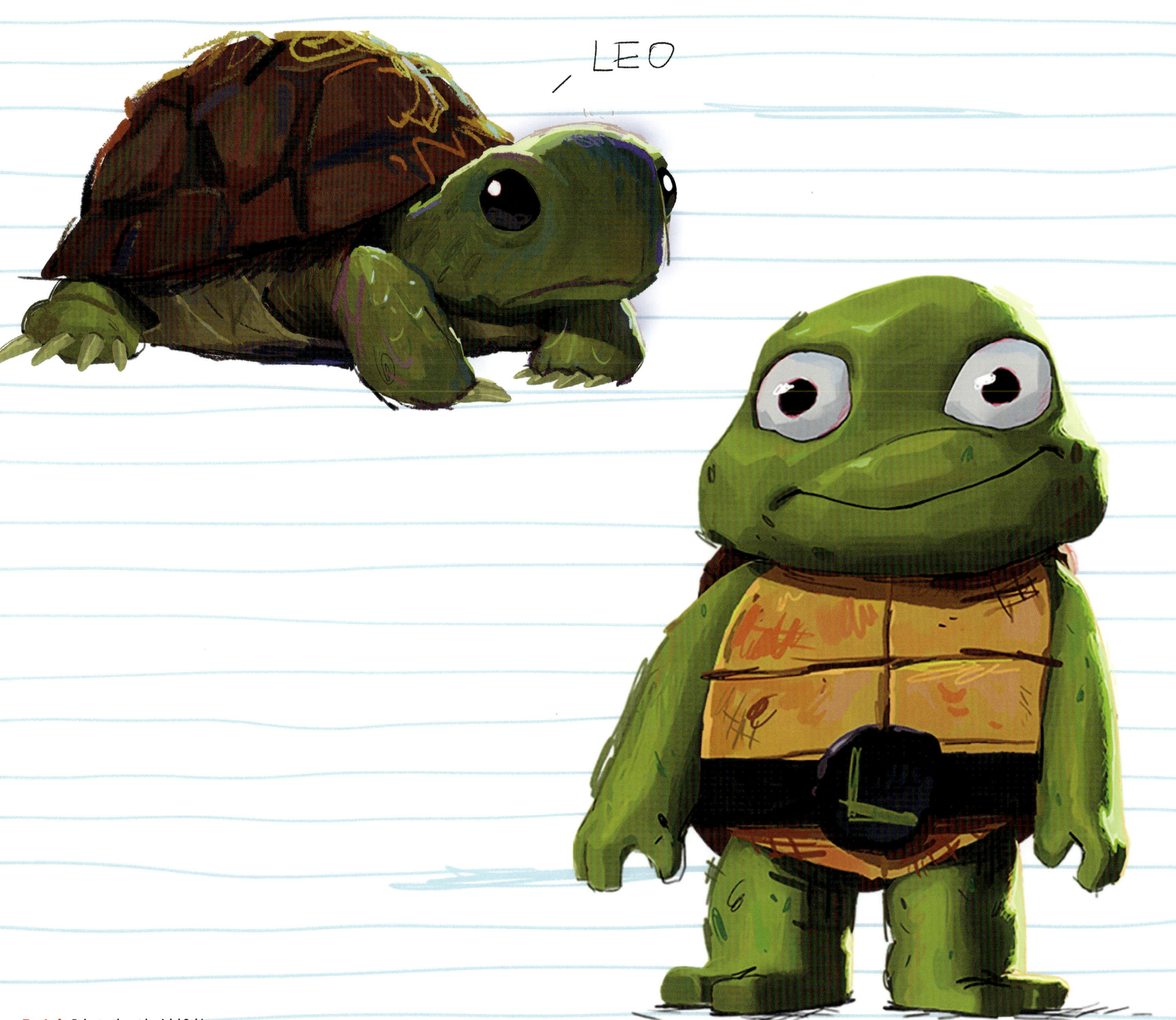

Top Left: Baby turtle art by Adel Sabi
Bottom Right: Toddler art by Alger Tam

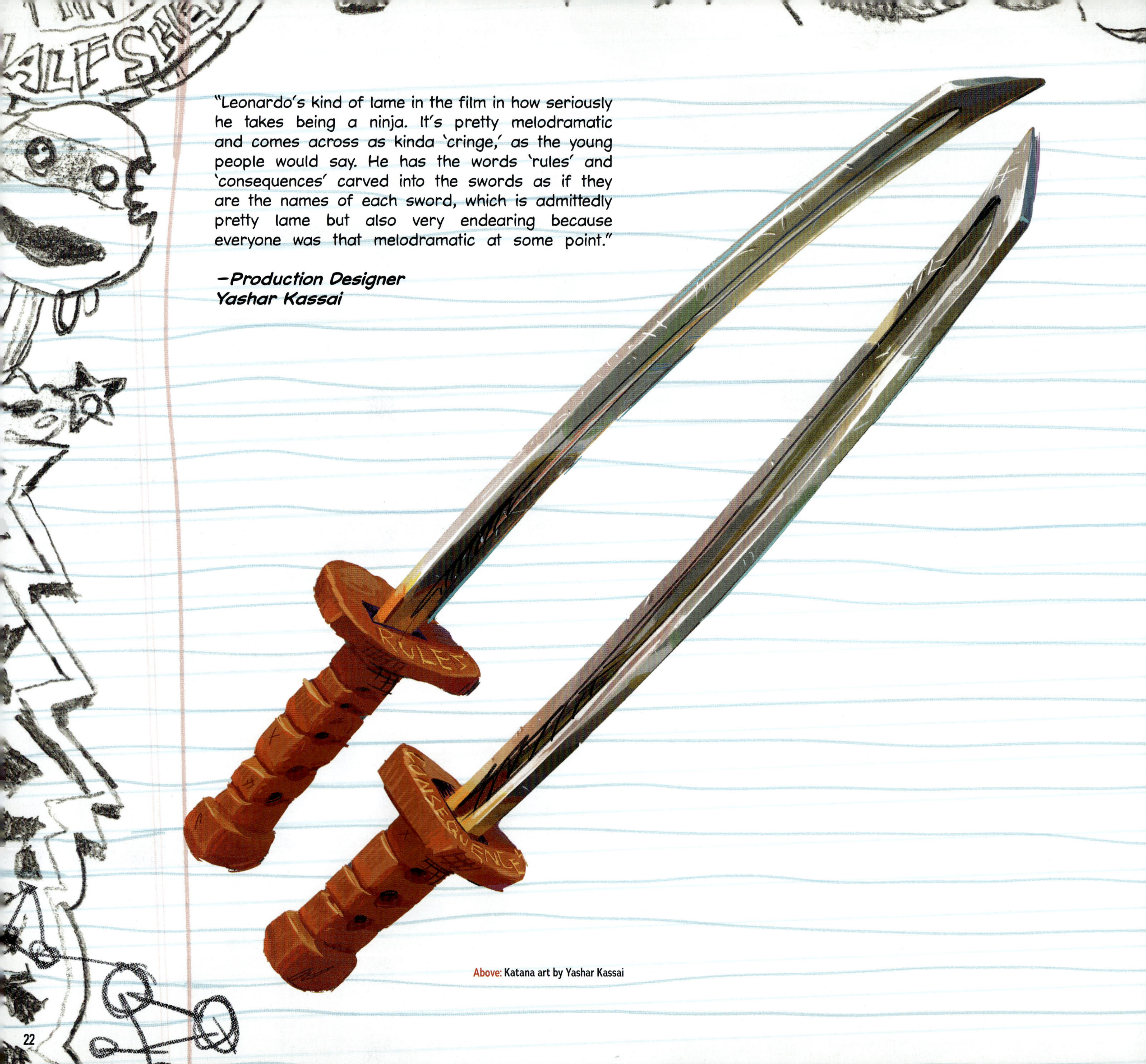

"Leonardo's kind of lame in the film in how seriously he takes being a ninja. It's pretty melodramatic and comes across as kinda 'cringe,' as the young people would say. He has the words 'rules' and 'consequences' carved into the swords as if they are the names of each sword, which is admittedly pretty lame but also very endearing because everyone was that melodramatic at some point."

—Production Designer Yashar Kassai

Above: Katana art by Yashar Kassai

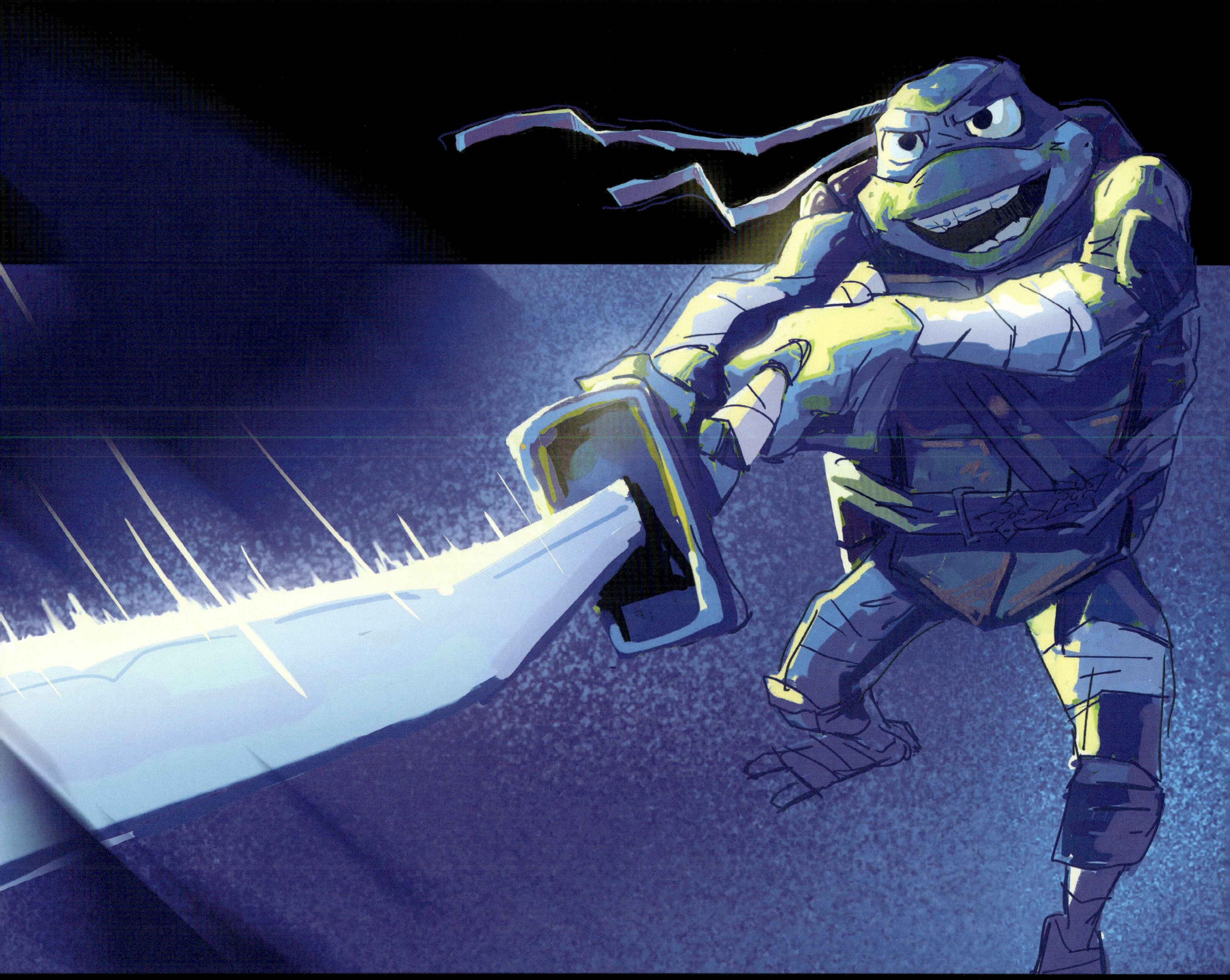

Above: Concept art by Lauren Airriess

DONNIE

VOICED BY
MICAH ABBEY

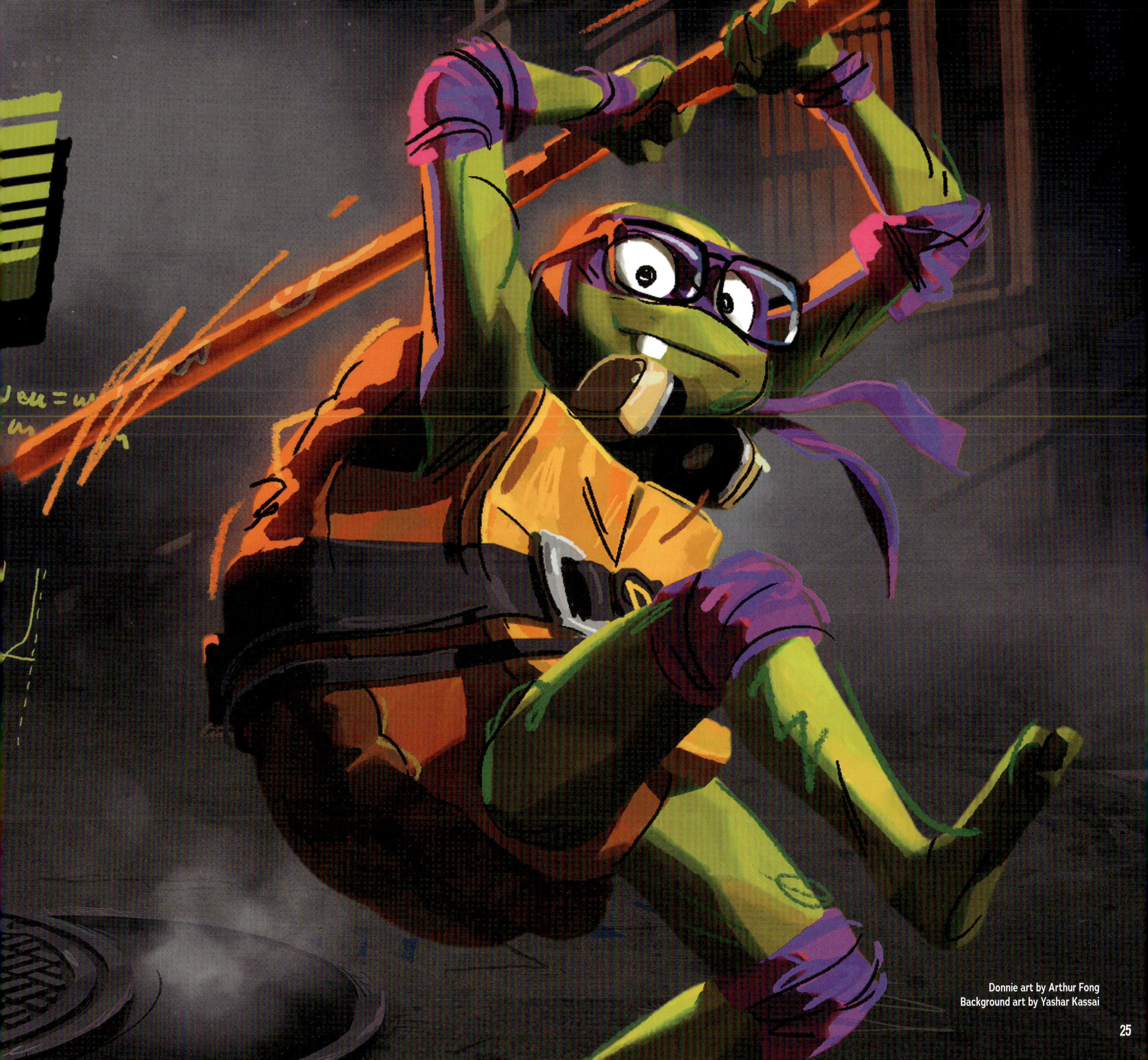

Donnie art by Arthur Fong
Background art by Yashar Kassai

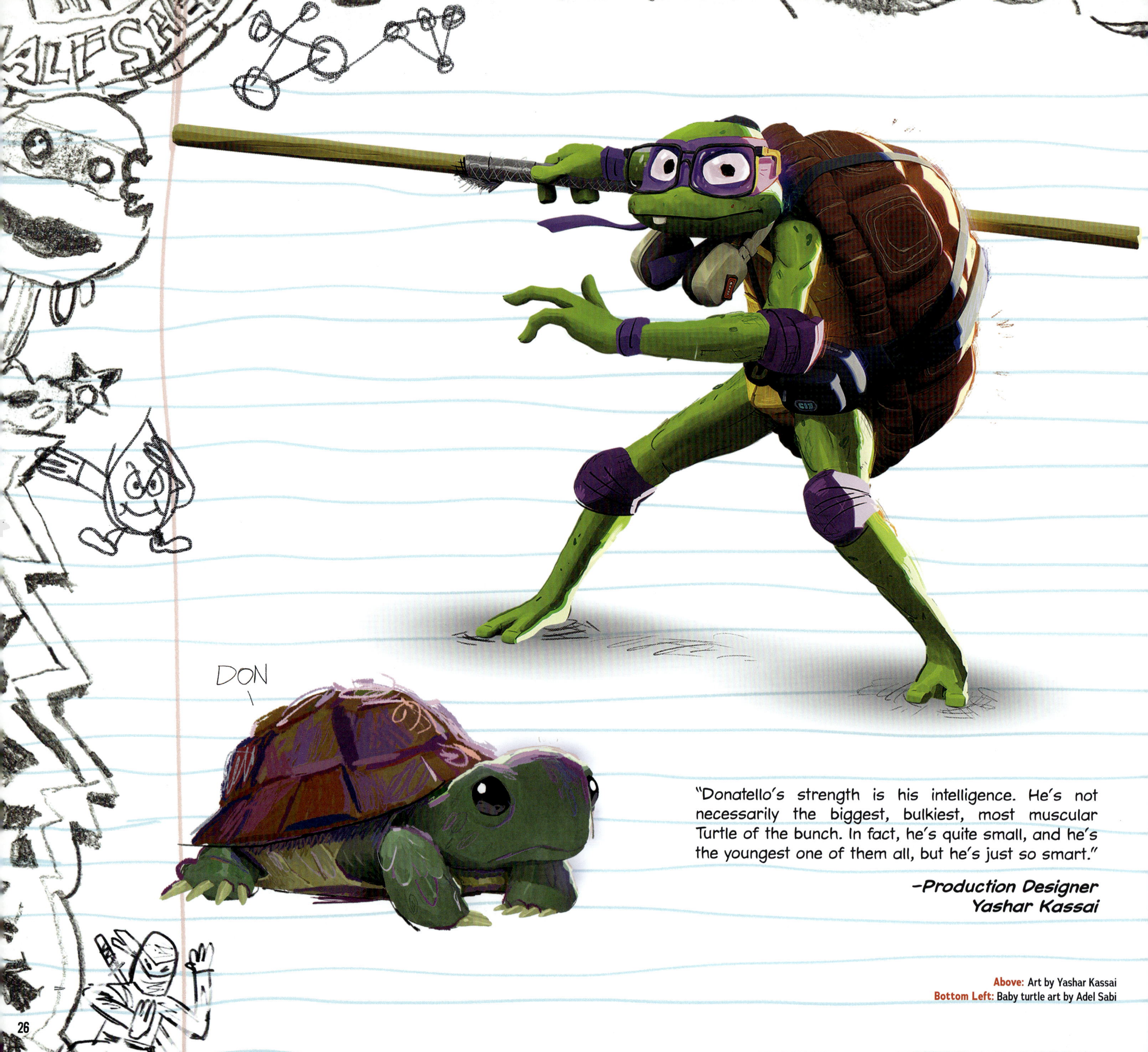

"Donatello's strength is his intelligence. He's not necessarily the biggest, bulkiest, most muscular Turtle of the bunch. In fact, he's quite small, and he's the youngest one of them all, but he's just so smart."

–Production Designer Yashar Kassai

Above: Art by Yashar Kassai
Bottom Left: Baby turtle art by Adel Sabi

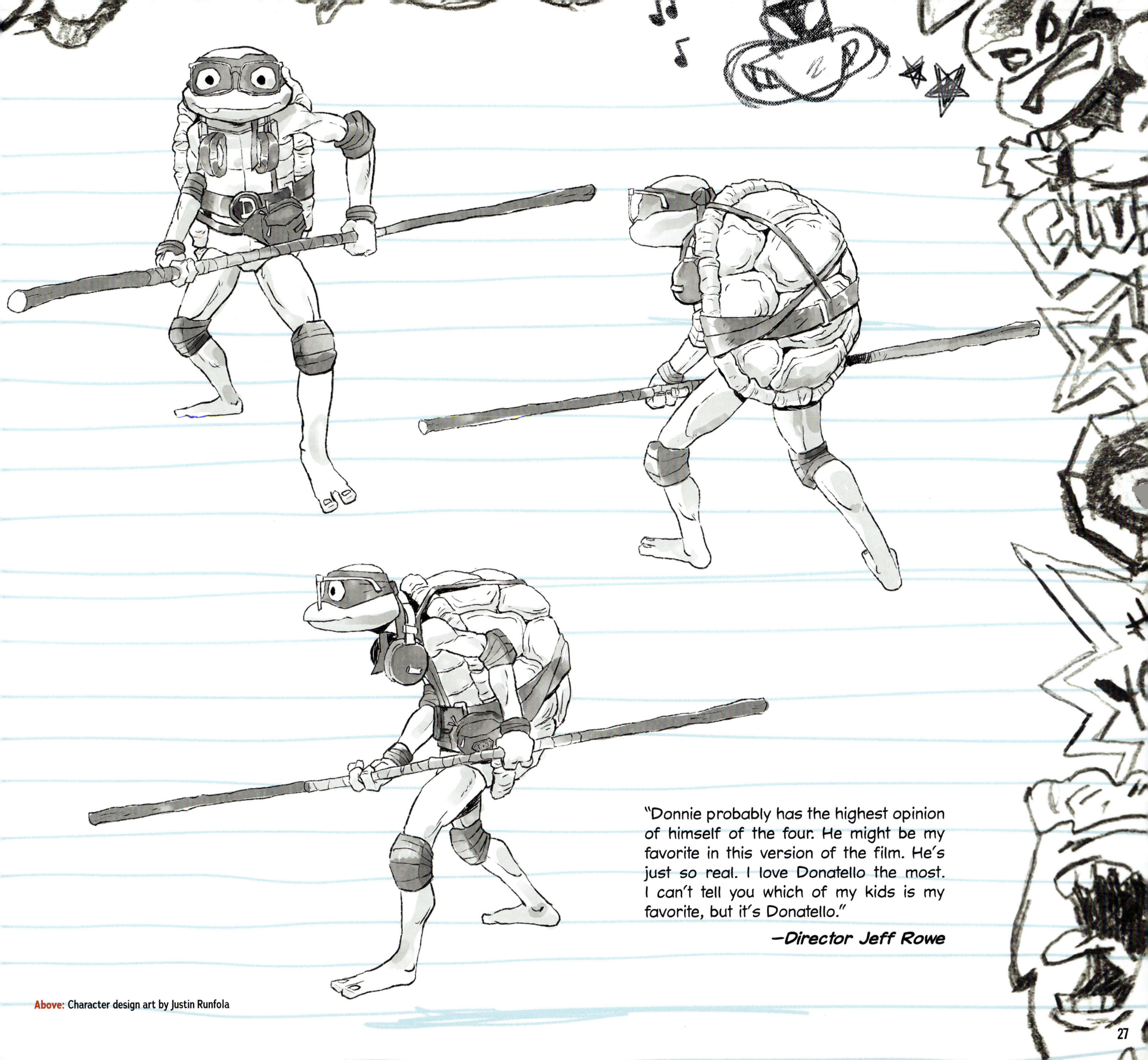

"Donnie probably has the highest opinion of himself of the four. He might be my favorite in this version of the film. He's just so real. I love Donatello the most. I can't tell you which of my kids is my favorite, but it's Donatello."

—*Director Jeff Rowe*

Above: Character design art by Justin Runfola

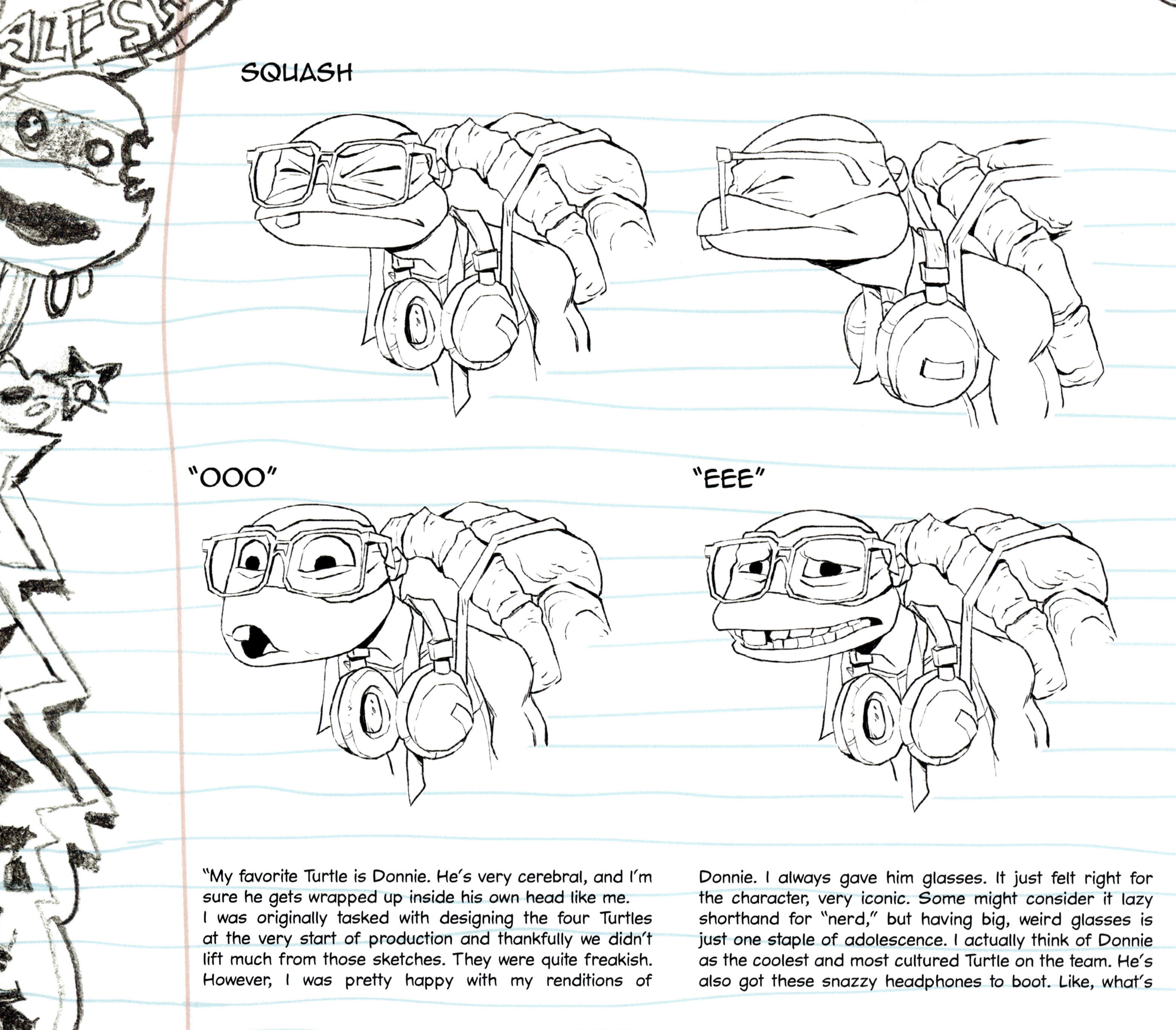

"My favorite Turtle is Donnie. He's very cerebral, and I'm sure he gets wrapped up inside his own head like me. I was originally tasked with designing the four Turtles at the very start of production and thankfully we didn't lift much from those sketches. They were quite freakish. However, I was pretty happy with my renditions of Donnie. I always gave him glasses. It just felt right for the character, very iconic. Some might consider it lazy shorthand for "nerd," but having big, weird glasses is just one staple of adolescence. I actually think of Donnie as the coolest and most cultured Turtle on the team. He's also got these snazzy headphones to boot. Like, what's

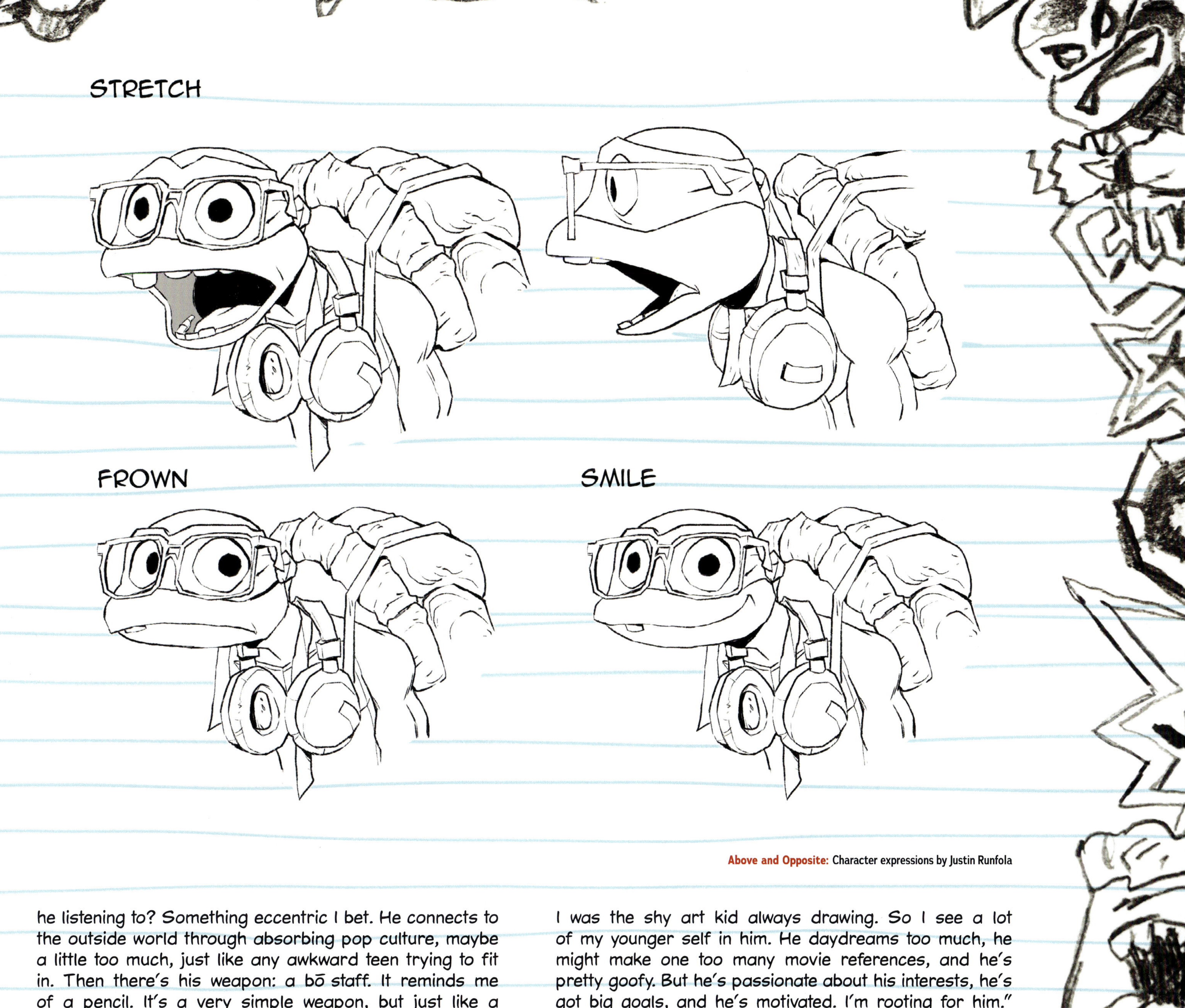

Above and Opposite: Character expressions by Justin Runfola

he listening to? Something eccentric I bet. He connects to the outside world through absorbing pop culture, maybe a little too much, just like any awkward teen trying to fit in. Then there's his weapon: a bō staff. It reminds me of a pencil. It's a very simple weapon, but just like a pencil, it's very effective if you know how to use it. And I was the shy art kid always drawing. So I see a lot of my younger self in him. He daydreams too much, he might make one too many movie references, and he's pretty goofy. But he's passionate about his interests, he's got big goals, and he's motivated. I'm rooting for him."

–Lead Character Designer Woodrow White

"We showcase Donnie's interest in technology. He's the one design that has the most gear on him. He's got a fanny pack with plenty of techie goods inside it. He's got his phone strapped to his belt so he always has it at the ready. He's got giant Bluetooth headphones around his neck. He's generally a bit smaller, uses a bō staff, which is traditional for him and isn't quite as brute-force a weapon as his brothers', who have swords and sai and nunchucks."

—Production Designer Yashar Kassai

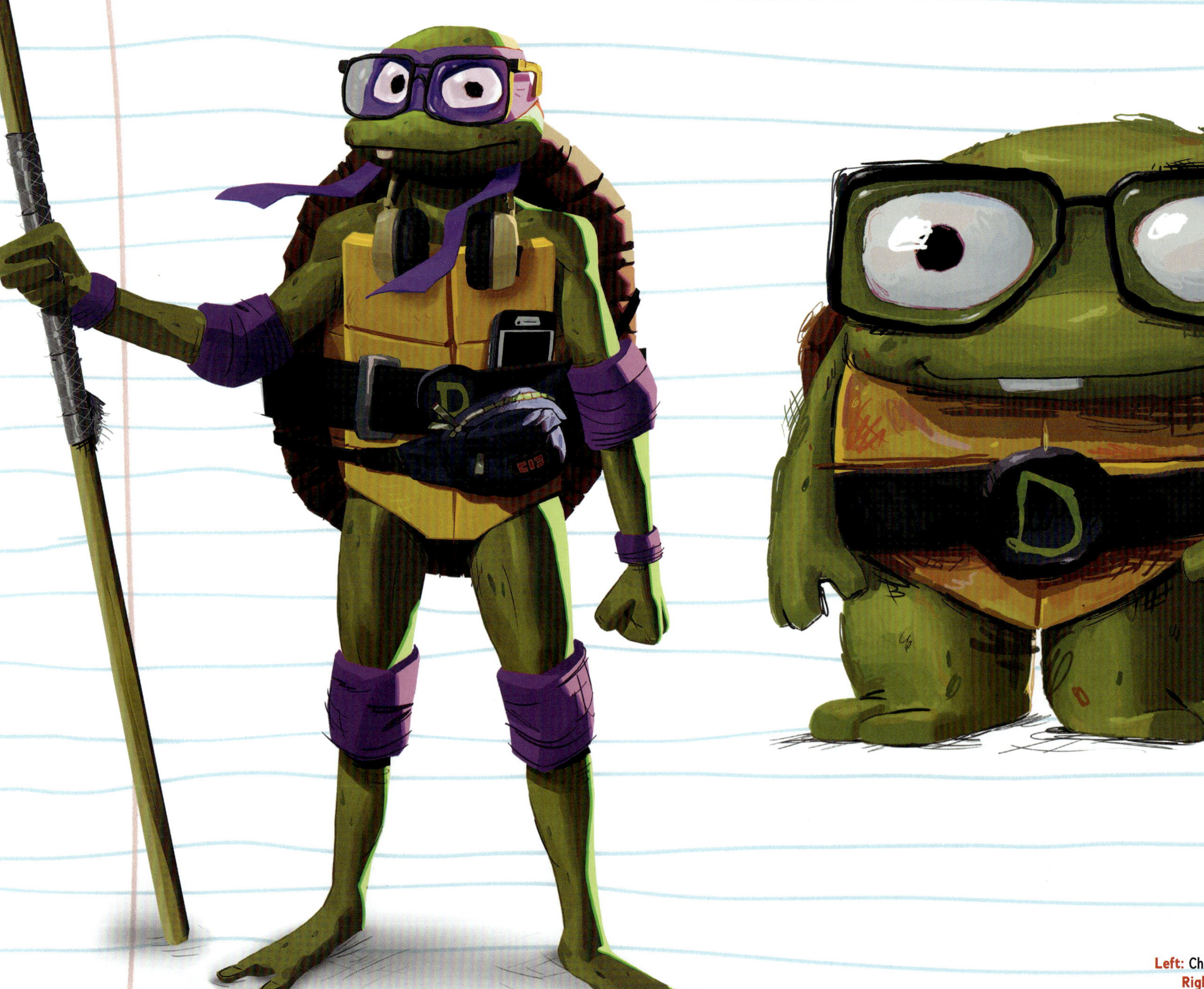

Left: Character art by Yashar Kassai
Right: Toddler art by Alger Tam

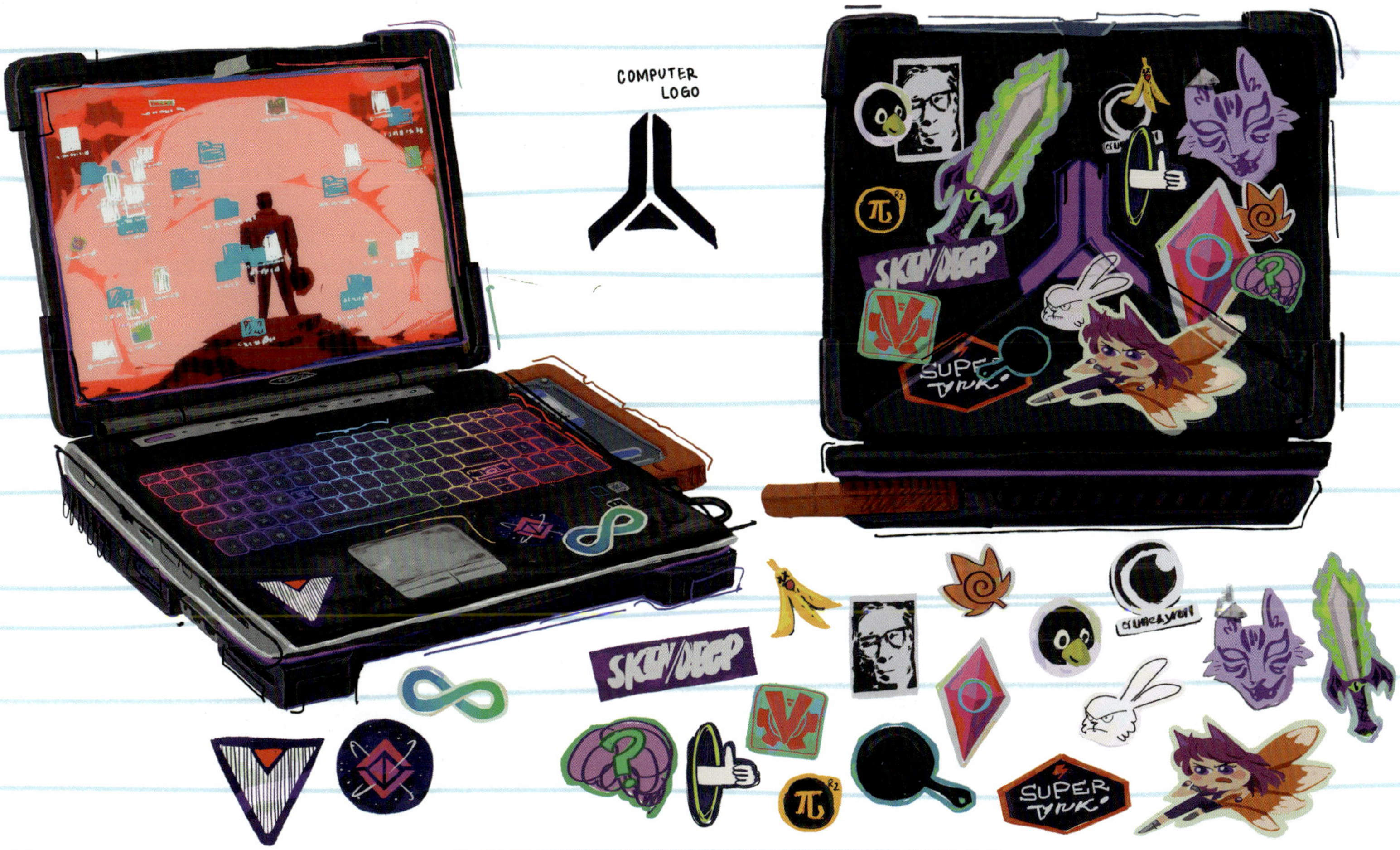

COMPUTER LOGO

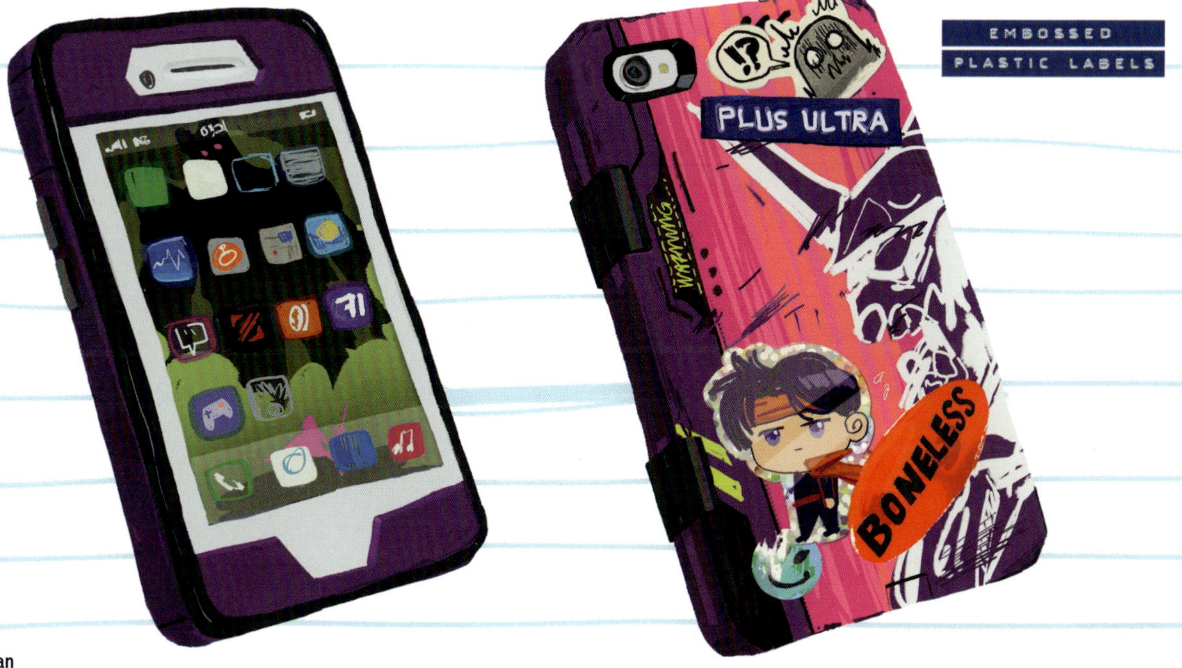

Above: Stickers art by Lily Nishita and Nikita Chan

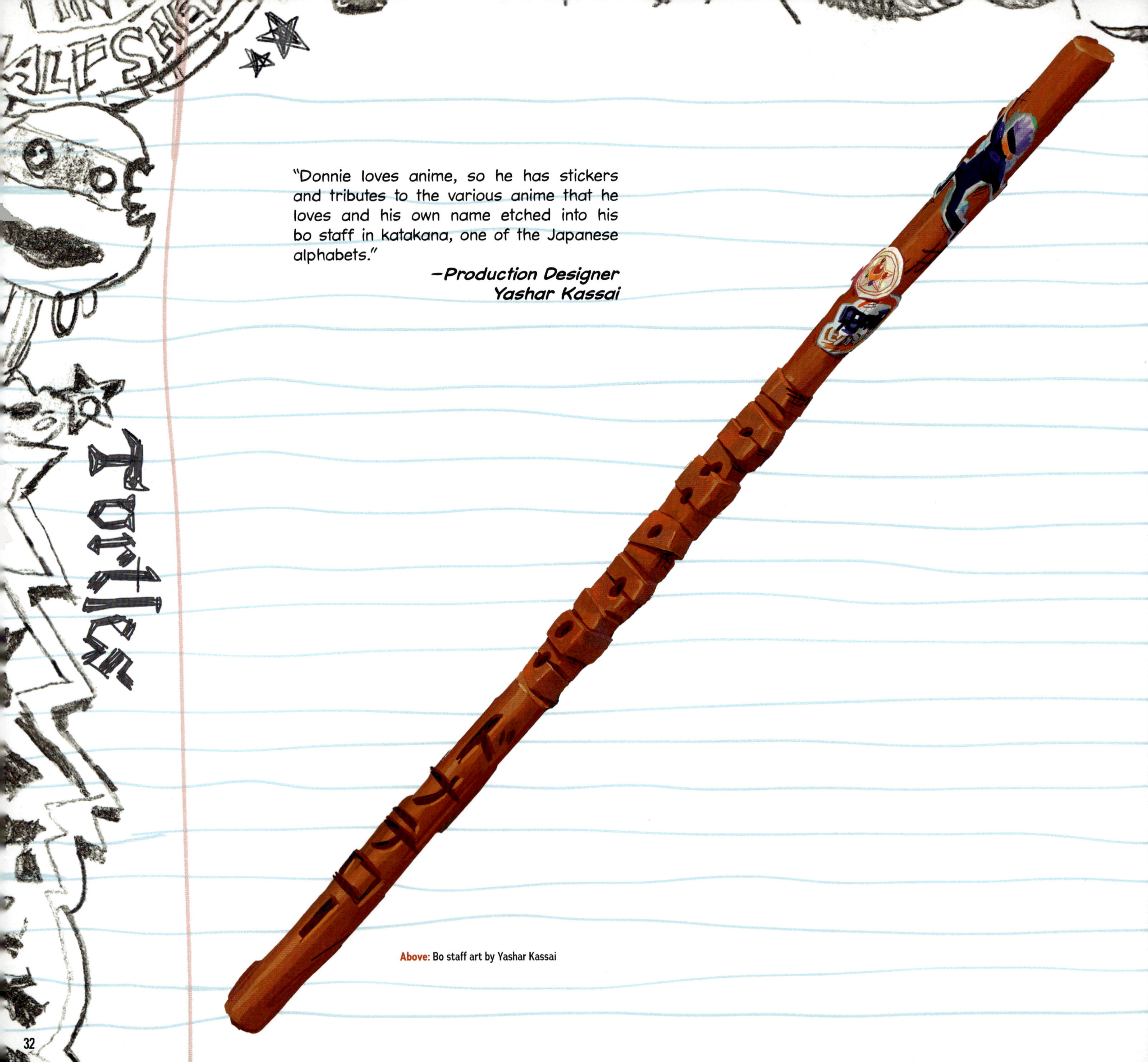

"Donnie loves anime, so he has stickers and tributes to the various anime that he loves and his own name etched into his bo staff in katakana, one of the Japanese alphabets."

—Production Designer Yashar Kassai

Above: Bo staff art by Yashar Kassai

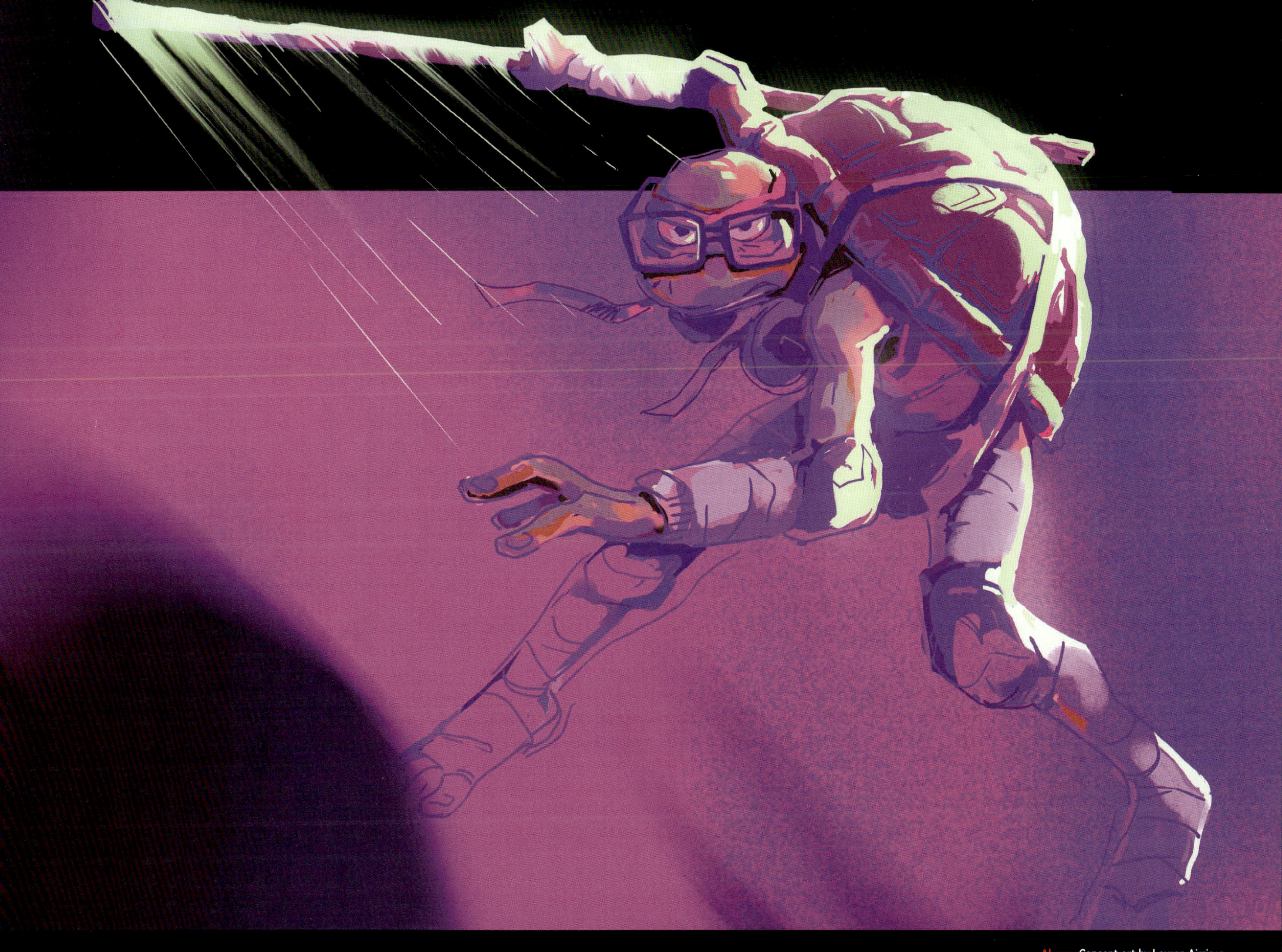

Above: Concept art by Lauren Airriess

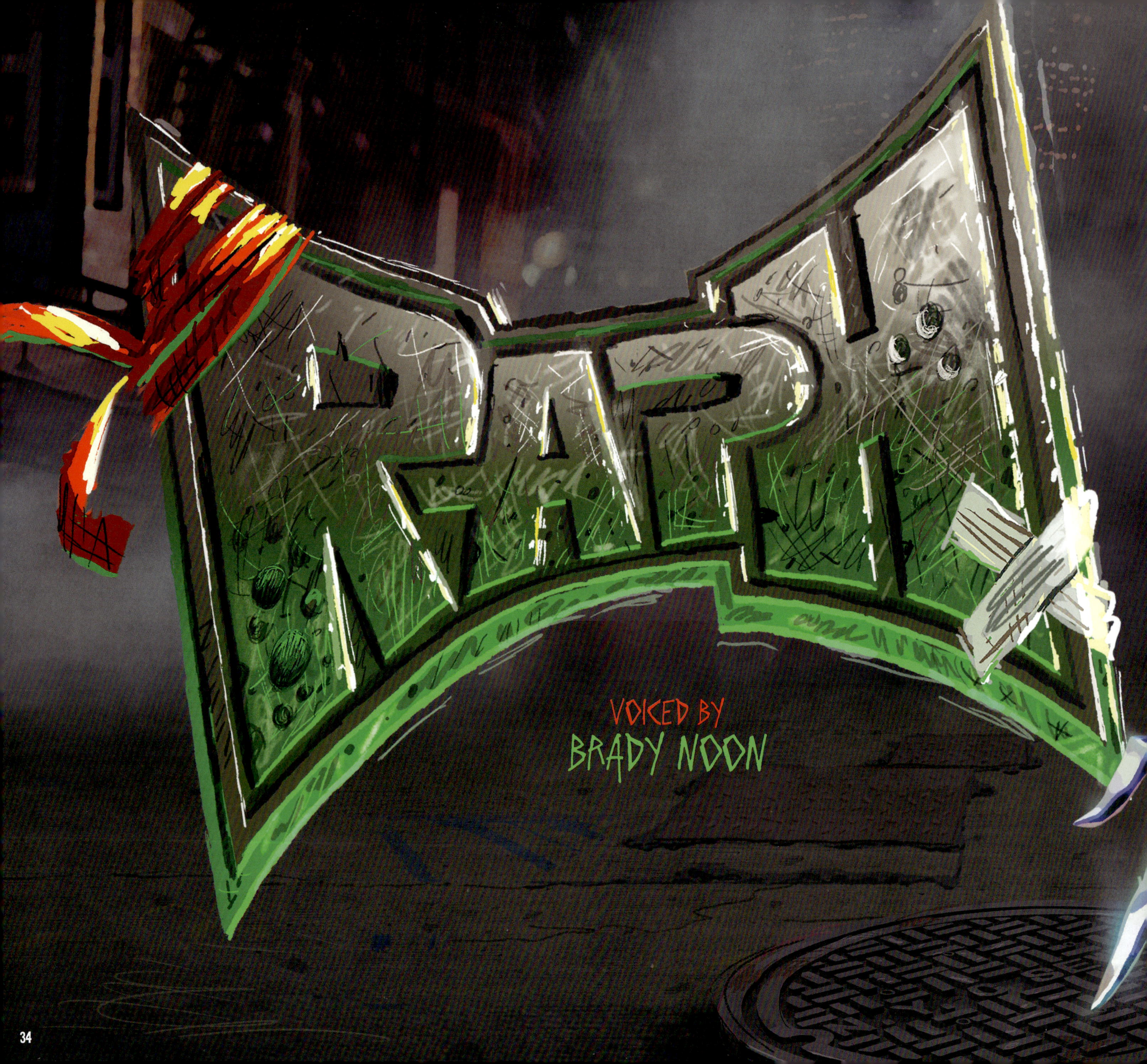
RAPH
VOICED BY
BRADY NOON

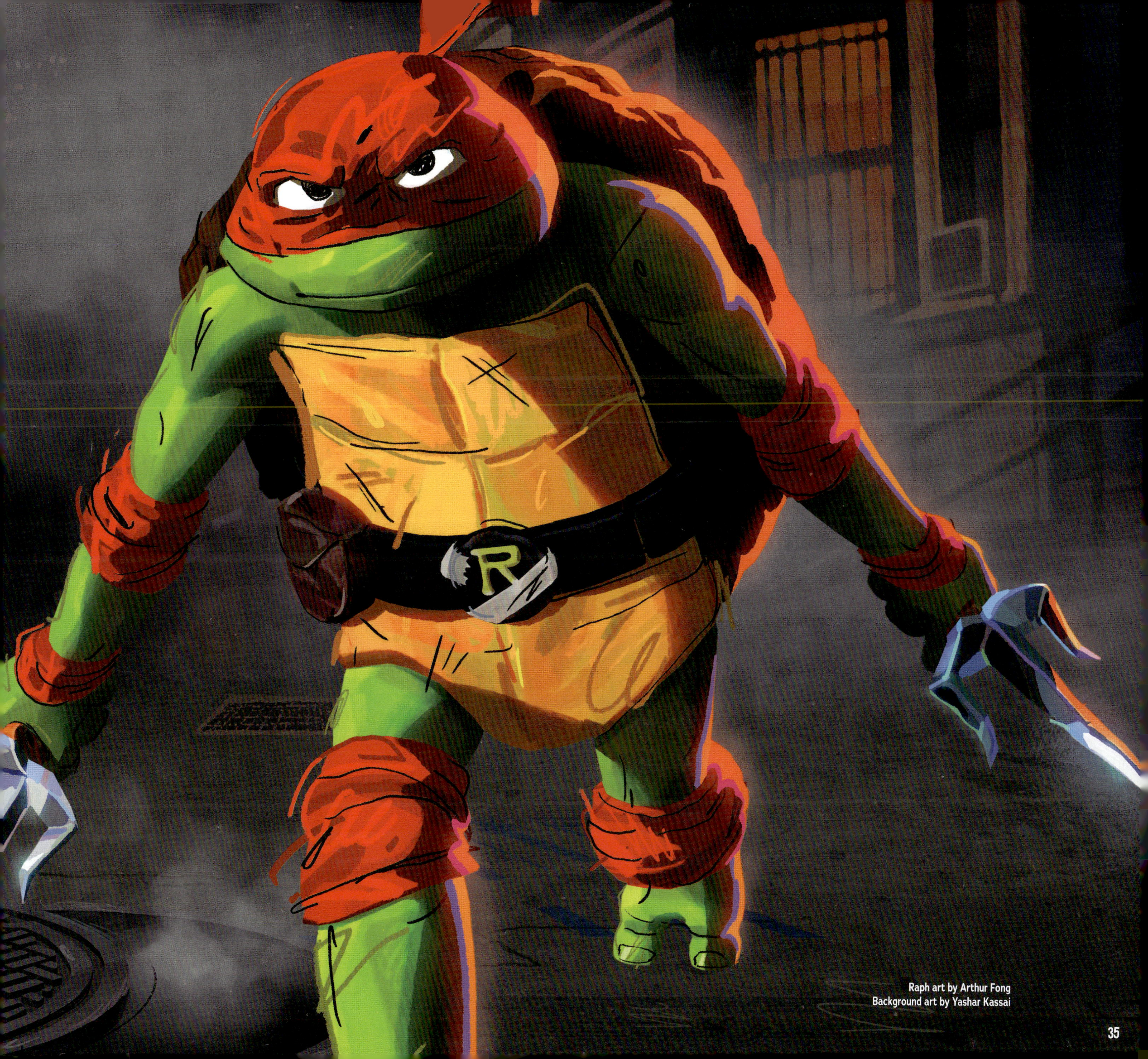

Raph art by Arthur Fong
Background art by Yashar Kassai

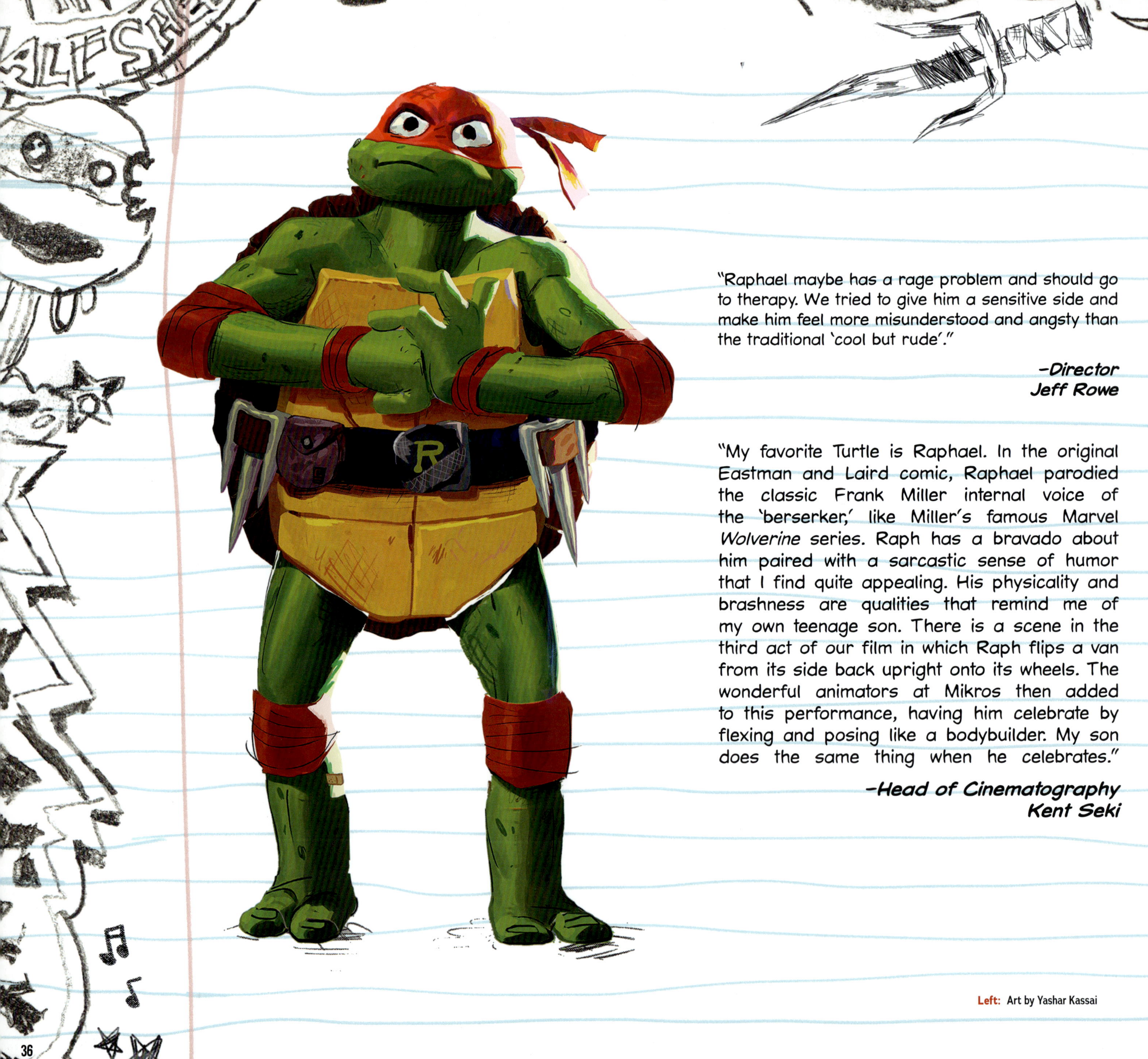

"Raphael maybe has a rage problem and should go to therapy. We tried to give him a sensitive side and make him feel more misunderstood and angsty than the traditional 'cool but rude'."

–Director
Jeff Rowe

"My favorite Turtle is Raphael. In the original Eastman and Laird comic, Raphael parodied the classic Frank Miller internal voice of the 'berserker,' like Miller's famous Marvel *Wolverine* series. Raph has a bravado about him paired with a sarcastic sense of humor that I find quite appealing. His physicality and brashness are qualities that remind me of my own teenage son. There is a scene in the third act of our film in which Raph flips a van from its side back upright onto its wheels. The wonderful animators at Mikros then added to this performance, having him celebrate by flexing and posing like a bodybuilder. My son does the same thing when he celebrates."

–Head of Cinematography
Kent Seki

Left: Art by Yashar Kassai

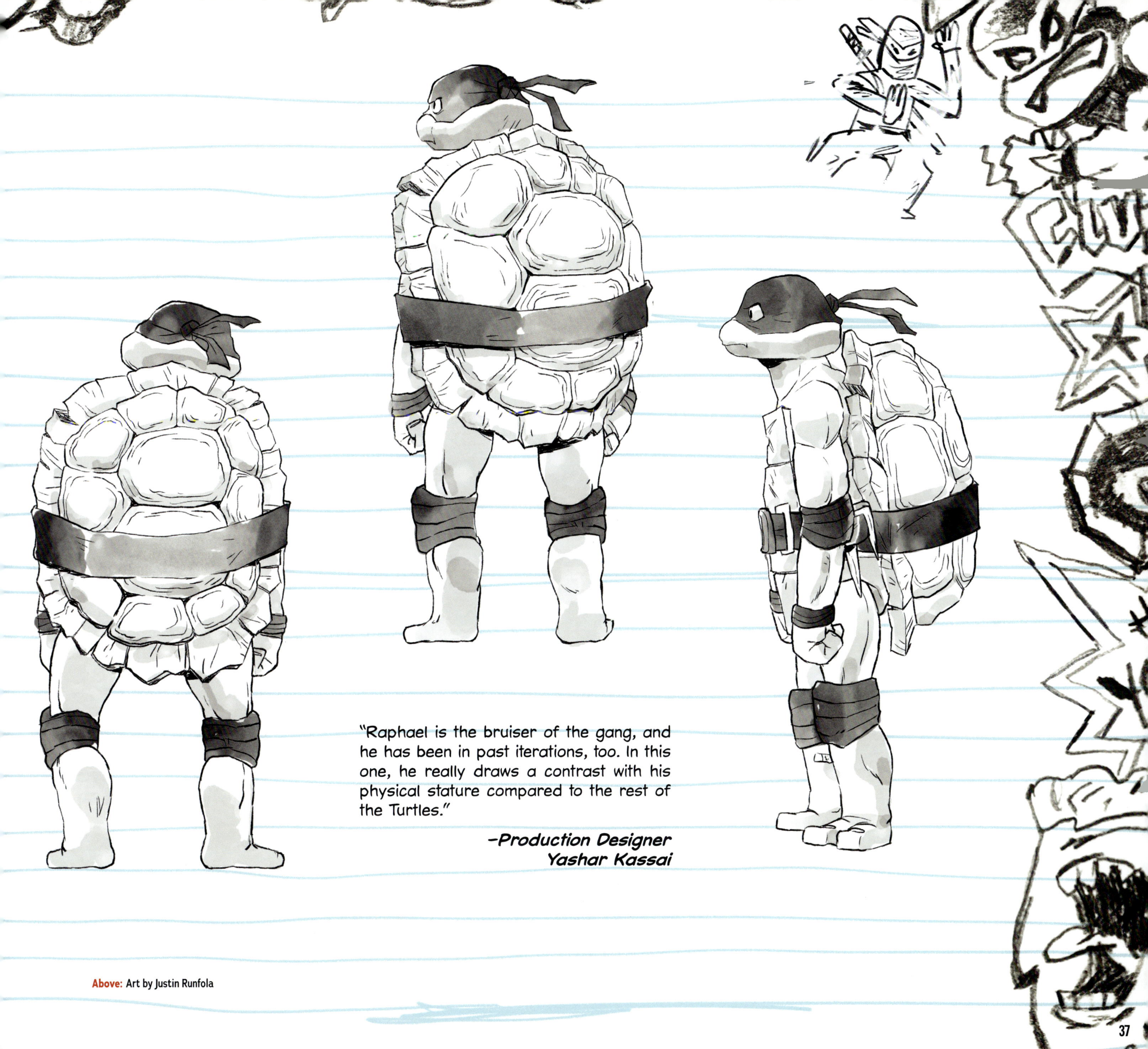

"Raphael is the bruiser of the gang, and he has been in past iterations, too. In this one, he really draws a contrast with his physical stature compared to the rest of the Turtles."

–Production Designer Yashar Kassai

Above: Art by Justin Runfola

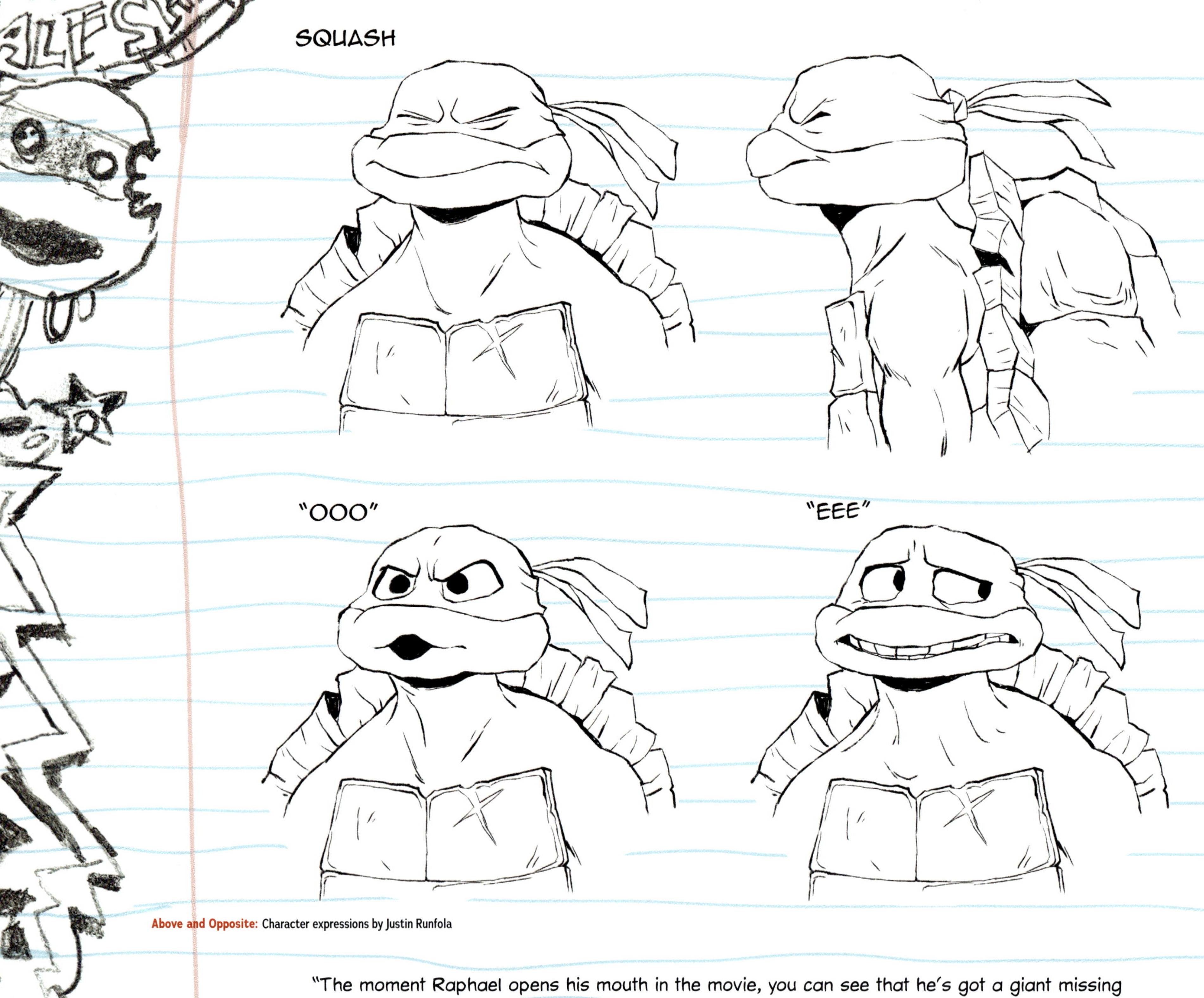

Above and Opposite: Character expressions by Justin Runfola

"The moment Raphael opens his mouth in the movie, you can see that he's got a giant missing tooth from the center of his top row of teeth (these are early design sketches without the missing tooth). His belt buckle has been handyman fixed with duct tape where it's been broken. He has a bunch of scrapes and scars all over his shell, so it's clear this dude has fought before."

–Production Designer Yashar Kassai

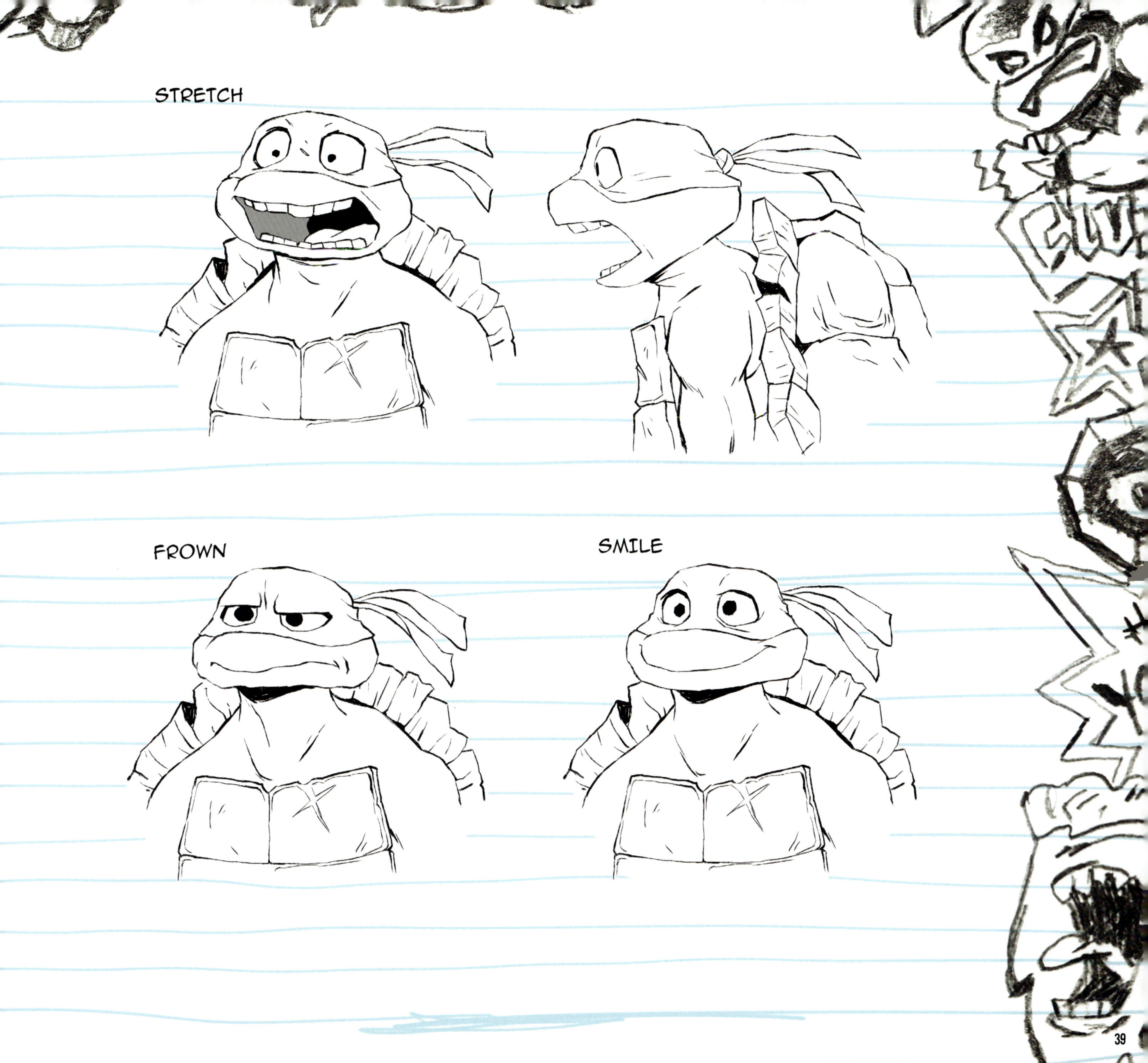
STRETCH
FROWN
SMILE

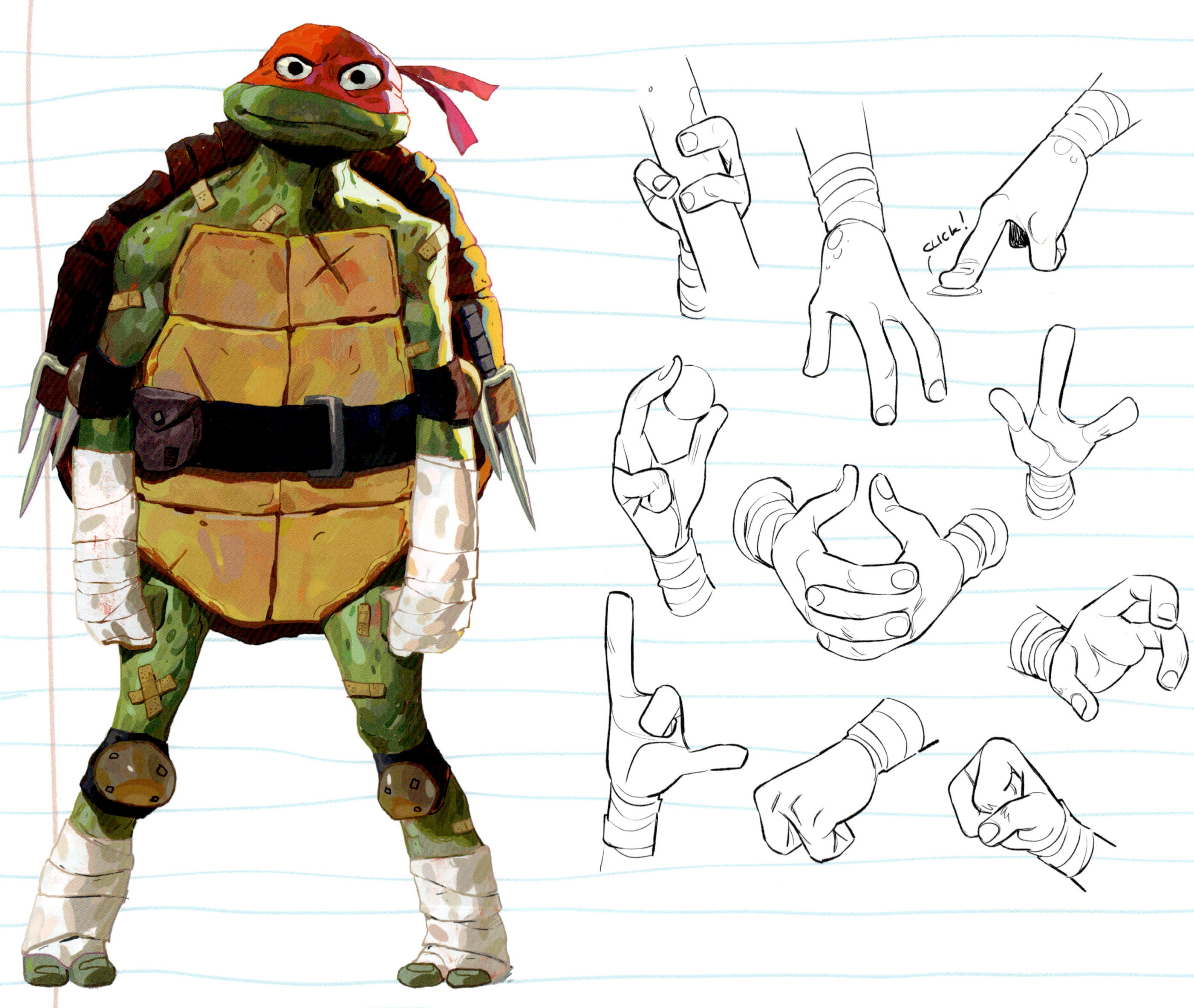

Left: Concept art by Yashar Kassai
Right: Hand design art by James A. Castillo

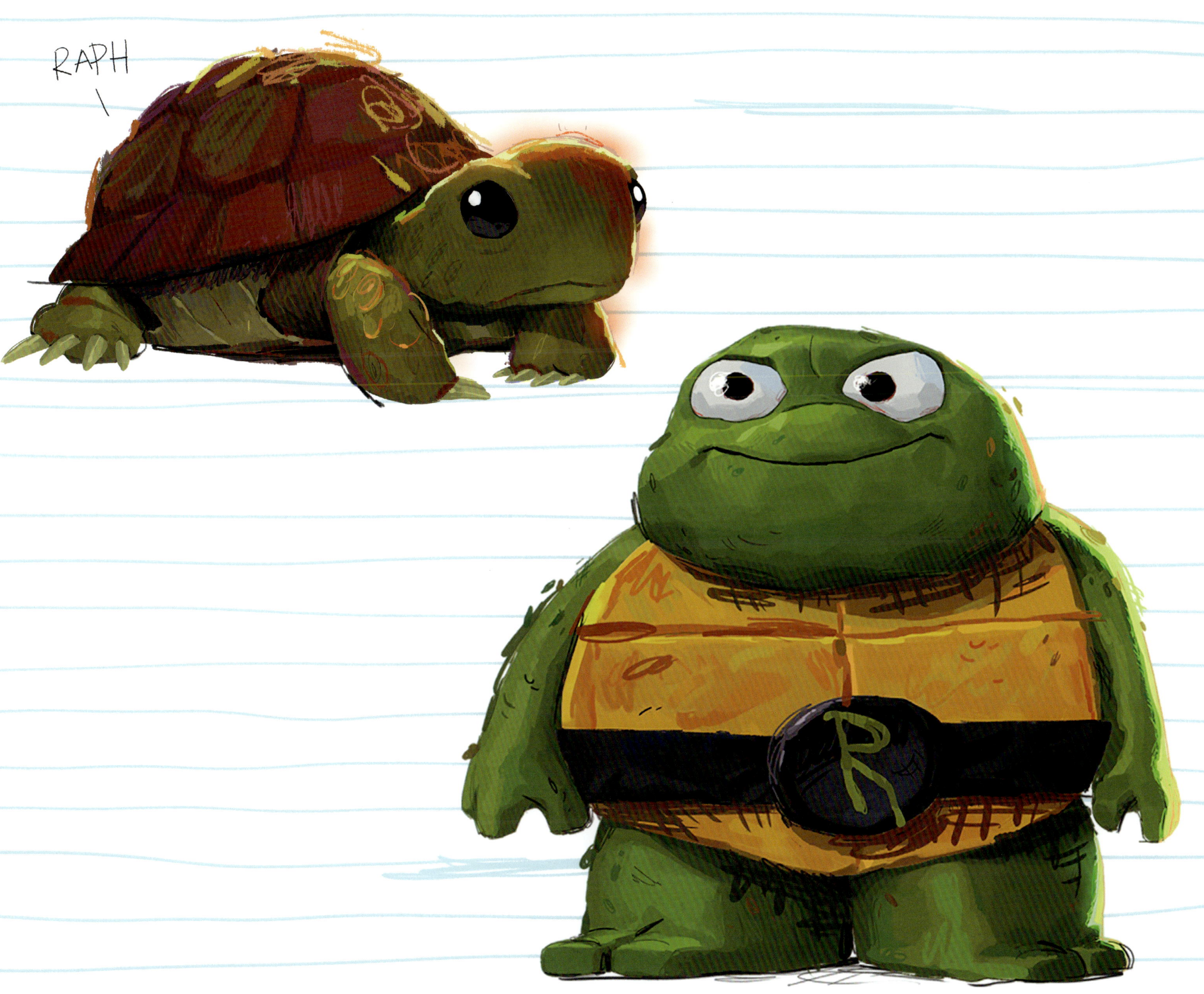

Top Left: Baby turtle art by Adel Sabi
Bottom Right: Toddler art by Alger Tam

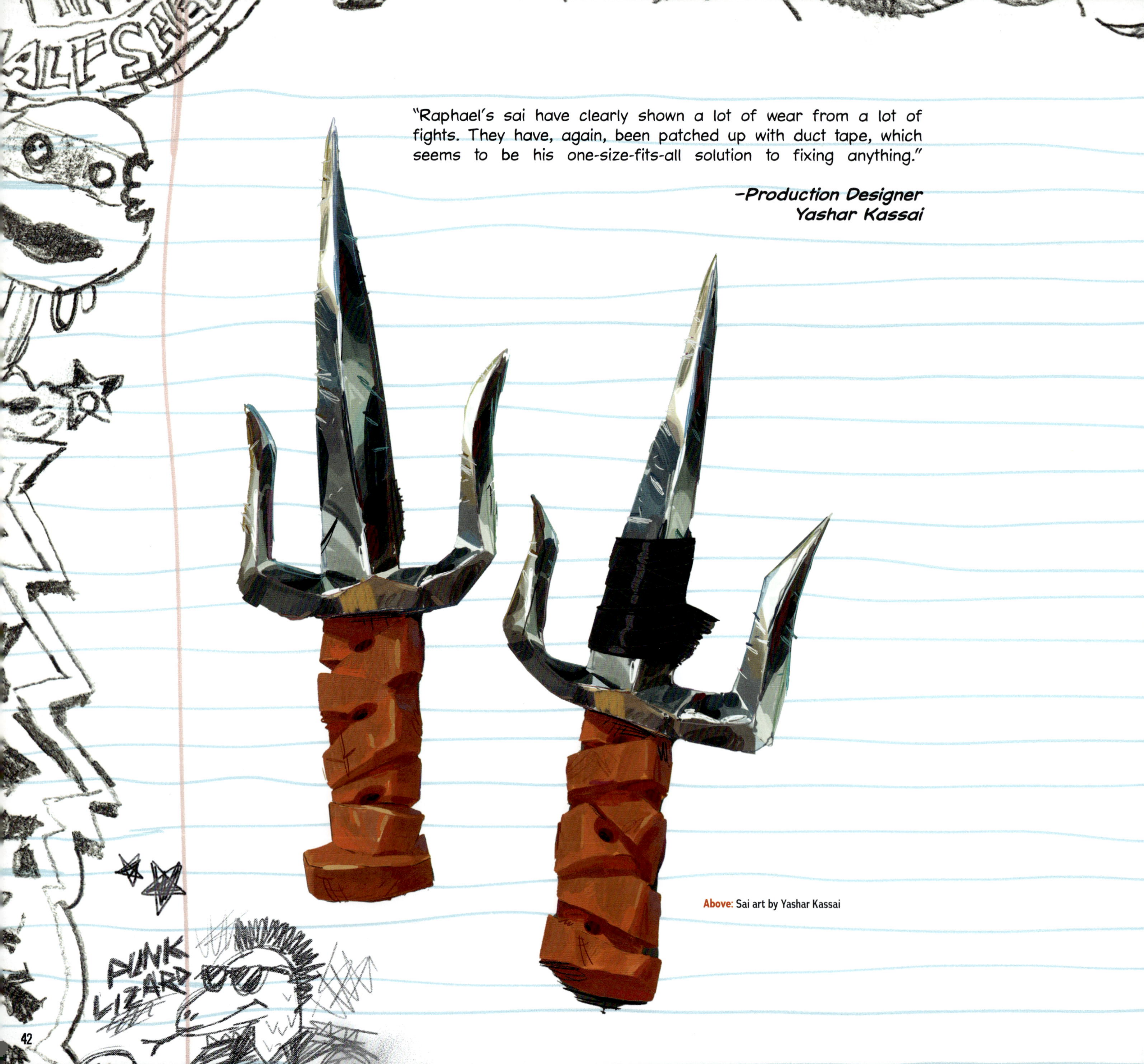

"Raphael's sai have clearly shown a lot of wear from a lot of fights. They have, again, been patched up with duct tape, which seems to be his one-size-fits-all solution to fixing anything."

–Production Designer Yashar Kassai

Above: Sai art by Yashar Kassai

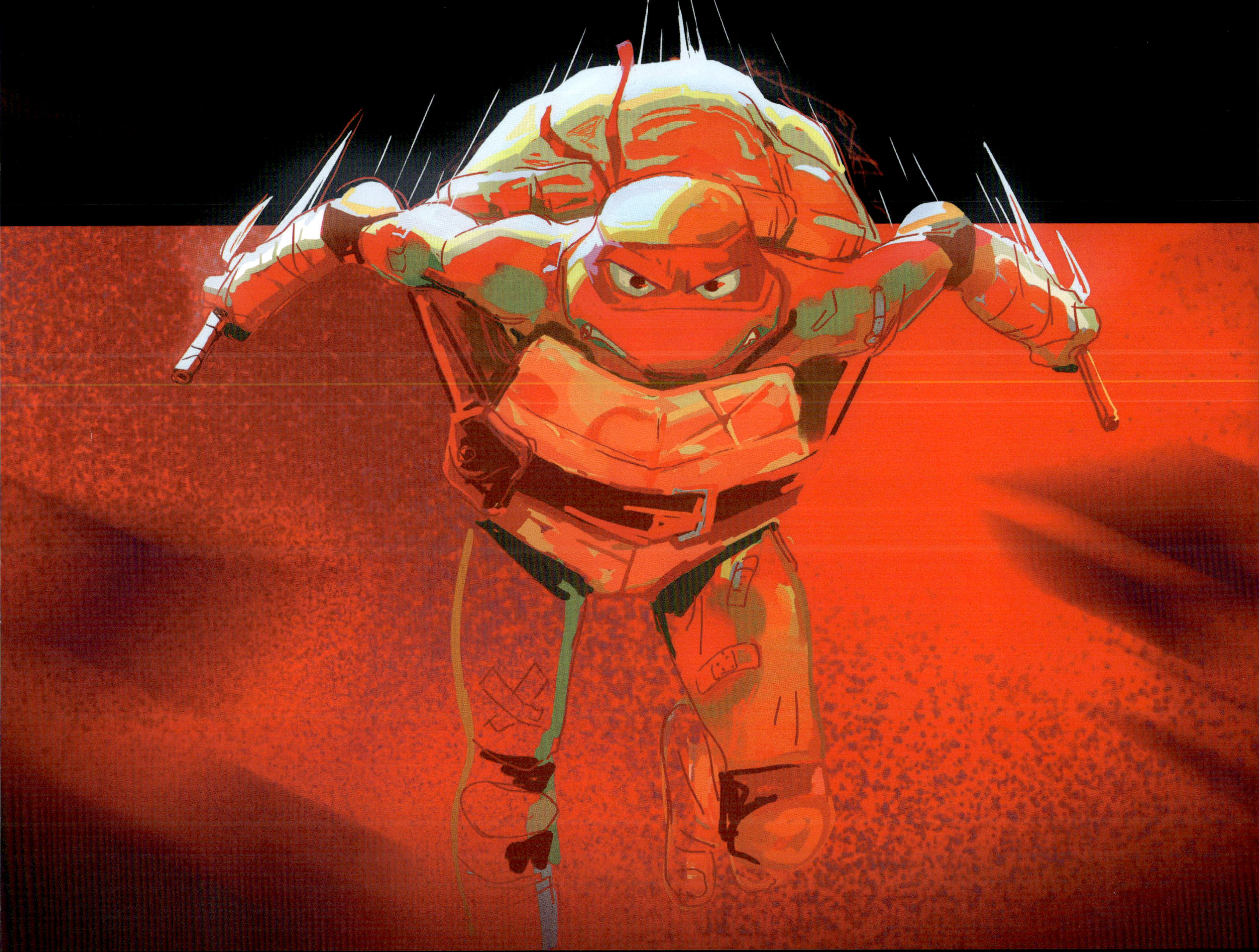

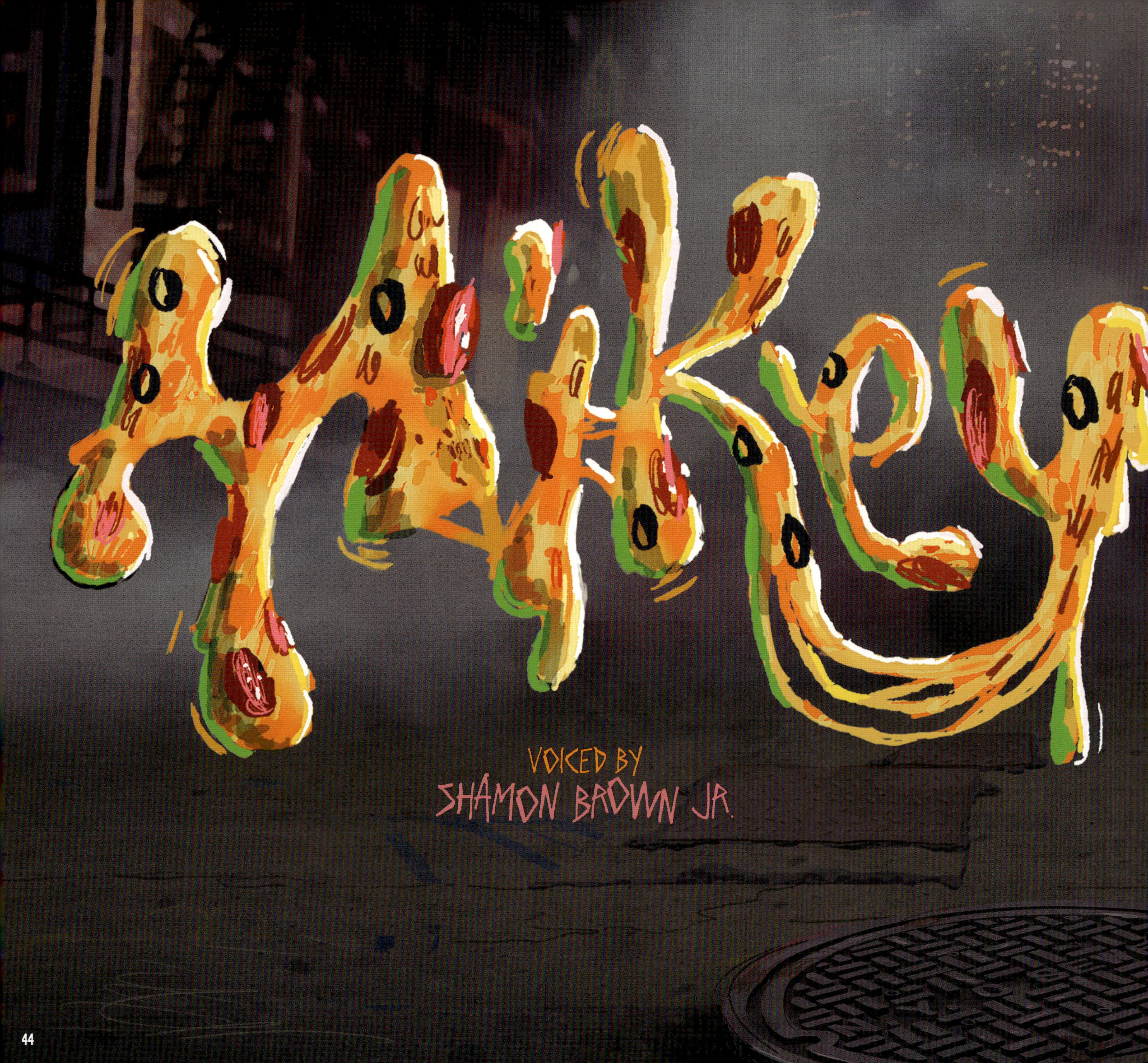
Mikey
VOICED BY
SHAMON BROWN JR.

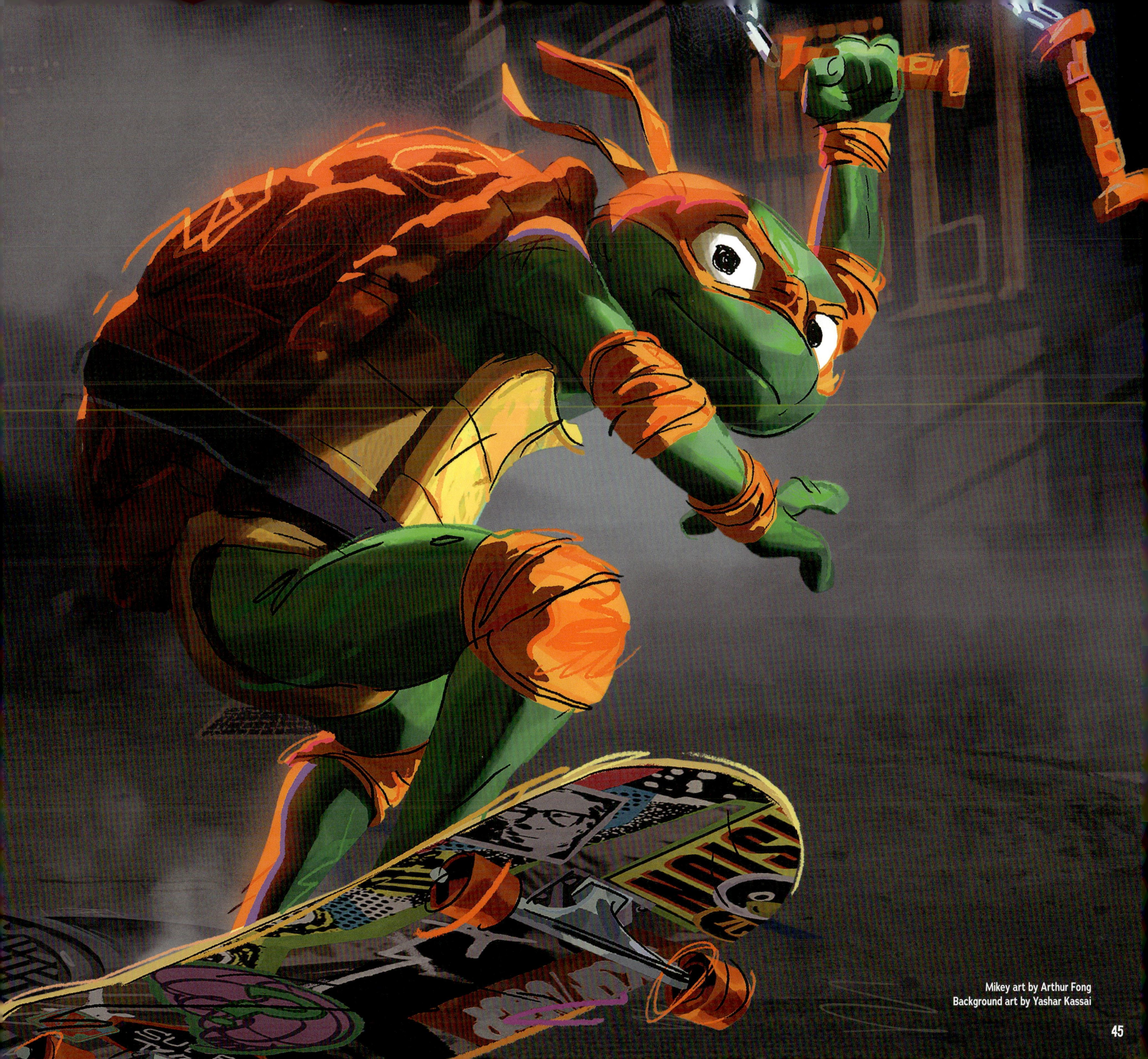

Mikey art by Arthur Fong
Background art by Yashar Kassai

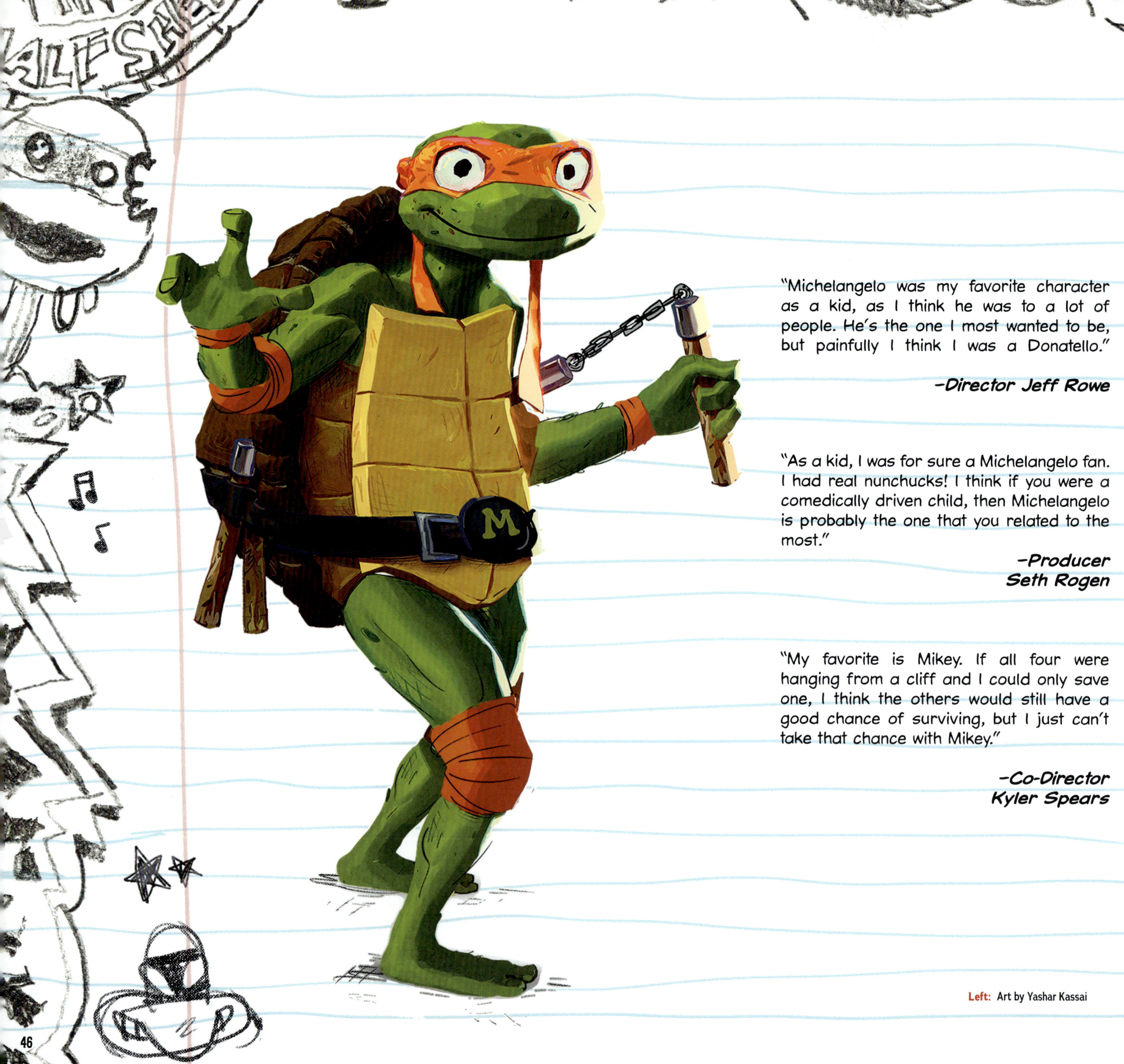

"Michelangelo was my favorite character as a kid, as I think he was to a lot of people. He's the one I most wanted to be, but painfully I think I was a Donatello."

–Director Jeff Rowe

"As a kid, I was for sure a Michelangelo fan. I had real nunchucks! I think if you were a comedically driven child, then Michelangelo is probably the one that you related to the most."

–Producer
Seth Rogen

"My favorite is Mikey. If all four were hanging from a cliff and I could only save one, I think the others would still have a good chance of surviving, but I just can't take that chance with Mikey."

–Co-Director
Kyler Spears

Left: Art by Yashar Kassai

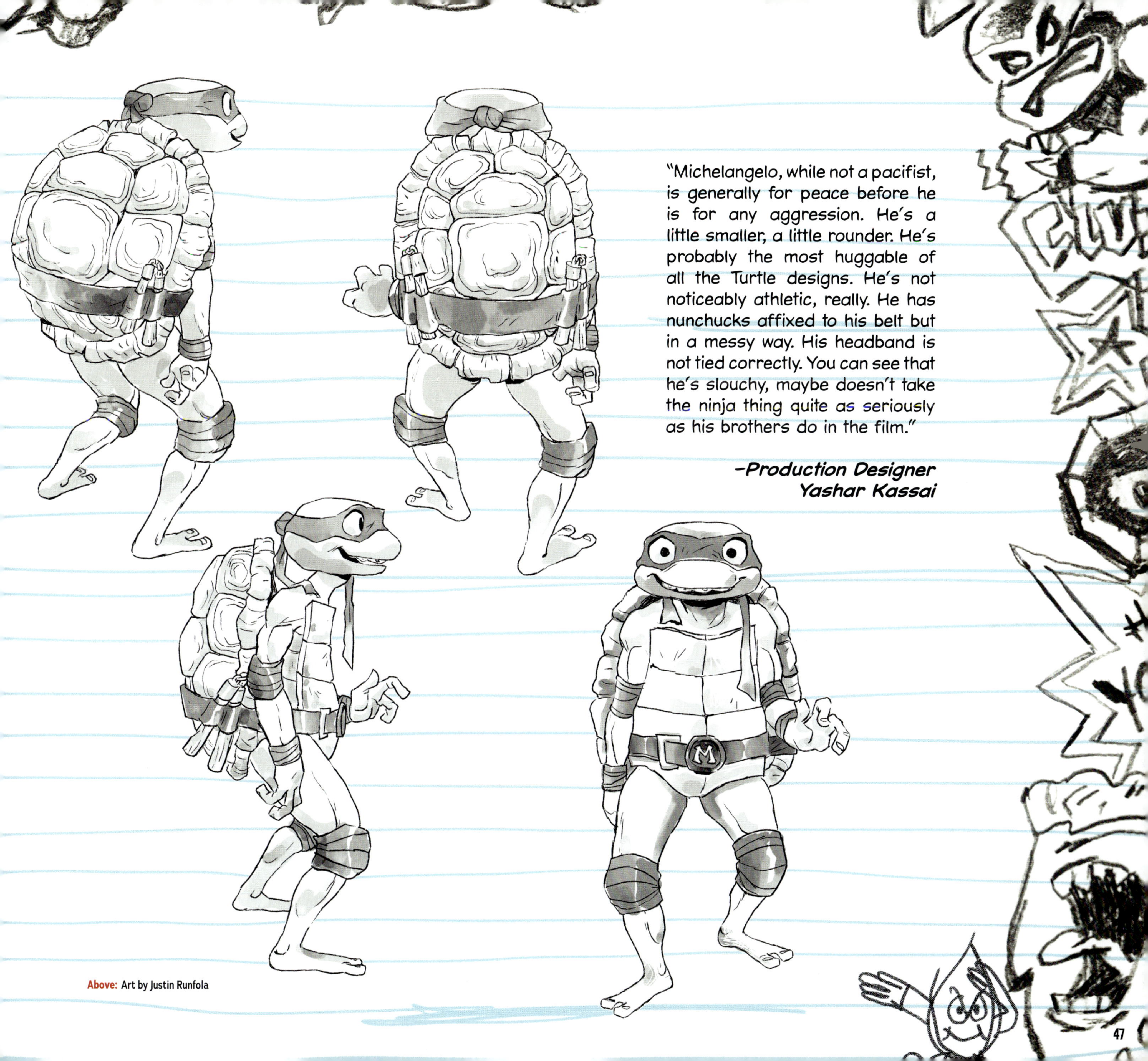

"Michelangelo, while not a pacifist, is generally for peace before he is for any aggression. He's a little smaller, a little rounder. He's probably the most huggable of all the Turtle designs. He's not noticeably athletic, really. He has nunchucks affixed to his belt but in a messy way. His headband is not tied correctly. You can see that he's slouchy, maybe doesn't take the ninja thing quite as seriously as his brothers do in the film."

–Production Designer Yashar Kassai

Above: Art by Justin Runfola

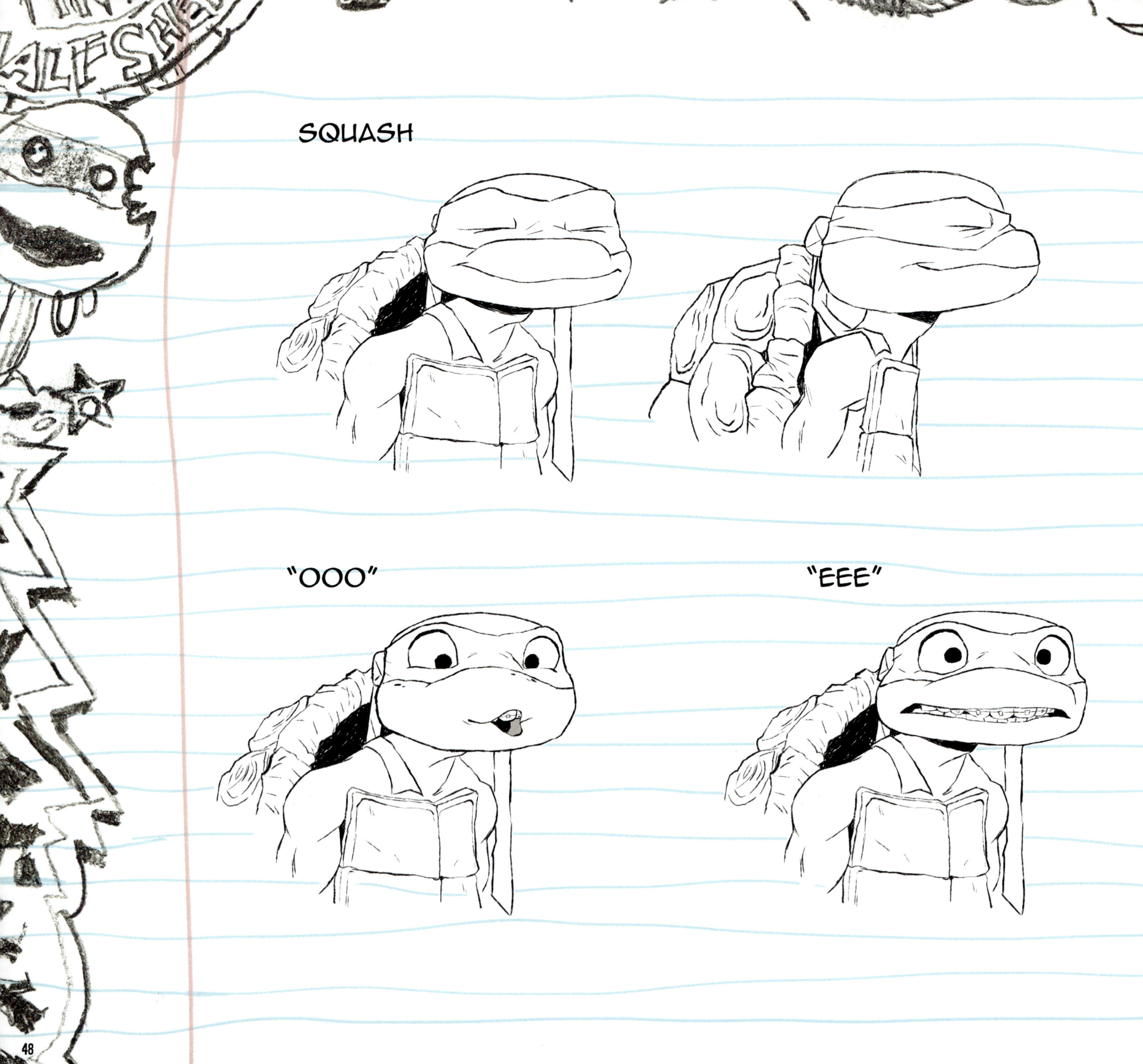

SQUASH
"OOO"
"EEE"

STRETCH

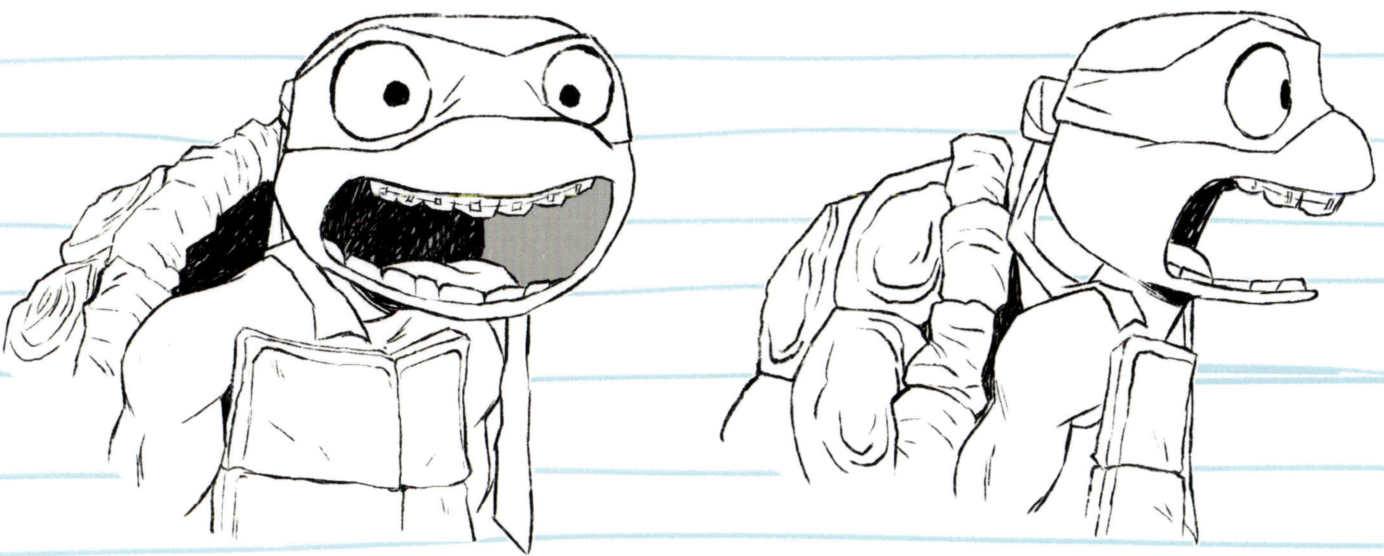

"Probably his most distinguishing feature, aside from just his proportions and the way he wears his clothing, is his braces. Very clear teenage braces across his teeth. Where those come from we choose not to say because we have no good answer, but we like the look of that on the character."

–Production Designer Yashar Kassai

FROWN

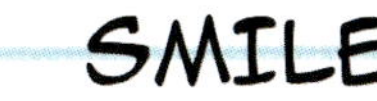

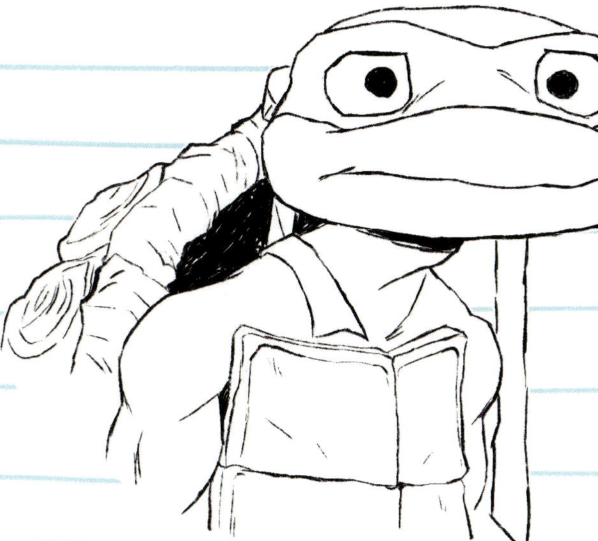

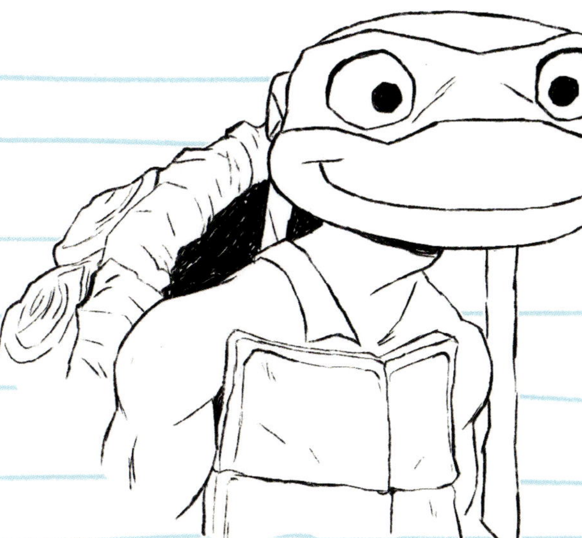

Above and Opposite: Character expressions by Justin Runfola

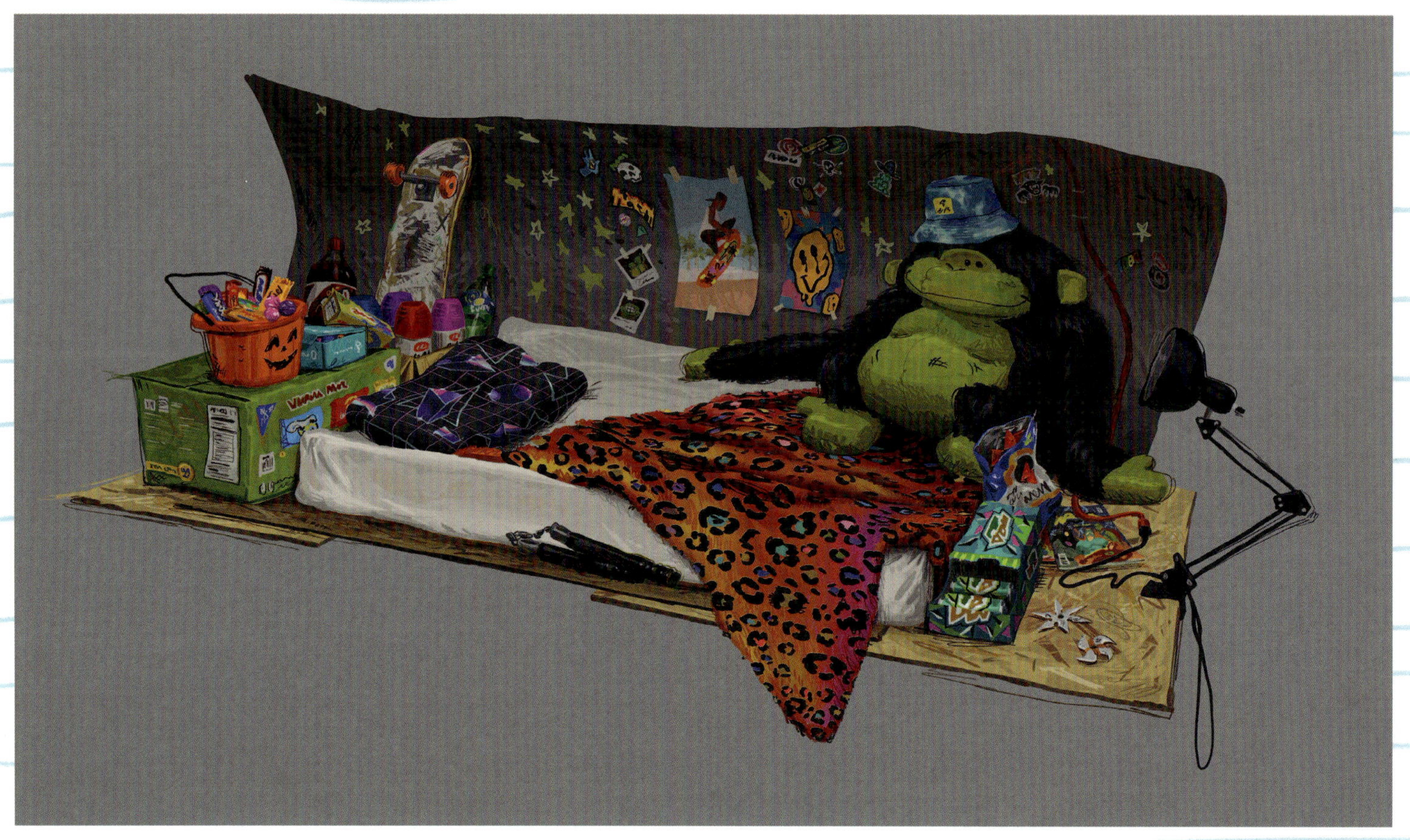

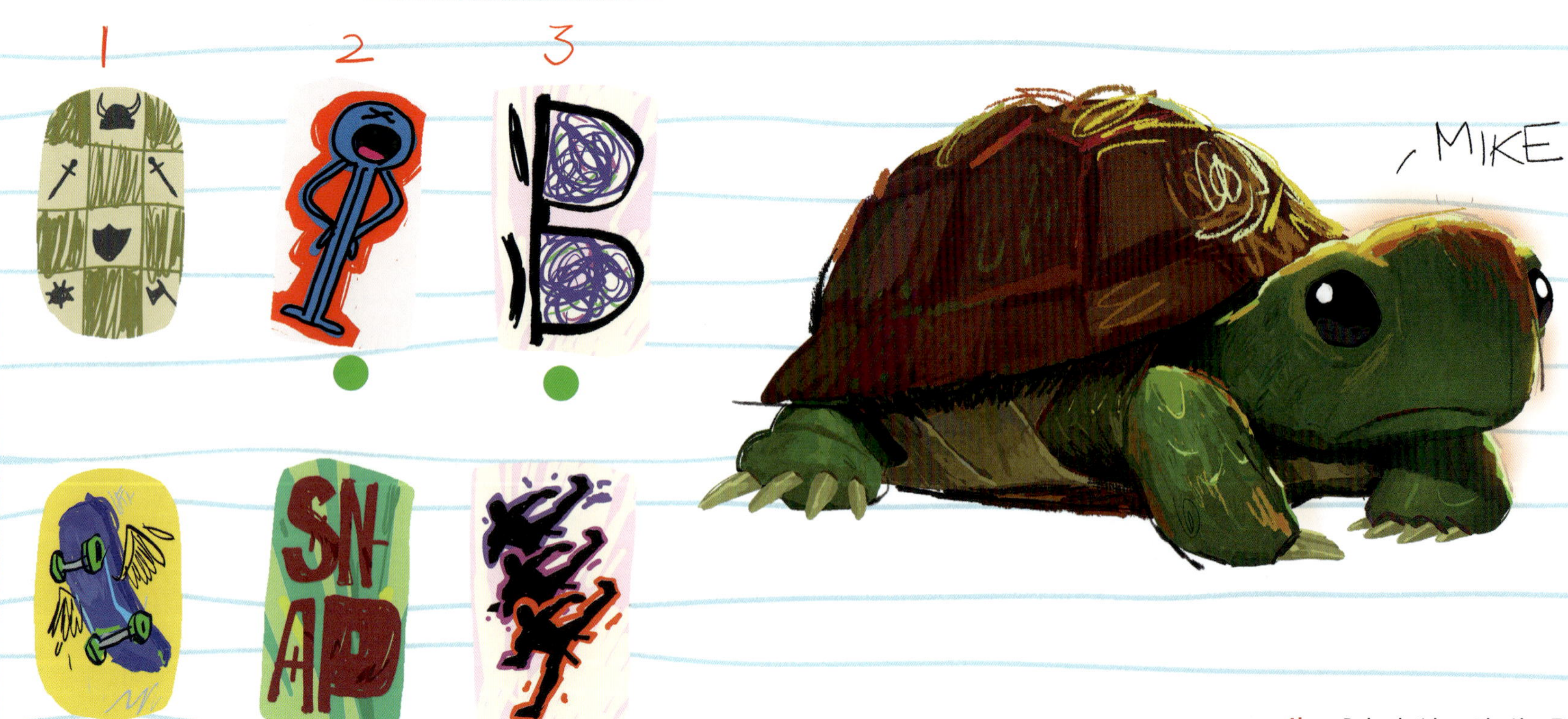

Above: Bed and sticker art by Alger Tam
Bottom Left: Stickers art by Tiffany Lam Almack
Bottom Right: Baby turtle art by Adel Sabi

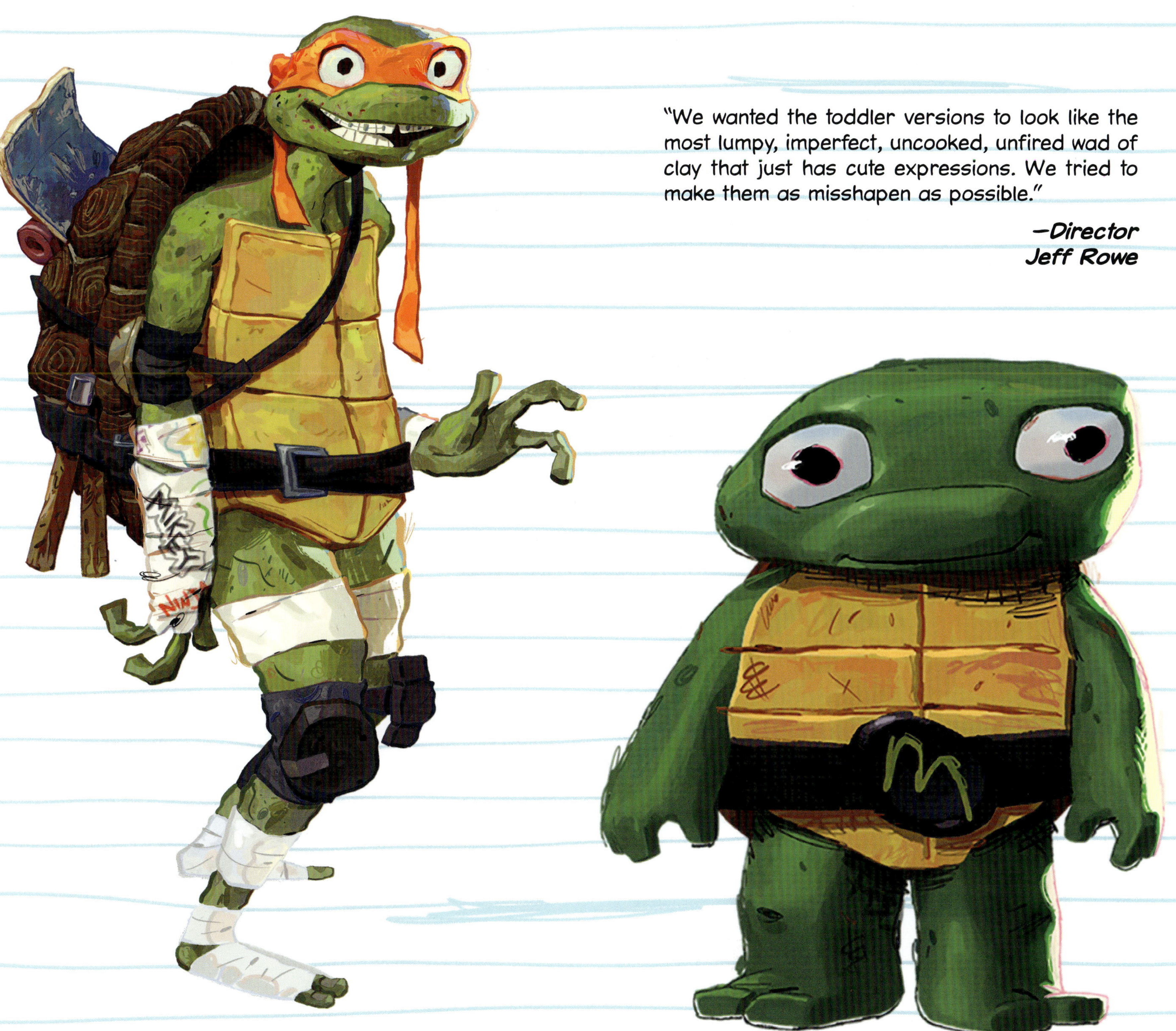

"We wanted the toddler versions to look like the most lumpy, imperfect, uncooked, unfired wad of clay that just has cute expressions. We tried to make them as misshapen as possible."

—Director Jeff Rowe

Left: Concept art by Yashar Kassai
Right: Toddler art by Alger Tam

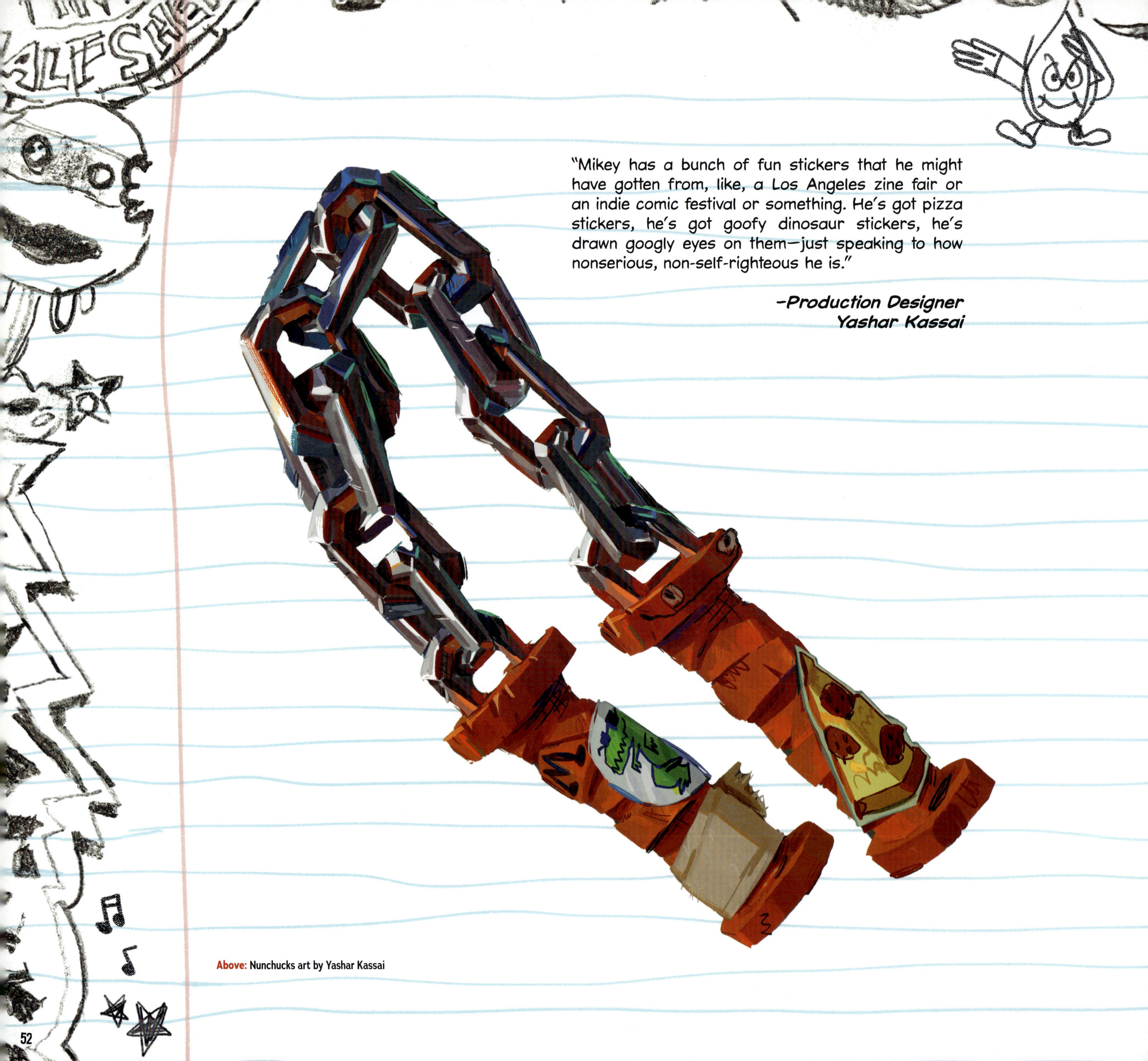

"Mikey has a bunch of fun stickers that he might have gotten from, like, a Los Angeles zine fair or an indie comic festival or something. He's got pizza stickers, he's got goofy dinosaur stickers, he's drawn googly eyes on them—just speaking to how nonserious, non-self-righteous he is."

–Production Designer Yashar Kassai

Above: Nunchucks art by Yashar Kassai

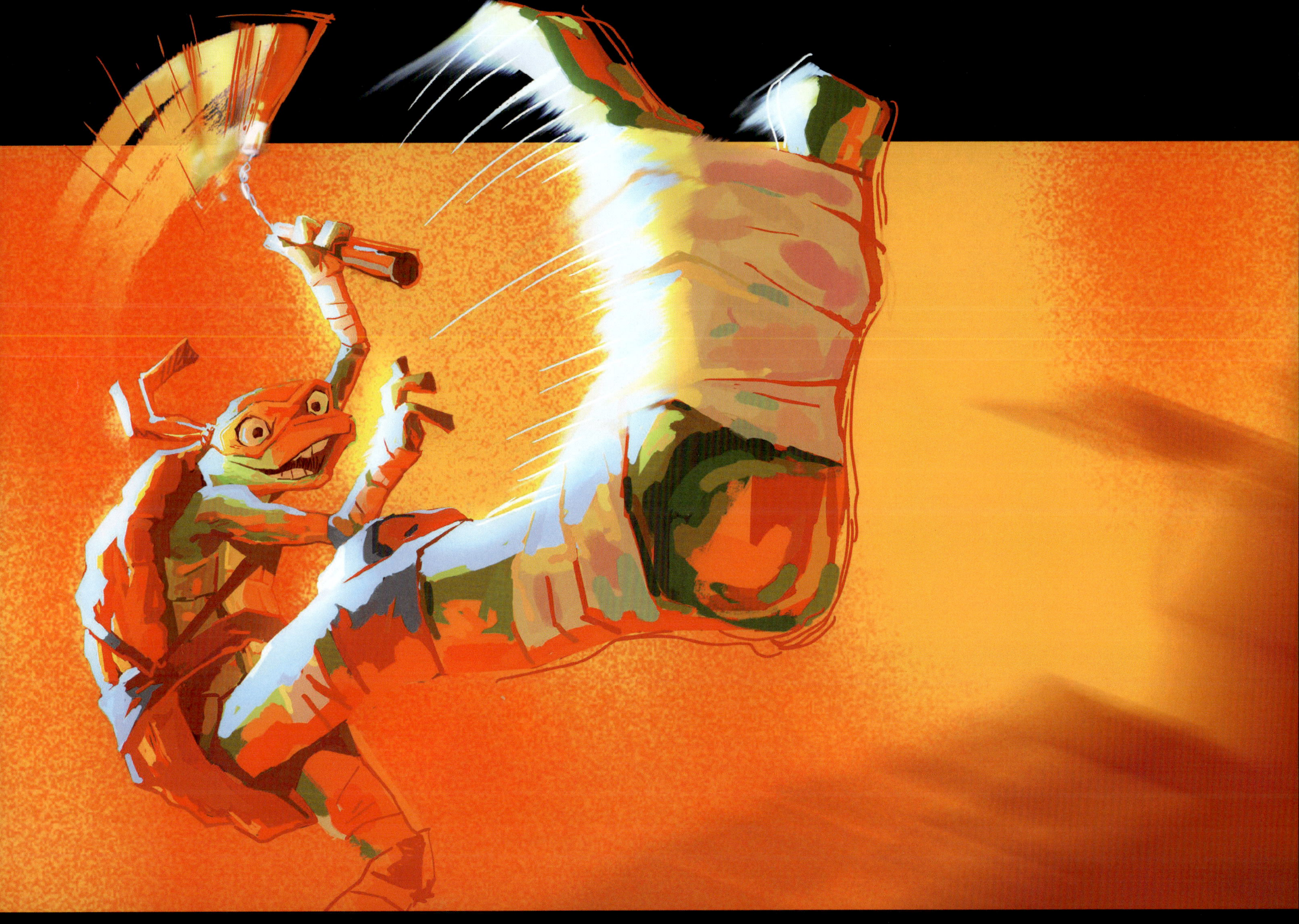

Above: Concept art by Lauren Airriess

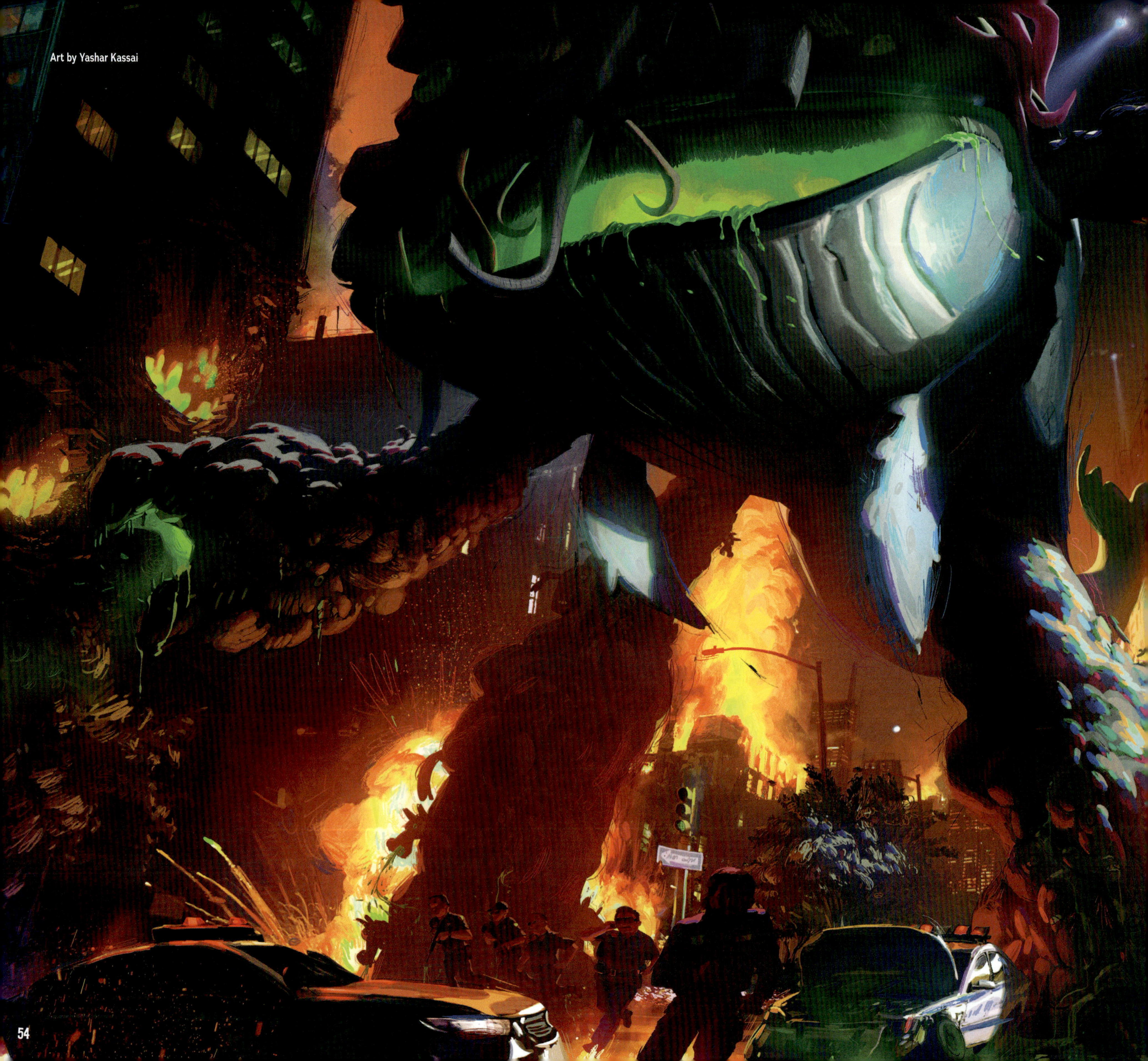

Art by Yashar Kassai

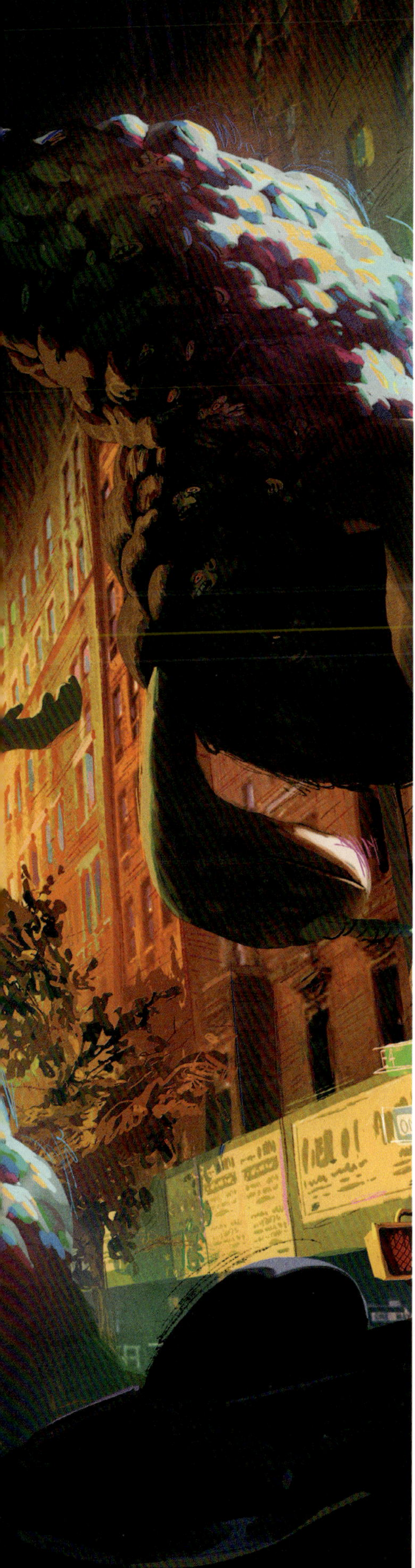

INTERVIEW WITH SETH ROGEN

Jim: The most obvious question is, what do the Turtles mean to you?

Seth: I grew up watching *Ninja Turtles.* I believe the animated show came out in, what, '89 or something like that?

Jim: '87.

Seth: '87, so I was five years old. The film came out in 1990. I was born in 1982, so it really came out when I was a kid, and I had all the toys, and I was obsessed with it, I just loved it. I did karate when I was a kid, probably inspired by the Teenage Mutant Ninja Turtles to some degree. My dad bought me a pair of nunchucks that I cracked my head open with.

Jim: Oh, no.

Seth: Yeah, actual nunchucks with a metal chain. He bought them at a flea market, and I seriously hurt myself with them. That's how much I love the Ninja Turtles. Honestly, it's something I've joked about for years, but I've always been such a big fan of teen driven material. *Superbad* was the first thing we wrote. *Freaks and Geeks* was the first thing I was on. This whole idea of teen-driven films and television shows was always my favorite genre. And I'd joke with my friends that the "teenage" part of the Teenage Mutant Ninja Turtles was always, to me, the most unexplored word of the Teenage Mutant Ninja Turtles. There was a lot of *mutant,* there was a lot of *ninja,* there was a lot of *turtle,* but the *teenage* part seemed to always fall through the cracks. As I got older, the idea of doing something that at once really spoke to the stuff that I was a huge fan of when I was a kid and really spoke to the kind of work I was really passionate about as an adult, and also the stuff that started my career when I was in my early twenties, there were a lot of things about it that I was really excited about.

Jim: And how do you make an interpretation of the Teenage Mutant Ninja Turtles that puts teenagers front and center?

Seth: You really look at it through a teenage lens, and you look at it through a character lens. What's great and kind of easy in a way and intuitive is that every teenager has an inherent desire to belong and to be accepted and to feel as though they are not outcasts or loners or losers and feel like they are a part of the group and that could not have more organically fit in with what you would project onto the personalities of teenage boys who are relegated to a life in the shadows, in the sewers, where they have been told that they'll never be accepted, probably rightfully! They probably wouldn't be! And so there were a lot of themes honestly, between being mutant crime fighters and just being awkward teenagers, that really overlapped much more naturally than maybe you would think. So, yeah, this story about these teenage boys who have always been told humans would hate them, and they've always wanted to be accepted by humans, and this idea that if they help humans maybe they will be accepted by them, lined up well to a nice convergence of emotional story and action movie plot.

Jim: It's an interesting metaphor, and to my knowledge, it's not one that any of the many, many interpretations of the Turtles has explored before.

Seth: It's a really intuitive way into it that I think really speaks to a lot of very relatable, growing-up themes, and it's always nice when you get to be the first one to do it.

Jim: What are other ways in which *Mutant Mayhem* is different from the Turtles projects that we've seen before?

Seth: Well, the look of the film is also directly inspired by the teenage element. Jeff Rowe, the director, was presenting a lot of concept art, and the kind of backstory, if you will, of the art was that a teenager scribbled it in the back of their binder or something like that. And that's actually where the original Teenage Mutant Ninja Turtles came from! The creators were just drawing things in notebooks and kind of scribbling them to make each other laugh. So Jeff brought us this imagery of concept art that was kind of done with the passion of a teenager where nothing's really staying in the lines, and the lines are inconsistent, and you're kind of pushing harder and more aggressively on the parts of the image you care about more, and in the background you're being a little rougher, and you're not that concerned with symmetry. Now, often, I've made a lot of animated things. You see the concept art and it does not translate that literally to the actual animation. Often the concept art is very painterly, kind of impressionistic, and then the animation is very clean, very rounded, all the roughness is removed from it.

Jim: I'm thinking of *Sausage Party*.

Seth: Exactly! And then, yeah, it actually all started with this mailbox. That was, I think the first thing that was rendered in 3D—this mailbox that had been drawn previously, and it was all rough and scribbly. And then they rendered it in 3D and it kind of looked like the drawing, and then I remember it rotated and it was unlike anything I'd ever seen. All the things that jutted out of the scribble were all dimensionalized in a way that really blew my mind. And then we started seeing more of it with the characters. And, again, the characters had this fun, kind of scribbled look, with the passion that a teenager would draw them in their notebook. And then we started to see them come to life! The whole look of the movie, the way the light moved and the way the explosions and smoke had these swirls, we started to see that stuff really early on. It actually made us—we were still working on the script for the movie, and that's what happens with these animated movies, is that you're often writing them in parallel as you're developing the look—it made us start to write to the look of the movie. It was a really inspiring look, and as one of the writers, I was thinking, like, "What do I want to see in this look? What do I want to see brought to life?" It was such a fun look that it also informed the storytelling. It made you think that the movie has to be fun, and it has to tonally fit into this adolescent, reckless, but very energetic style of art. Yeah, it really informed the structure and the tone and all that of the actual writing of the movie, which was really interesting.

Jim: Can you give me some examples of specific choices that were inspired by the art style?

Seth: I think including more and more mutants was inspired by the art style. At first, there weren't that many of them, and then we really started to lean in to, structurally, making a movie that required a lot of mutants and creatures. We really re-outlined the movie with the idea of adding more creatures into it because it was just so fun and exciting and they looked so cool. And they really were inspired by all my favorite toys when I was a kid, which was really fun to bring to life as well. The setting, the action, the car chases, things like that, the giant monster at the end of the movie, a lot of that stuff was really inspired by, honestly, just me thinking, what do I want to personally see brought to life in this aesthetic.

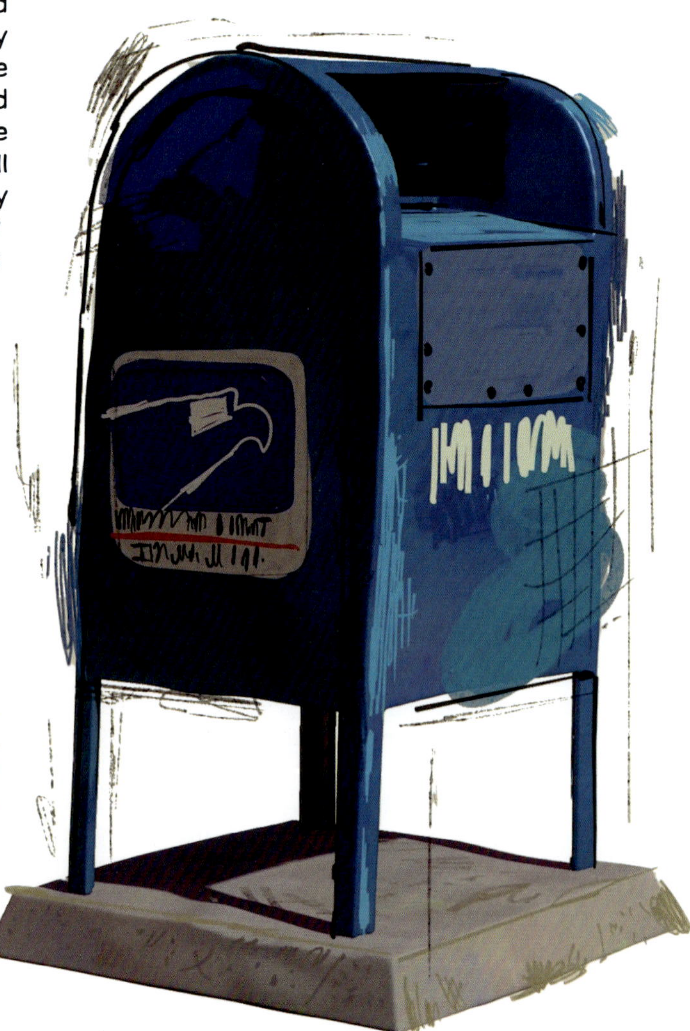

3D mailbox test by Yashar Kassai

Jim: When did the title *Mutant Mayhem* get attached to the project?

Seth: I think around that same time. We were pretty deep into the writing process as that title came about. It had a few other titles up until then, but there was a moment when this storyline, this plot, these arcs for the characters really synthesized and came together as the art style and animation was really getting realized as well. We had done a few recordings with the cast and we started to get to know them better, and the guys were playing the Turtles and we started to understand their dynamic, and that actually heavily informed the tone as well. It all kind of came together a year and a half into the process. Luckily, it's a four-year process so we had plenty of time to work after that.

Jim: I'm glad you brought up the cast. I'm seeing a lot of excitement in the Turtles fandom about the absolutely spectacular group of actors you've brought together. How did that come about?

Seth: I'm a fan of big casts! I came up watching movies where I was dazzled by the prospect of seeing all these performers I loved together in something. I'm a fan of all these people. I genuinely think that whether you have five lines or 500 lines in something, if you're able to get the funniest people you can and the best performers you can, then just go for it. All the people we got were the people we spoke about while designing the characters as well. It was really a dream situation in that we were able to tailor-make the characters and their styles and their jokes to the performers we wanted and, ultimately, got.

Jim: Is there a lot of improv in the film, or is it mostly scripted?

Seth: No, there's TONS of improv. We actually recorded with a lot of the actors together almost all the time. I think every time the Turtles recorded, except for a few pickup lines here or there, all four of them were together in a group. When we had Ice Cube come in he was with them a lot of the time. There was one time when it was all four of the Turtles, Ice Cube, me, Rose Byrne, and Natasia Demetriou, and maybe even one more person, again, all in the same session together. Every time Paul Rudd recorded, I would record as well. It's specifically so we can play off each other, improvise, and riff. The movie has a hypernaturalistic energy to it, and we really wanted to feel like everyone is kind of talking over each other. We tried to eliminate a lot of the rigidity that's associated with animated movies and infuse a naturalism that is almost impossible to obtain in animated movies because they essentially never record people in the same place at the same time, and once you do that it really opens up a tone that is not possible unless you're doing that.

It really was this idea of making sure that people were together. I remember the first time we recorded, they were all together but it wasn't being done in a way that they were all recording simultaneously, talking over each other. I remember we would record at this place in the Valley and we did it for like an hour and it was like fine and it was funny. Then we took a lunch break, and then I saw the kids, the four guys who were the Turtles, sitting together at a little table eating lunch together. They were all talking over each other, making fun of each other, clowning each other, just unrelentingly disrespectful to one another, interrupting each other. I remember going and being like, "That's what it needs to be like." The way they just *are* when they're together, that's what real teenagers feel like. What we're doing is *fine,* but I don't think we're capturing this lightning in a bottle that you get when you actually have four teenagers really being themselves around each other and really interacting with each other in the way that they would normally. That became a big revelation.

It was honestly really hard. Most recording is not set up to have four people record simultaneously. It took us a while to actually drill down on the best way to do it. There were a few sessions where we tried and we weren't getting good enough, clean sound on everybody, things like that. We eventually drilled down on a very good system, but that was a real revelation. I remember calling the other producers and saying that this has to be how we do it. We can never just record one line and the next line and the next line. Once you see what we can get when we're all together, it'll never feel good when they're not together.

Jim: What's the most fun thing that's happened in the course of putting the film together?

Seth: Honestly, I'm a huge Jackie Chan fan. If you ask me who the greatest living comedian is at this moment, I would say Jackie Chan. I love Jackie Chan. I'm obsessed with him. I will put him in a Charlie Chaplin, Buster Keaton category. He has abilities that are impossible to obtain by many and is truly a marvel. What's almost more amazing, though, in this movie is that it's voice work, and so you're kind of stripping away all the things that you would assume make him the funny, charismatic performer he is, and that's not true! He steals the entire movie, he's the funniest person in the entire movie, he's by far the audience's favorite character, and it only speaks more to what a powerhouse comedic talent he is, truly one of the greatest of all time. I've been in every one of his recording sessions I think, and it's truly amazing to watch him work. His timing, his emotionality, his delivery, he's *so* good. I'm so lucky to have gotten to do it honestly.

Jim: What would you like the fans to walk out of the movie theater and take away from the film?

Seth: I really want people to love the movie. Even if it's not their favorite Turtles movie, I want them to love it. It was made by people who genuinely love Ninja Turtles, so I think we're trying to do ourselves justice, and in turn, I hope we're doing the fans justice as well.

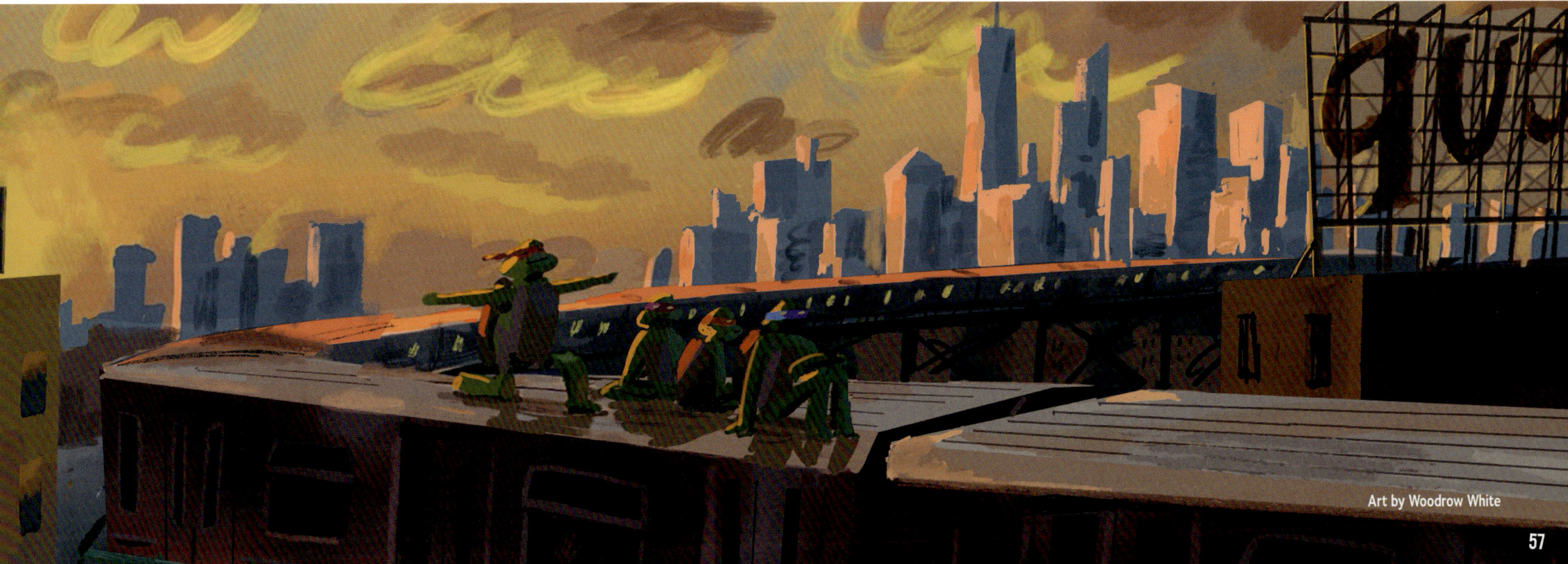

Art by Woodrow White

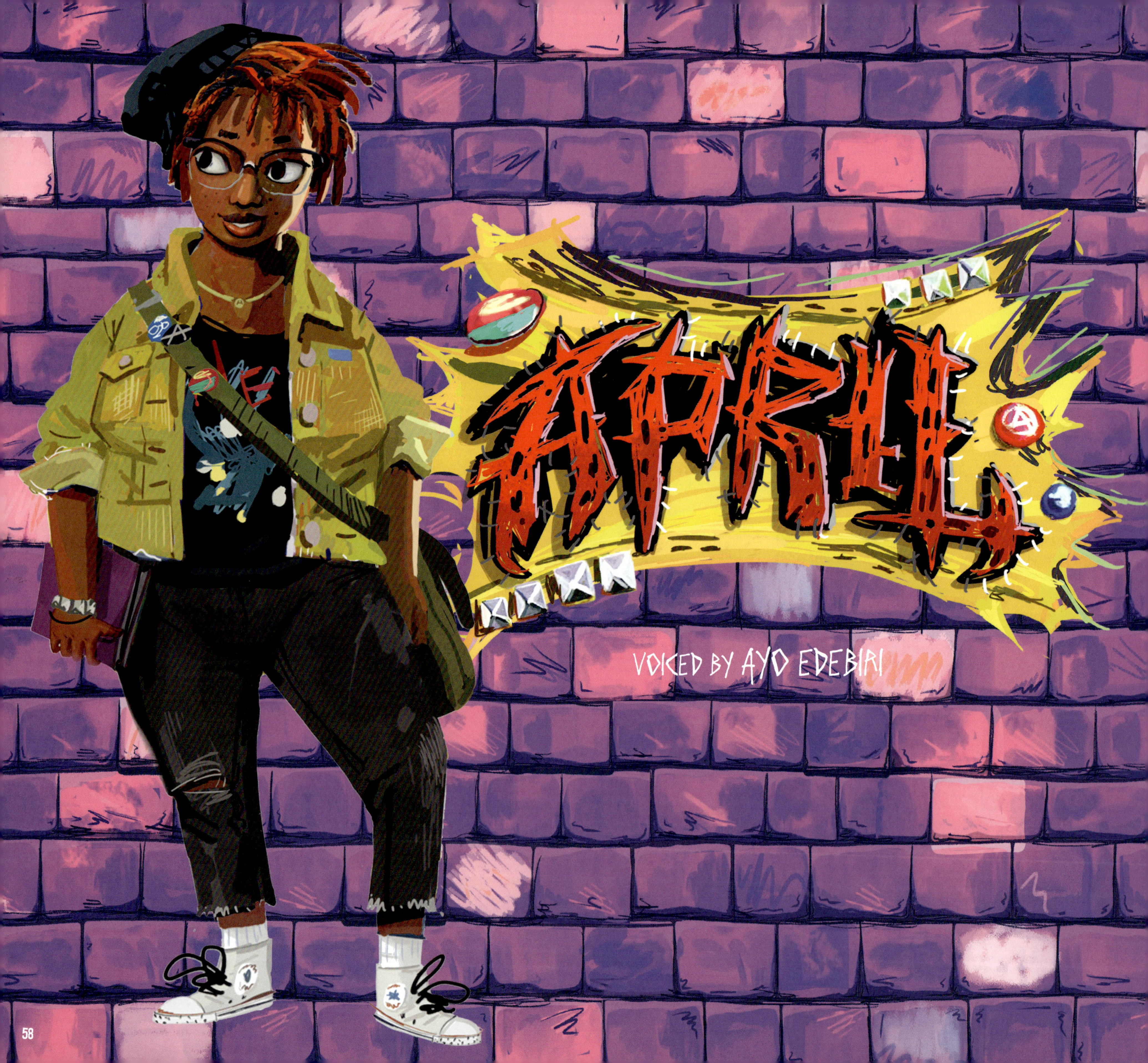
APRIL
VOICED BY AYO EDEBIRI

"There's a trend in animation to be like 'she's the girl character and she's like cool and tough, kicking doors and taking names.' We just wanted her to feel like a real actual teenager who is flawed like the Turtles and has hopes and dreams of her own and is navigating the painful and difficult experience of being a human just as much as anyone."

–Director Jeff Rowe

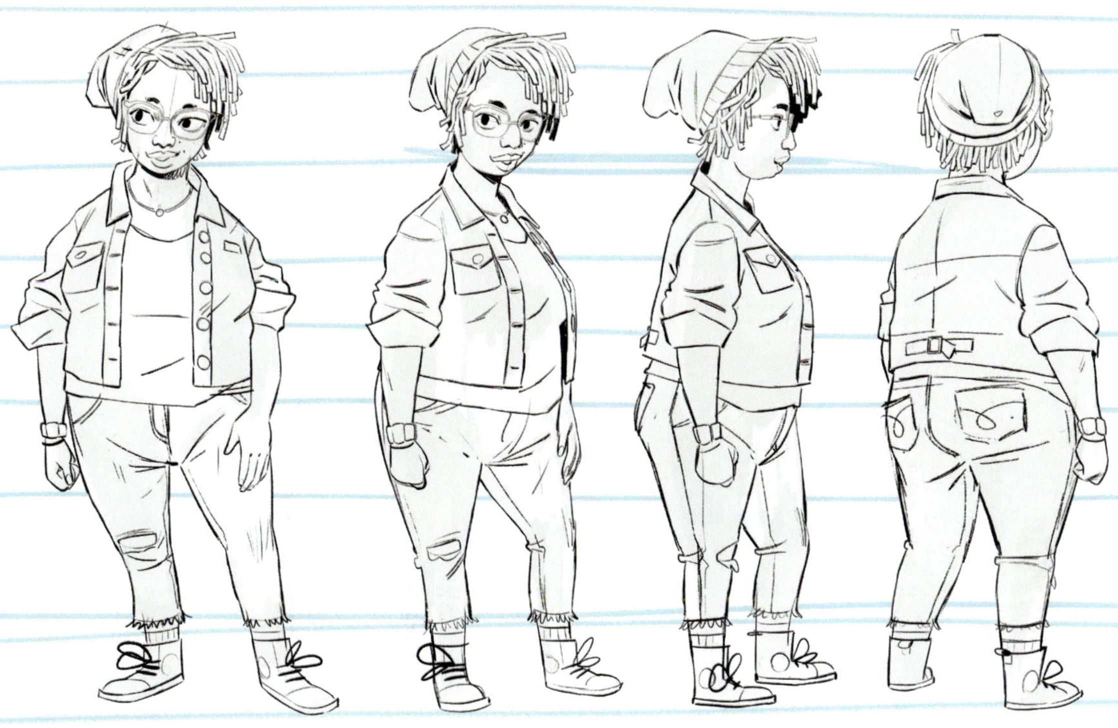

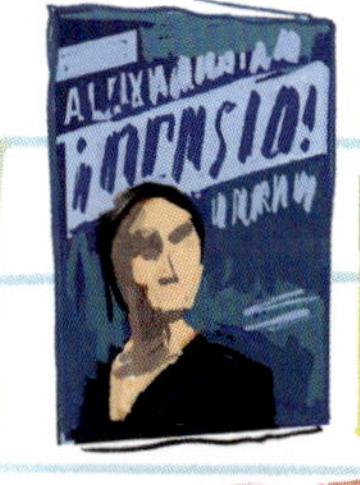

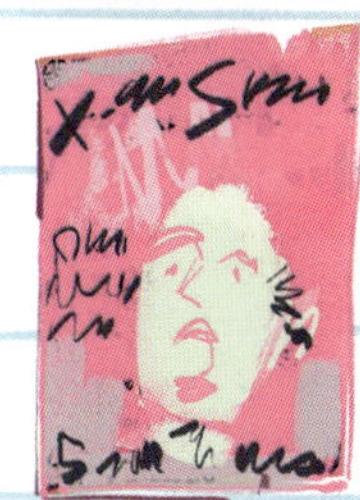

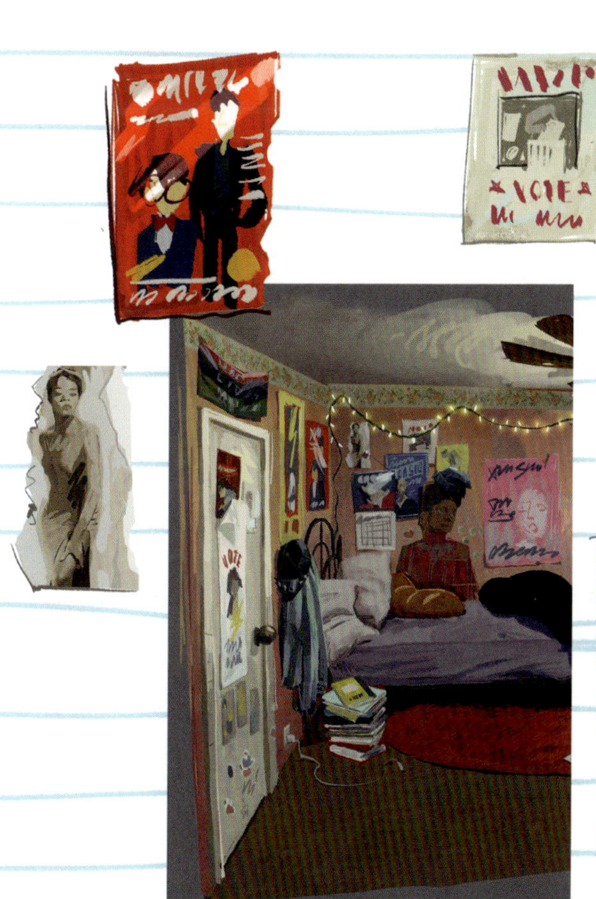

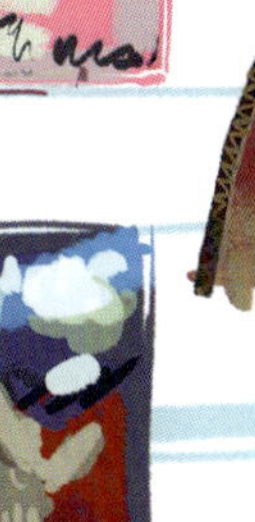

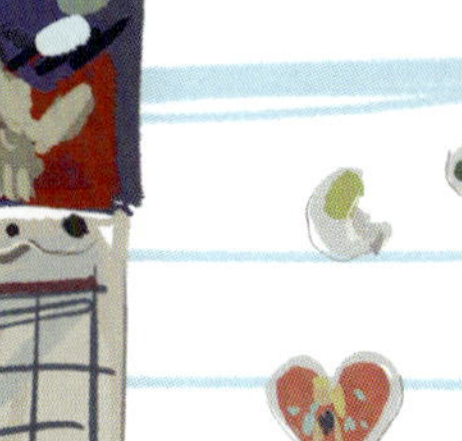

"April is a pretty cool, stylish young teen, maybe inspired by the current *Gen Z*. We see a lot of people in Los Angeles that dress like April.

We wanted to ground the character in something that was clear to us first off. She has things like a cool graphic tee that alludes to an alt-indie band she might listen to."

–Production Designer Yashar Kassai

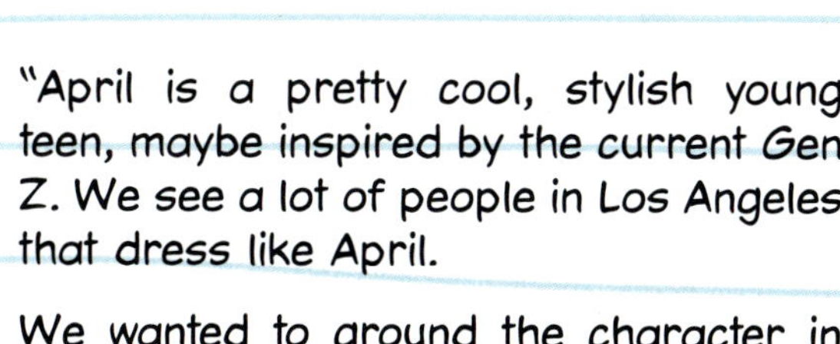

Above: Character design art by James A. Castillo
Below: Bedroom concept art by Chalky Wong and Lily Nishita
Opposite: Character art by Lauren Airriess

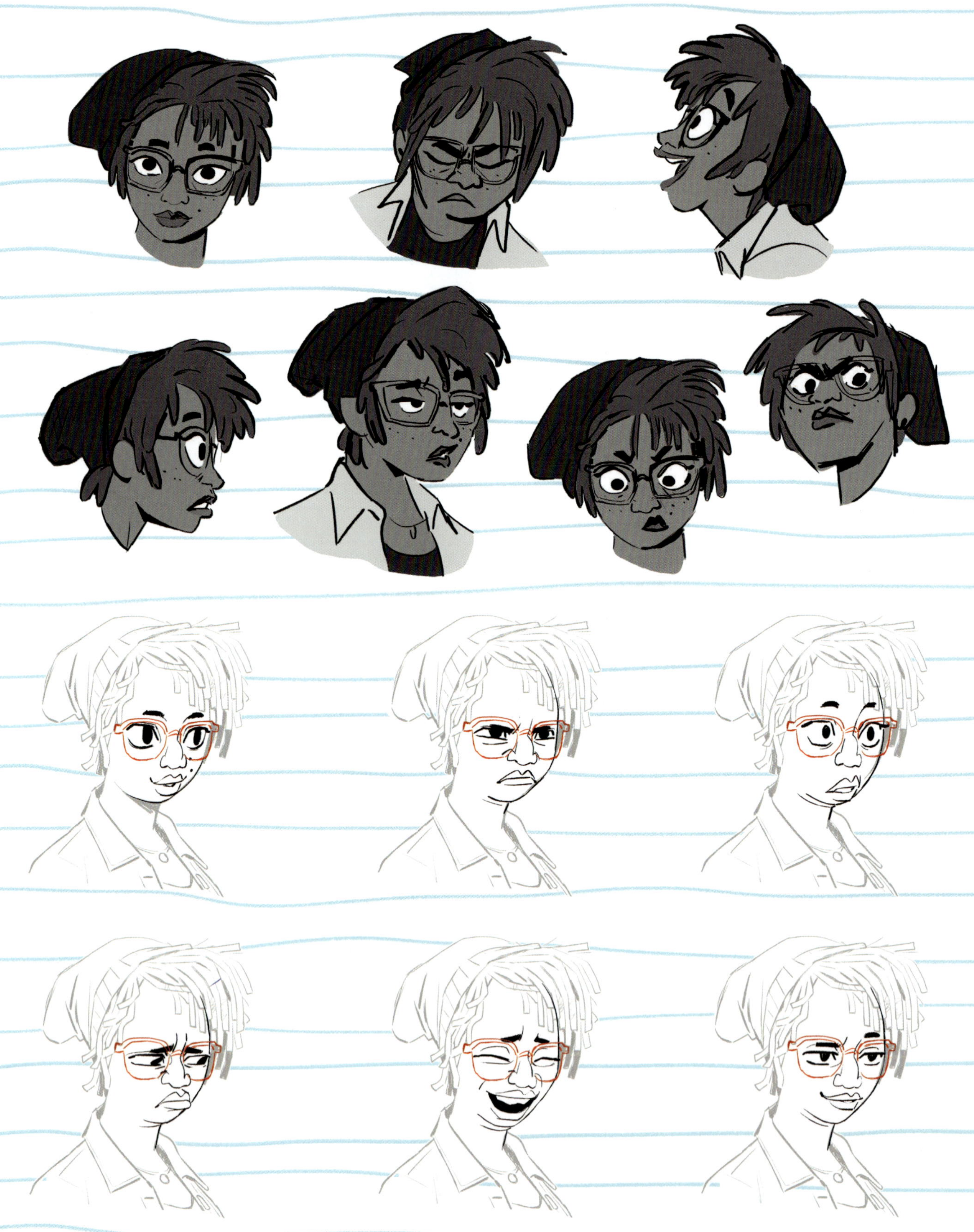

Top: Character expressions by Andrew Ross
Bottom: Character expressions by James A. Castillo

Below: Key art byTom Eichacker

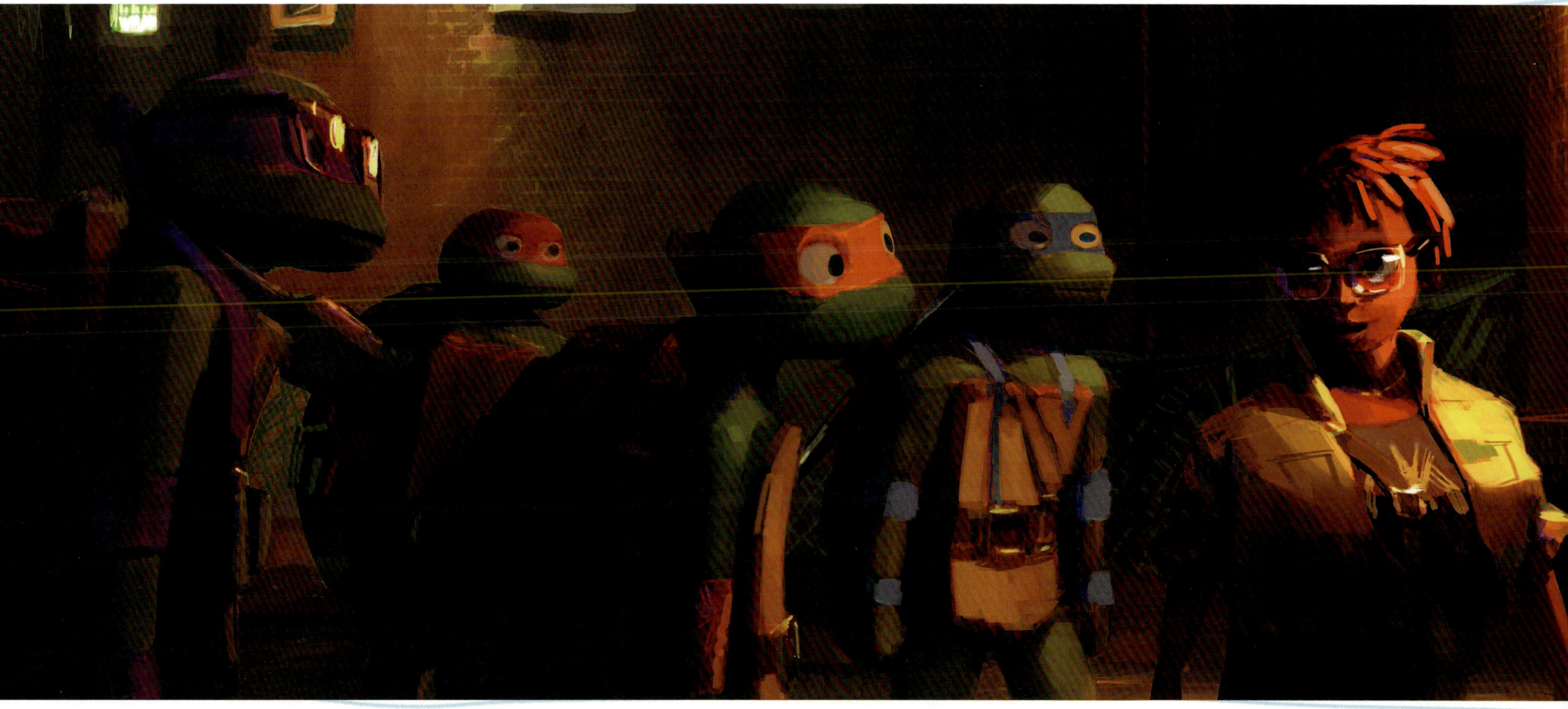

"One of the things that I've liked about the reaction to the trailer is that there have been girls that look very similar to April that feel surprised and represented by the character.

To me, more than anything, that speaks volumes to the care of the specificity and honesty with which every character has been treated in the movie.

We want to make sure that New York is represented in the movie. Any generic choices would almost always get lost in the process. Any choice that was a little more specific, more genuine, would be celebrated. Jeff created an environment in which everyone felt comfortable pushing and making risky choices."

–Character Designer James A. Castillo

"I wanted to play with the colors of April. Like with the mutants, I wanted to pay homage to the original characters and their colors but place them in different weird ways, using colors as a signifier to represent these already well-established members of the Turtles universe.

With April, it was red and yellow. I remember looking at a lot of hairstyles and finally settling on dyed red hair."

–Lead Character Designer Woodrow White

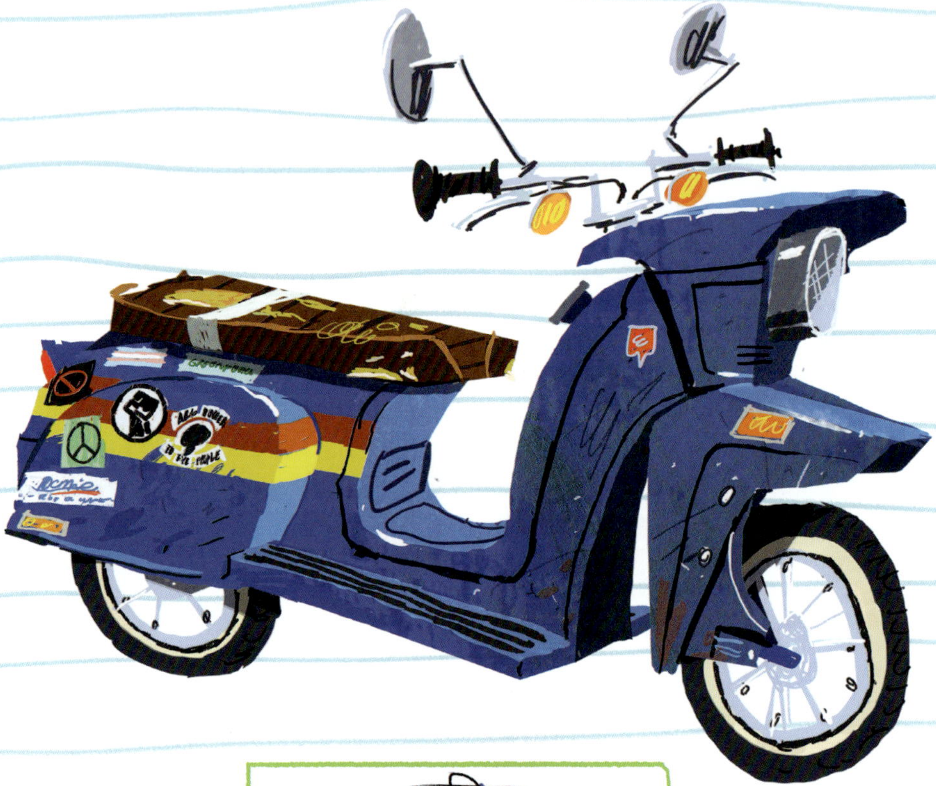

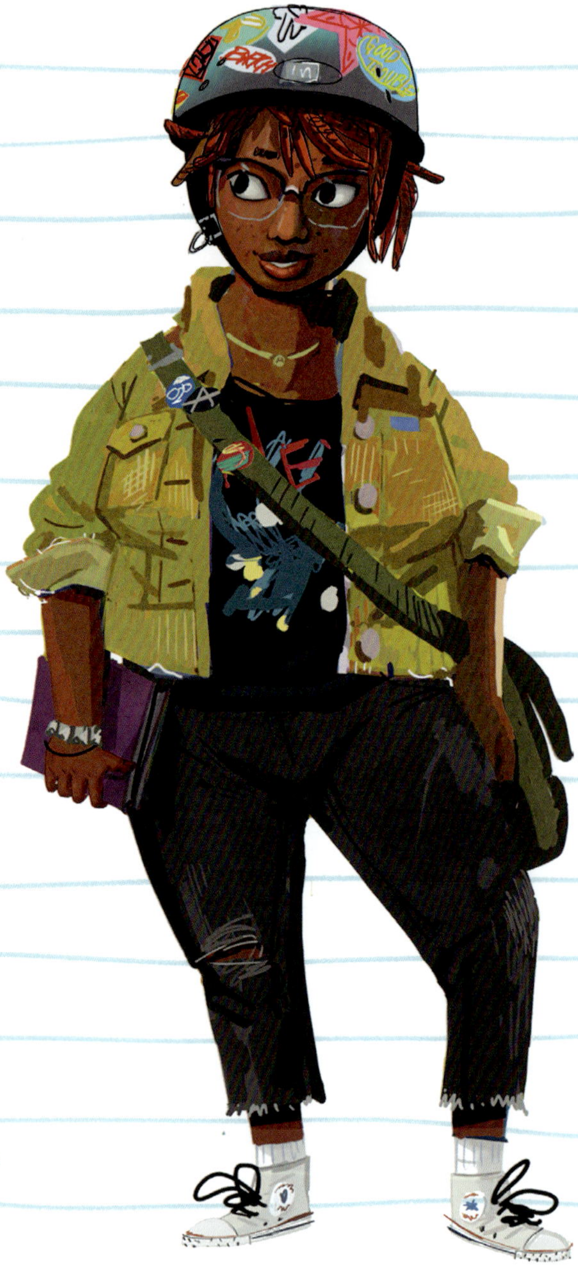

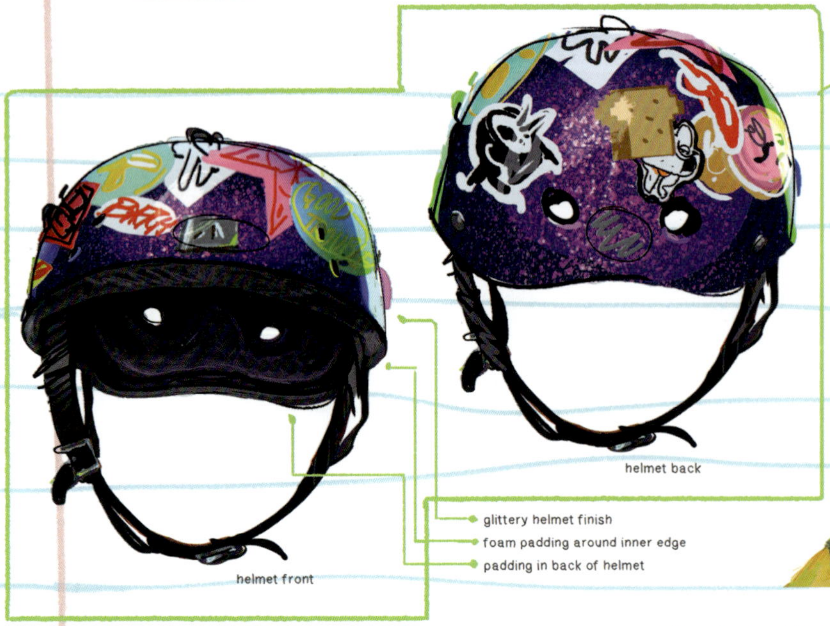

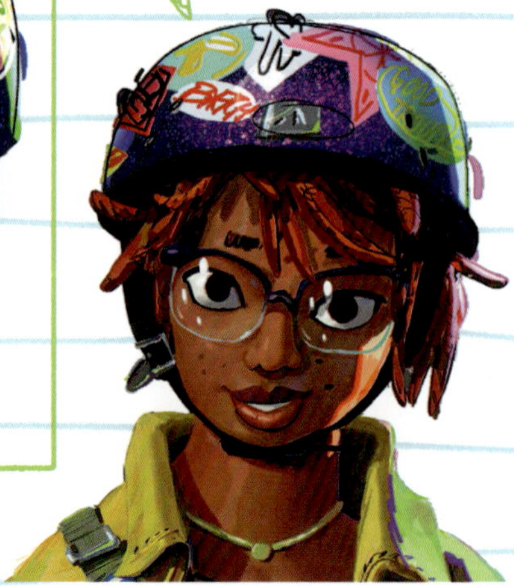

helmet front

helmet back

glittery helmet finish

foam padding around inner edge

padding in back of helmet

Top Left: Moped concept art by Woodrow White
Below Left: Helmet designs art by Sean Sevestre
Right: Concept art by Lauren Airriess

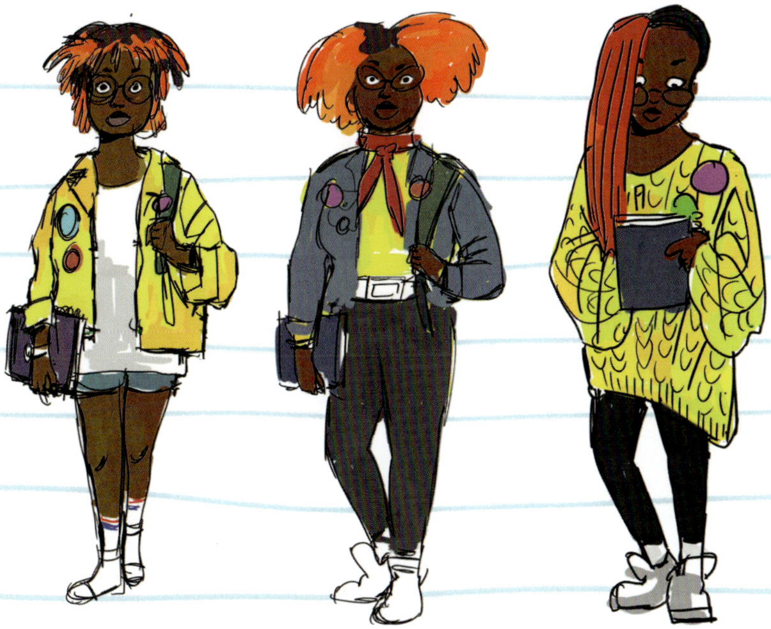

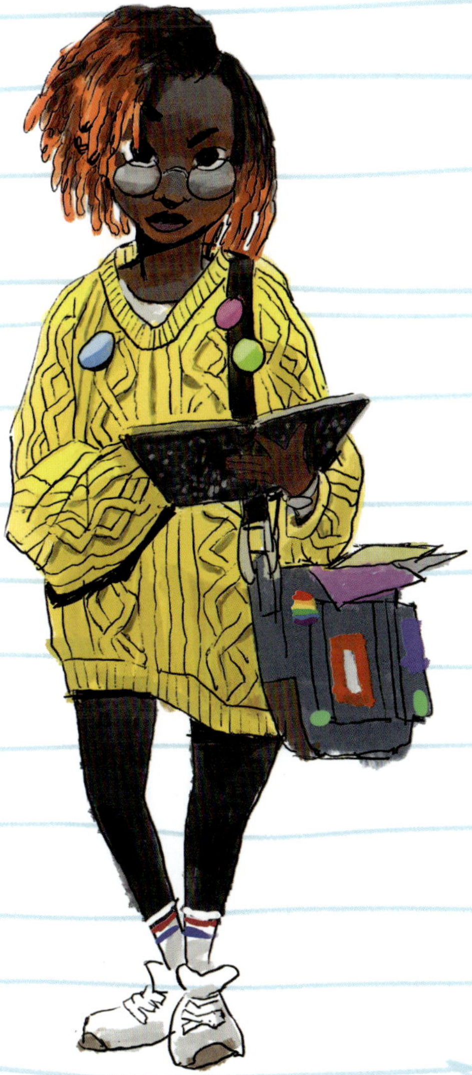

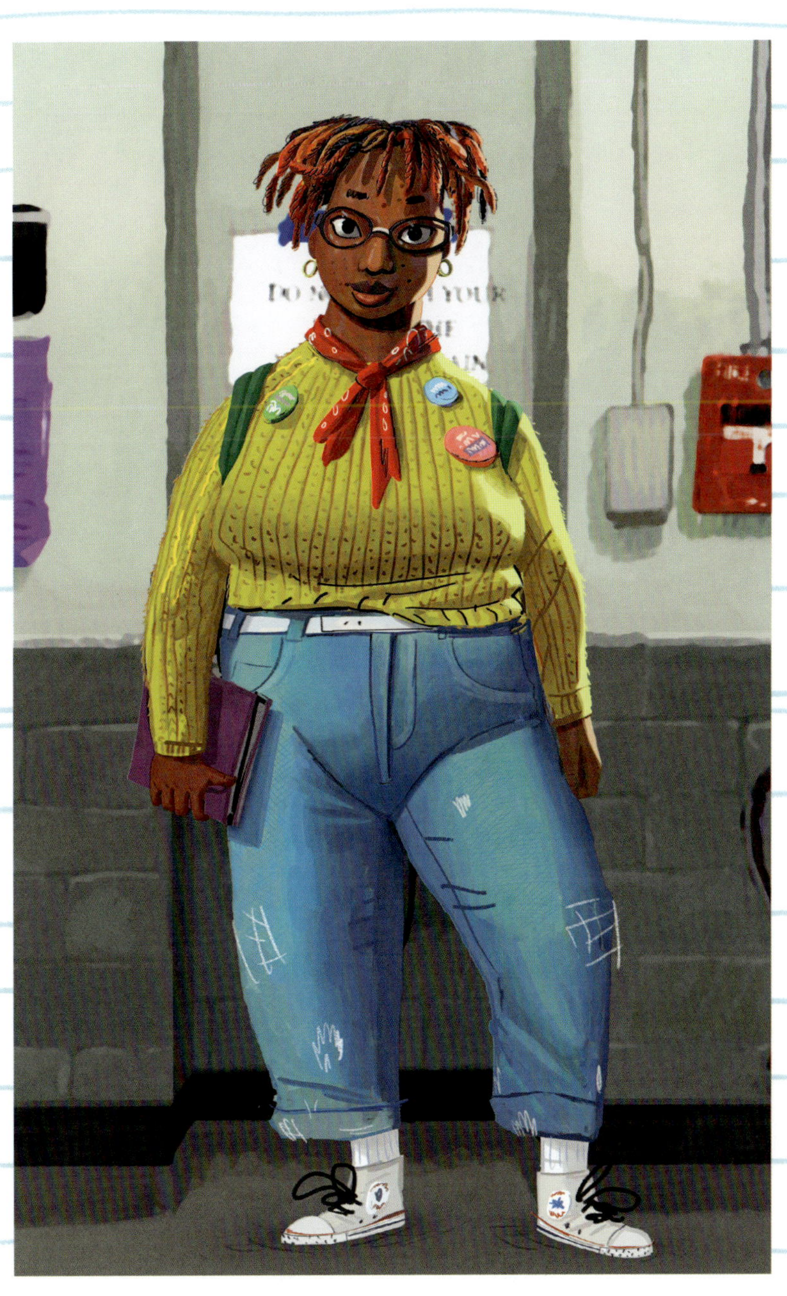

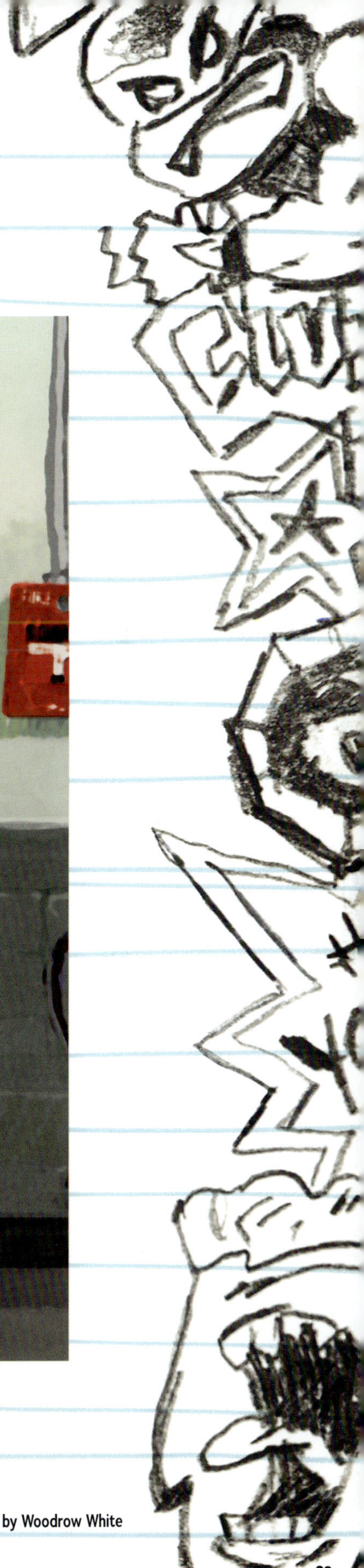

Above: Concept art by Woodrow White

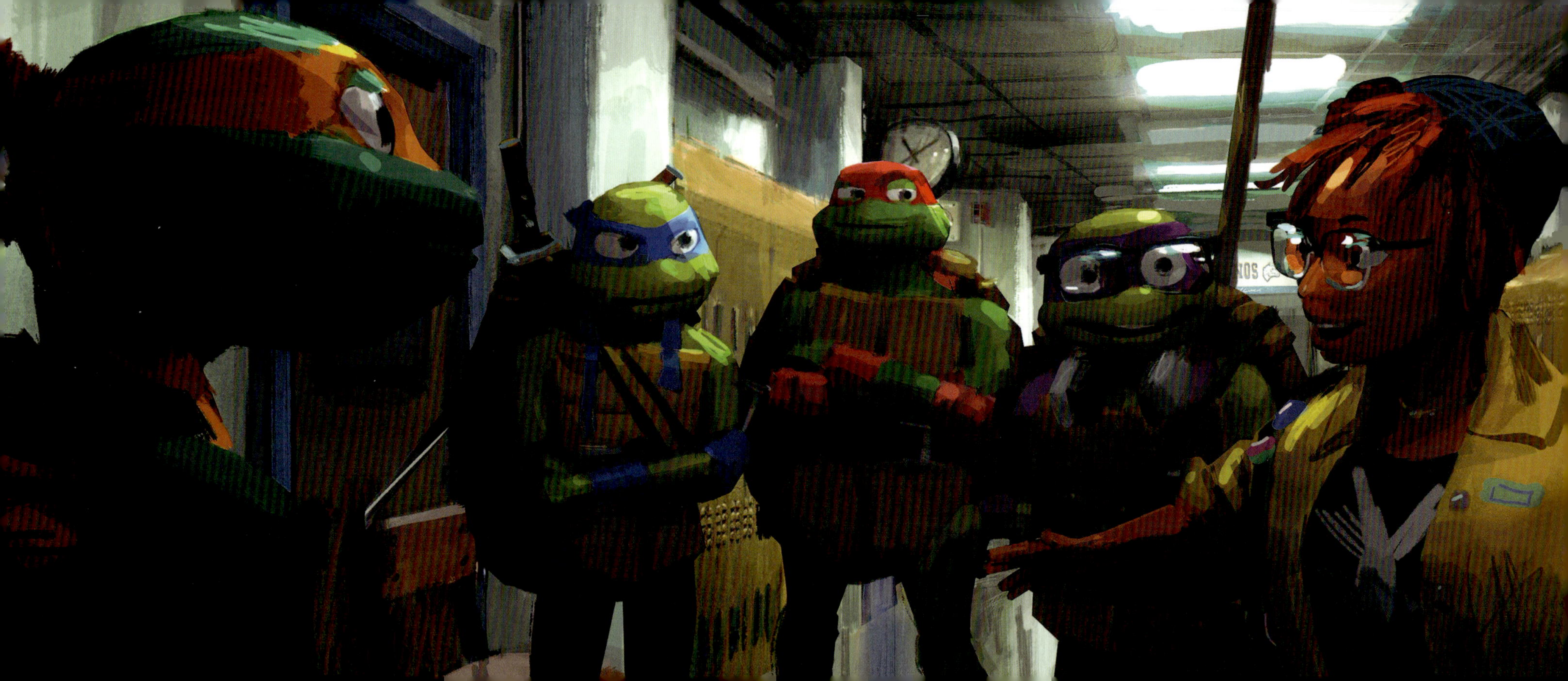

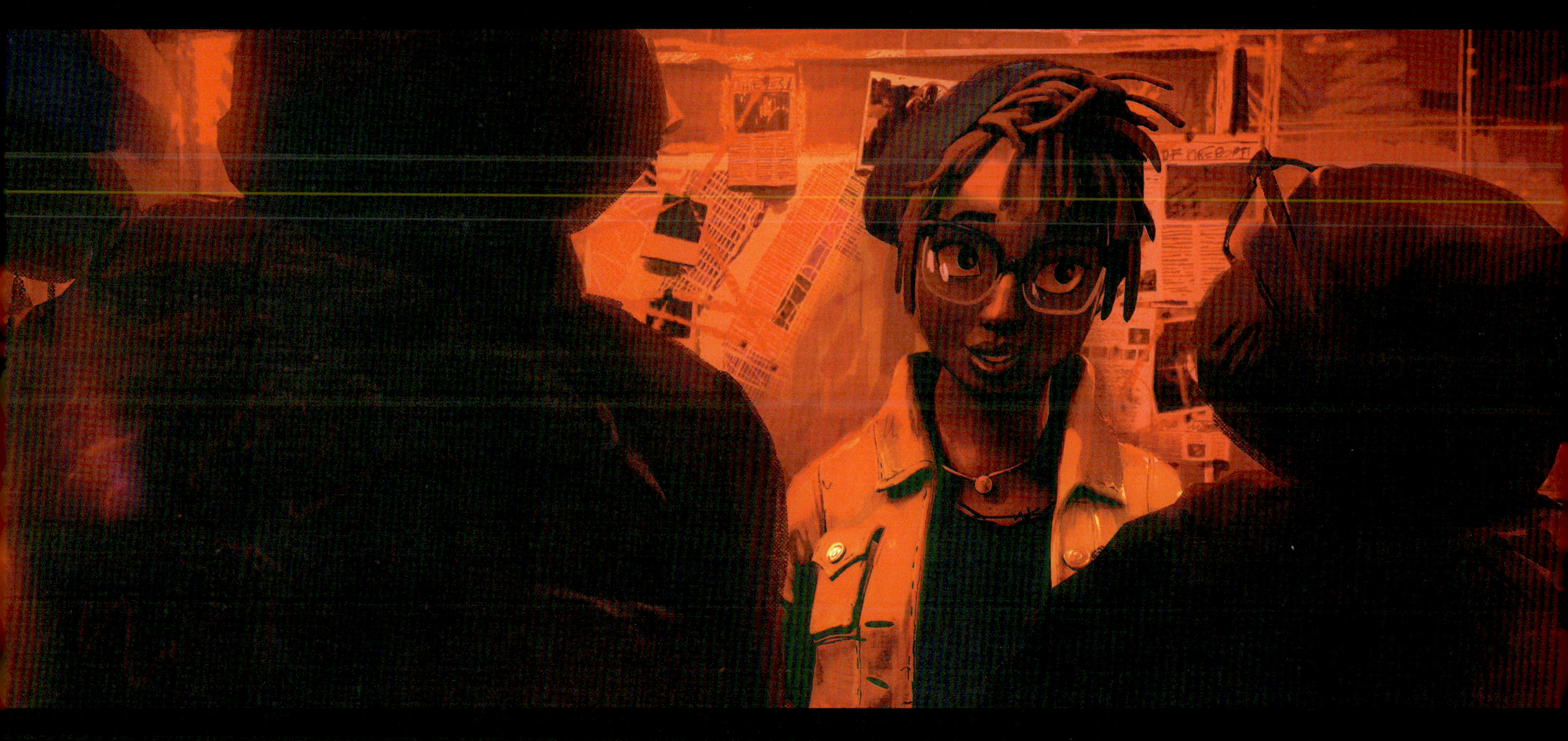

Key art by Yashar Kassai

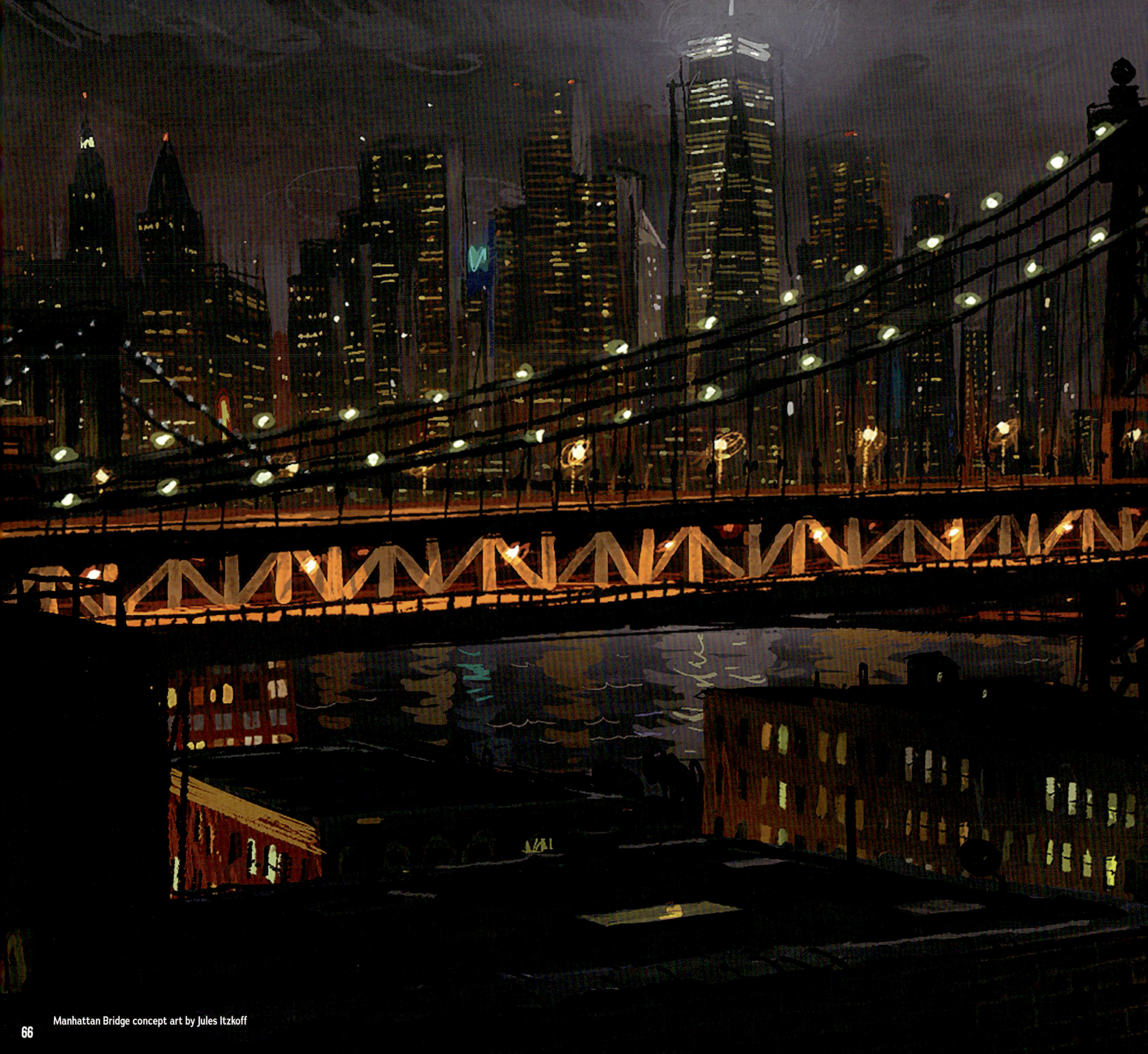
Manhattan Bridge concept art by Jules Itzkoff

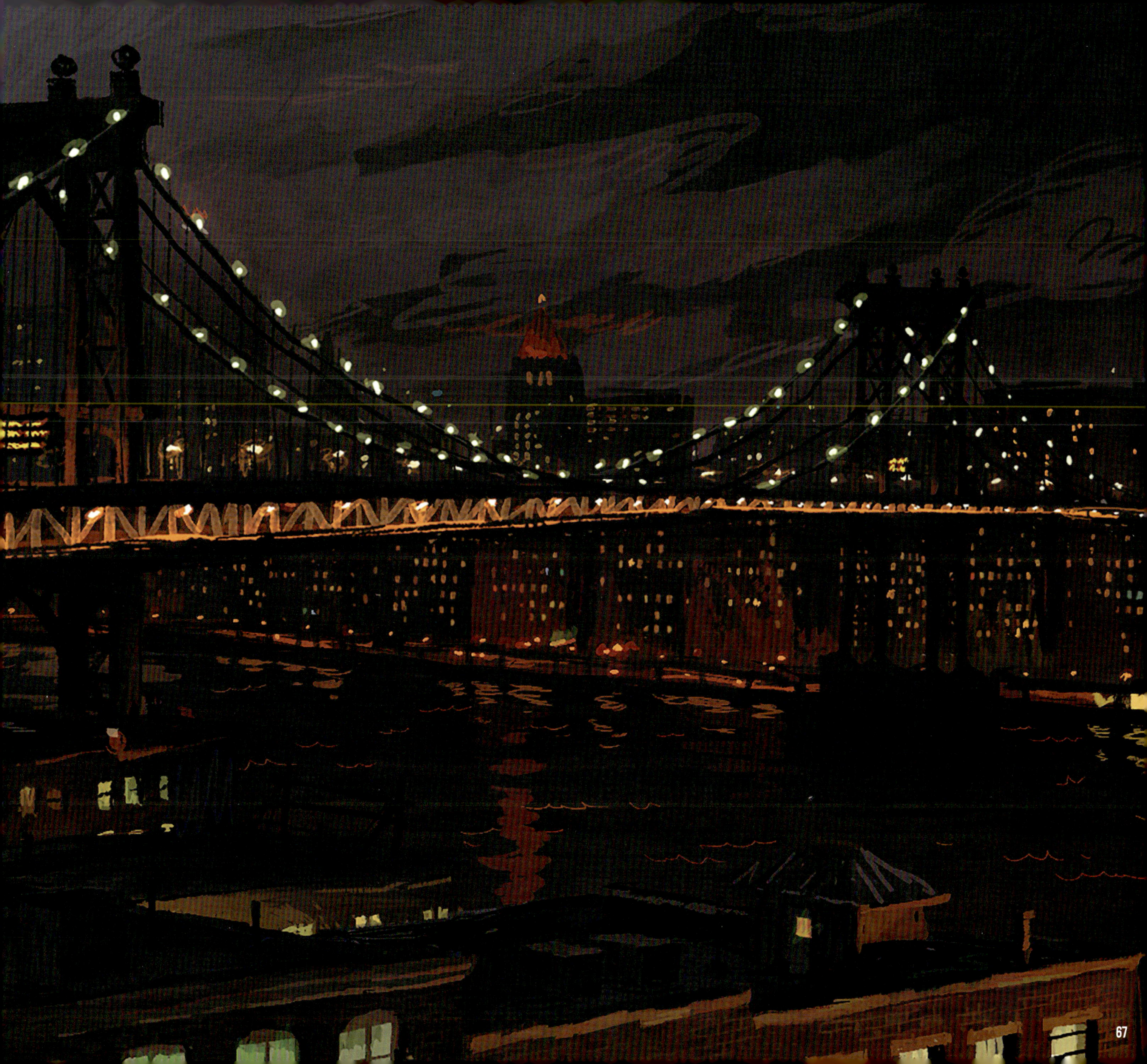

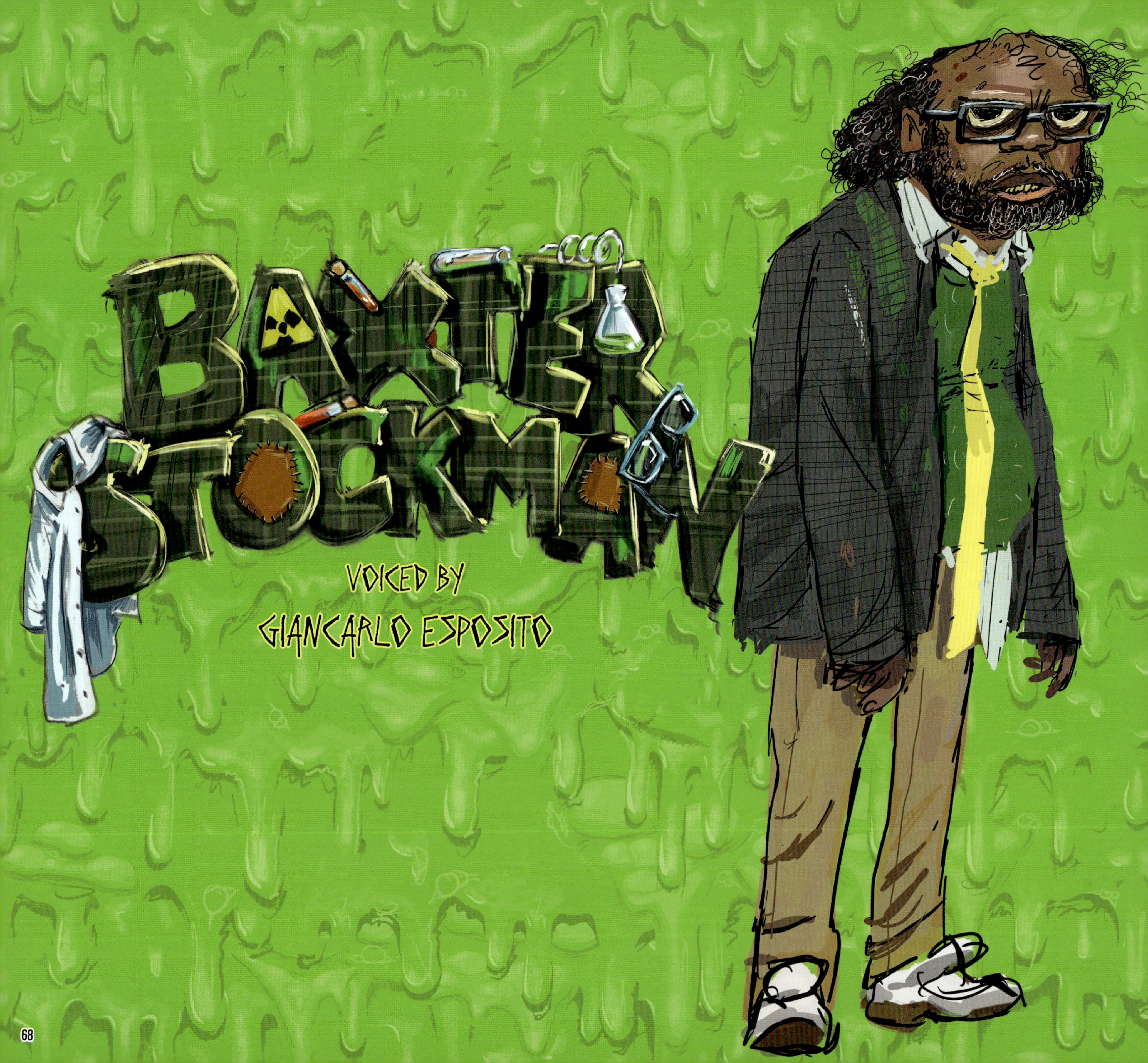
BAXTER STOCKMAN
VOICED BY
GIANCARLO ESPOSITO

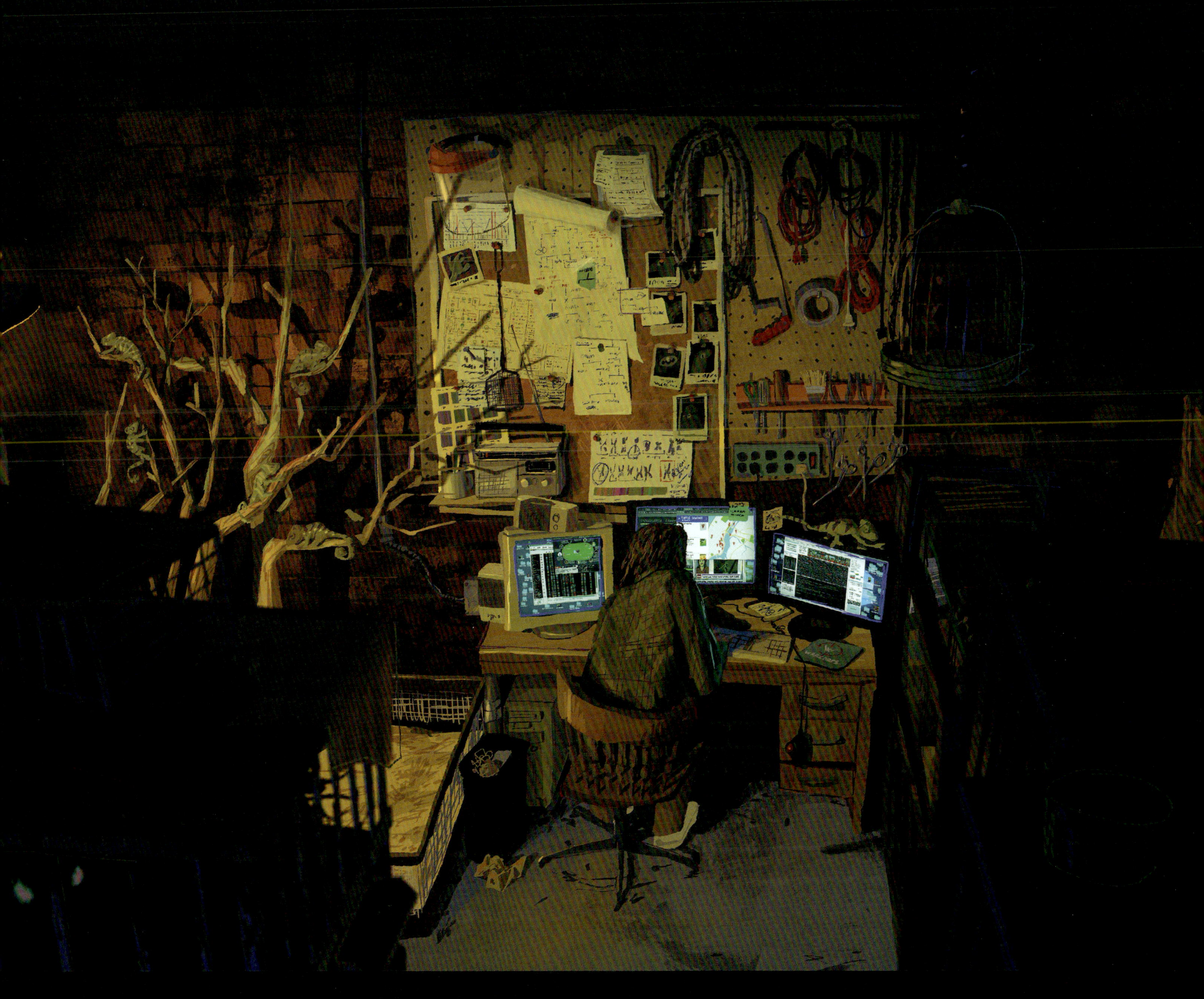

Above: Basement art by Garrett Lee
Opposite: Character art by Woodrow White

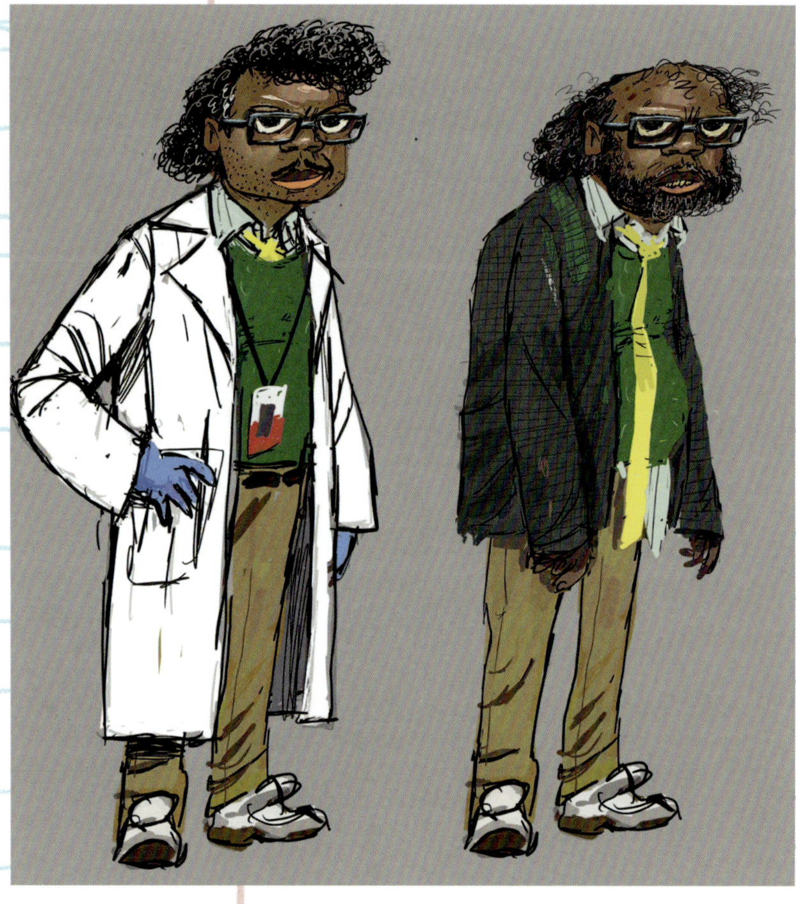

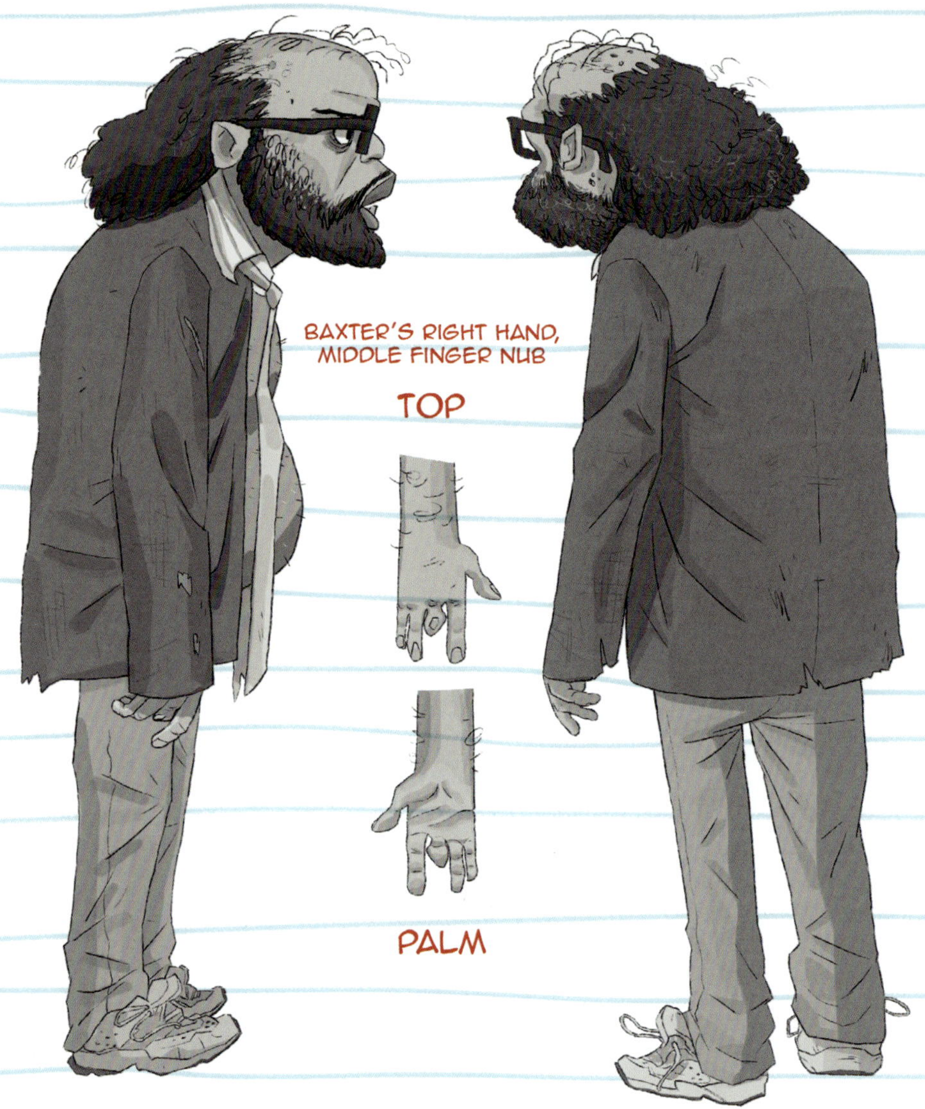

"Baxter Stockman was one of the hardest human characters to crack. I want to say we went through like 60 Baxters before we got to the final version.

In very, very early versions, he was supposed to be a sort of tech mogul, head of TCRI. Soon after that, he became a disgruntled scientist turned madman. He was meant to be very nerdy, very selfish and self-obsessed, egotistical, more bitter than the way you see him in the final movie where he's a lot more sympathetic.

Maybe a little crazy but still a sympathetic character. The beard really clicked for me, and it almost made him even more fly-ish, like the hairs on a fly."

–Lead Character Designer
Woodrow White

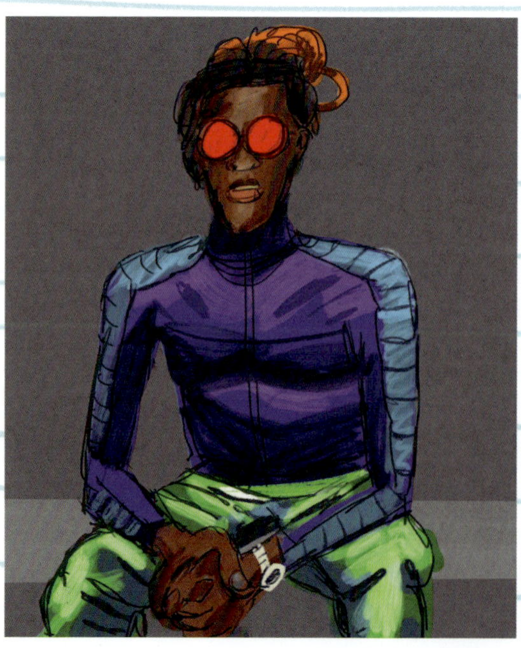

Top Left: Flashback concept art by Woodrow White
Top Right: Character design art by Justin Runfola
Bottom Right: Concept art by Woodrow White

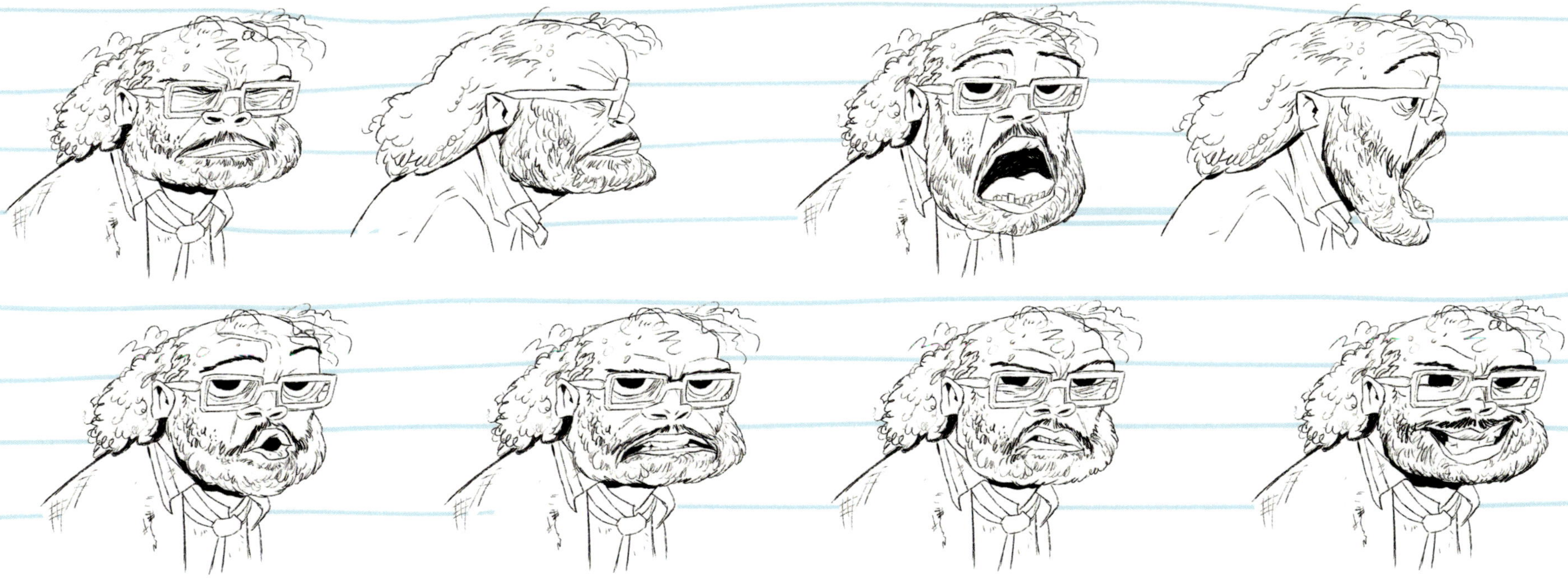

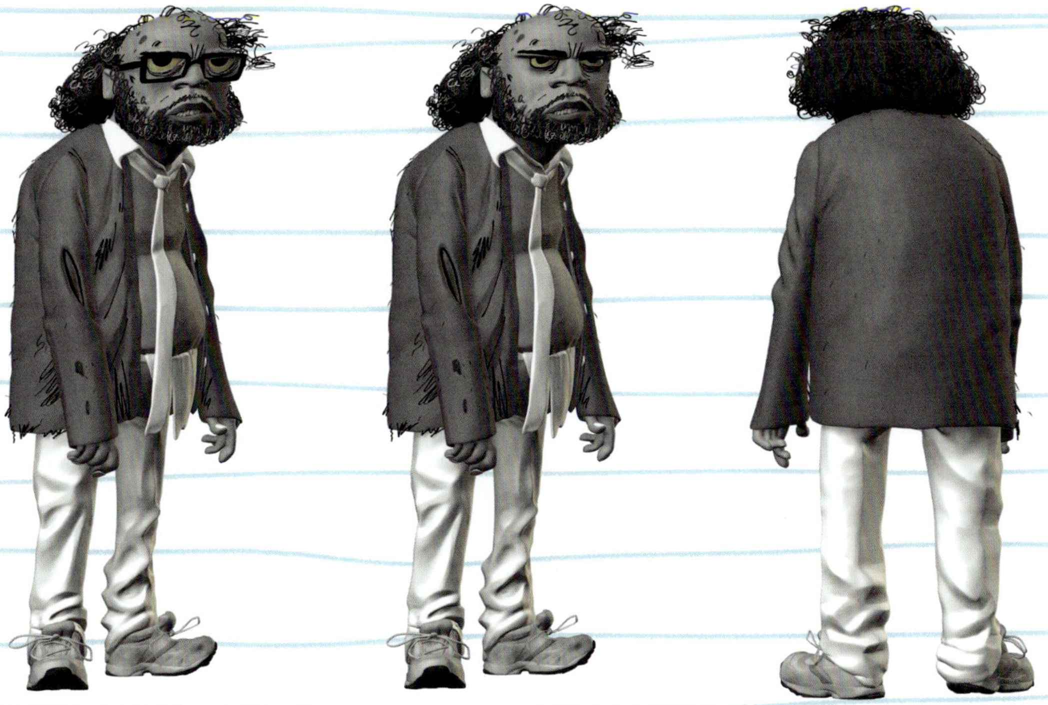

"I knew I wanted to make him very fly-like, give him fly characteristics, thus the coke-bottle glasses that make his eyes bigger. He's diminutive, a shorter guy, kinda hunched over. He's got the original colors of Baxter Stockman's outfit, which I wanted to incorporate into this design.

I was doing a lot of that in Photoshop, just eyedropping the original designs for the colors and using those exact color palettes for all the characters."

–Lead Character Designer
Woodrow White

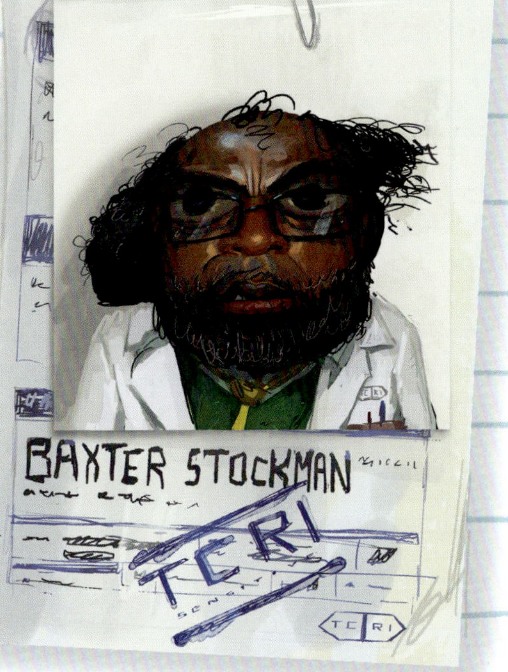

Above: Character expressions by Justin Runfola
Middle Left: Character art by Paulette Emerson
Below Right: TCRI dossier concept art by Sean Sevestre

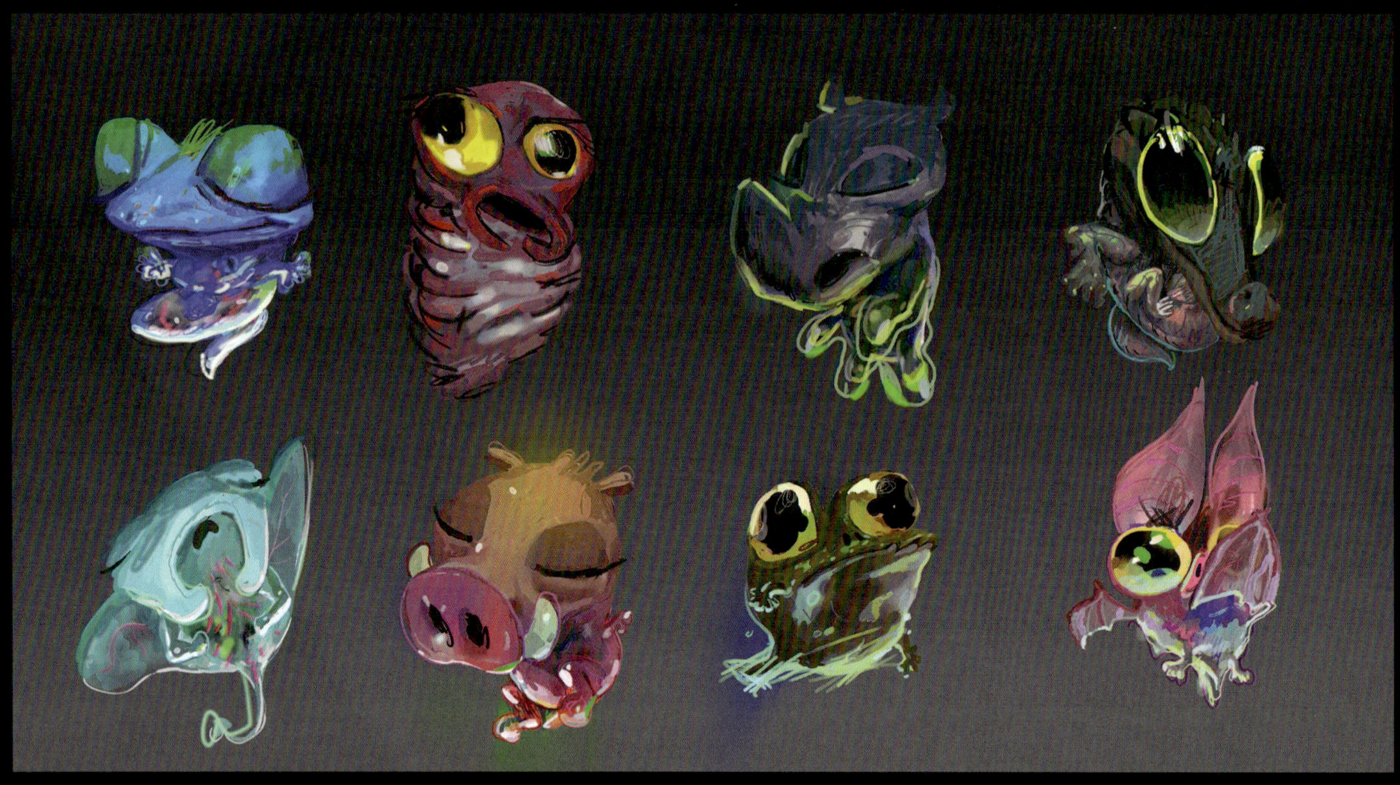

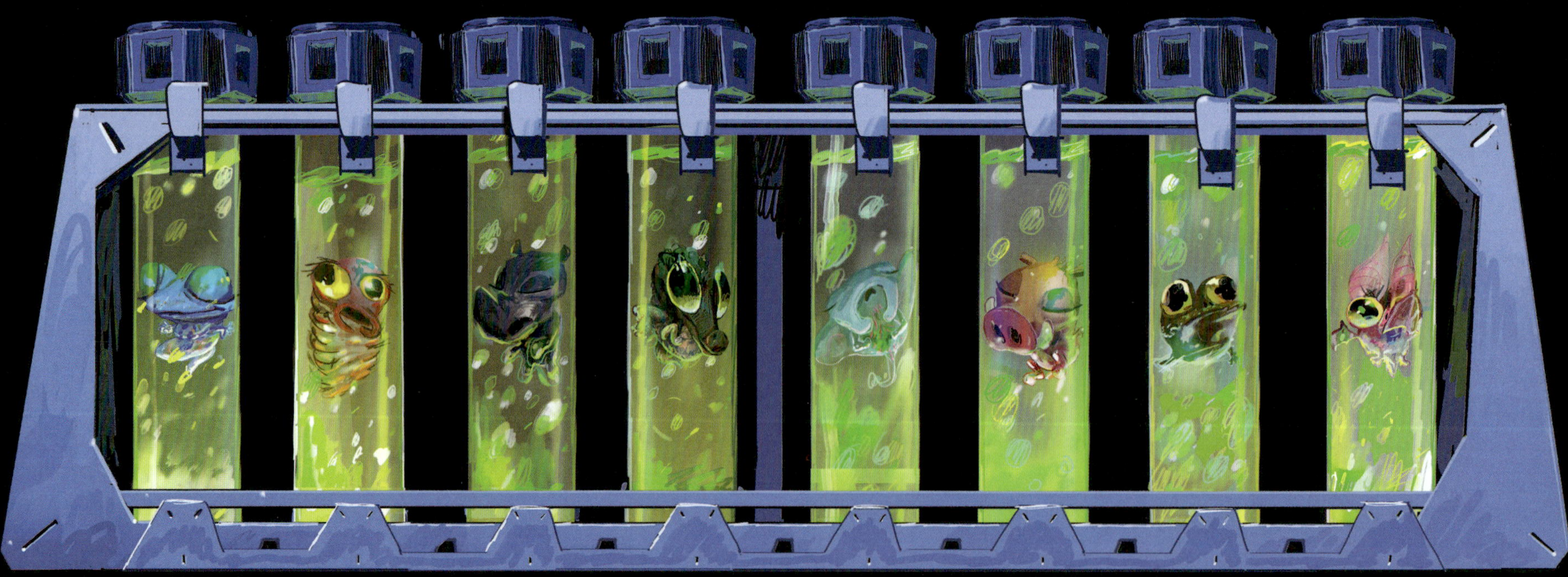

Above and Below: Mutant embryo art by Kellan Jett

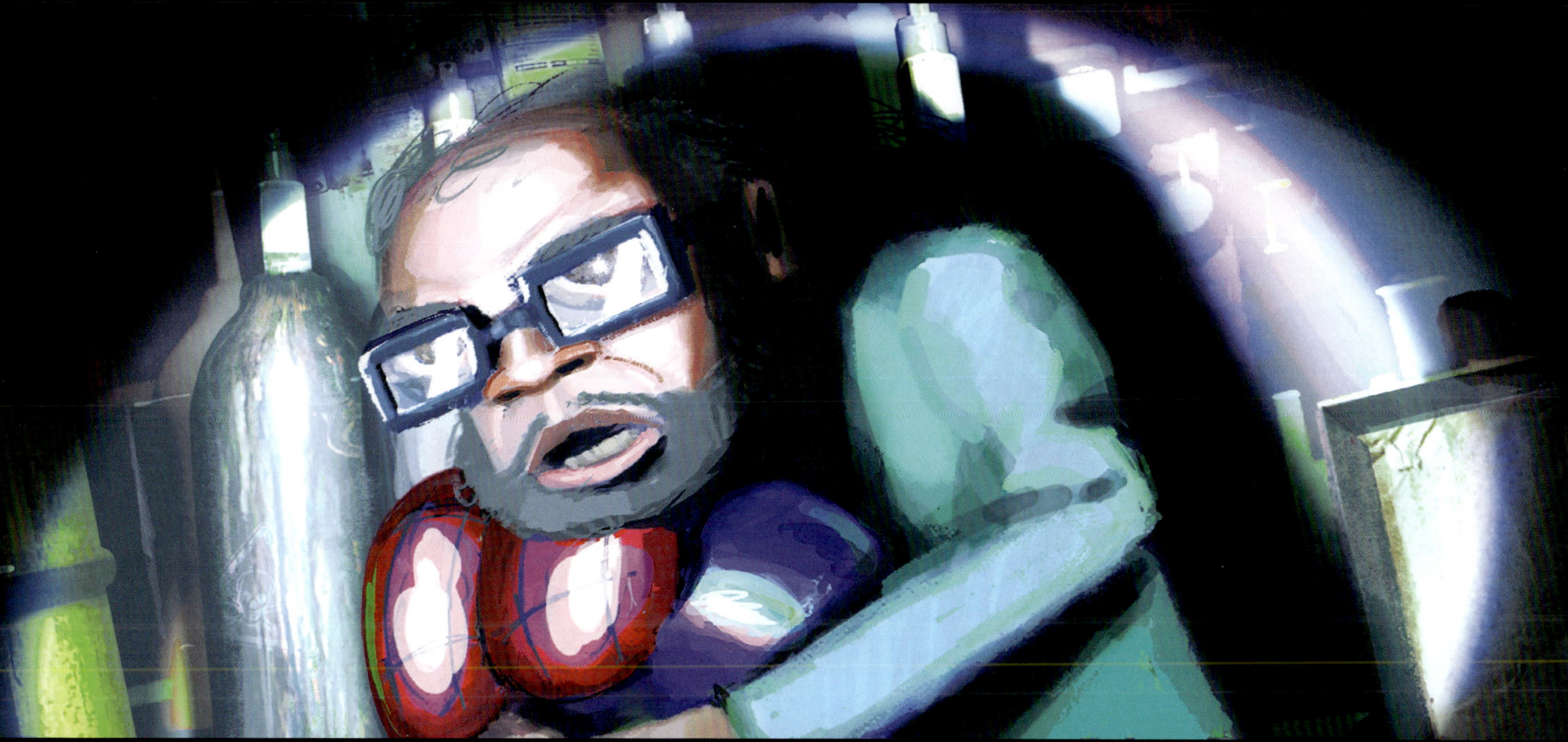

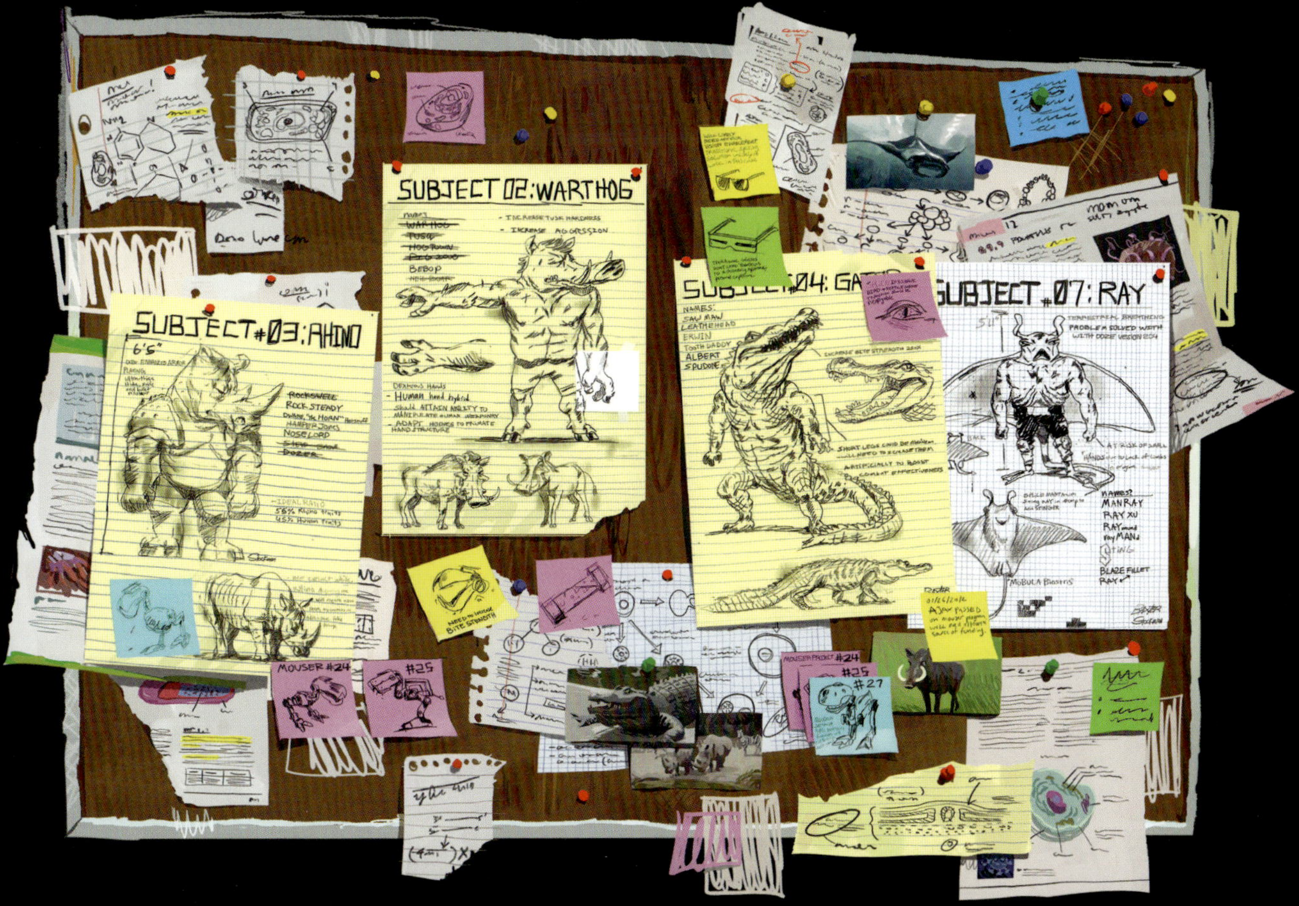

Above: Key art by Jules Itzkoff
Below: Basement board concept art by Kellan Jett and Garrett Lee

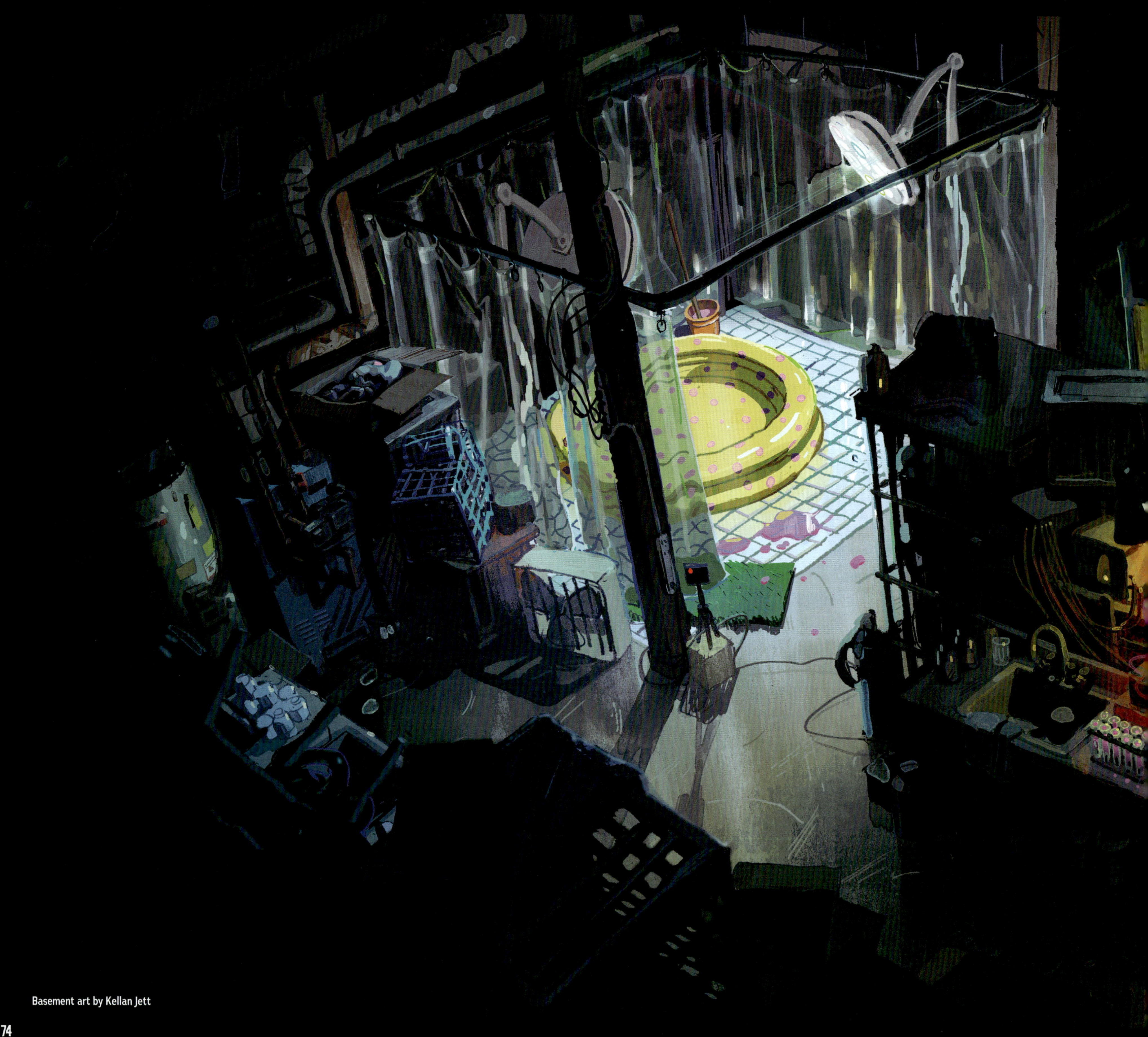

Basement art by Kellan Jett

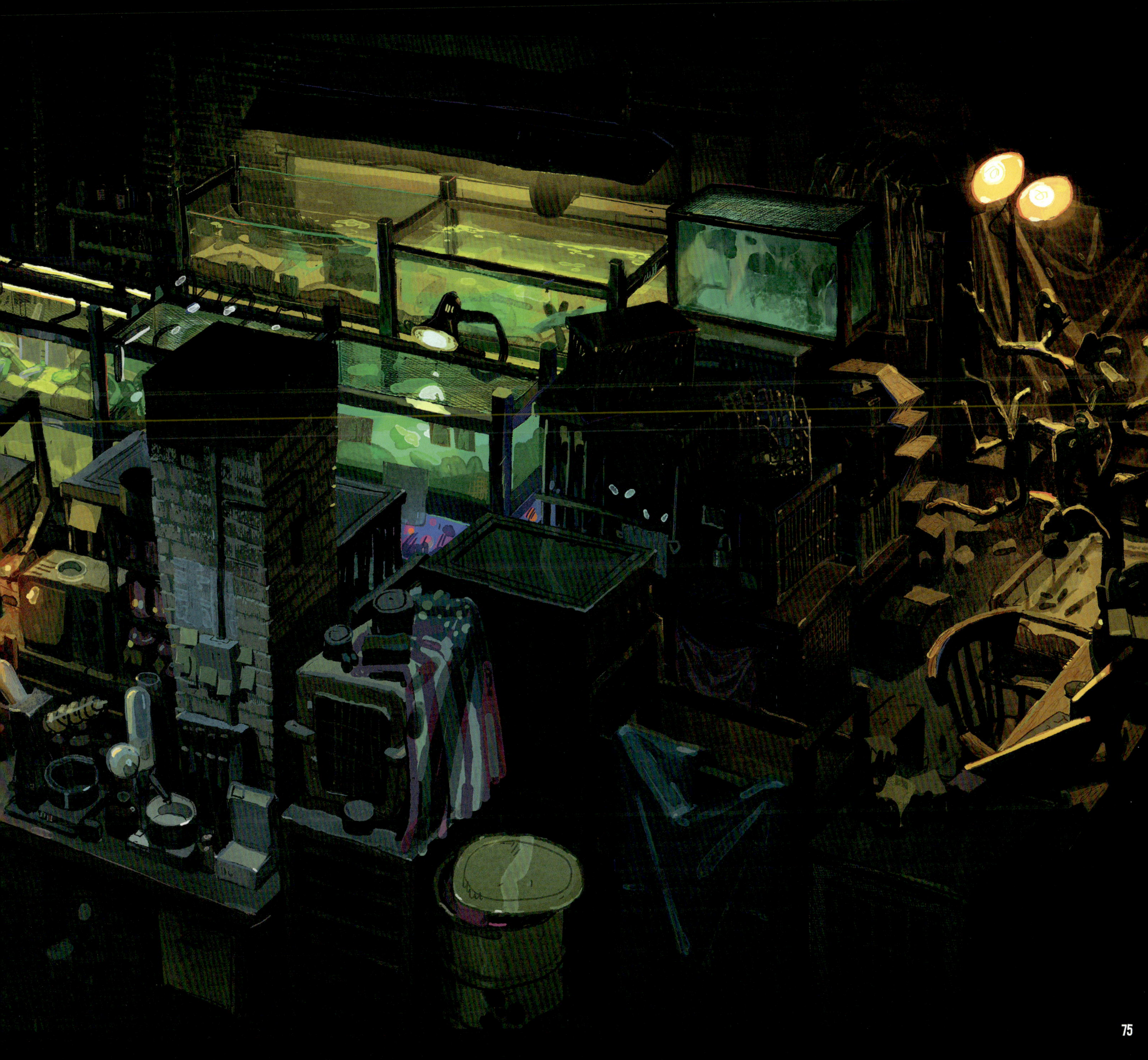

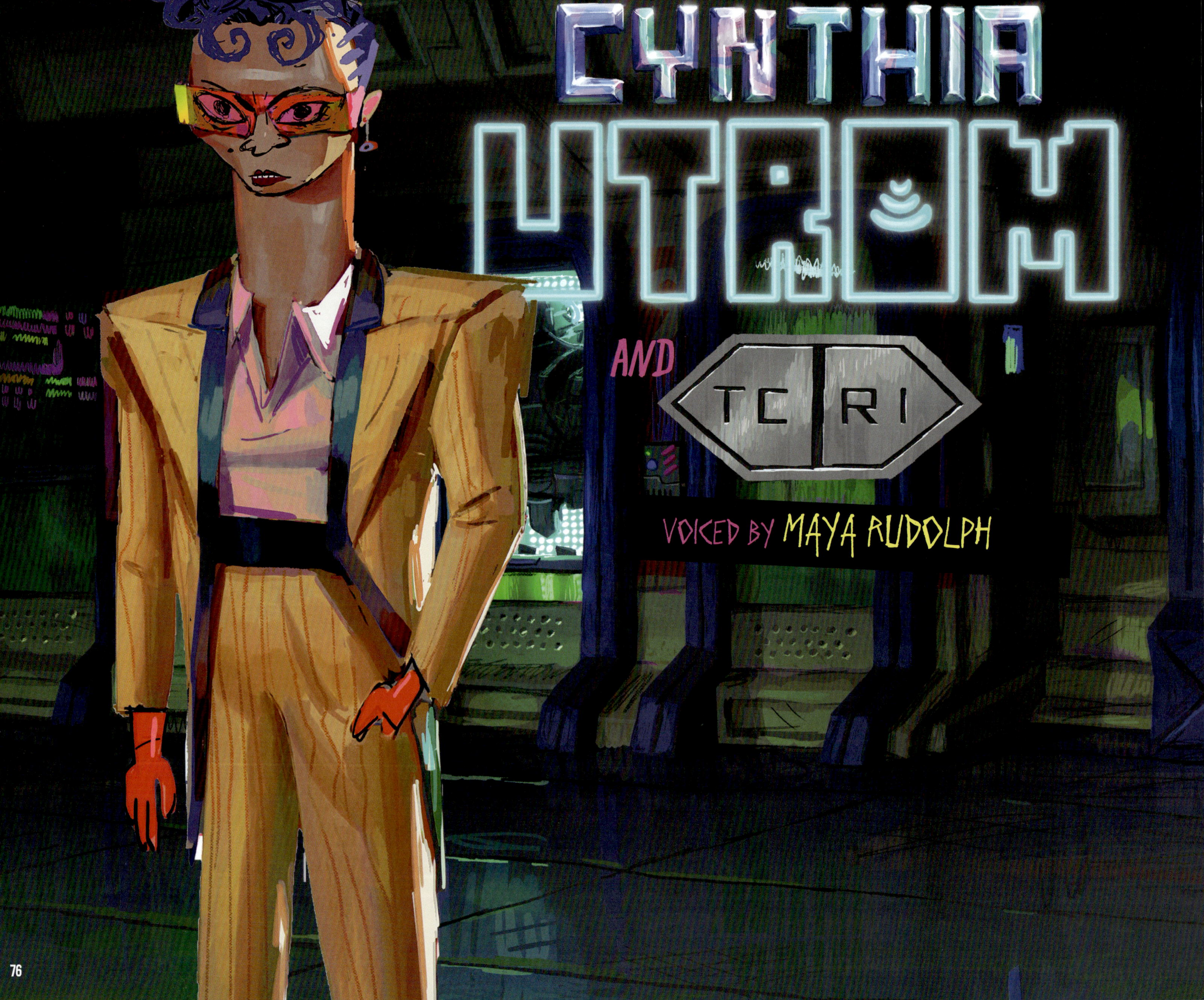
CYNTHIA
UTROM
AND
TCRI
VOICED BY MAYA RUDOLPH

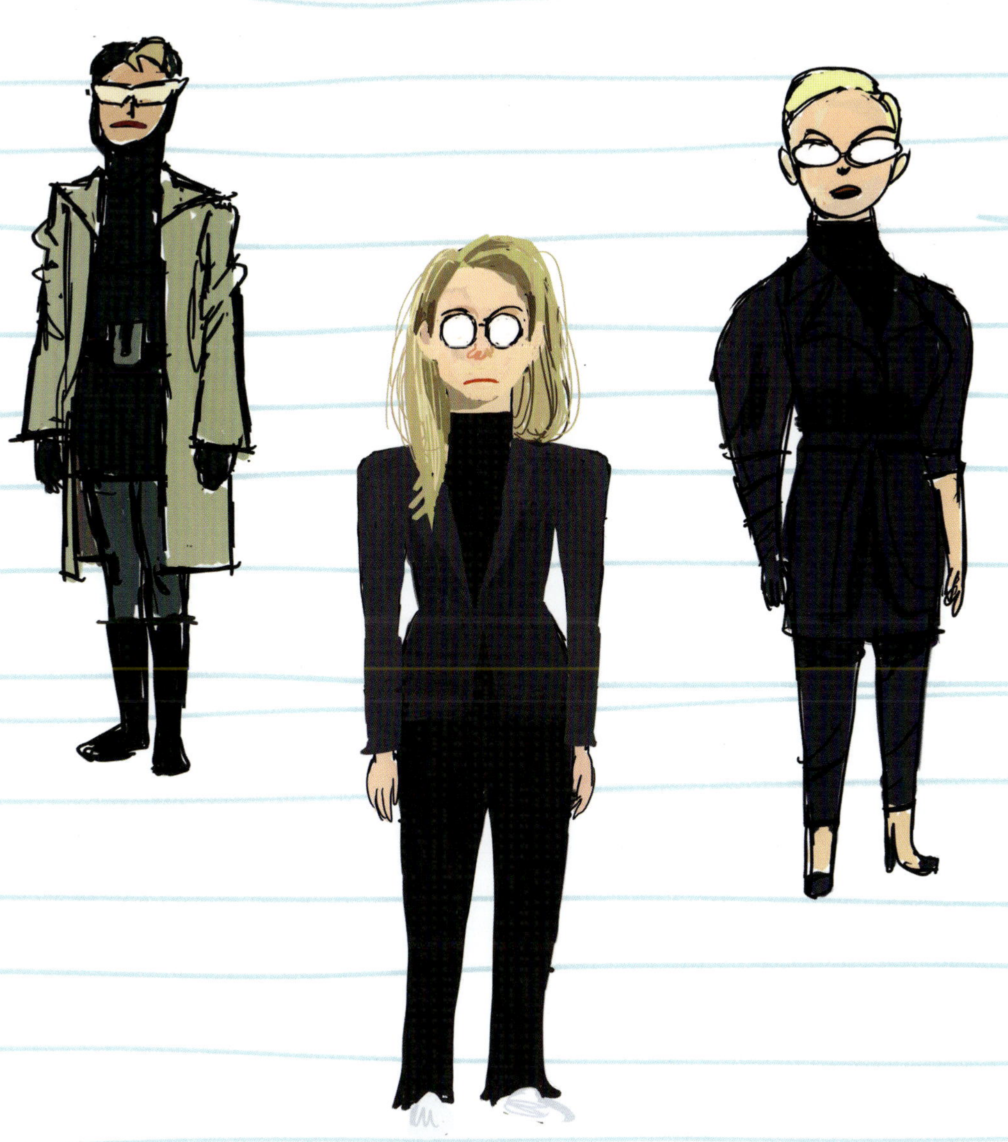

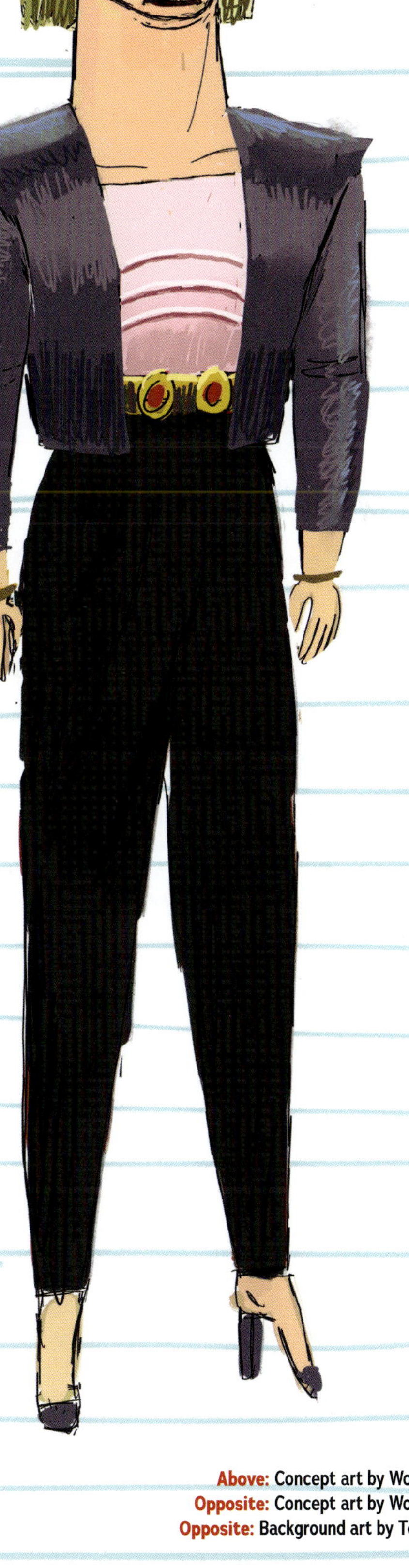

"Cynthia Utrom took a lot of work as well. Jeff was describing her as very conservative, businesslike, and ruthless. I looked at a lot of tech-world female CEOs like Facebook COO Sheryl Sandberg and Elizabeth Holms, the Theranos woman. I gave her a very alien feel, which lends itself to her name, which is an homage to the alien Utrom race in the original *TMNT*.

She's cold and icy and disconnected from everyone else. I wanted to play with the ways she could stand out among all the other human characters. She's way more put-together than the other humans. She's very rich, and she has this very sleek outfit."

–Lead Character Designer
Woodrow White

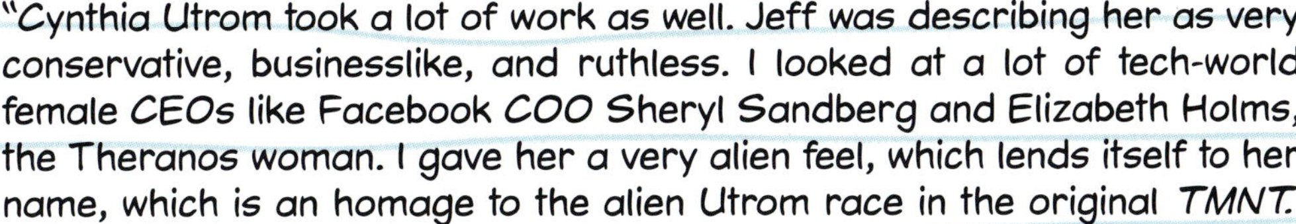

Above: Concept art by Woodrow White
Opposite: Concept art by Woodrow White
Opposite: Background art by Tom Eichacker

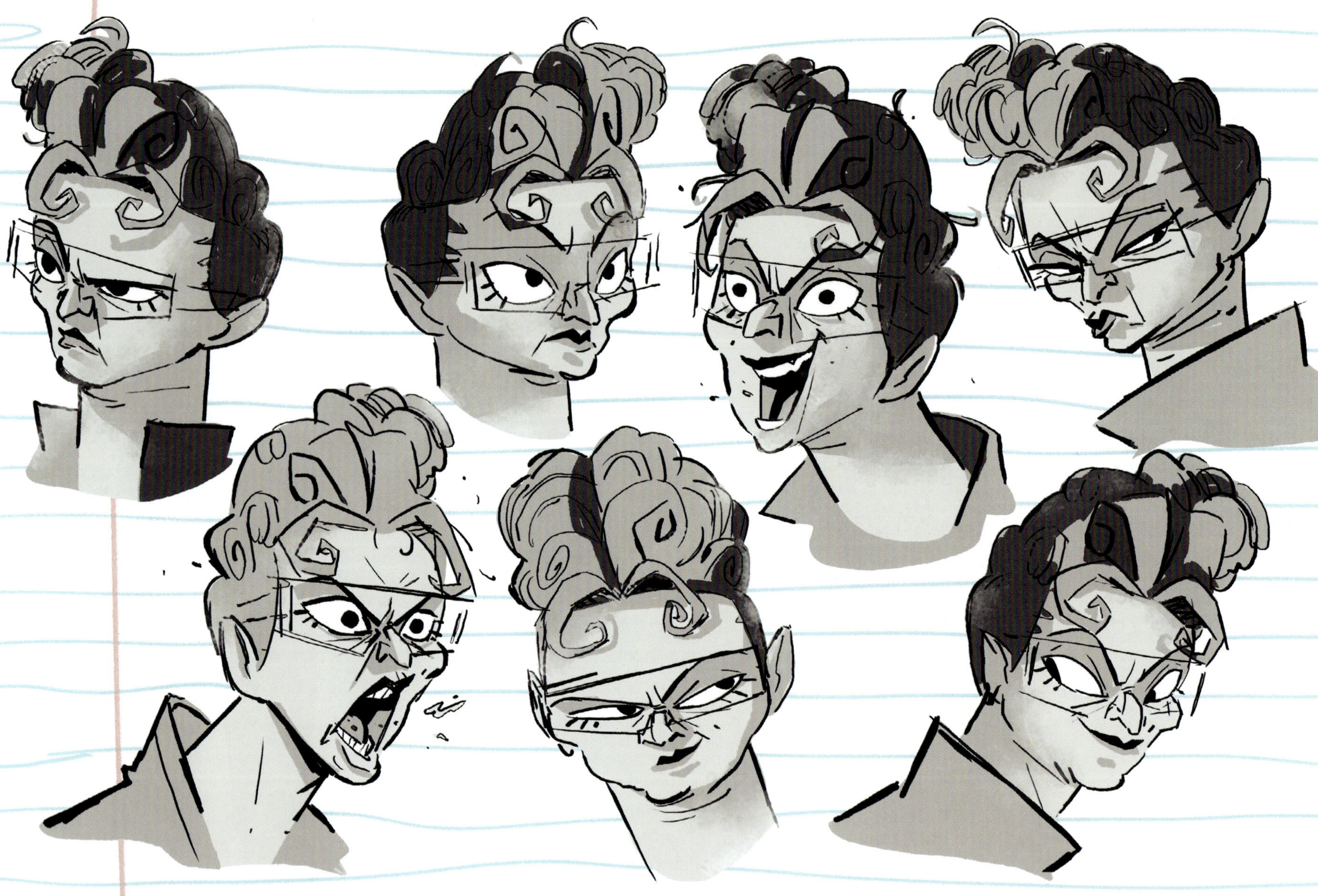

"I wanted to incorporate aspects of Krang's exoskeleton character, the giant body he inhabits. You can see certain shapes appear in her dress; I wanted to give as many callbacks to the original TCRI as possible. Her hair, for instance, is another callback to Krang. It's very tentacle-y. She's a very corporate, futuristic, cold, ruthless character. I made her proportions weird on purpose because she's meant to be esoteric and strange and unlike any of the other humans we see because she's not supposed to be very human herself."

–Lead Character Designer Woodrow White

Above: Character expressions by Andrew Ross

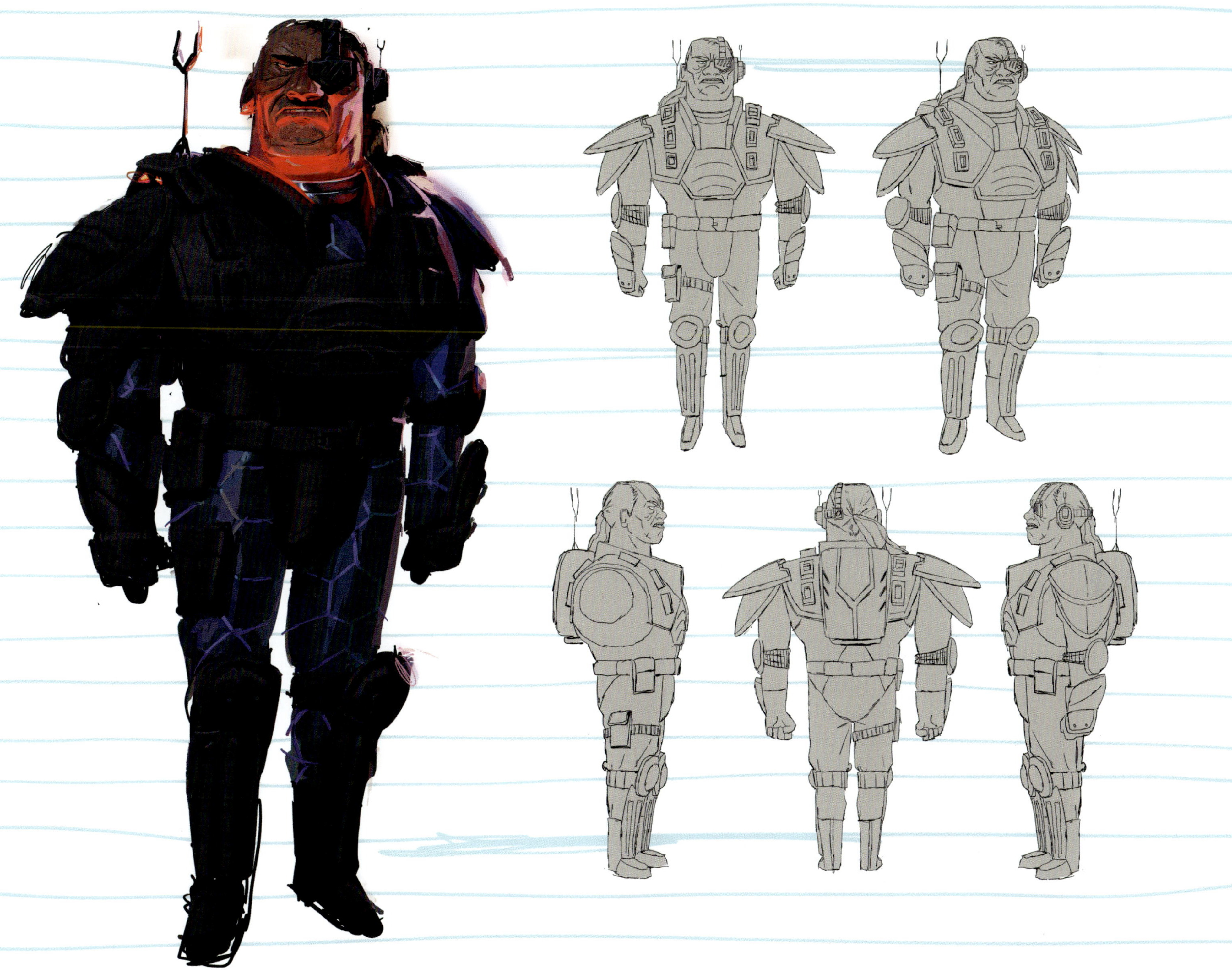

Left: Spider character paint by Sean Sevestre
Right: Spider character turn by Adel Sabi

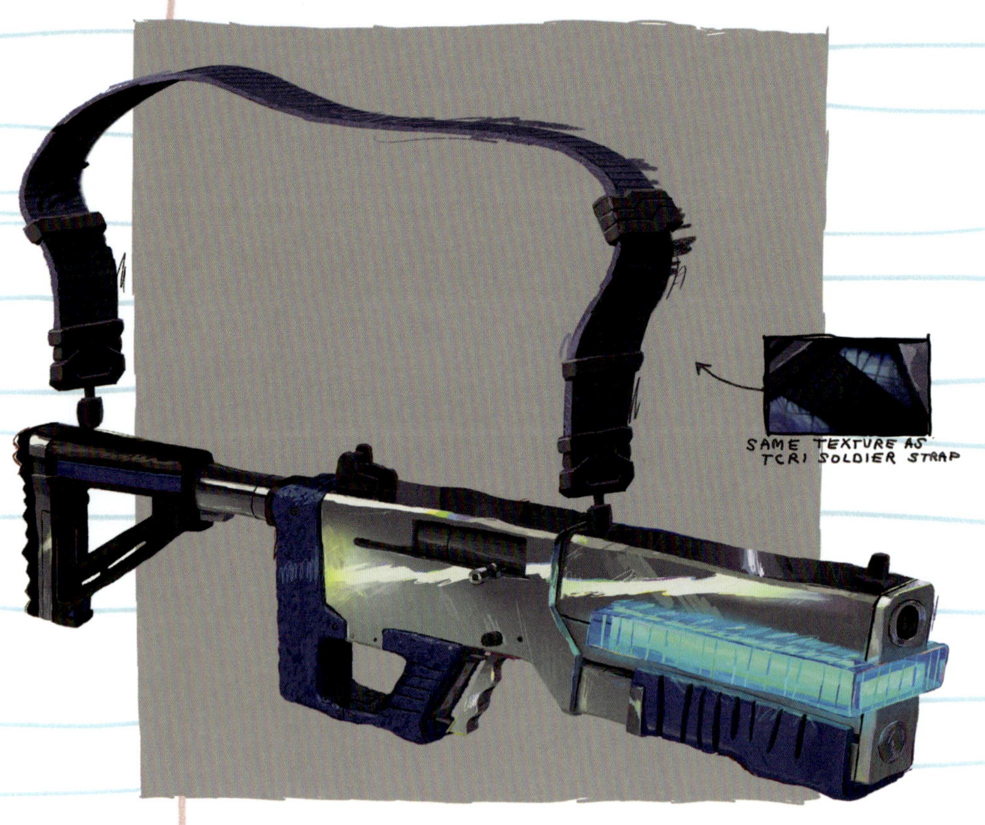

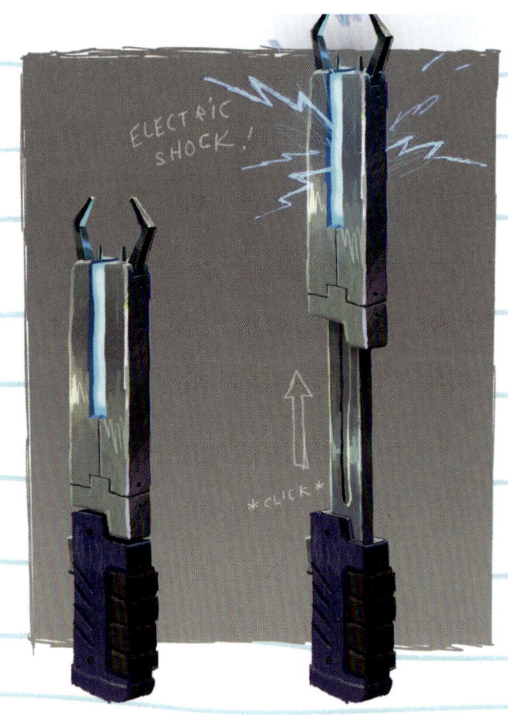

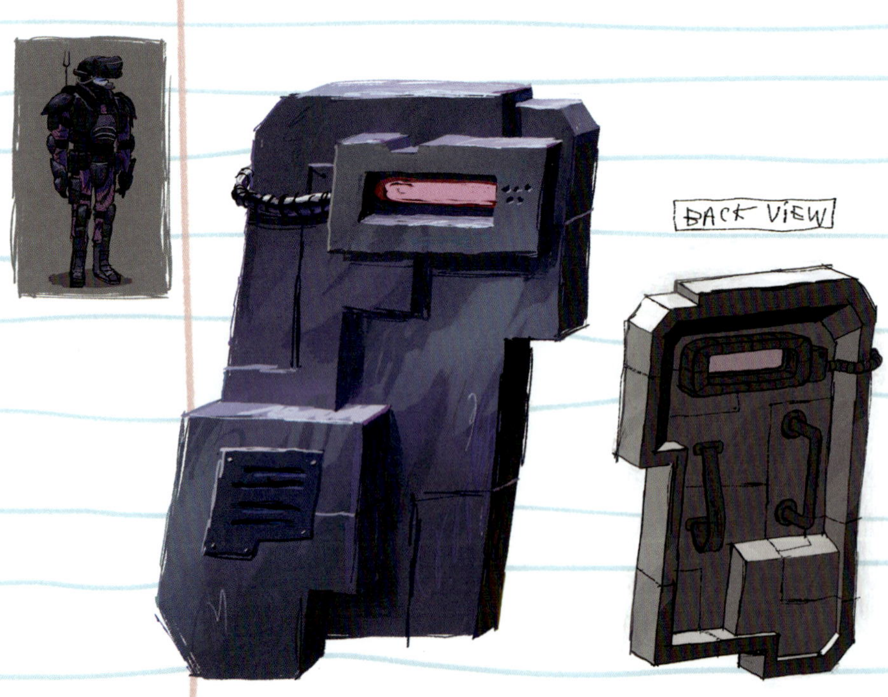

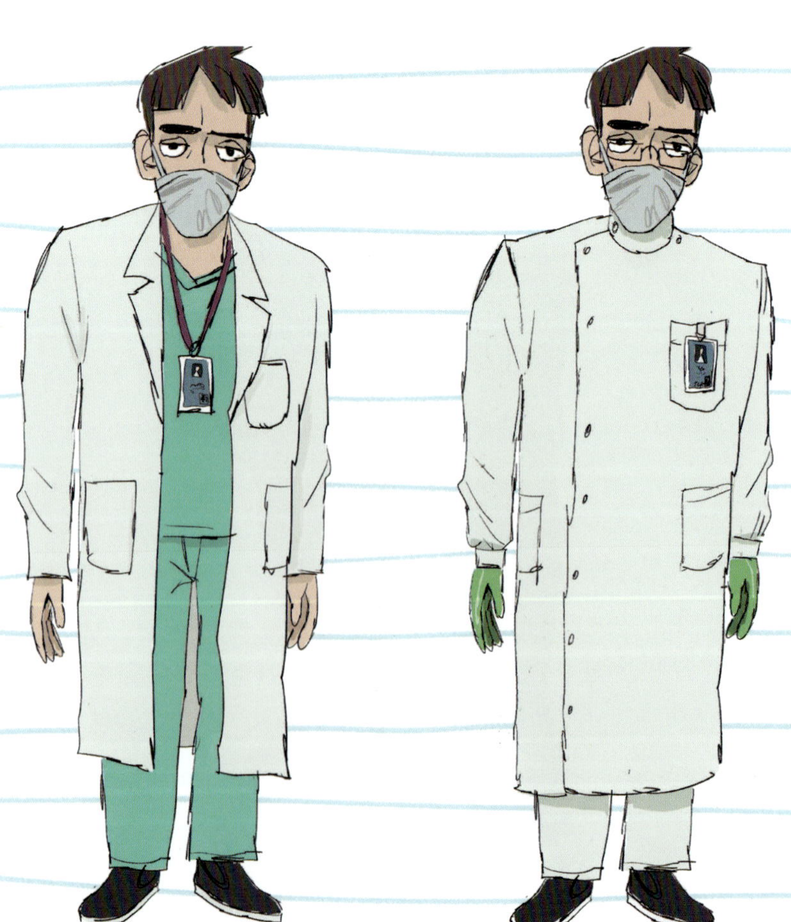

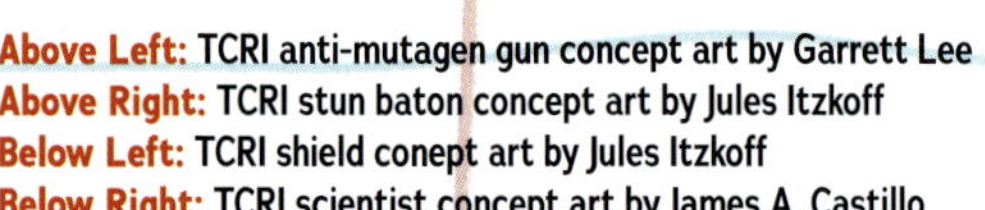

Above Left: TCRI anti-mutagen gun concept art by Garrett Lee
Above Right: TCRI stun baton concept art by Jules Itzkoff
Below Left: TCRI shield conept art by Jules Itzkoff
Below Right: TCRI scientist concept art by James A. Castillo

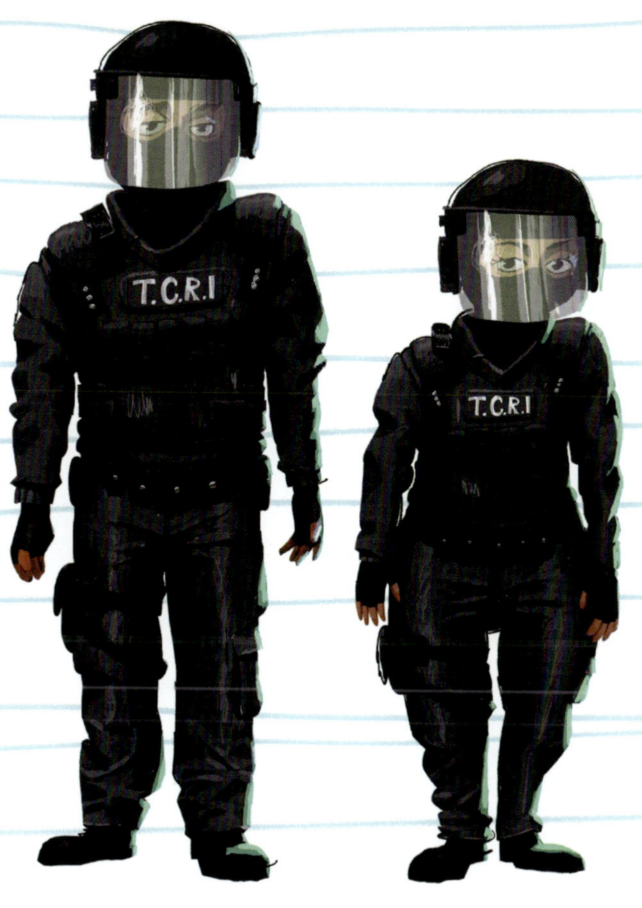

"The TCRI soldiers were really fun [to design]. I was looking at a lot of manga and anime and the way soldiers dress in cartoons and video games. I gave them an overall cool, cyberpunk feel to them. I was looking at VR headsets when designing their headsets, giving them a robotic feel to them. Their antenna, in particular, is a callback to Krang's original exosuit."

–Lead Character Designer Woodrow White

Left: TCRI SWAT uniform concept art by Adel Sabi
Below: TCRI security room art by Tom Eichacker

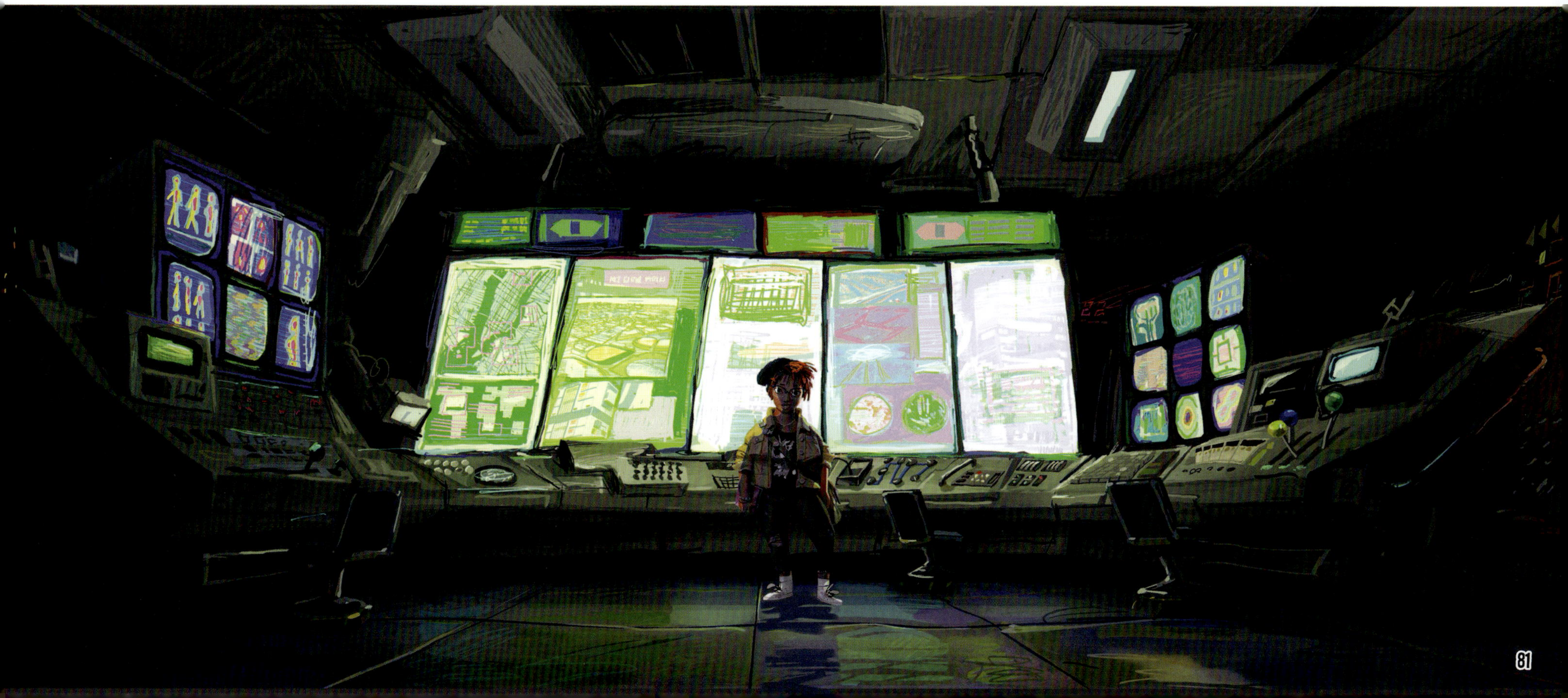

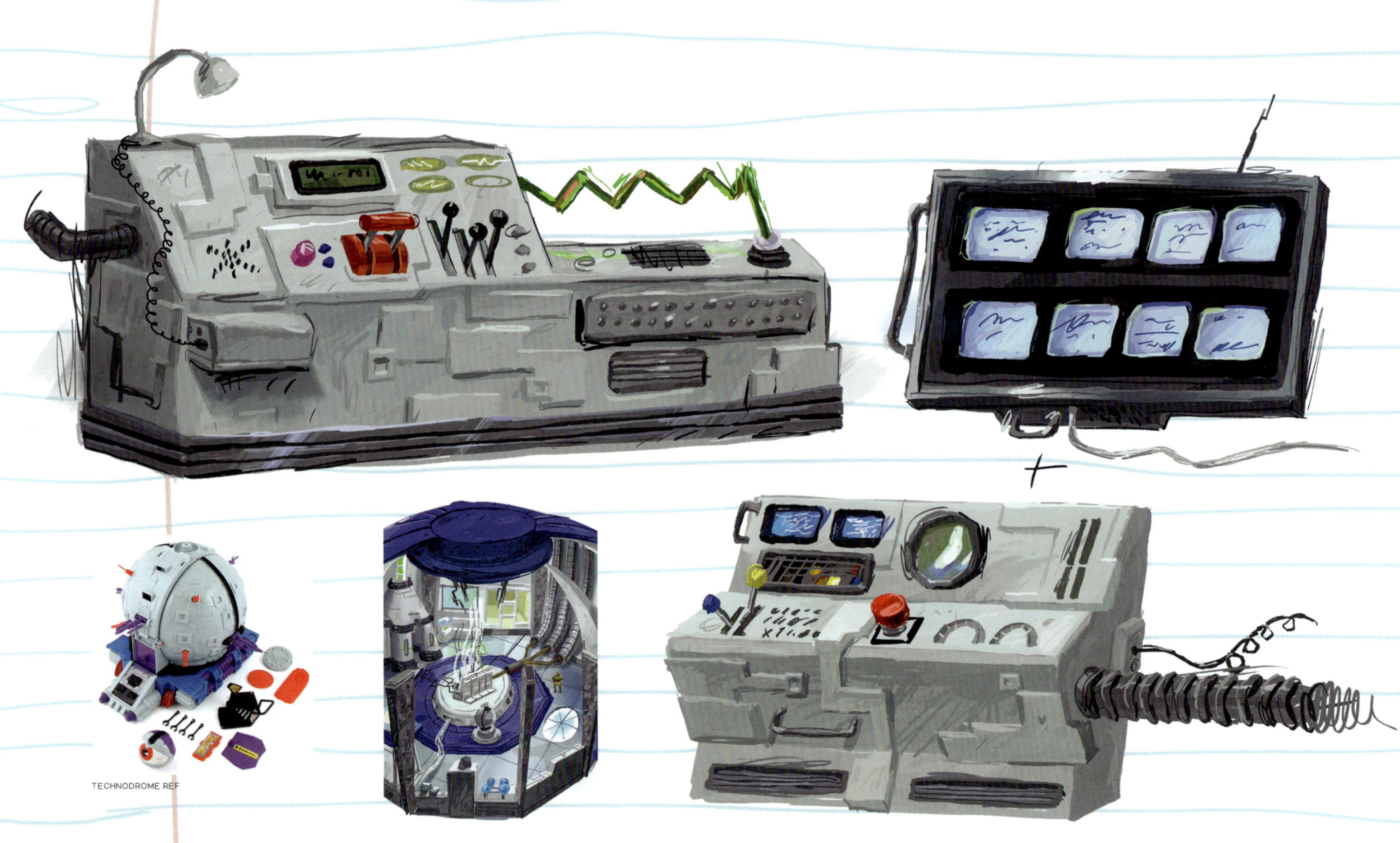

Above: TCRI lab concept art by Tiffany Lam Almack

"My favorite environment to design was TCRI. All I knew was that it was supposed to be an ultra-bizarre-techy science lab-like environment. It was supposed to feel as different from the sewers and the rest of New York as much as possible. I was directed to the Technodrome, something that unfortunately was not in my library of knowledge. When I started to do some research, I also saw a lot of the old TMNT shows, movies, concept art, and I especially honed in on the quirky '90s TMNT playsets. I asked myself, 'How can I use these bulky, plasticky, childish sets and bring that visual language into this TCRI world?' It was so, so fun to design because I've never really designed a sci-fi tech environment, so it really was new territory for me.

It's possible that not knowing much about the Technodrome world allowed me to see it in a new and fresh light. The original TMNT designs were funky and bizarre, didn't have that much rhyme or reason, and honestly was perfect for the low brow aesthetic that we were attracted to anyway."

–Art Director (Environments)
Tiffany Lam Almack

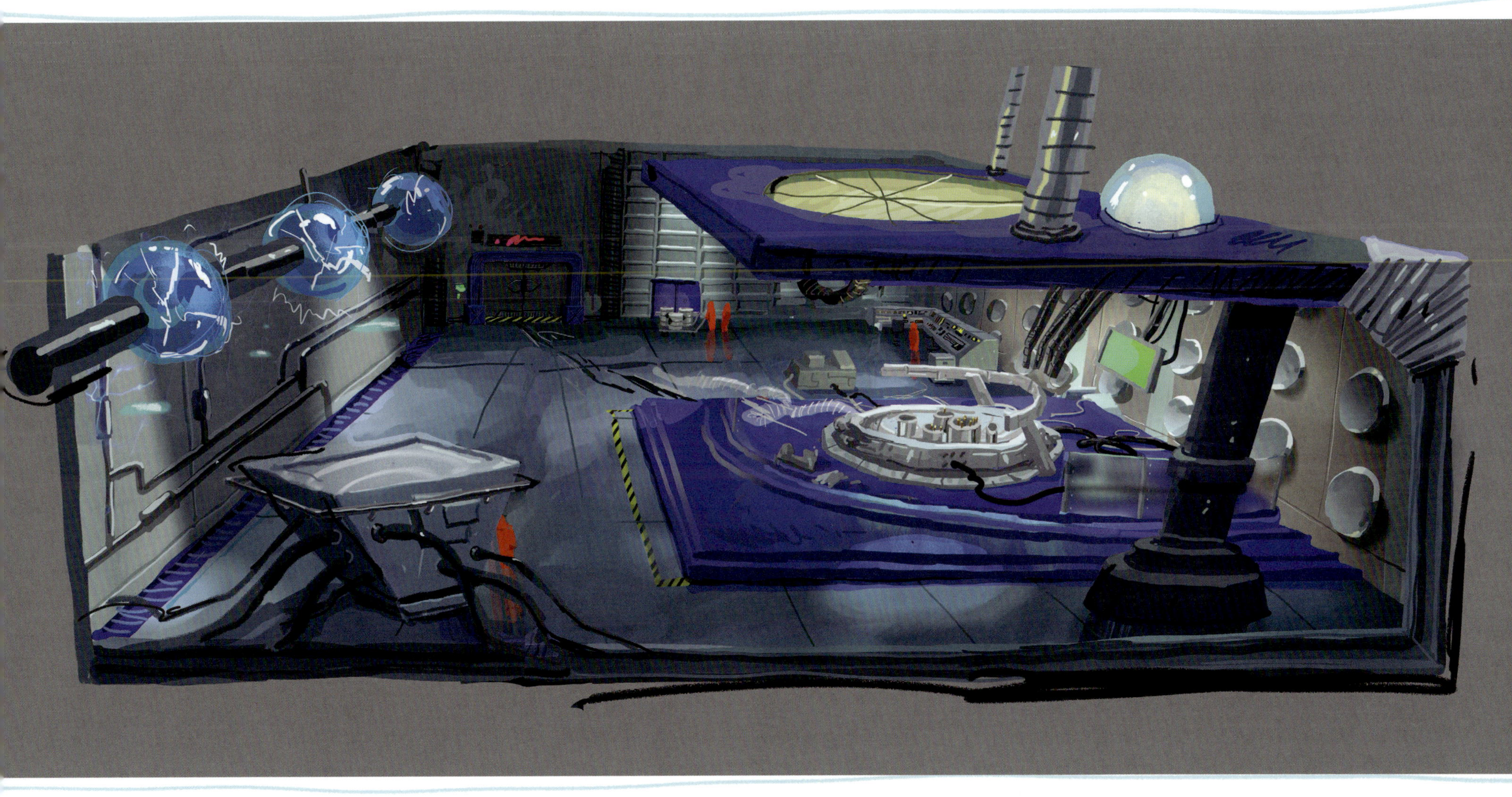

Above: TCRI lab concept art by Tiffany Lam Almack

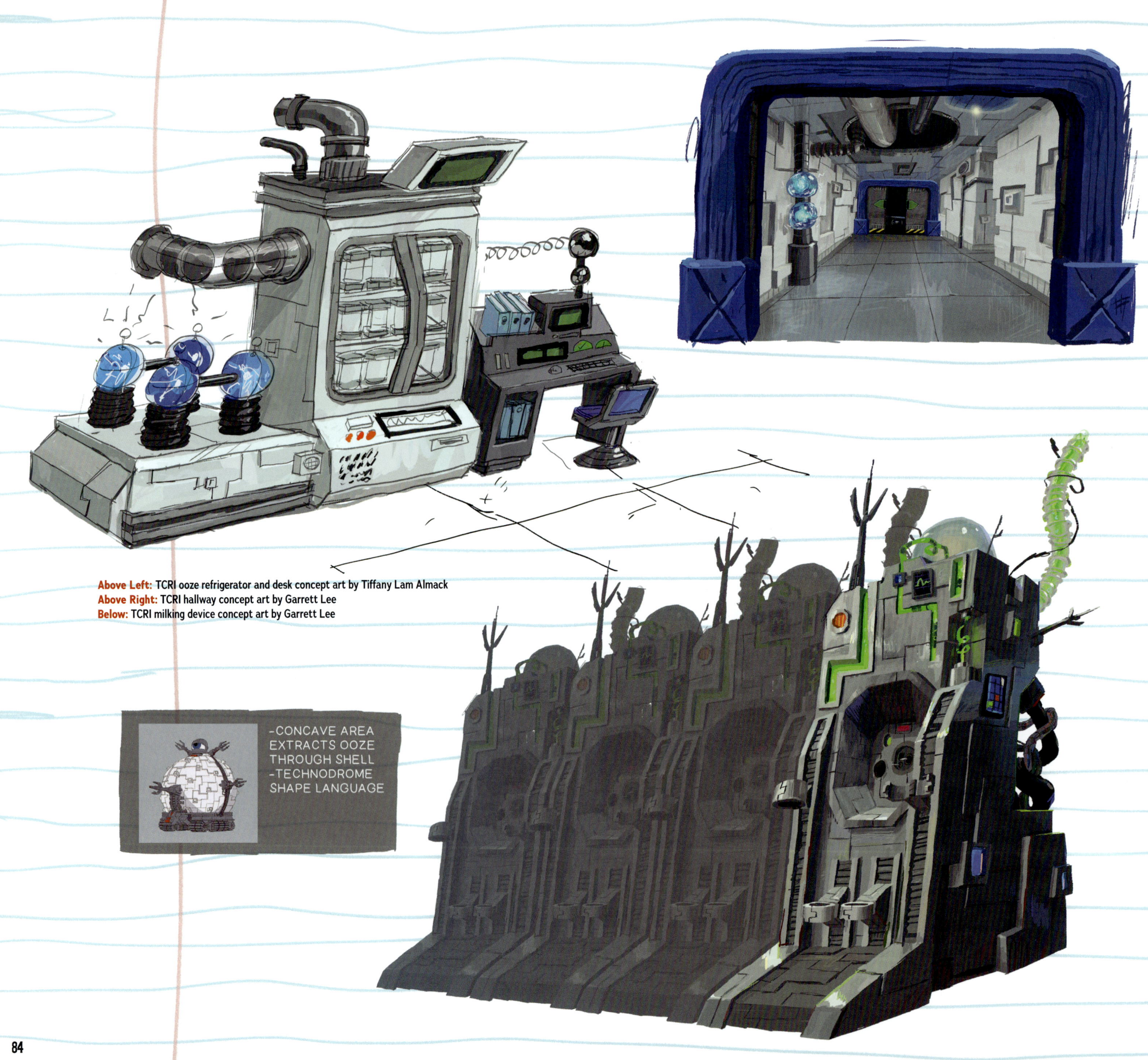

Above Left: TCRI ooze refrigerator and desk concept art by Tiffany Lam Almack
Above Right: TCRI hallway concept art by Garrett Lee
Below: TCRI milking device concept art by Garrett Lee

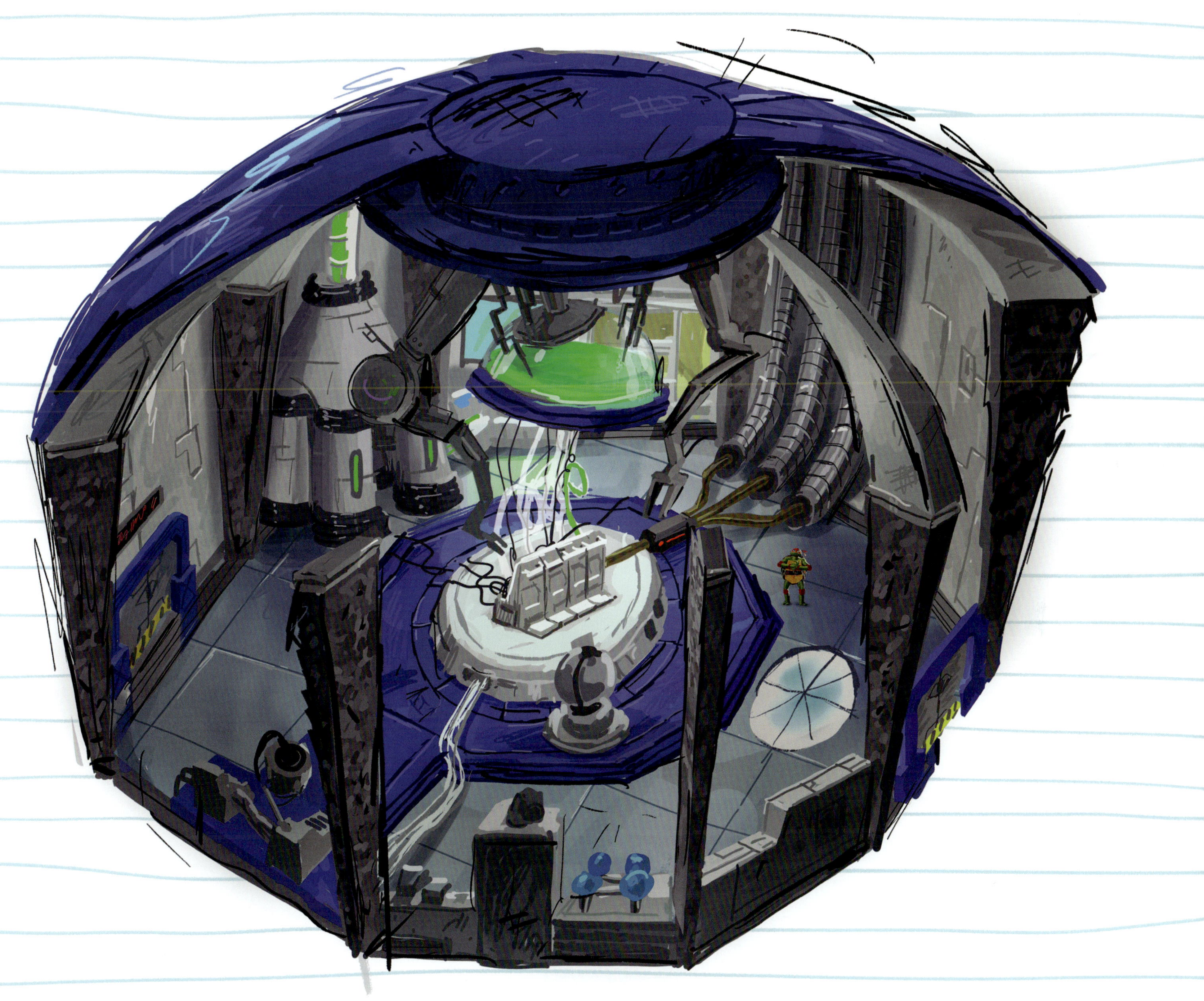

Above: TCRI lab concept art by Tiffany Lam Almack

New York City

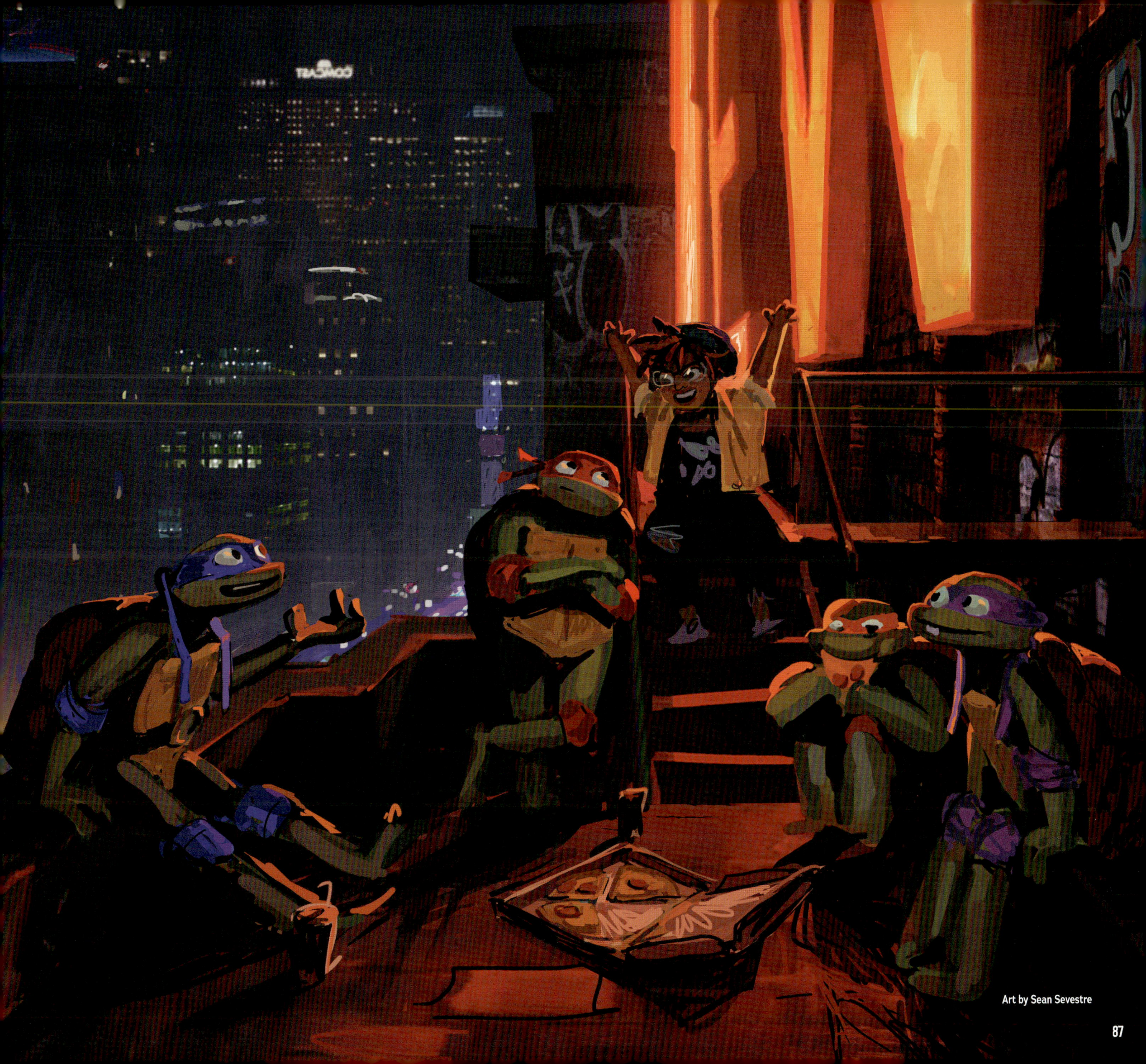

Art by Sean Sevestre

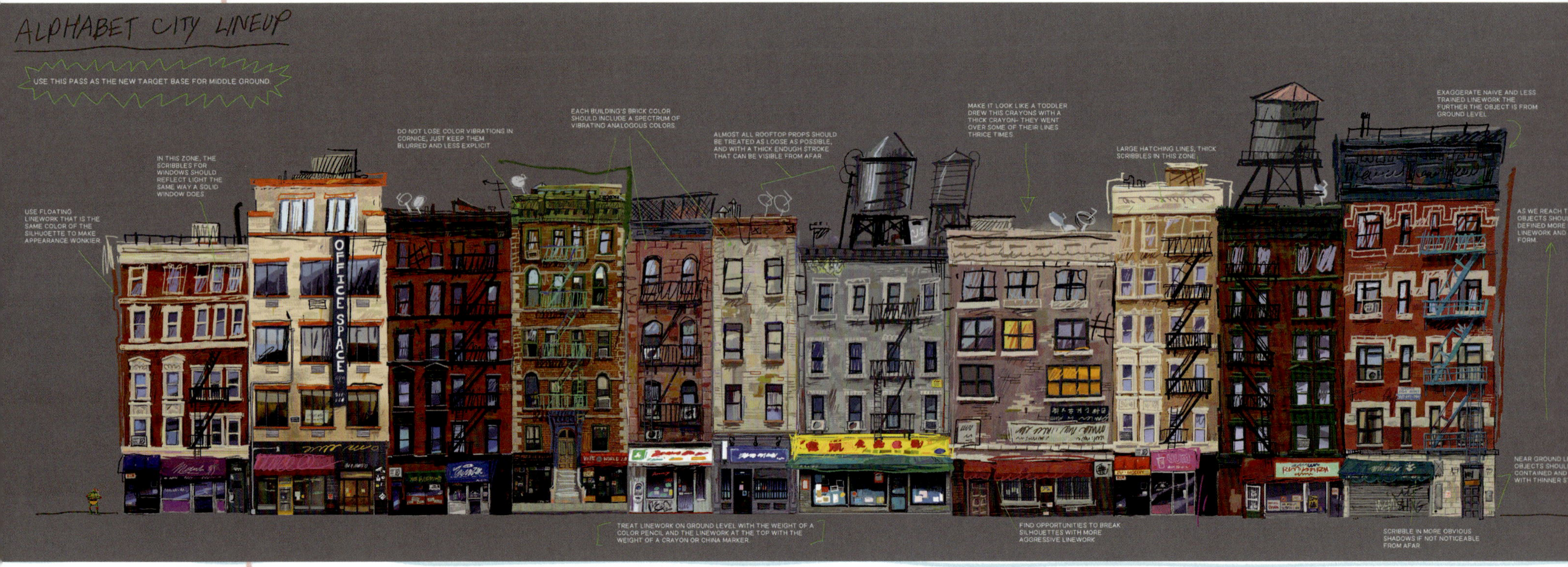

"The turtles have to want to be a part of New York. There was a story imperative that they had to aspire to be normal people in this city so we had to glamorize New York in a really realistic way, and realistically New York is not that glamorous, especially if you're living in the sewers. Things like the quality of the sunlight late in the day, and those hard shadows, and thinking about what it would be like to live in the sewers your entire life, and then be able to step into the sunlight. At its core it's realistic, it's beautiful in its mundanity, and hopefully it's aspirational."

—Director Jeff Rowe

Above: Initial design by Kellan Jett, final paint by Lily Nishita, Garrett Lee, Nikita Chan, and Tiffany Lam Almack

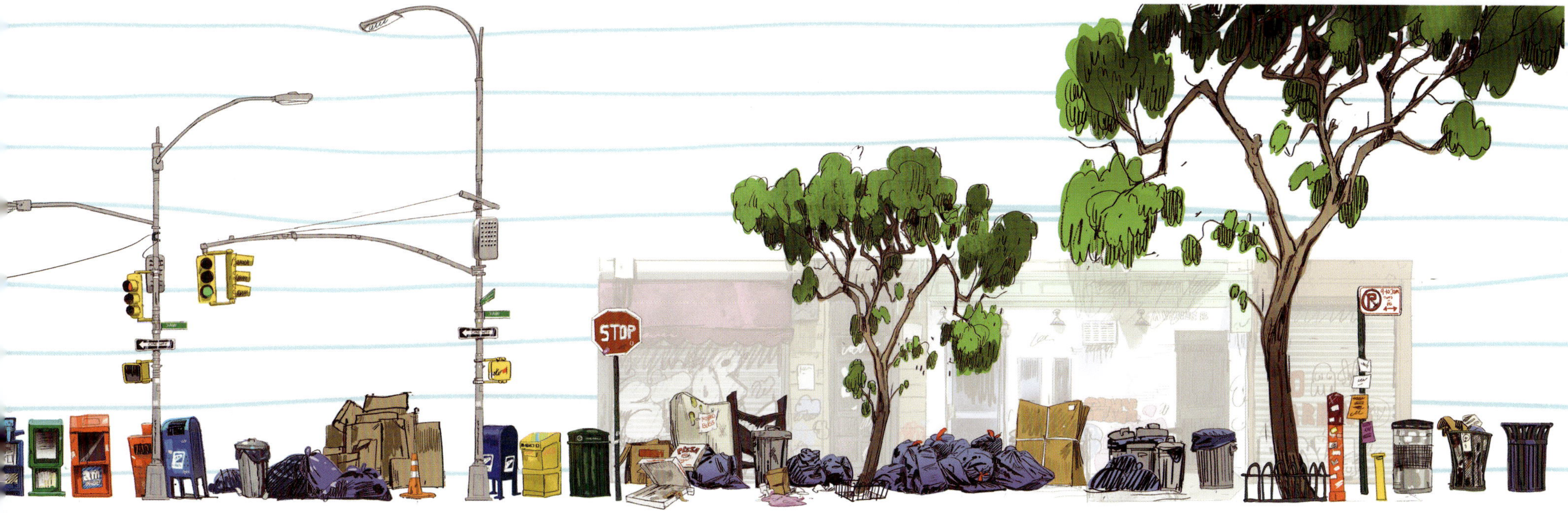

"New York City is multifaceted and multilayered. It can be glamorous and glitzy, expensive and flashy, but there are also the grimy, dirty, graffitied, unplanned parts of New York. That part of New York is home to the Turtles and Splinter. It was fun to be able to explore and world build just because it's so rare for this side of New York to be featured in an animated film. It's an undeniable part of the city that we tried really hard to make feel observed and authentic."

–Art Director (Environments)
Tiffany Lam Almack

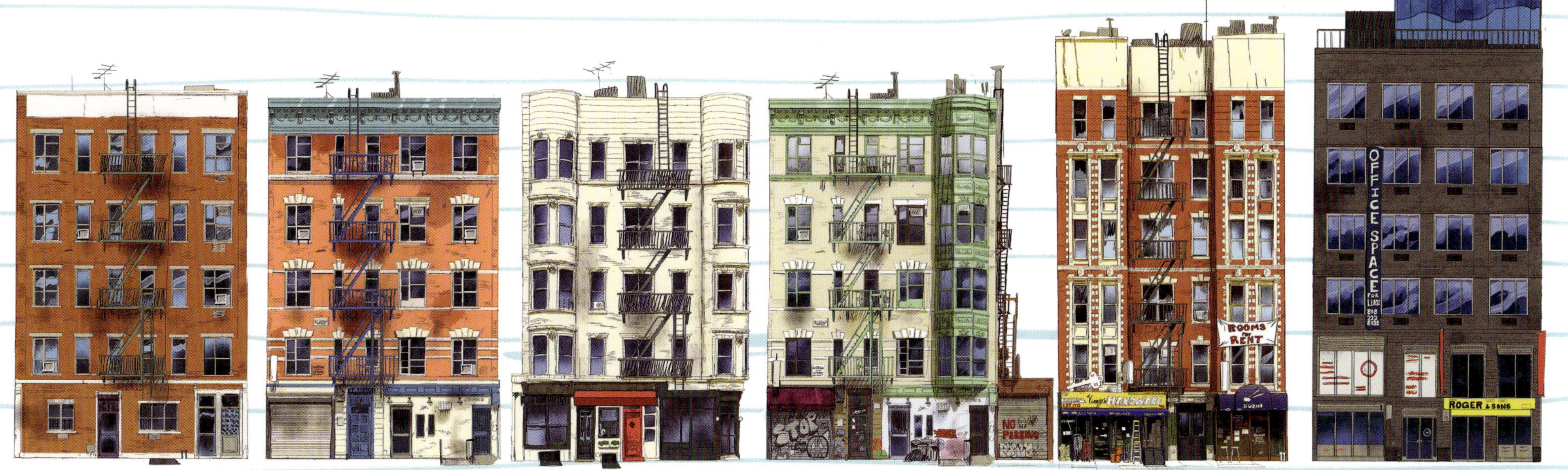

Above: City street designs by Kellan Jett
Below: City block building designs by Kellan Jett

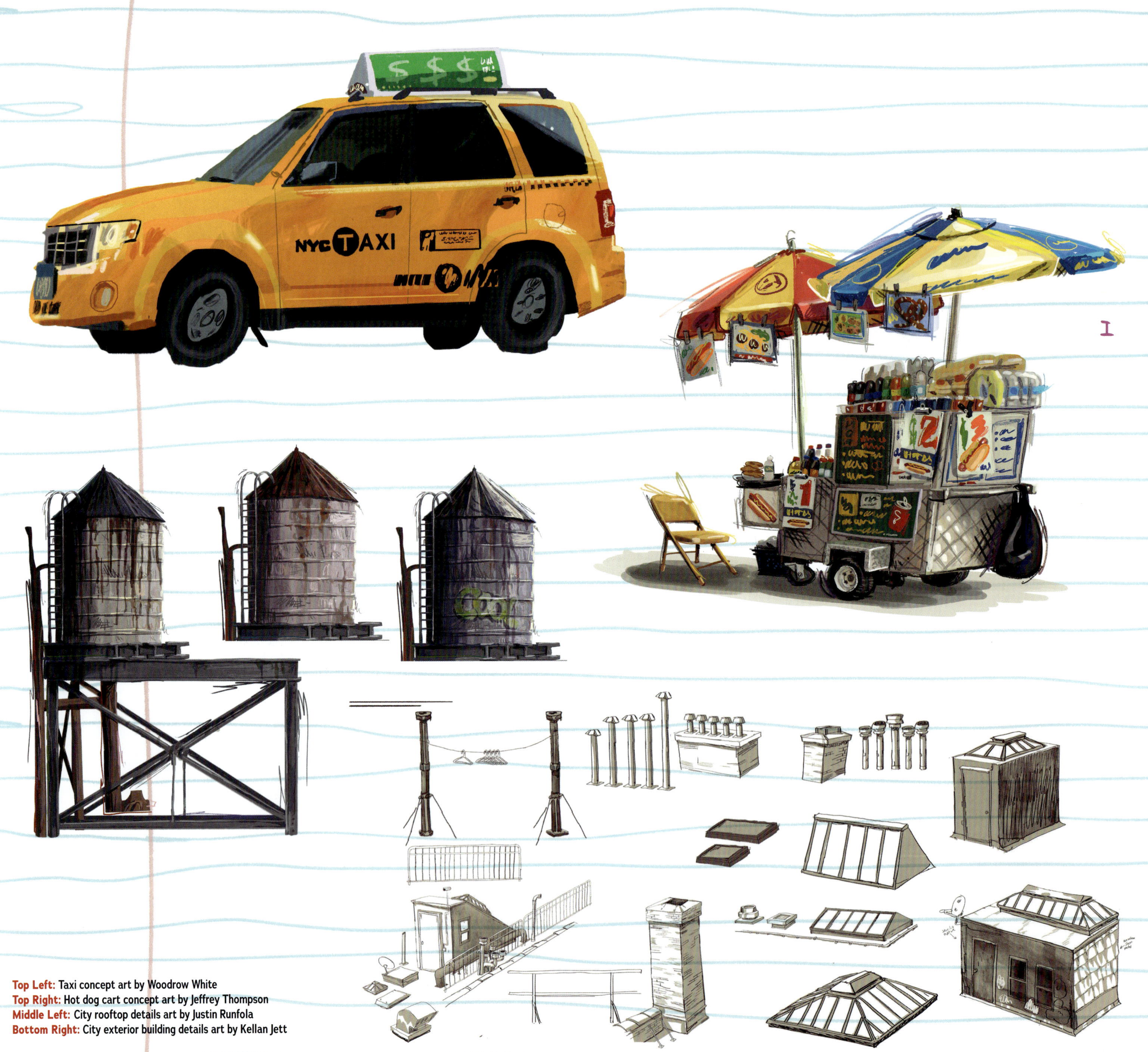

Top Left: Taxi concept art by Woodrow White
Top Right: Hot dog cart concept art by Jeffrey Thompson
Middle Left: City rooftop details art by Justin Runfola
Bottom Right: City exterior building details art by Kellan Jett

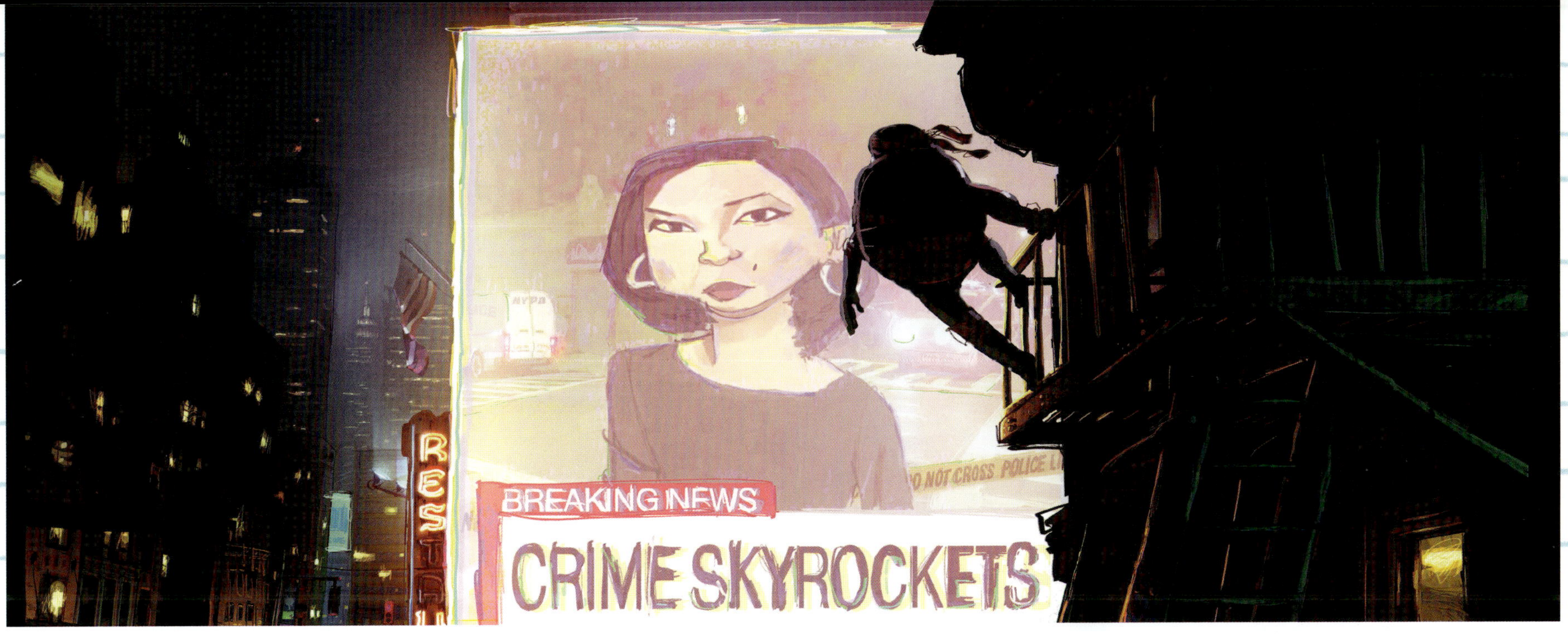

Above: Fire escape concept art by Jeffrey Thompson
Below: Chop shop interior concept art by Nikita Chan

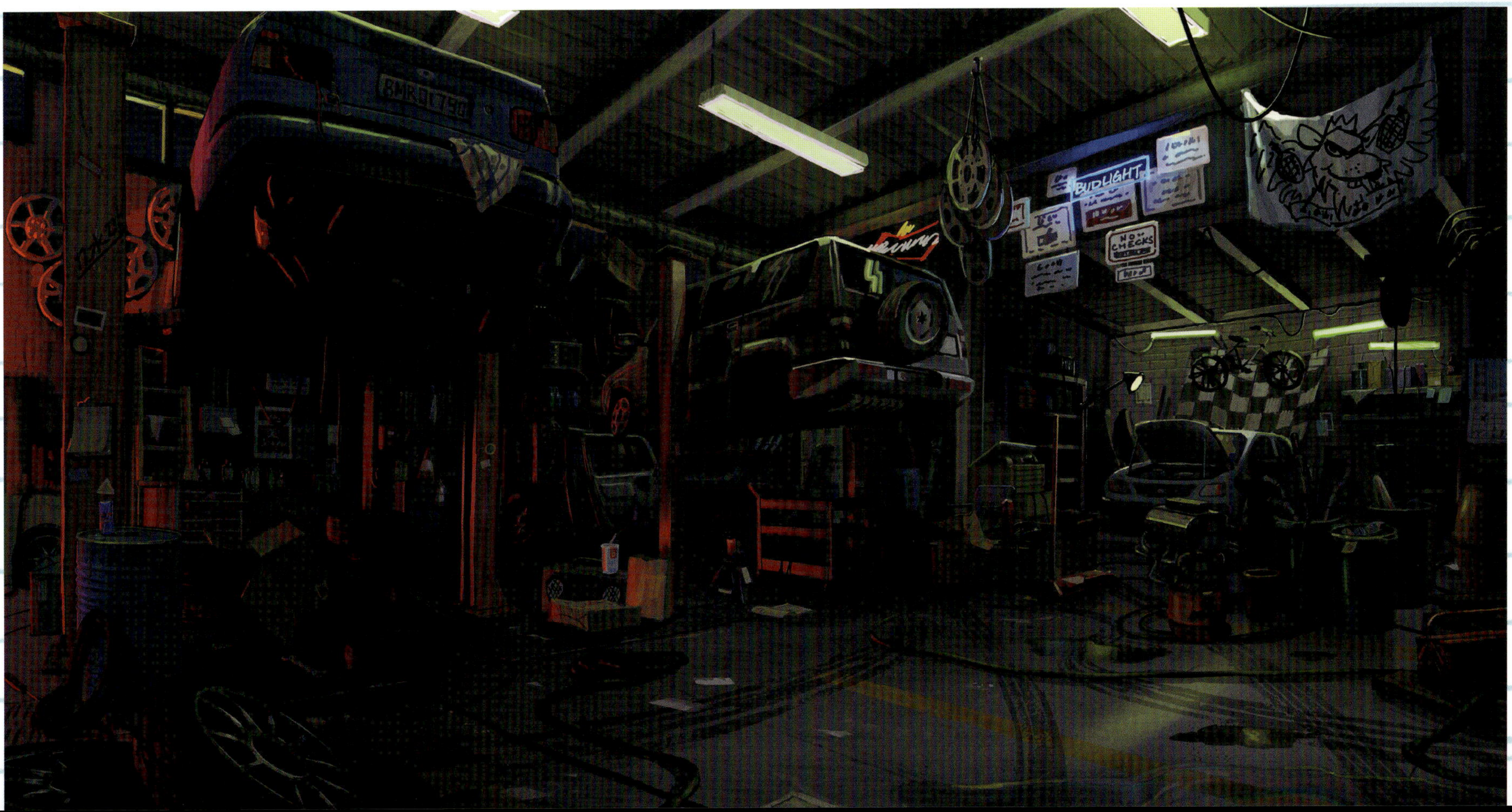

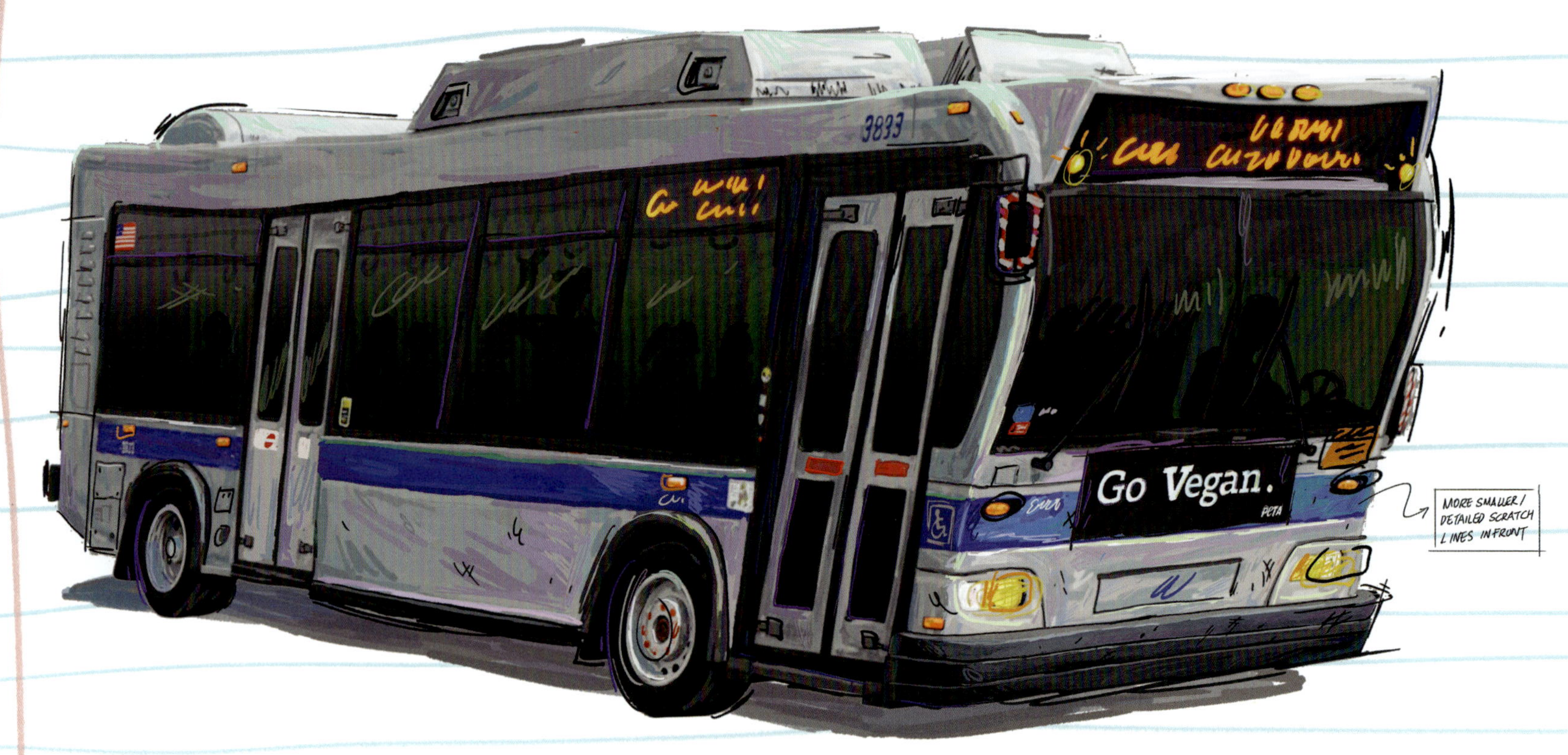

Above: City bus art by Dustin d'Arnault and Nikita Chan
Below: Police car concept art by Dustin d'Arnault

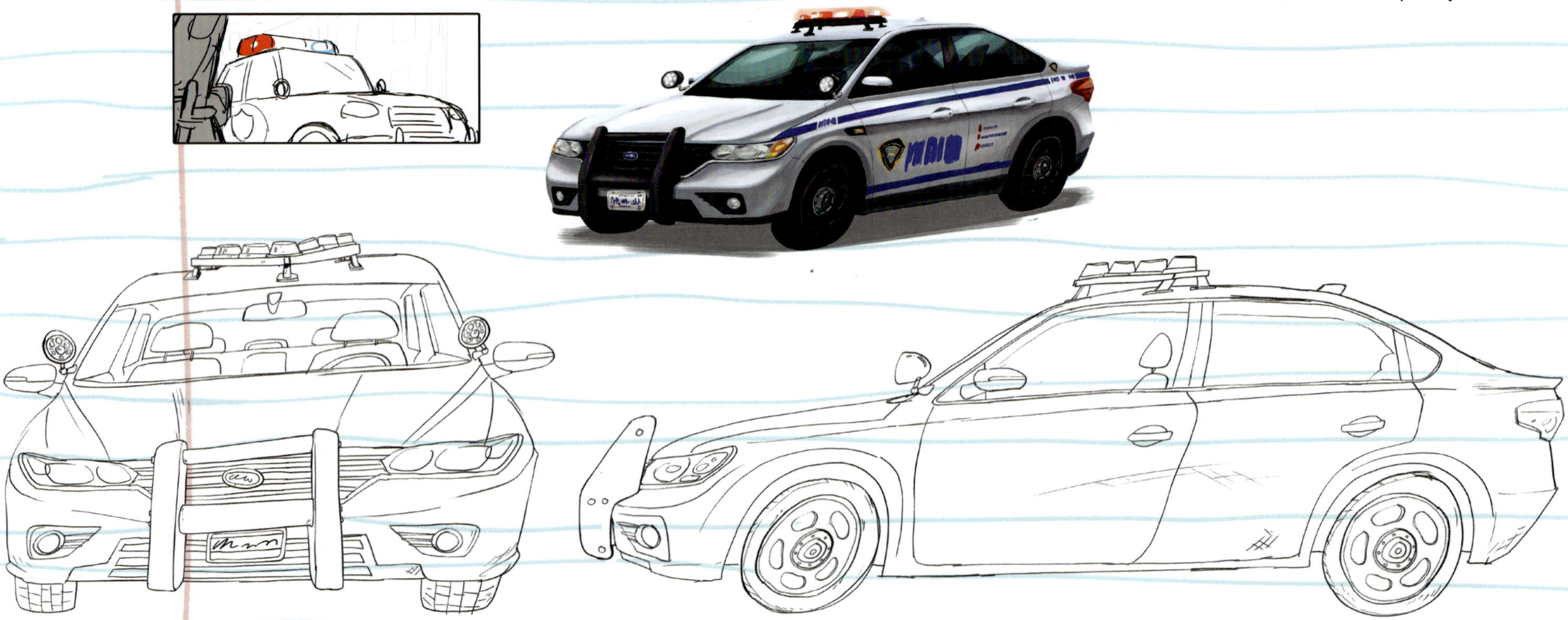

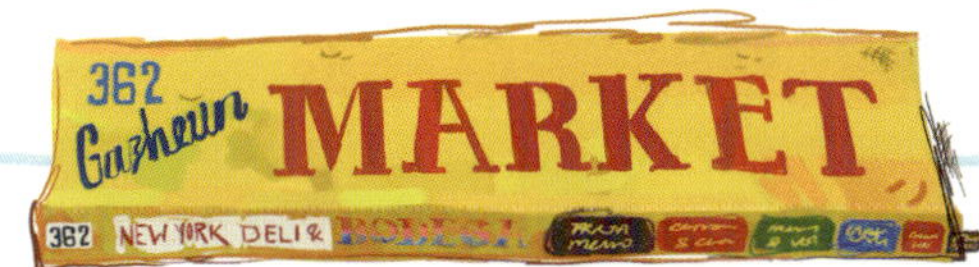

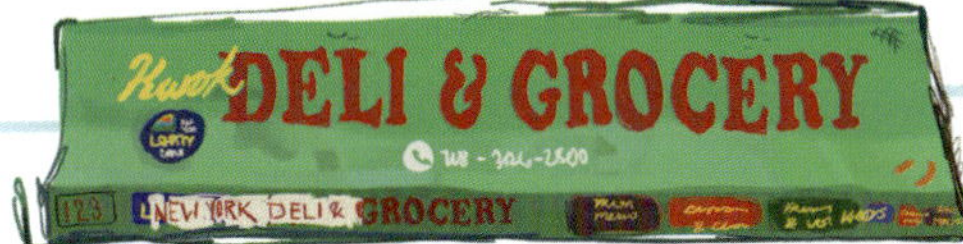

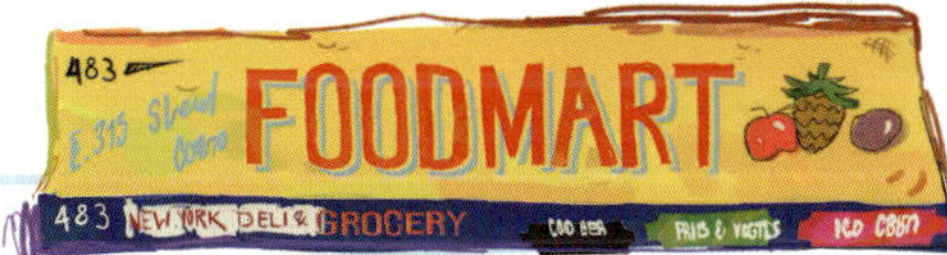

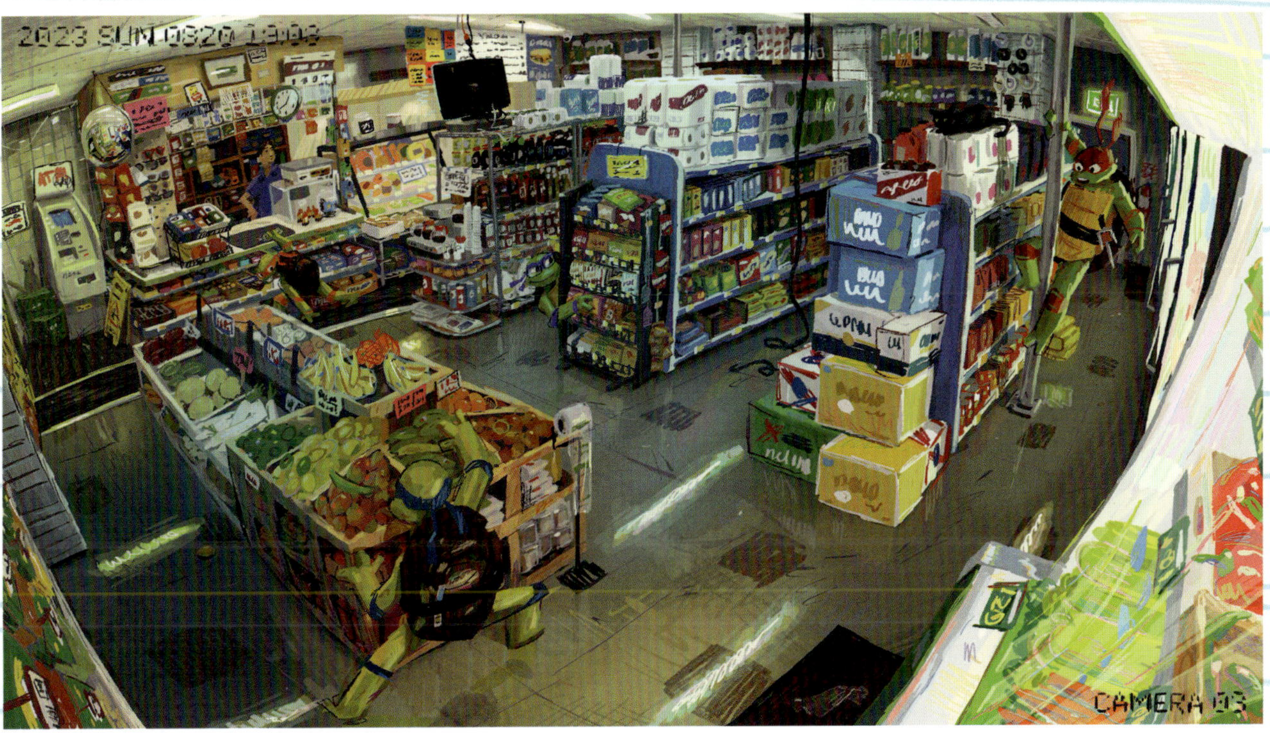

Top Right: Bodega interior concept art by Garrett Lee
Top Left: Bodega exterior concept art by Alger Tam
Below: Outdoor movie concept art by Kellan Jett

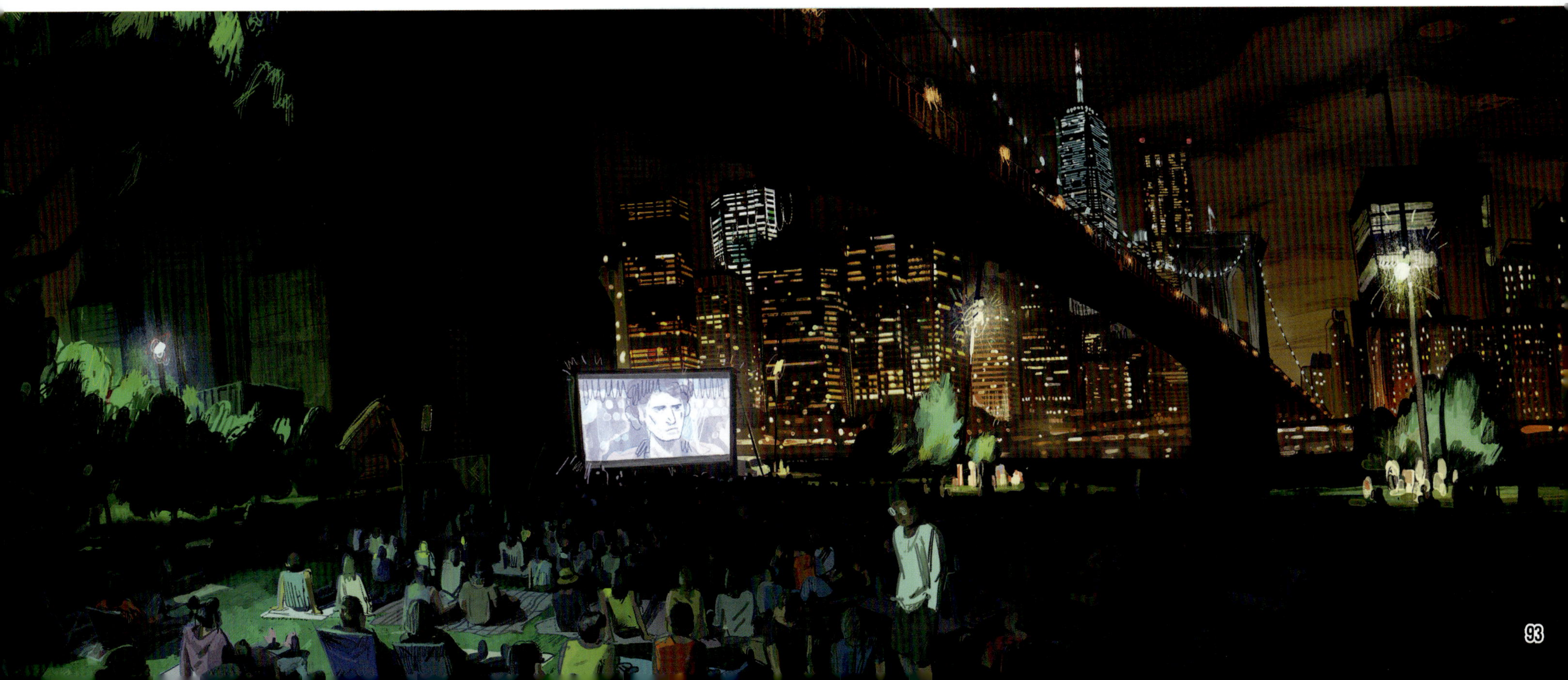

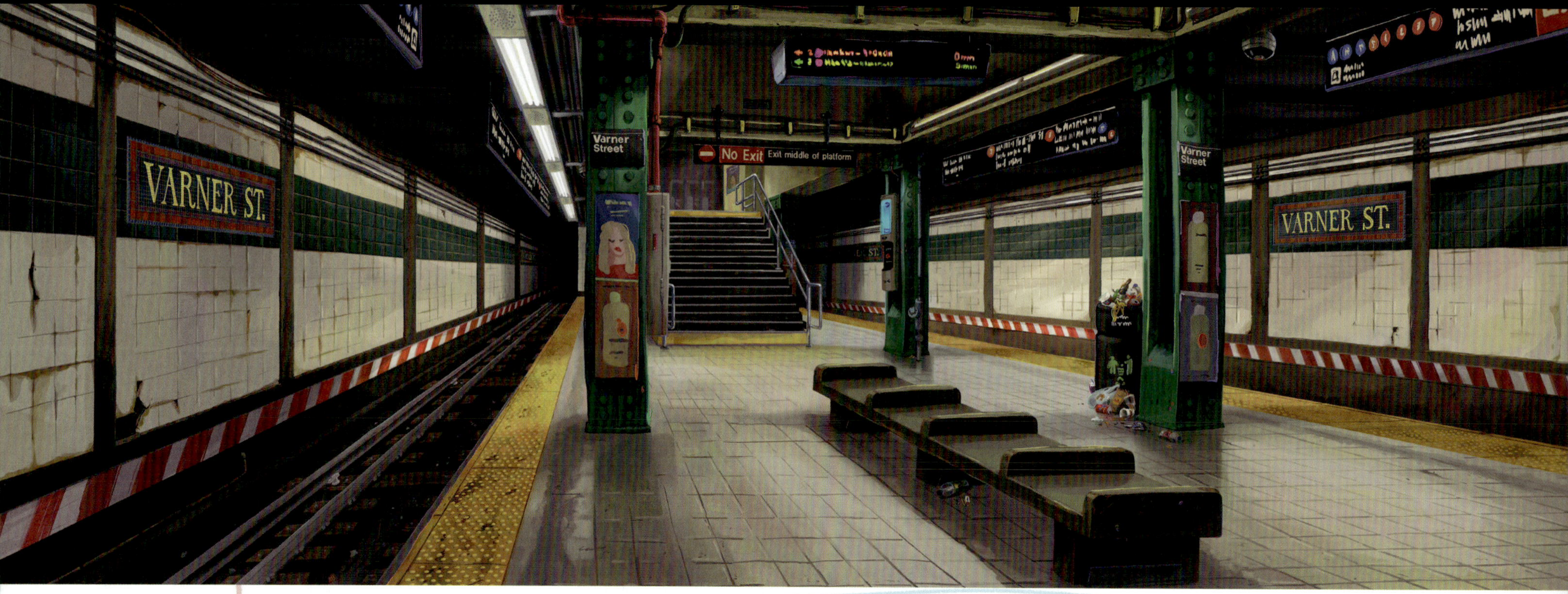

"Figuring out how these buildings would look in a 3D space was initially challenging. When you look upwards, typically what you would do to give the illusion of depth is to use a blur effect. But that kind of perfect CG look didn't match our show style. Instead, we developed a system where the further the buildings got in x, y, or z space, the crazier the scribbles got. The windows on the tenth floor and up would get increasingly more abstract and more messy, breaking the silhouette. I think that really helped with the style of the movie."

–Art Director (Environments)
Tiffany Lam Almack

Above: Subay concept art by Dustin d'Arnault
Below: City rooftop concept art by Nikita Chan

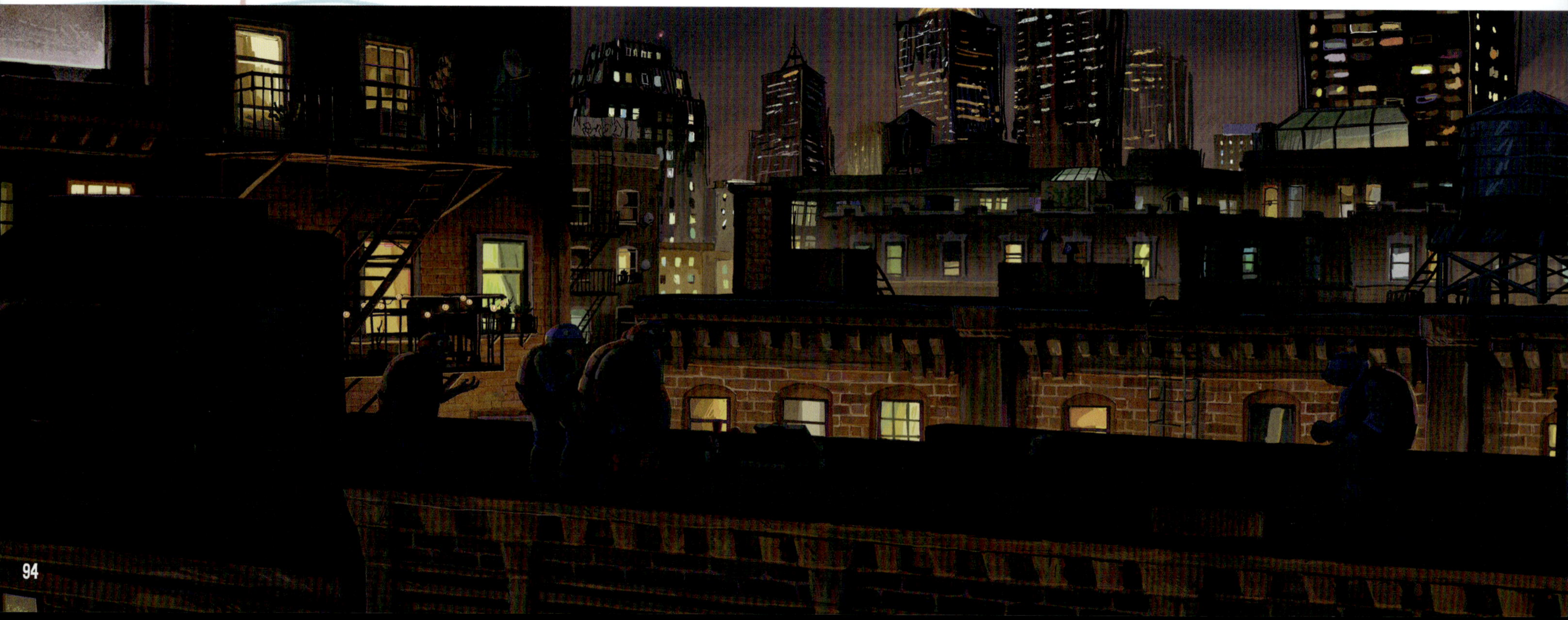

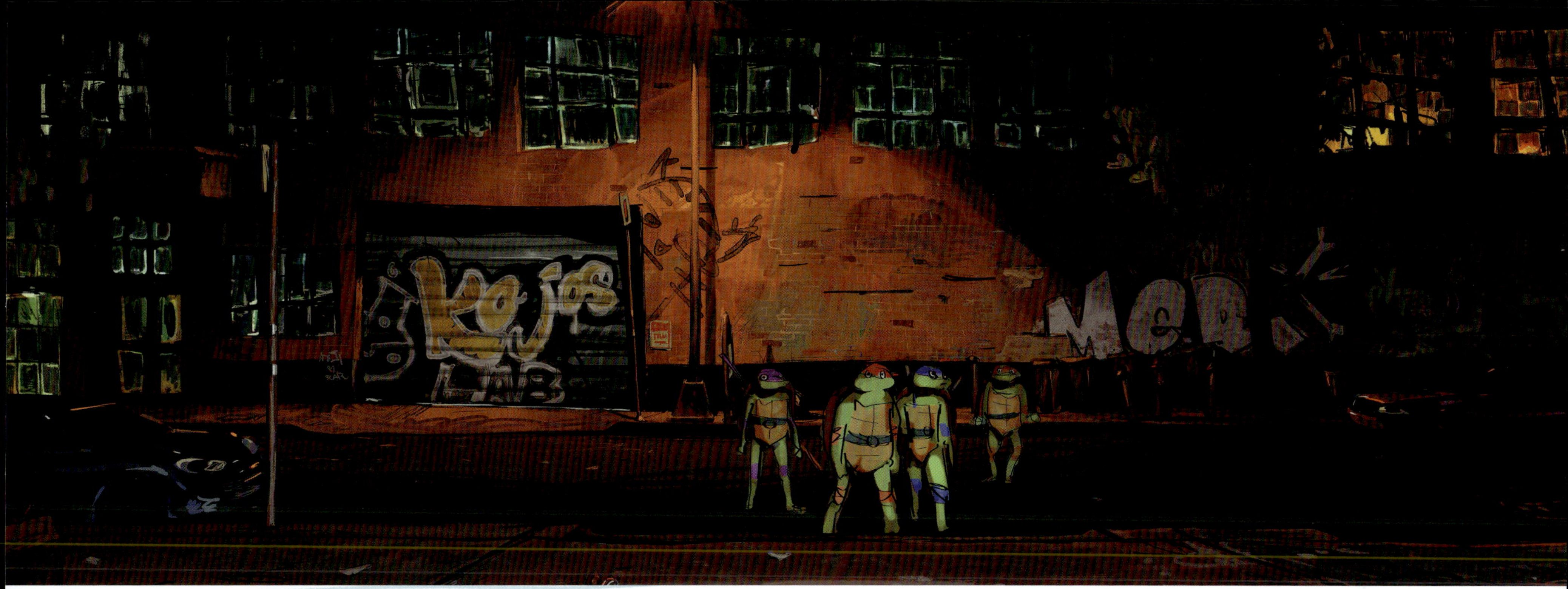

"Google Earth was truly a lifesaver on this movie. You get to pick a location and you get plopped down onto the street and suddenly you have a plethora of crucial information."

–Art Director (Environments) Tiffany Lam Almack

Above: Exterior chop shop art by Sean Sevestre
Below: Residential city block art by Lily Nishita

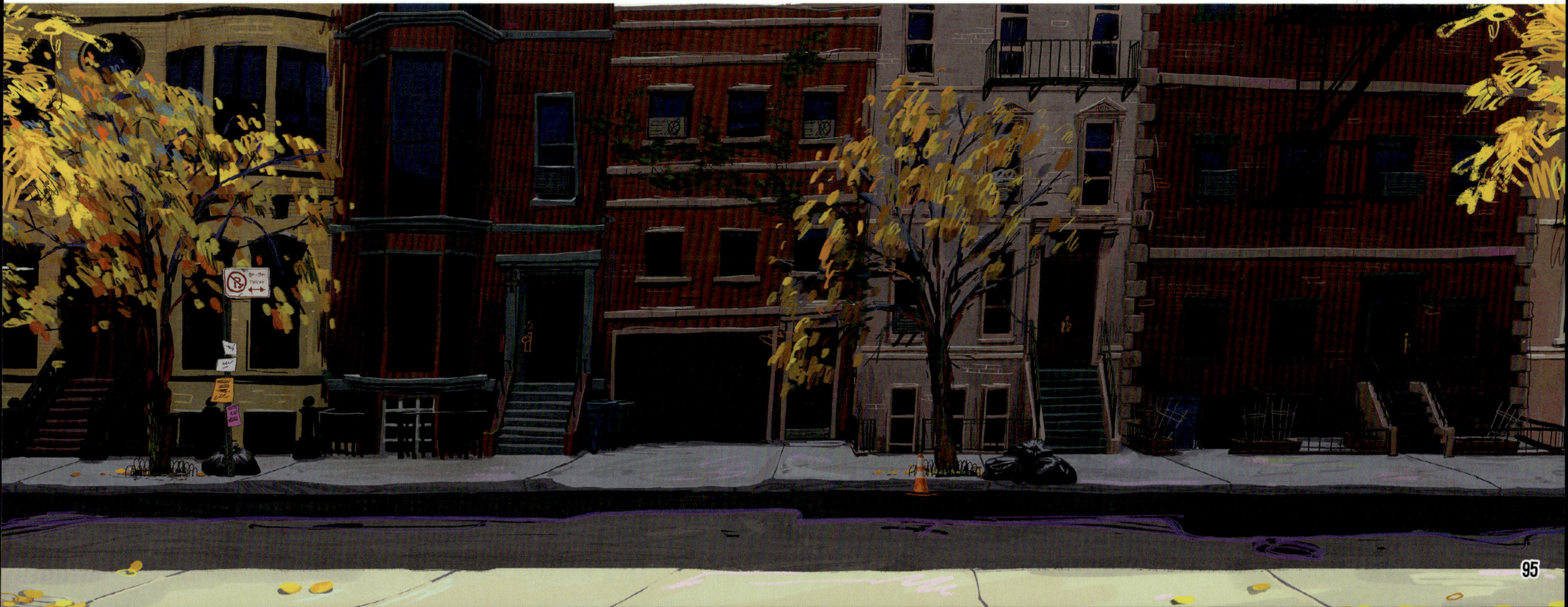

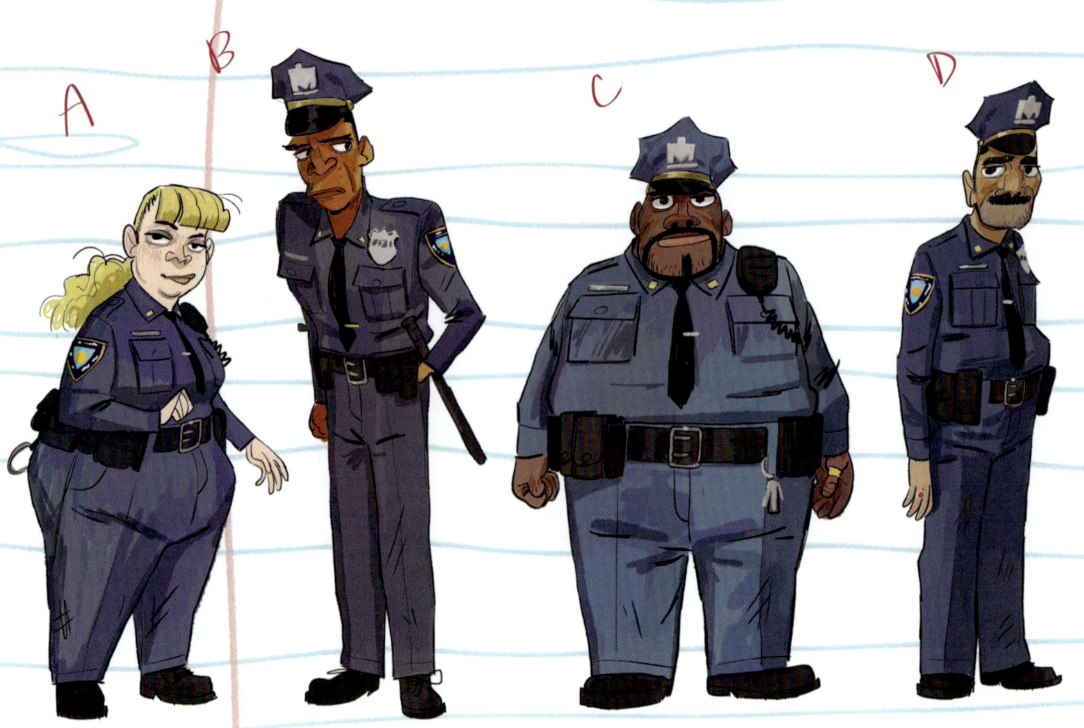

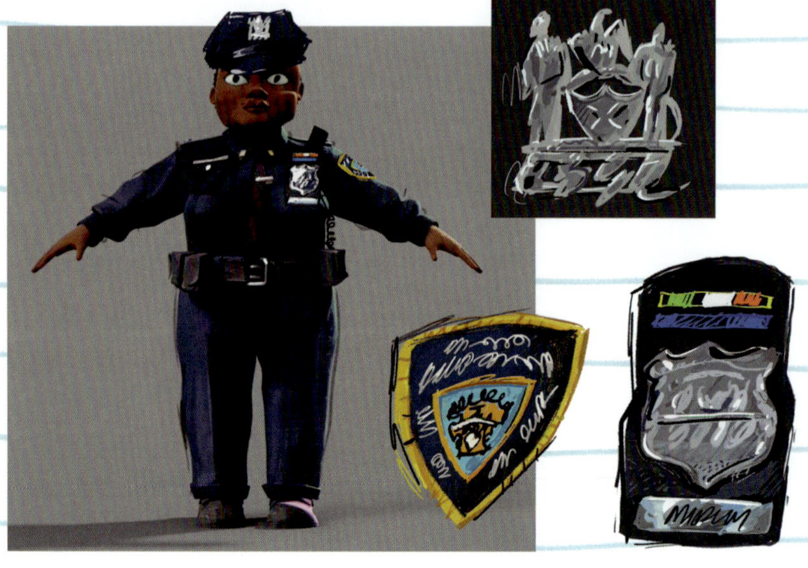

Above Left: Police officer concept art by James A. Castillo
Above Right: Poice officer and badge concept art by Tiffany Lam Almack
Below Left: News anchors concept art by Woodrow White
Below Right: News anchors concept art by Yashar Kassai

"Populating New York was really fun. For a very long time, no humans had been designed for the movie; it was just the Turtles. The question becomes, how do you design not just humans who can live in this world as the Turtles, because the style is so unique and so new, but also make characters that are generally New Yorkers?

Because NY is such a specific part of the DNA of *Teenage Mutant Ninja Turtles,* I started just watching people who have created five-hour-long videos walking through the streets of downtown. What's the vibe, what's New York like now, because they also wanted the movie to be very current, very much of the modern age. There was a lot of attention to detail as to creating characters that could represent the New York that we know and love today."

–Character Designer James A. Castillo

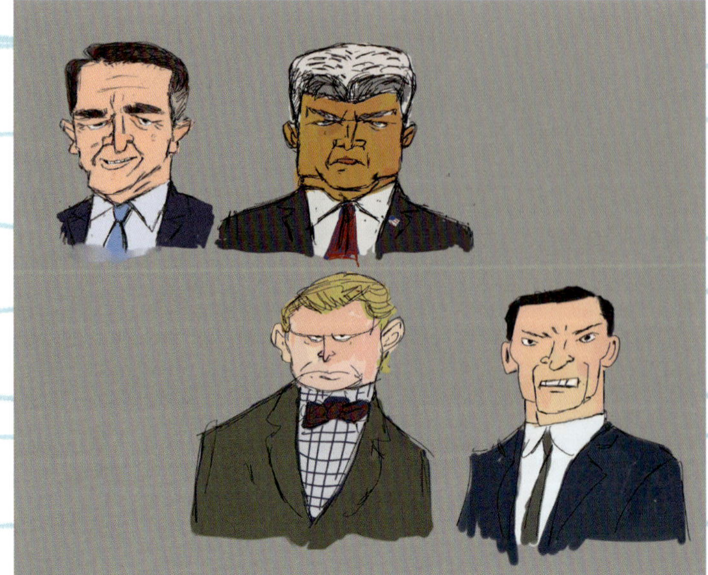

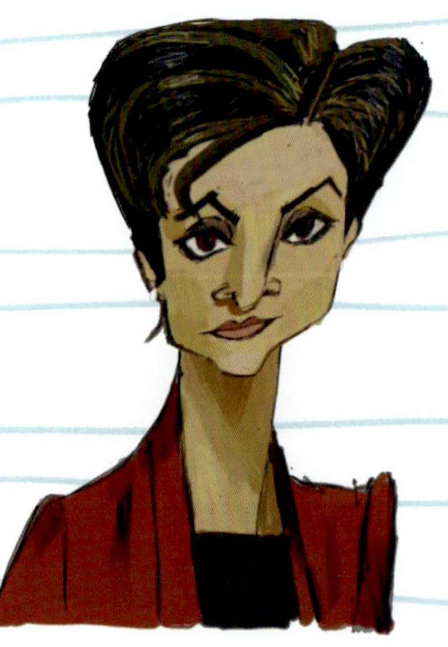

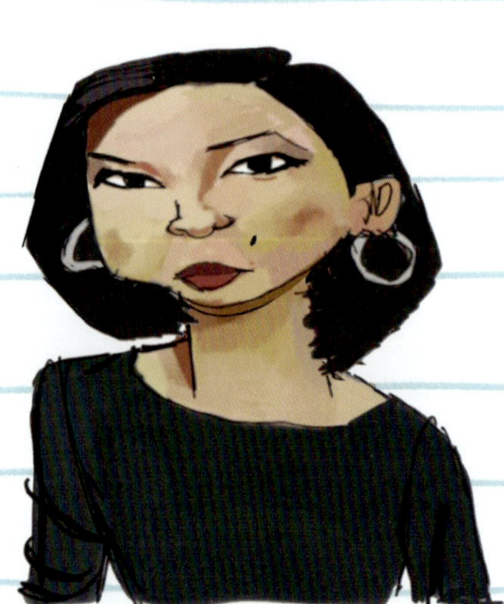

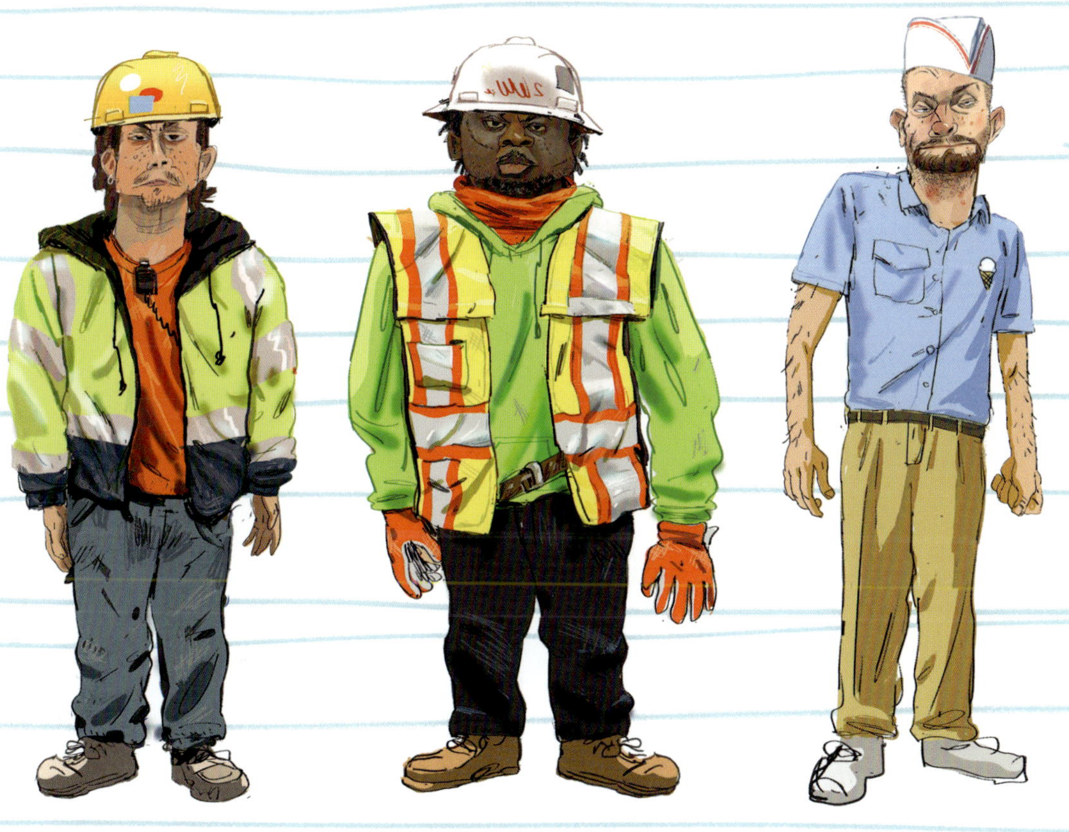

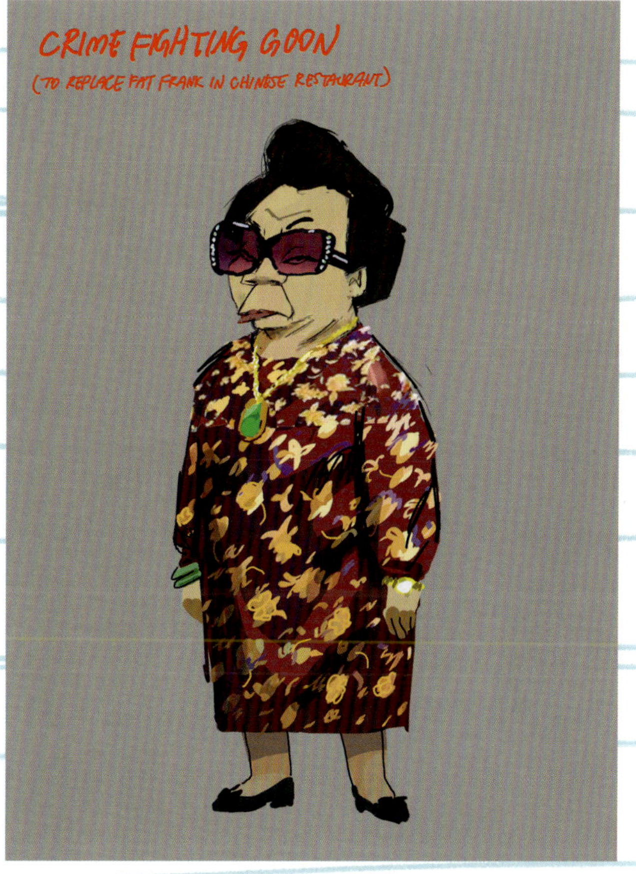

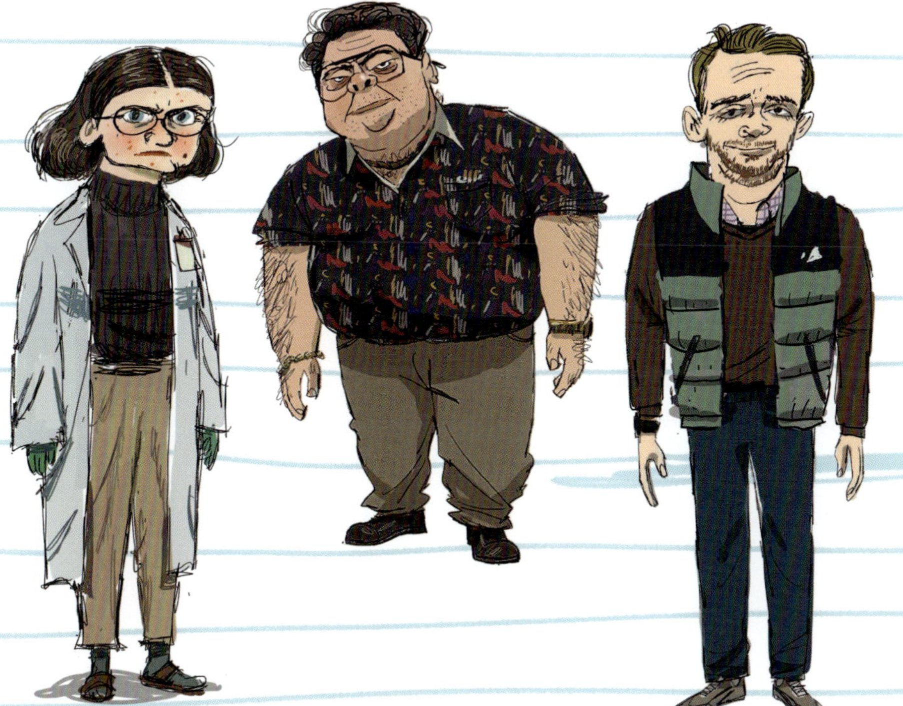

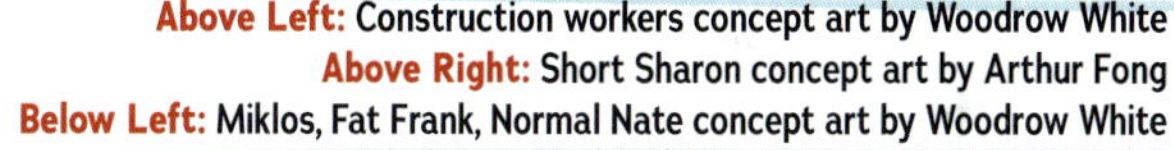
Above Left: Construction workers concept art by Woodrow White
Above Right: Short Sharon concept art by Arthur Fong
Below Left: Miklos, Fat Frank, Normal Nate concept art by Woodrow White

"A couple crew members and I took a trip to New York during production and did a lot of people watching. The way they dress, their postures, the sort of faces you see. That was very helpful.

Another thing, too, we wanted to make the humans look just as weird as the mutants. That was a very conscious decision, these themes of fitting in and alienation. To make the humans uglier gives a very deliberate perspective shift, putting you in the shoes of the mutants and helping you to feel how strange humans must be to these four ninja turtles."

–Lead Character Designer Woodrow White

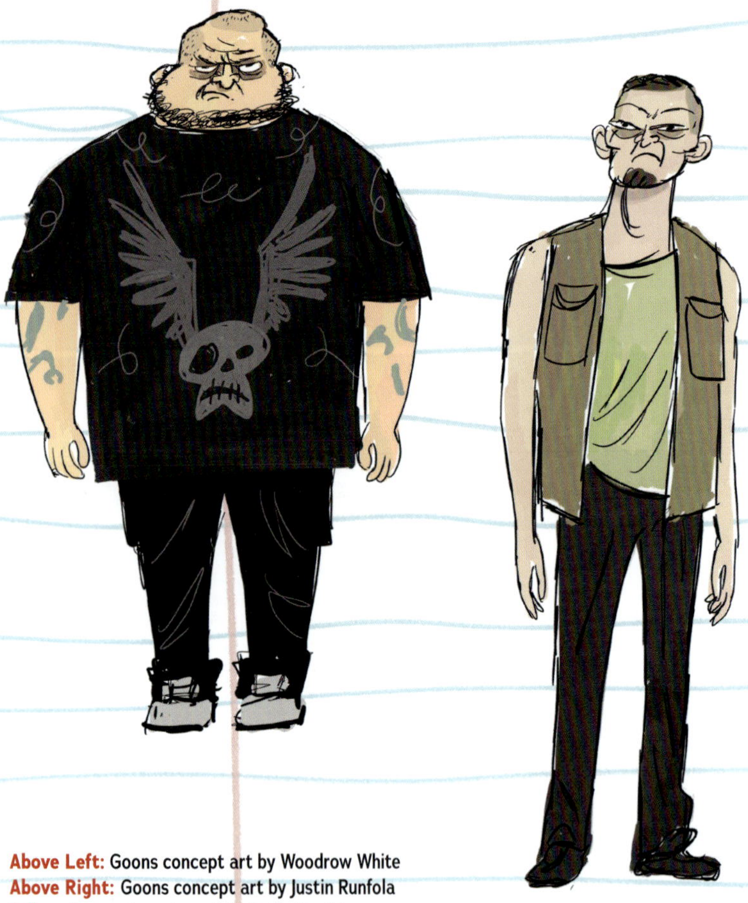

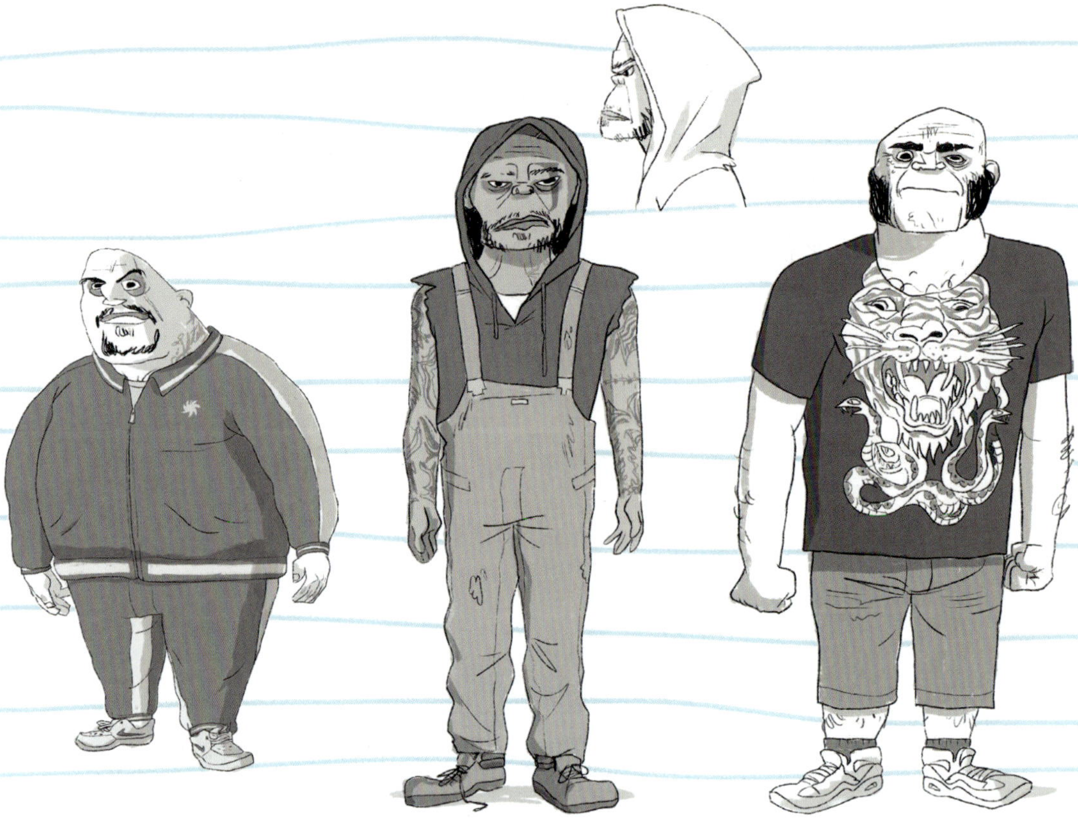

"The mob bosses were really fun because it was a very *Dick Tracy*-esque exploration. With names like Bald Bronson and Normal Ned, their names were the prompts. Like, I knew Bald Bronson had to be an extremely bald guy with a really shiny head."

–Lead Character Designer Woodrow White

Above Left: Goons concept art by Woodrow White
Above Right: Goons concept art by Justin Runfola
Below: Goons character art by Justin Runfola

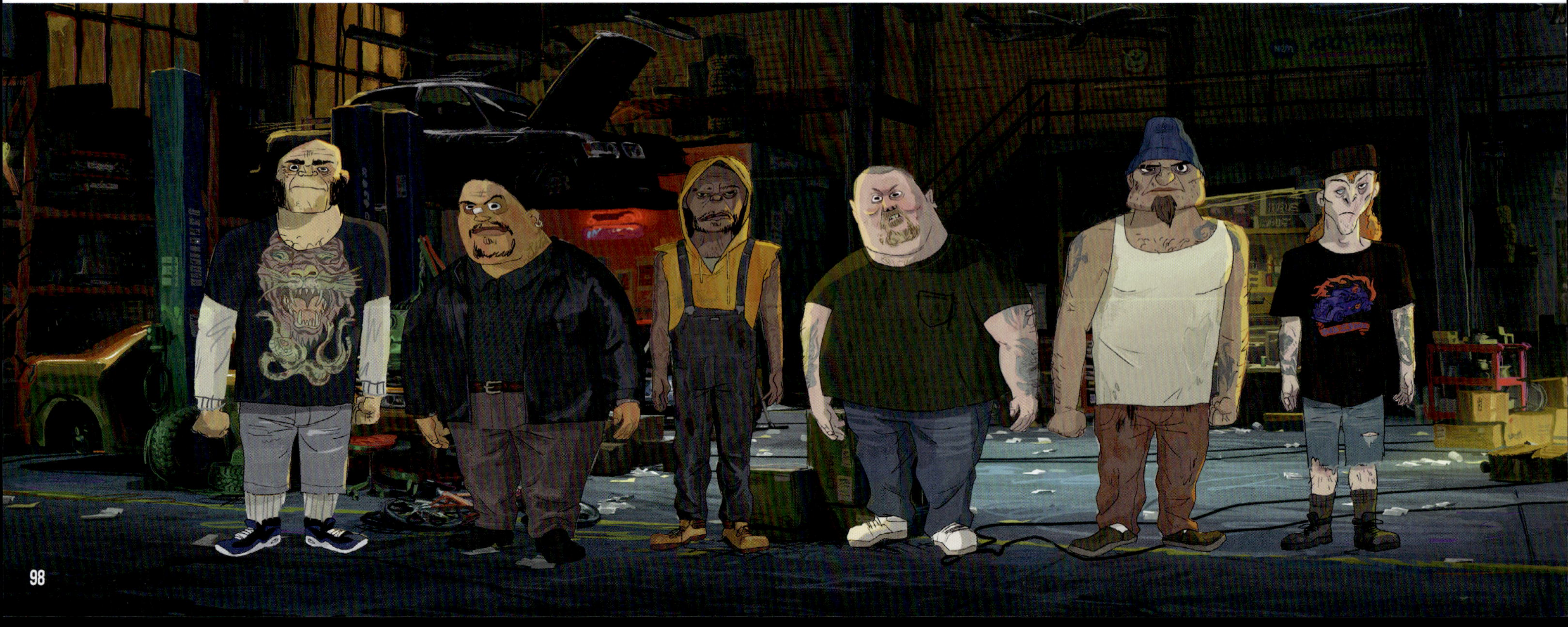

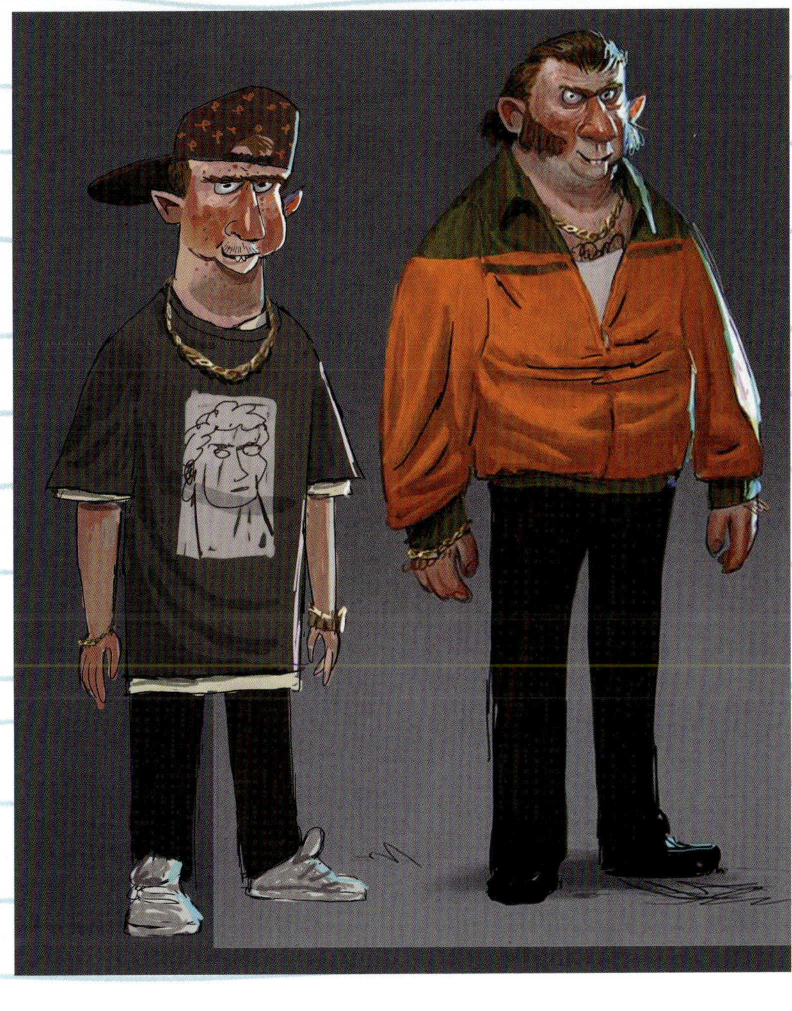

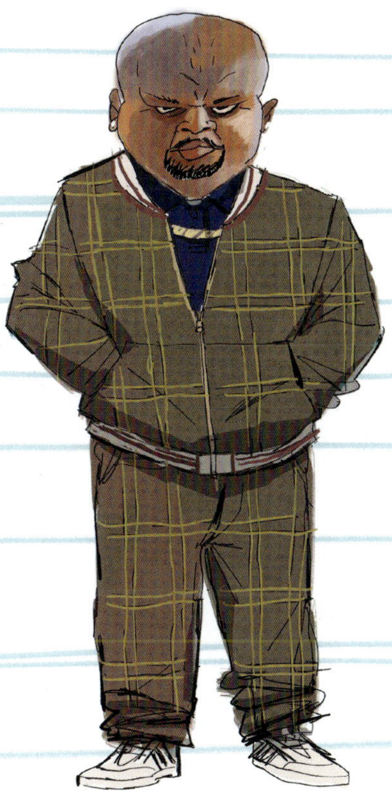

Above Left: Bad Bernie and Bad Bernie Jr. concept art by Woodrow White
Above Right: Bald Bronson concept art by Woodrow White
Below Left: Armored truck driver concept art by Kellan Jett
Below Right: Firefighter concept art by Kellan Jett

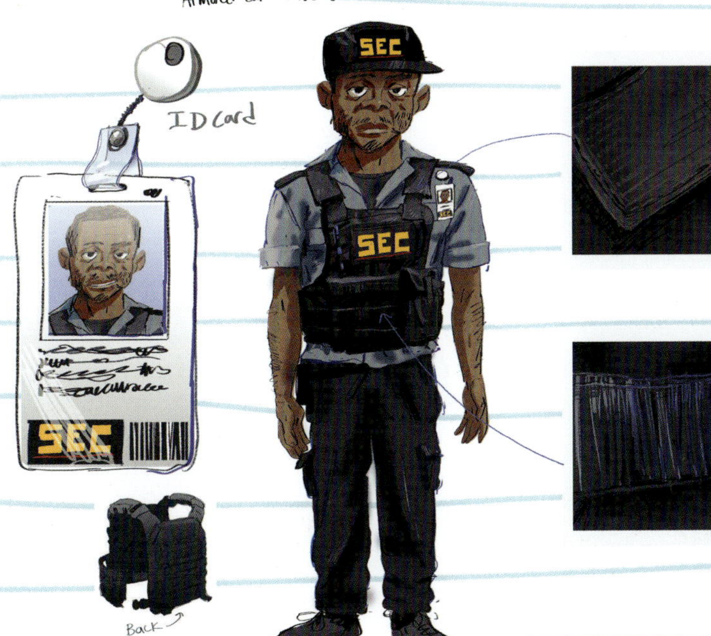

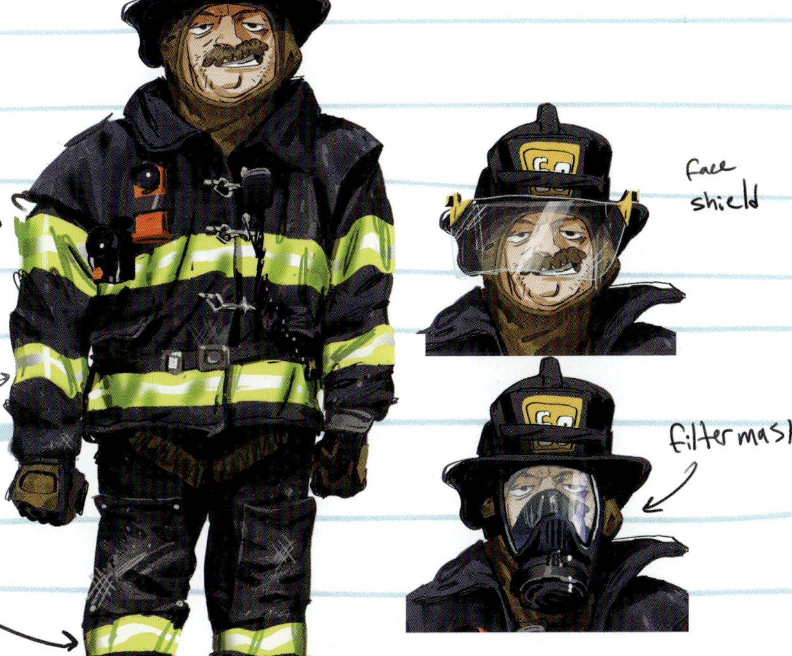

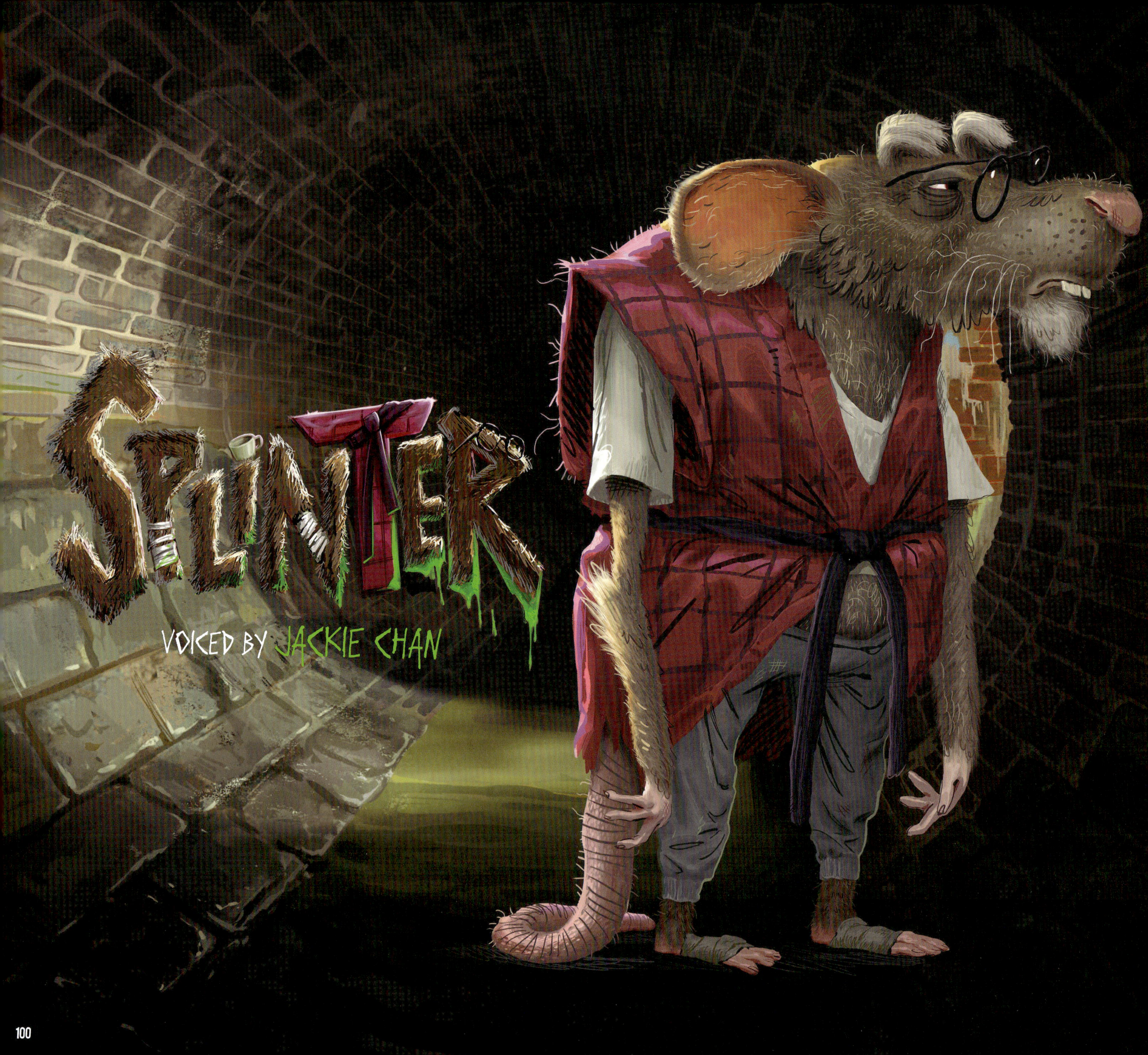
SPLINTER
VOICED BY JACKIE CHAN

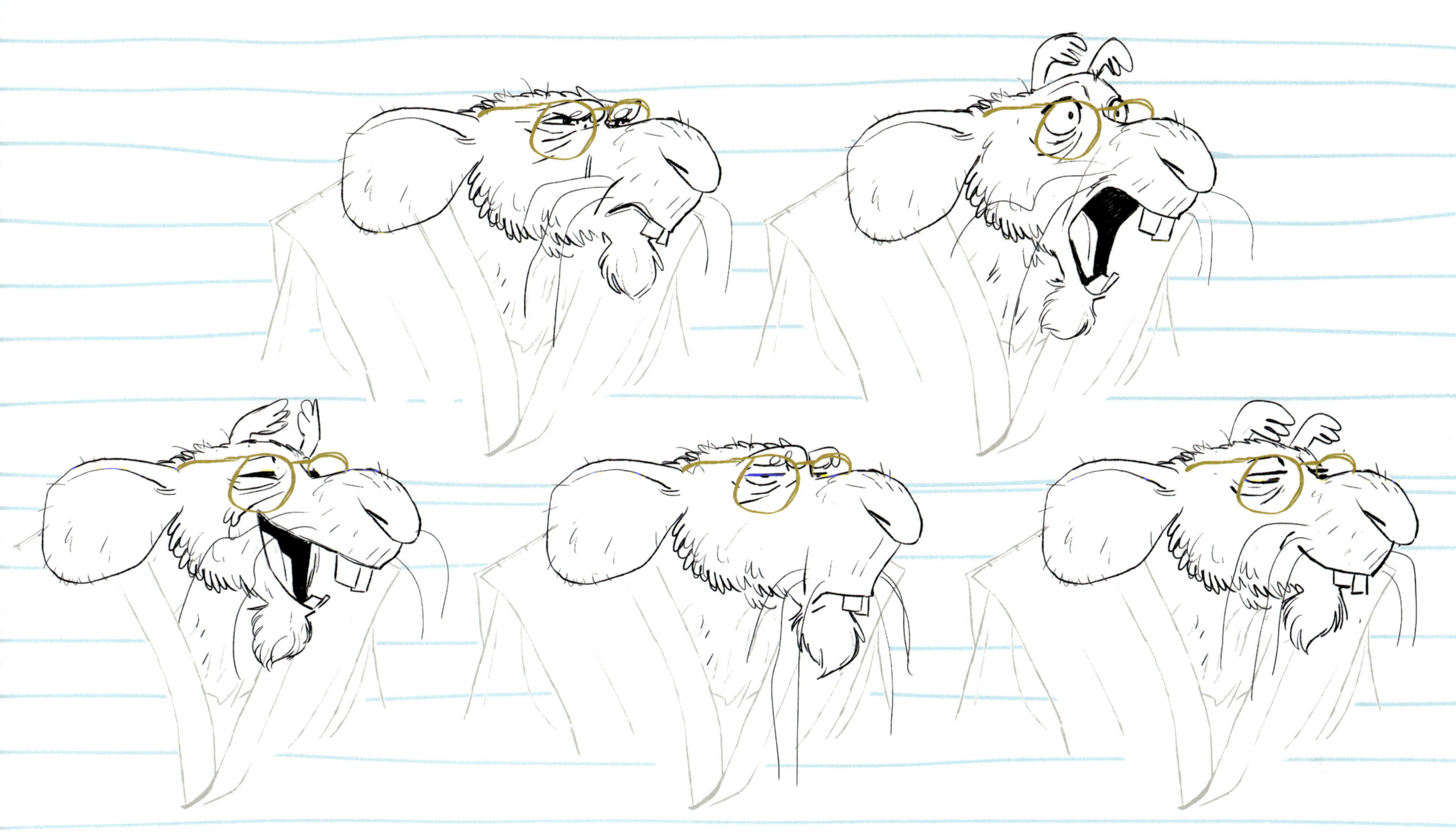

Above: Character expressions by James A. Castillo
Opposite: Character design by Woodrow White, final paint by Sean Sevestre
Opposite: Background art by Alger Tam

"I've always loved the character of Splinter as a sort of Rat Dad in the sewers. In this movie, he's like a very concerned older parent. I loved the way the writers wrote him. I looked at earlier versions of Splinter and there were things I loved and things I wanted to change.

One thing I wanted to change was how he never quite resembled what I imagined a rat mutant should look like. He lacked rat characteristics. I wanted to bring the rat features front and center. Big ears, nose, lots of whiskers, thick fleshy tail, matted fur. I wanted to make him extra gross. On the other hand, I also wanted to make him charming and cute.

Our goal was to make him a real dad-type character. So, I went about making adjustments to how Splinter normally dresses while keeping archetypal elements in place, like how he wears faded burgundy. I was looking at old prints of samurai and there's the traditional *kataginu* that samurai wear, and I thought about how I could make it makeshift, how I could turn it into something he could have made with a bedsheet, so I added plaid to his outerwear."

–Lead Character Designer Woodrow White

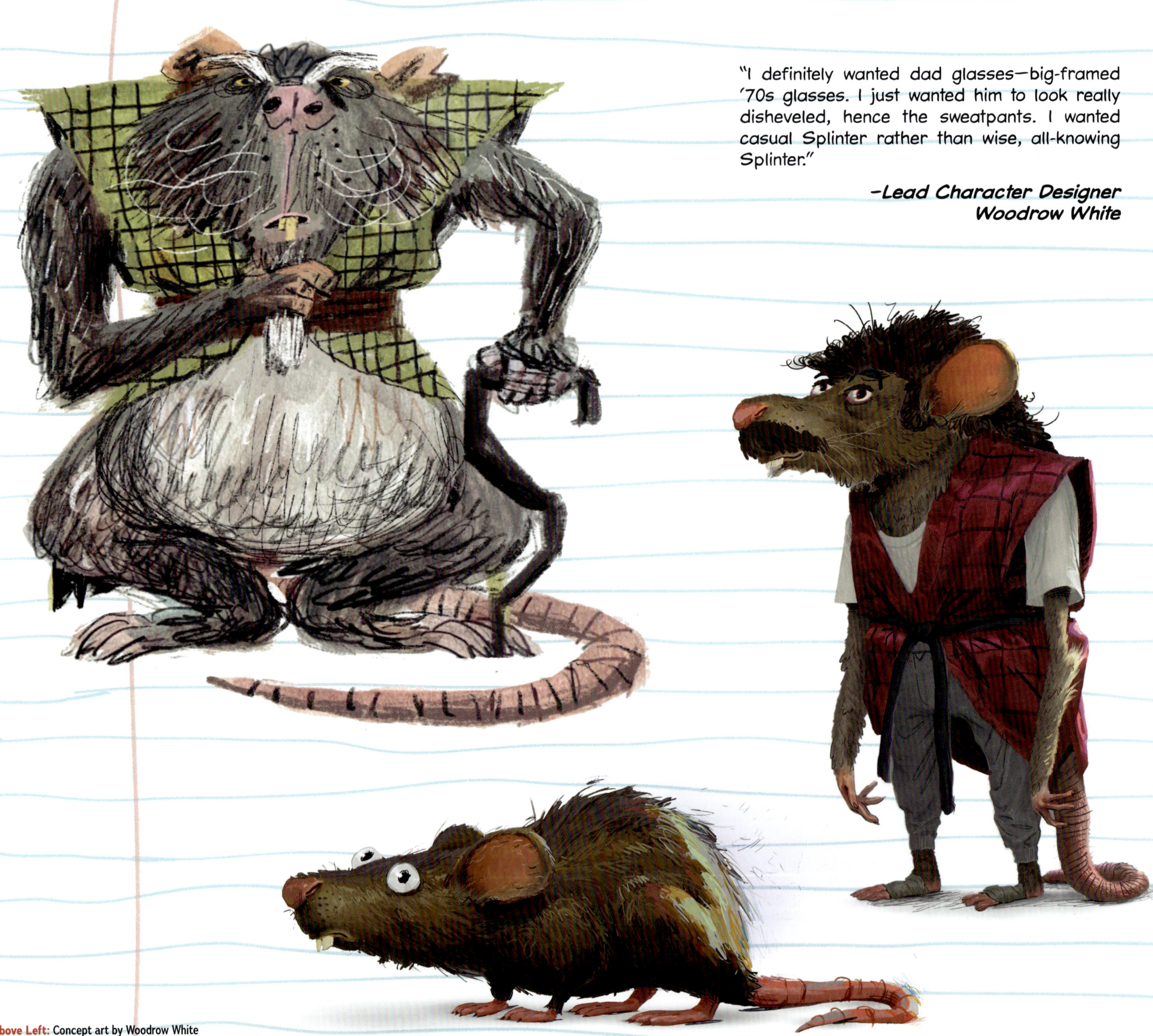

"I definitely wanted dad glasses—big-framed '70s glasses. I just wanted him to look really disheveled, hence the sweatpants. I wanted casual Splinter rather than wise, all-knowing Splinter."

–Lead Character Designer Woodrow White

Above Left: Concept art by Woodrow White
Right: Young Splinter concept art by Arthur Fong and Woodrow White
Bottom: Un-mutated Splinter concept art by Yashar Kassai

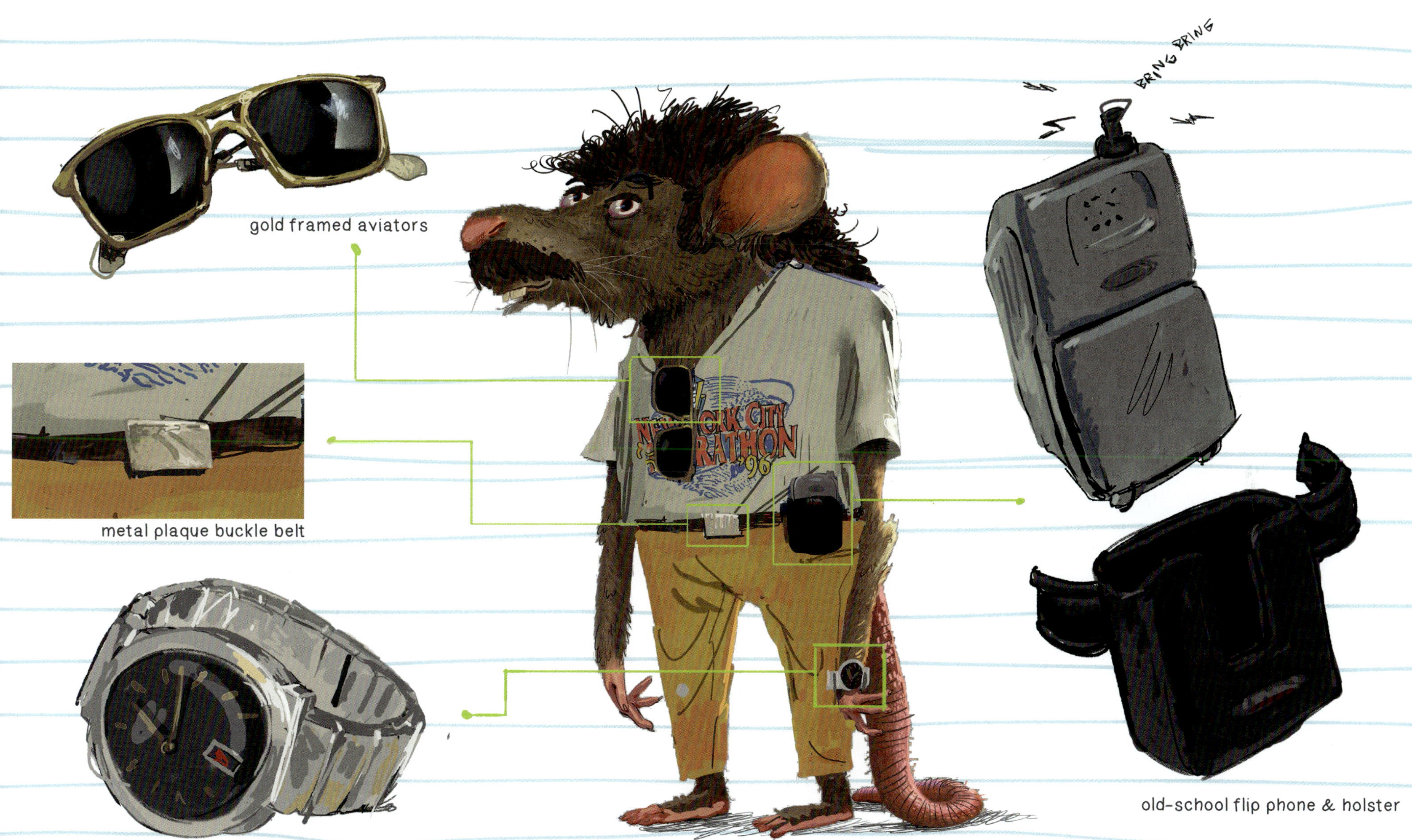

"First, I had to get over the excitement of working on Splinter because he's such an iconic character. Especially with him, he has such a specific feel in this movie. It's a different Splinter from other films we've seen.

He's more human, a bit more flawed, more driven by emotions than in other versions. It was very fun to be able to explore how a character like that would live his day-to-day life.

A lot of my explorations were around not just how does he move, how does he fight, but also how does he wash dishes, how does he raise the Turtles, how does he clean the home?

I think that was the most endearing. Sometimes Splinter can be simplified as just a grumpy old master, but in this one, there's a little more growth to the character. That was the most compelling part of the job for me."

–Character Designer
James A. Castillo

Above: Young Splinter art by Woodrow White and Yashar Kassai, props by Alger Tam

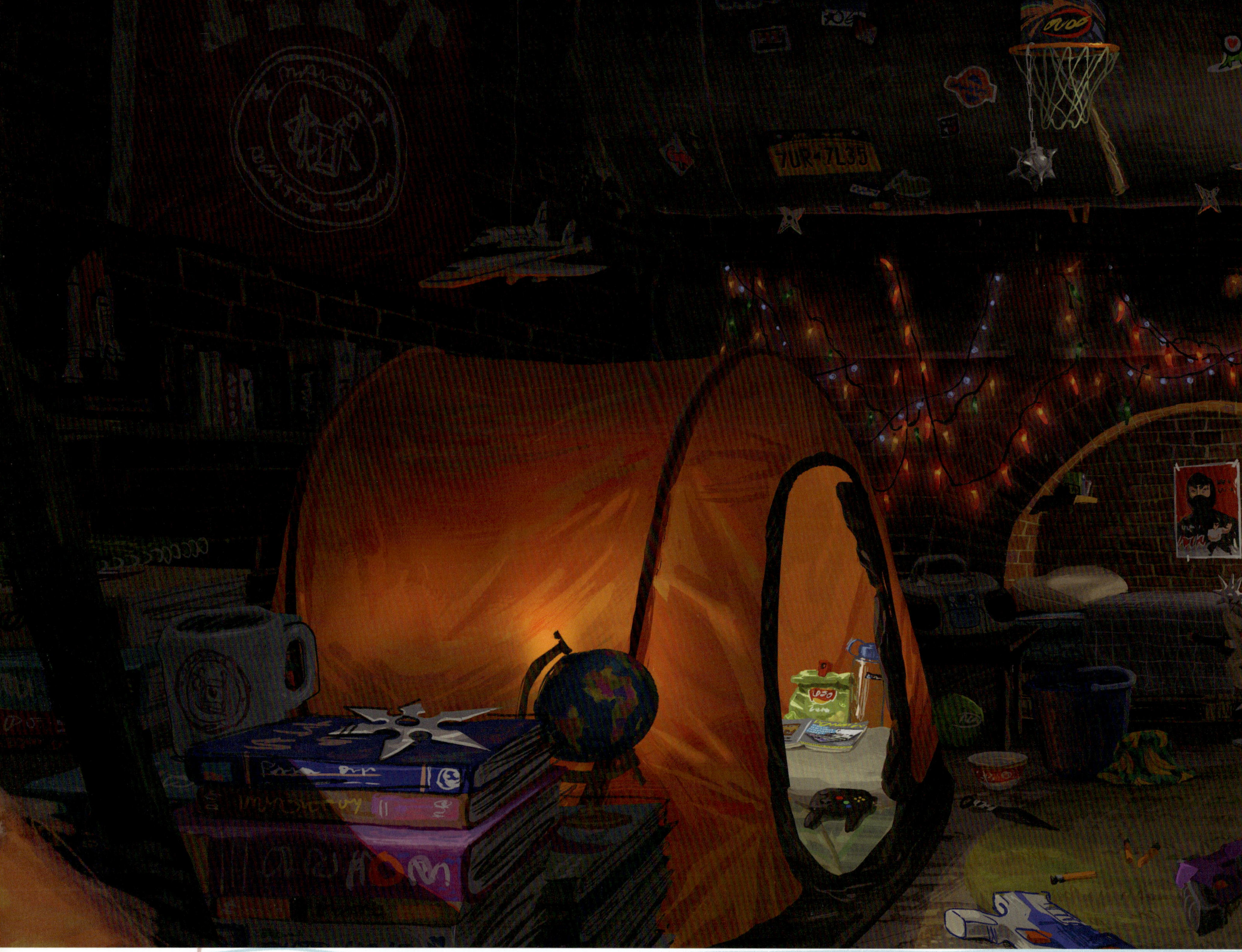

Above: Sewer lair bedroom concept art by Alger Tam

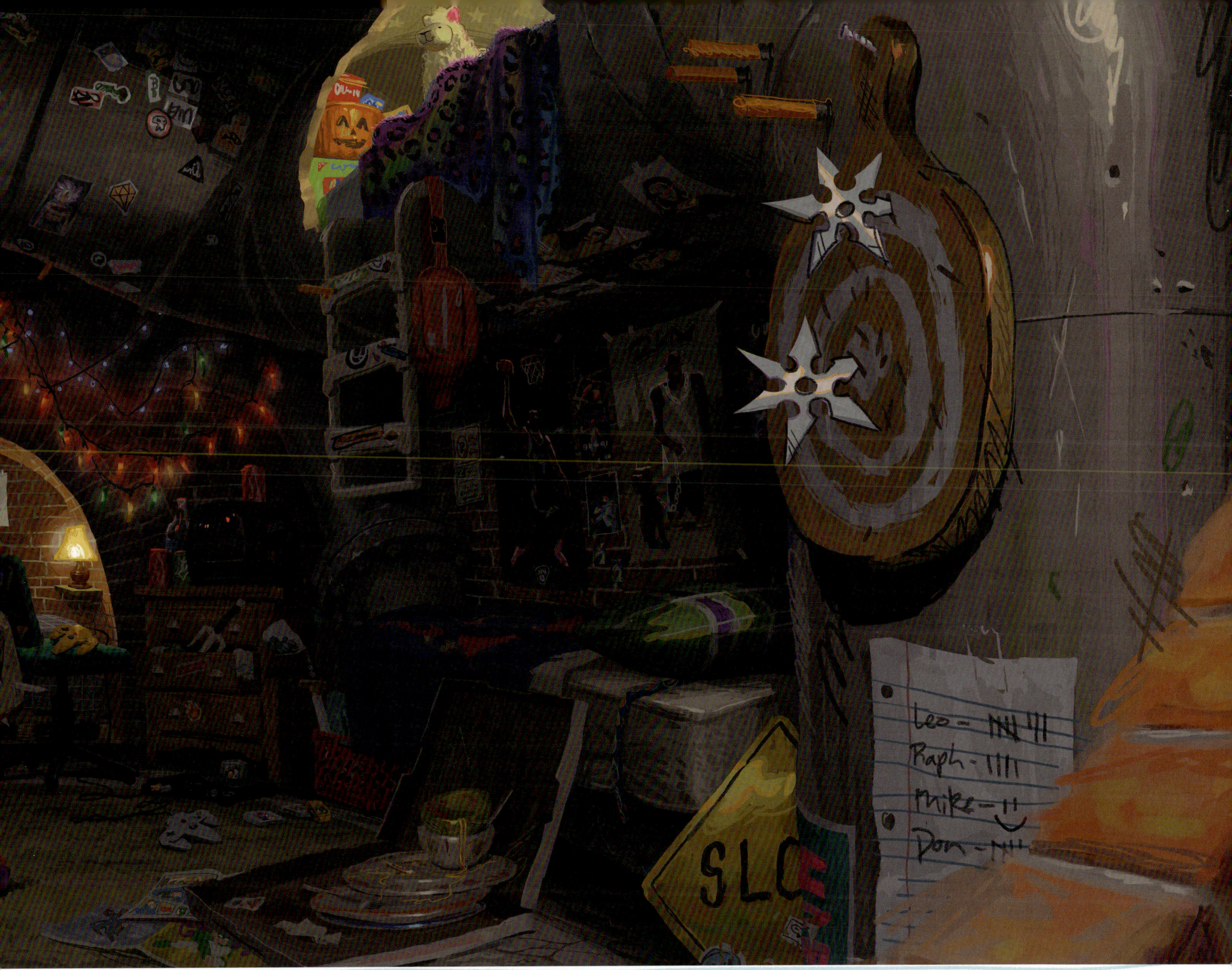

"Kids can take any environment and they'll make it their own. You can't make anything minimalist. You've got these four boys and their dad all sharing a space together, and they've been living together for years. They're going to make it their own, and they'll make sure that they've got all their favorite things accessible to them at all times."

–Visual Development Artist
Lauren Airriess

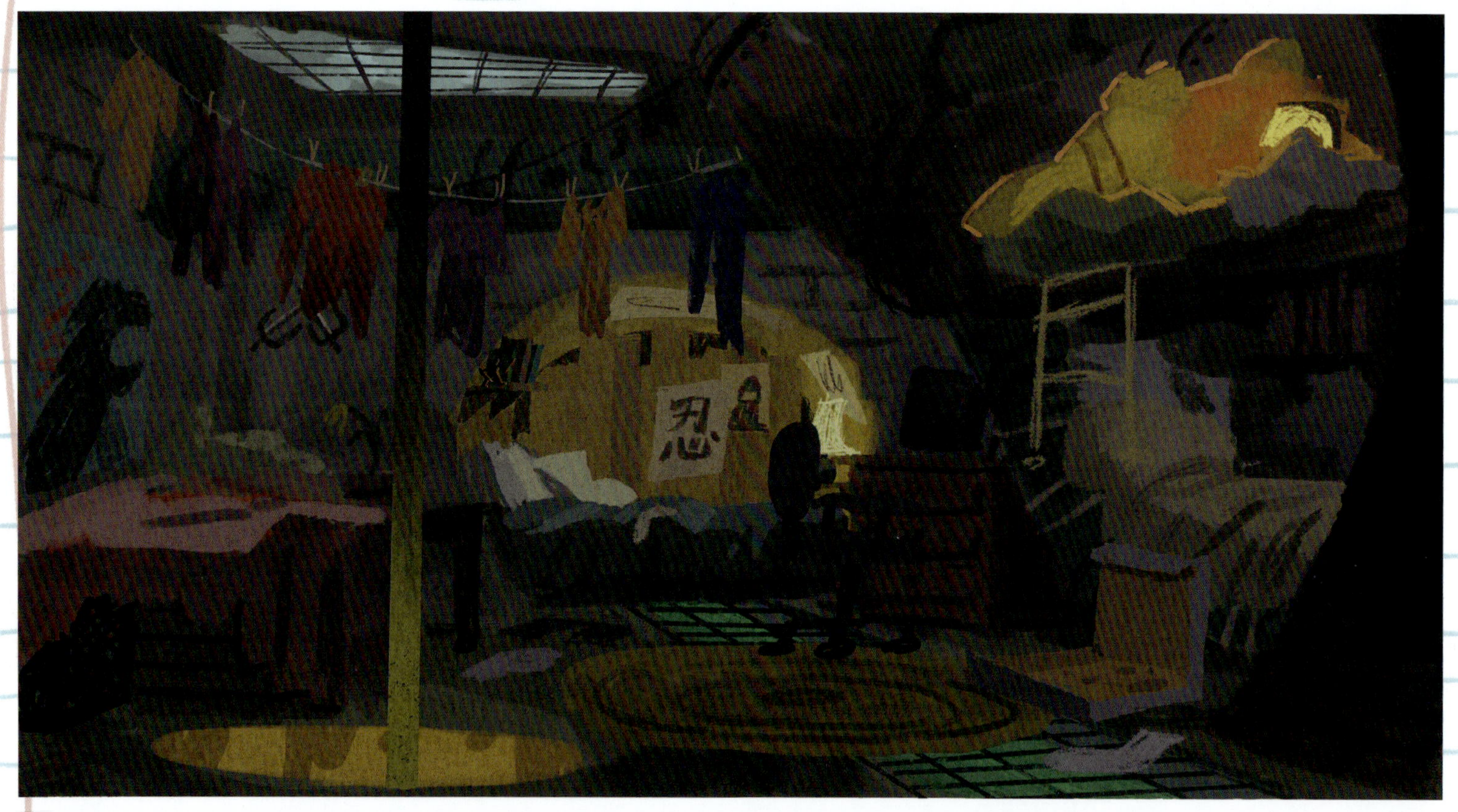

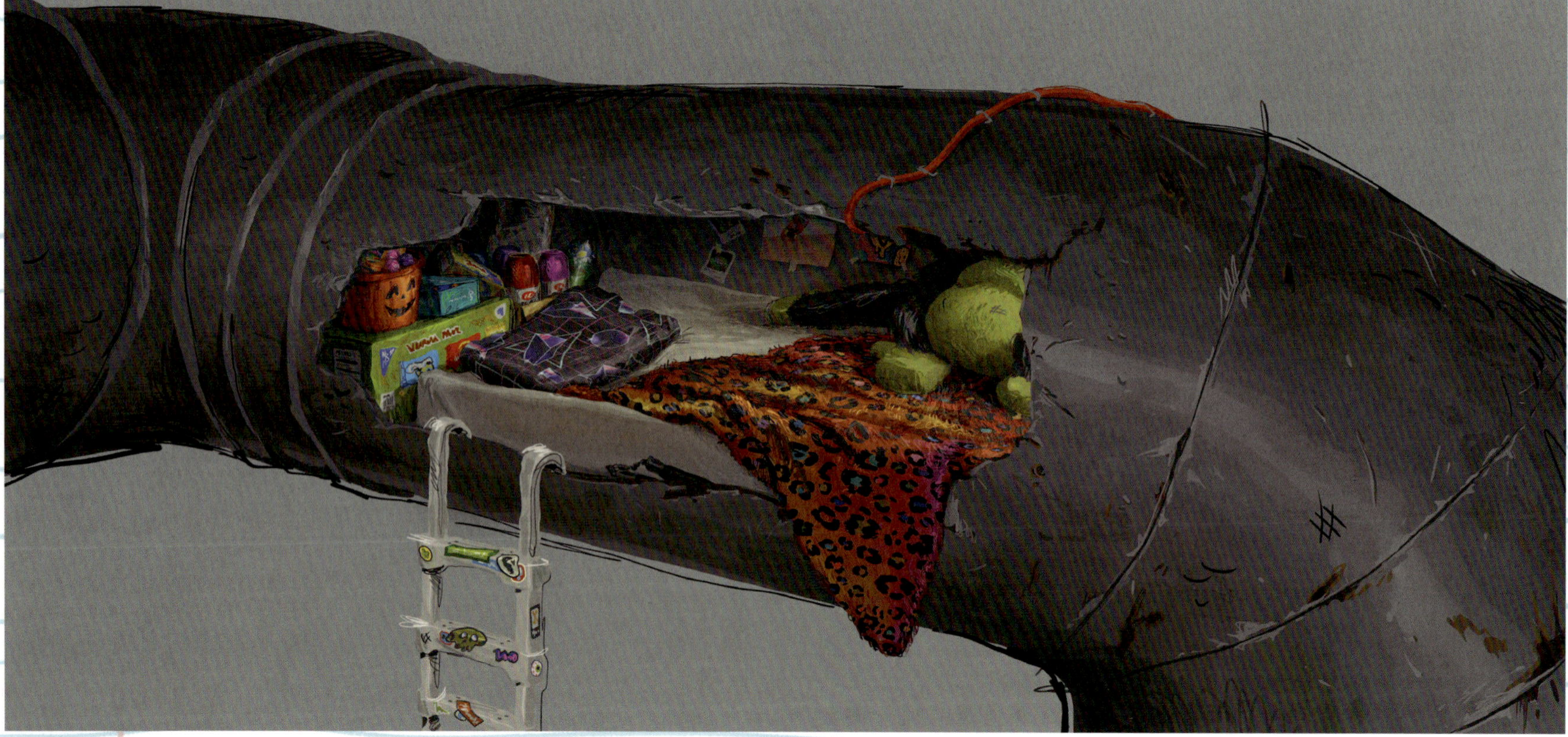

Above: Sewer lair bedroom concept art by Woodrow White
Below: Sewer lair bedroom design by Alger Tam

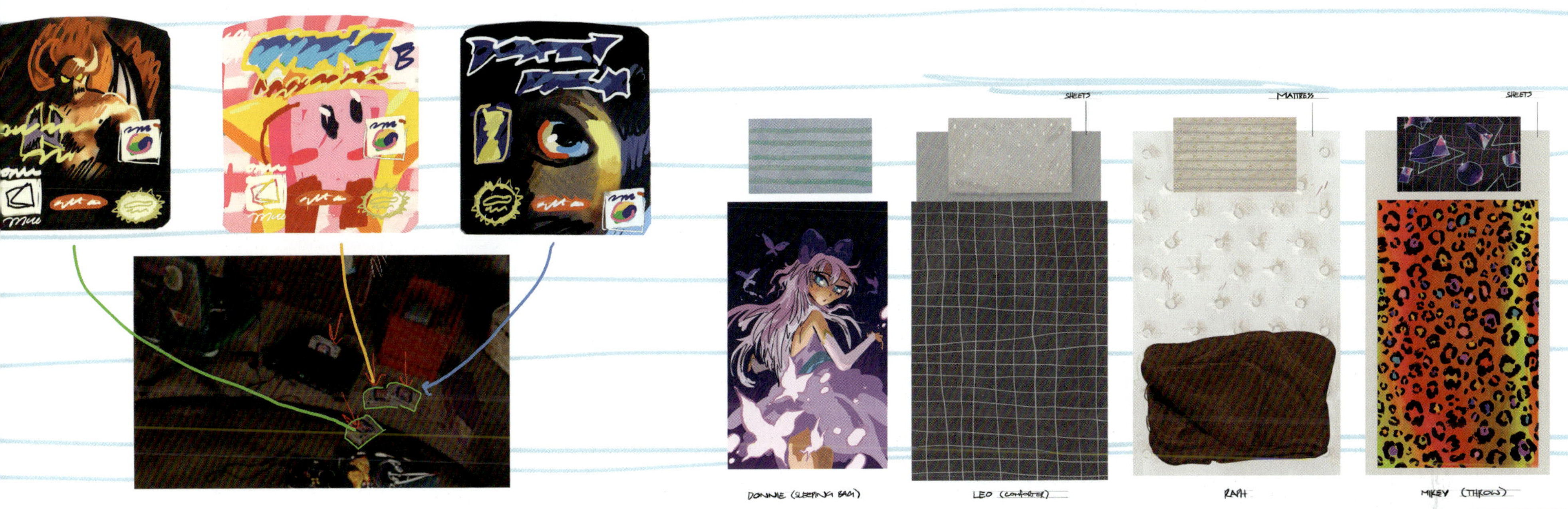

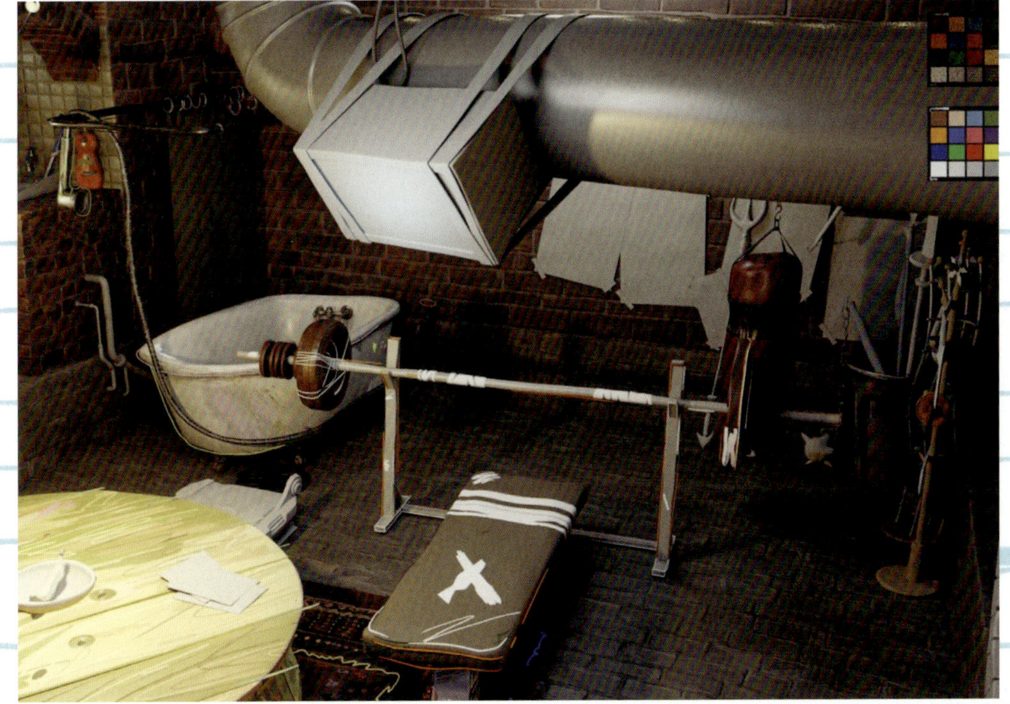

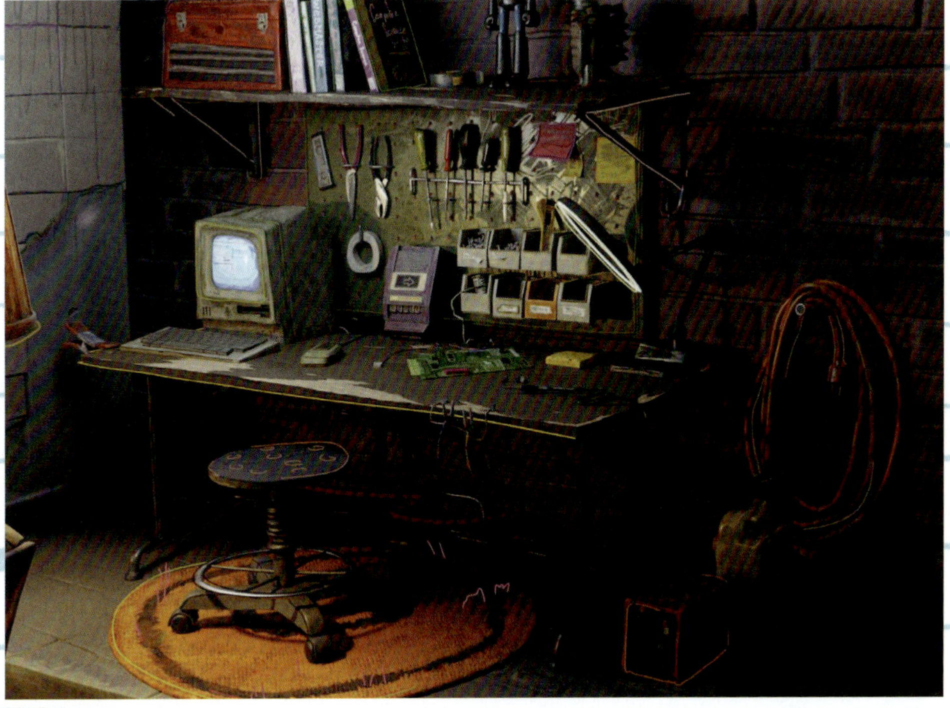

Top Left: Sewer lair bedroom designs by Arthur Fong
Top Right: Sewer lair bedroom designs by Alger Tam
Bottom: Donnie workstation and Raph workout area render by Mikros Animation

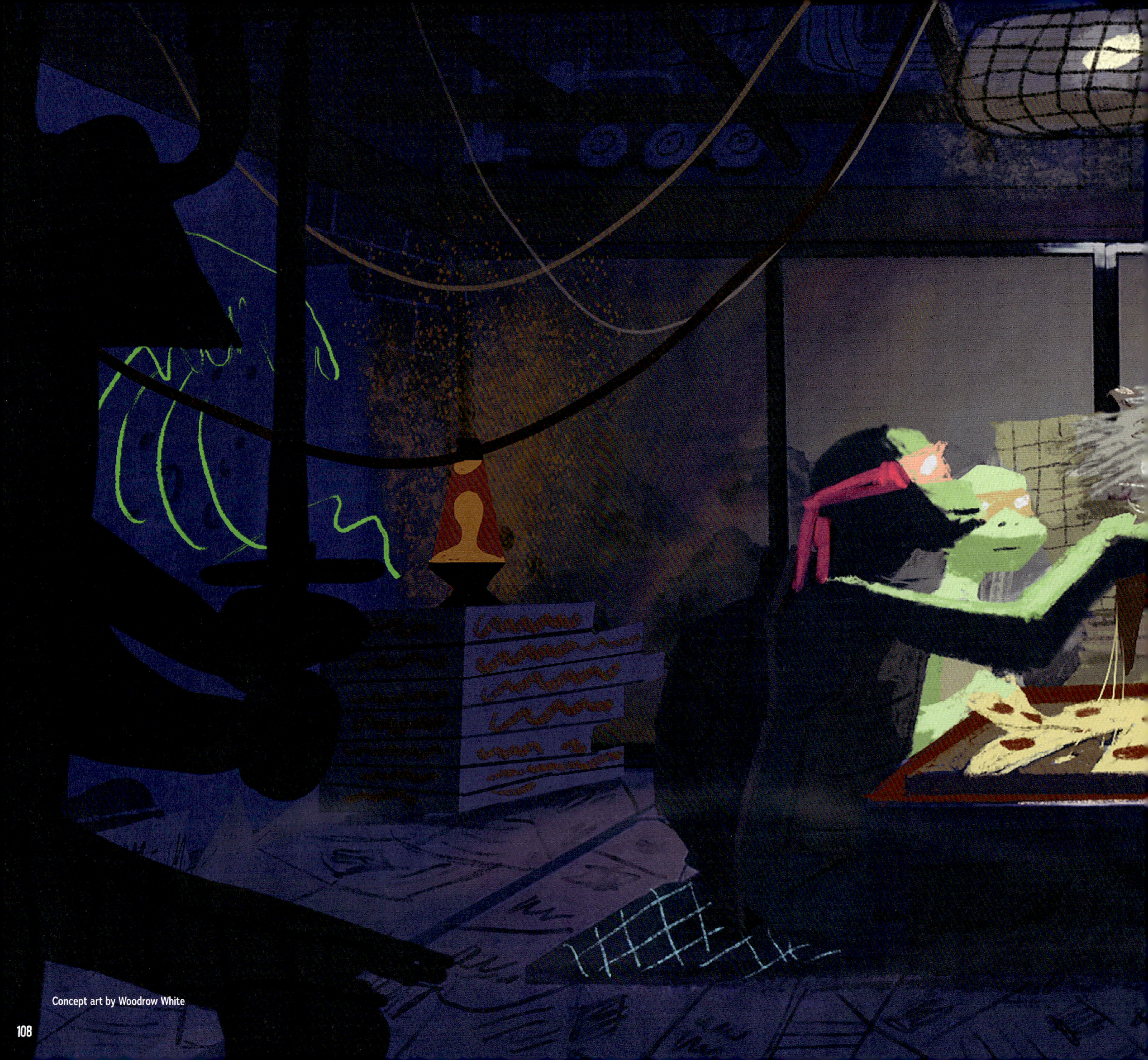

Concept art by Woodrow White

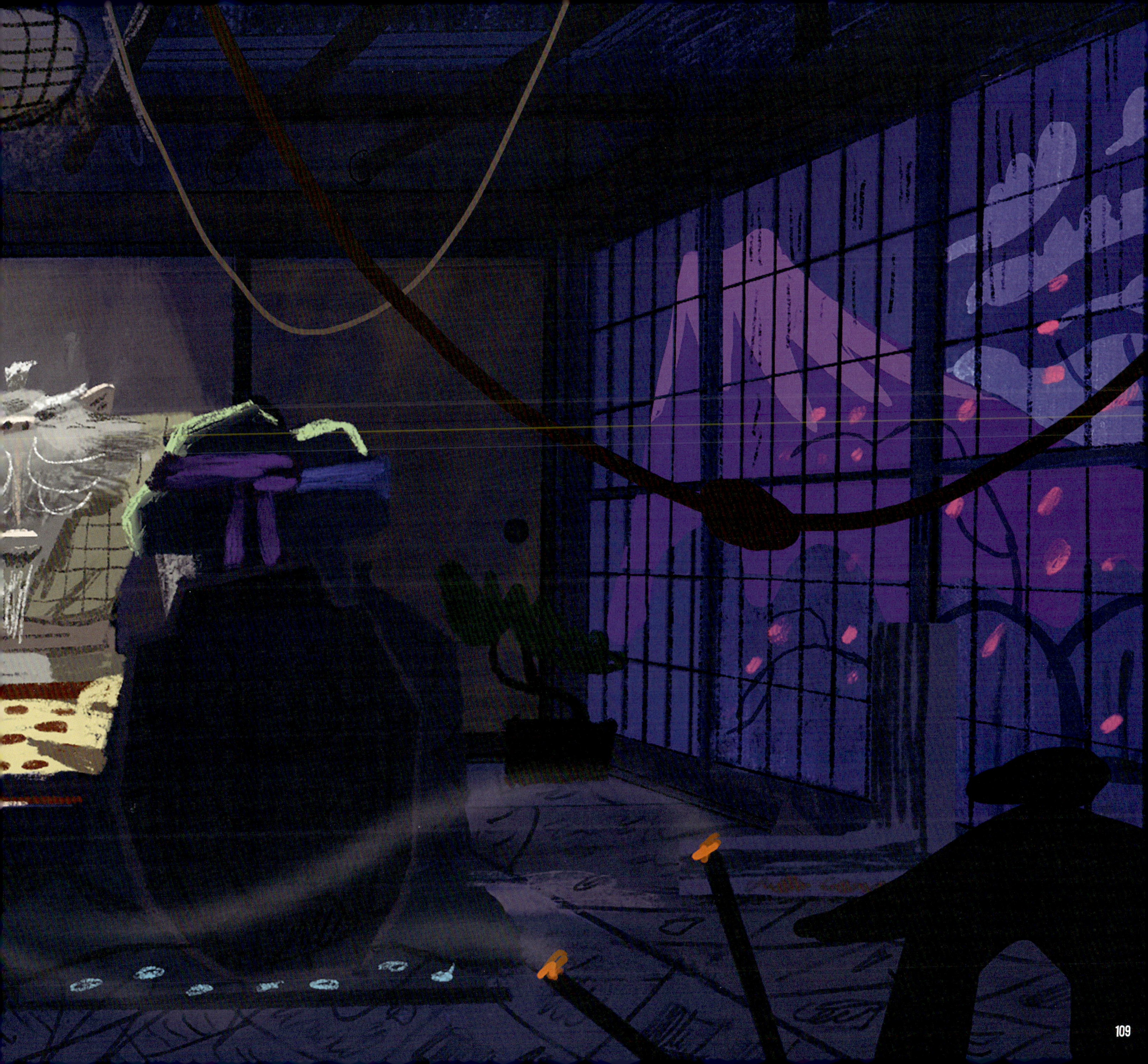

STORYBOARDS

One of the most critical steps in the creation of a film—any film, but especially an animated one—is the process of storyboarding. In it, sequences are taken from the script to the visual realm, with the action plotted out and dialogue paired to visuals.

In animation, the storyboards offer the first chance to direct the action and can make or break a sequence. We've chosen two sequences by John Jackson, Hanna Cho, and Kyler Spears, to give a small taste of how storyboards help shape the narrative.

Scene	Duration	Panel	Duration
0060	18:00	9	01:00

Scene	Duration	Panel	Duration
0060	18:00	10	01:00

Scene	Duration	Panel	Duration
0060	18:00	11	01:00

Scene	Duration	Panel	Duration
0060	18:00	12	01:00

Scene	Duration	Panel	Duration
0060	18:00	13	01:00

Scene	Duration	Panel	Duration
0060	18:00	14	01:00

Scene	Duration	Panel	Duration
0060	18:00	15	01:00

Scene	Duration	Panel	Duration
0060	18:00	16	01:00

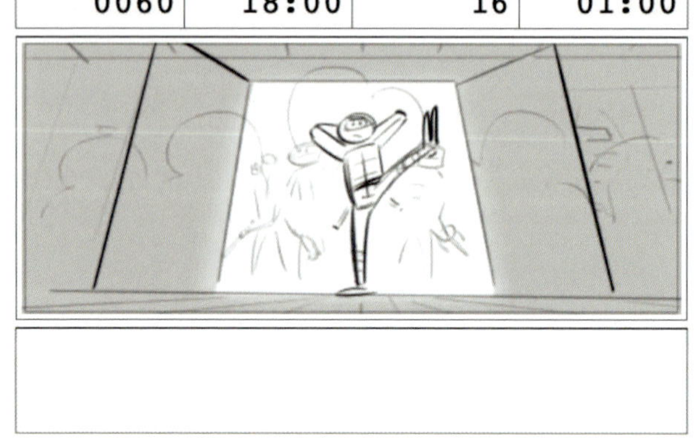

Scene	Duration	Panel	Duration
0060	18:00	17	01:00

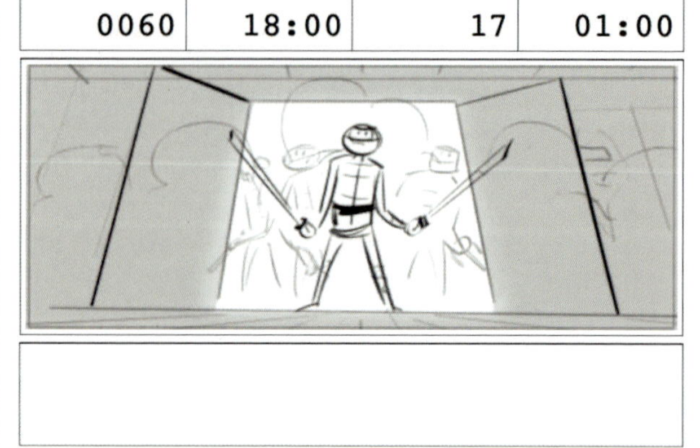

Above and Opposite: Storyboards by John Jackson

"One sequence I'm particularly proud of is the crime-fighting montage boarded initially by story artist John Jackson. Though it's changed a bit since then, the style and energy from that initial pitch still carries through to the final cut. Everyone always talks about it as a highlight. Who doesn't love to see the Turtles fighting, kicking butt, set to a good track?" ***-Co-Director Kyler Spears***

Scene	Duration	Panel	Duration
0100	01:14:00	24	01:00

Scene	Duration	Panel	Duration
0100	01:14:00	25	01:00

Scene	Duration	Panel	Duration
0100	01:14:00	26	01:00

Scene	Duration	Panel	Duration
0100	01:14:00	27	01:00

Scene	Duration	Panel	Duration
0100	01:14:00	28	01:00

Scene	Duration	Panel	Duration
0100	01:14:00	29	01:00

Scene	Duration	Panel	Duration
0100	01:14:00	30	01:00

Scene	Duration	Panel	Duration
0100	01:14:00	31	01:00

Scene	Duration	Panel	Duration
0100	01:14:00	32	01:00

"Splinter's story, the flashback about why he keeps the Turtles underground, was boarded many, MANY, times but the core of it was done by story artist Hanna Cho. She was instrumental in showing us who these Turtles were and how they interacted with each other. For the whole story team an emphasis was put on not just getting coverage of who is talking, but who is listening. Seeing the Turtles emote and pantomime to things said offscreen. How their body language could communicate their personalities and emotions better than exposition. The goal was to make them grounded, relatable teenagers, and Hanna hit the nail on the head." ***-Co-Director Kyler Spears***

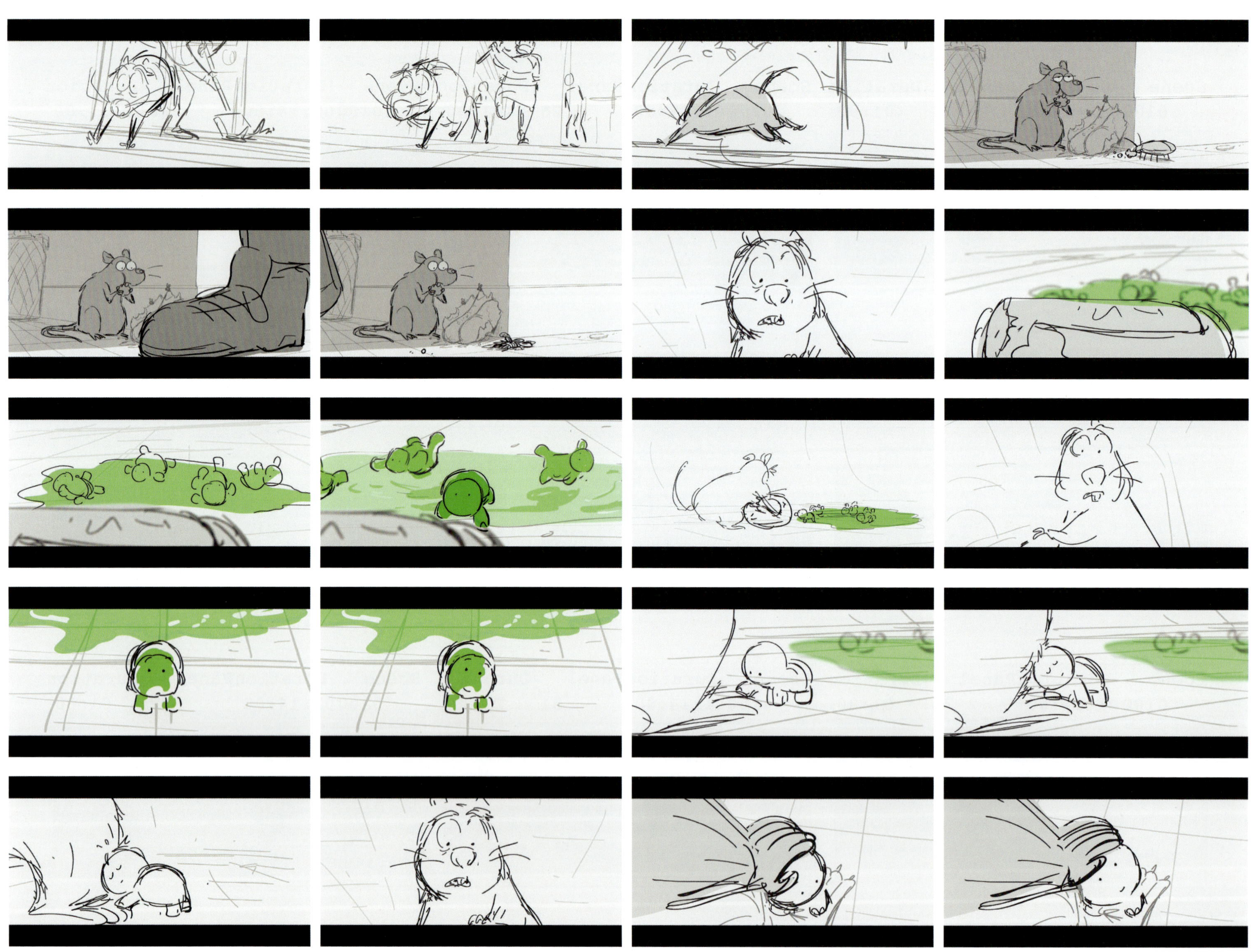

Above: Storyboards by Hanna Cho

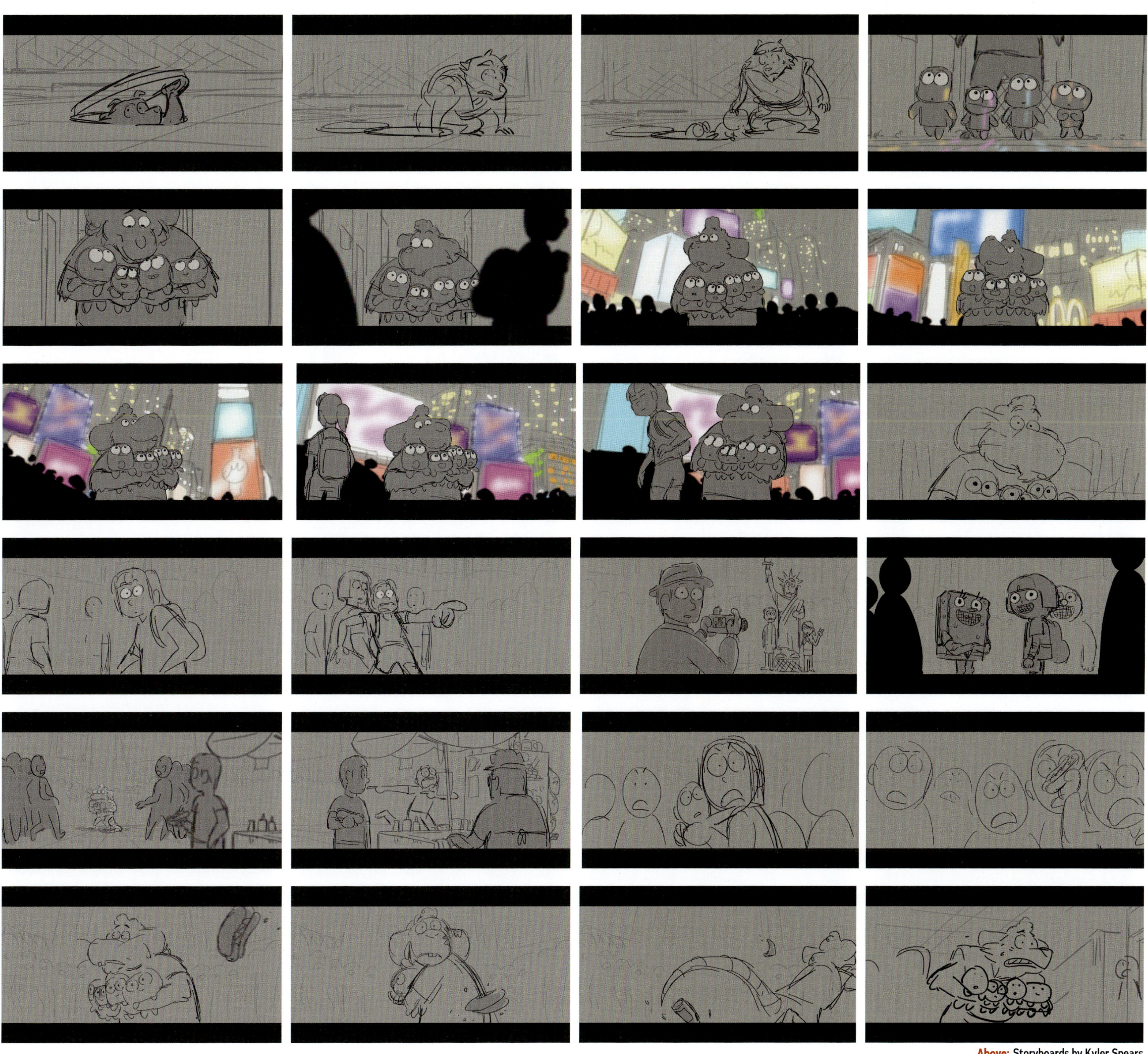

Above: Storyboards by Kyler Spears

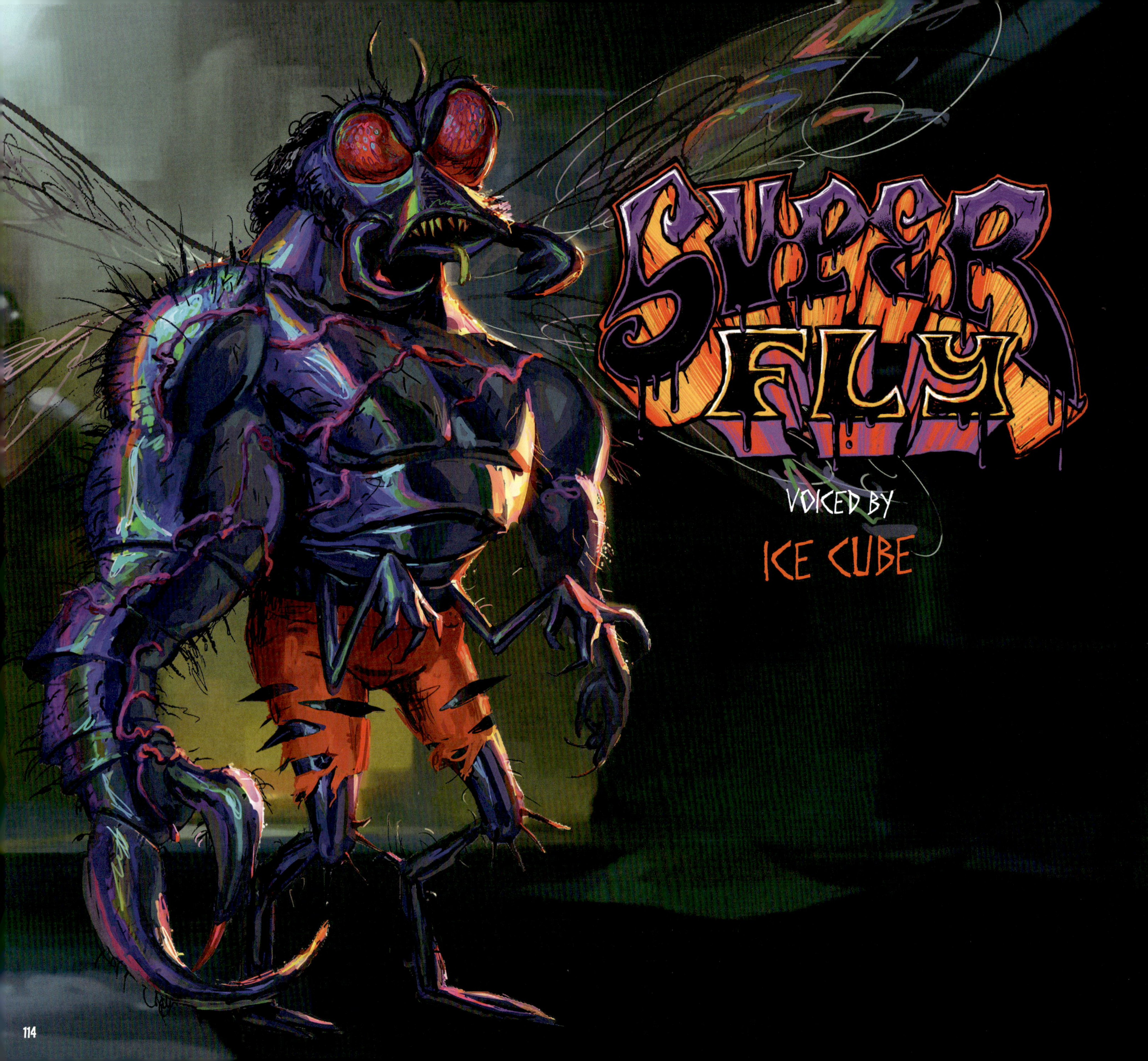
SUPER FLY
VOICED BY
ICE CUBE

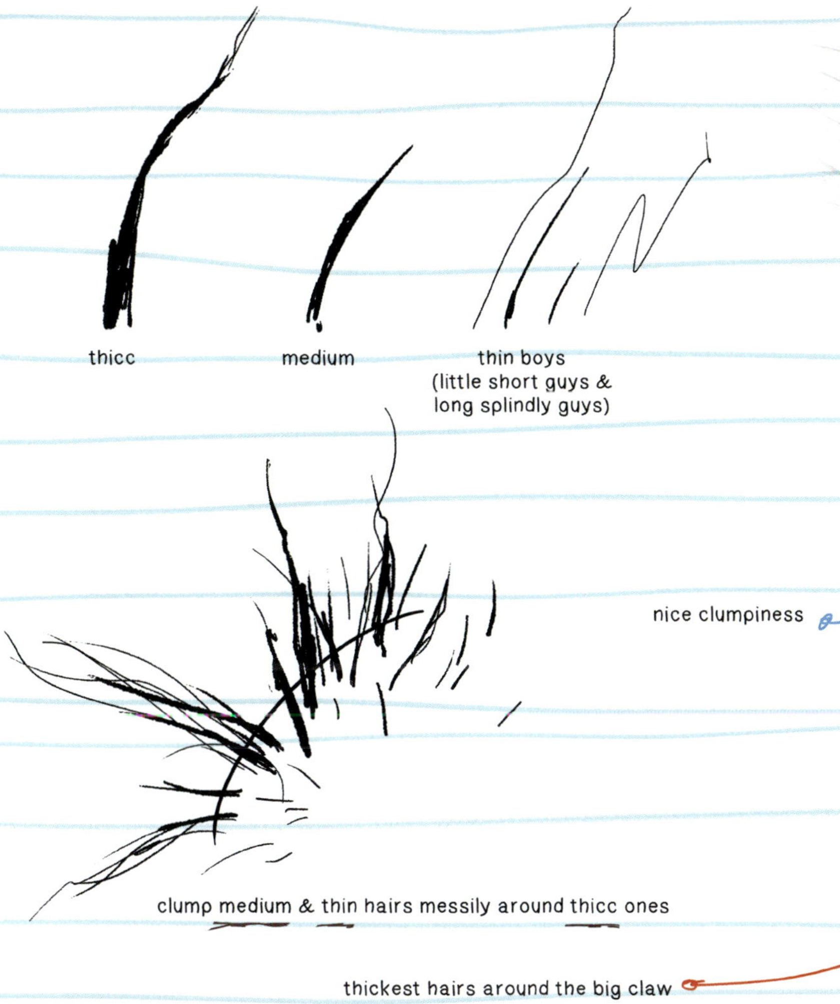

thicc

medium

thin boys
(little short guys &
long splindly guys)

clump medium & thin hairs messily around thicc ones

nice clumpiness

thickest hairs around the big claw

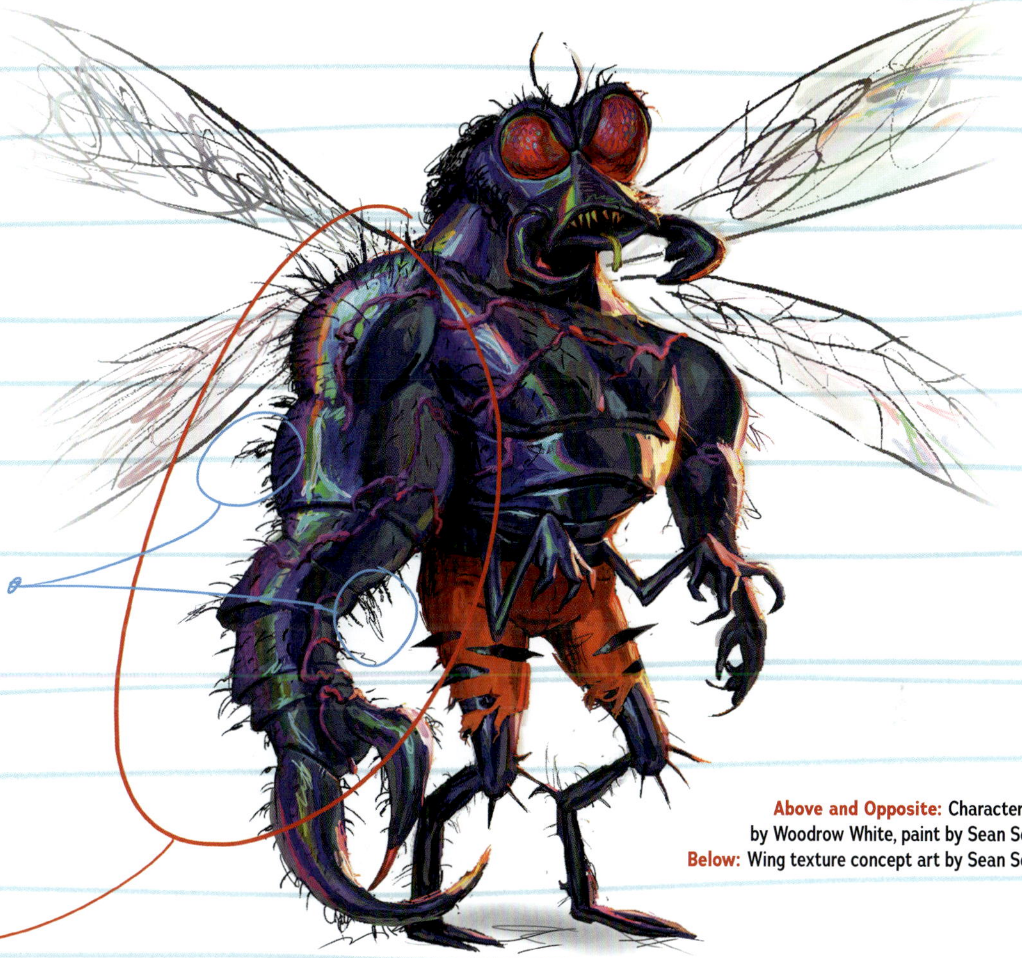

Above and Opposite: Character design by Woodrow White, paint by Sean Sevestre
Below: Wing texture concept art by Sean Sevestre

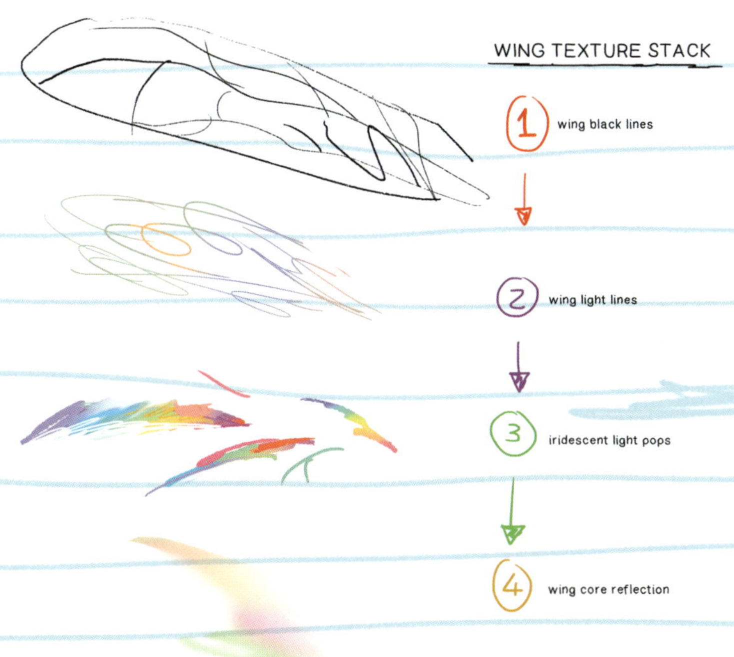

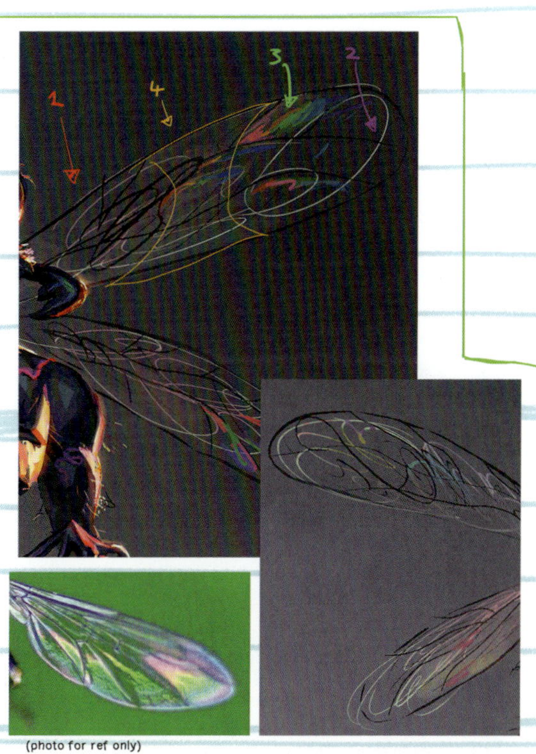

"I was looking at a lot of Japanese monster designers when creating Superfly, particularly this one monster designer Yasushi Nirasawa, who is just an absolute madman genius monster designer from Japan. He has these characters with a big, bulky arm and a smaller arm. He loves playing with breaking up character symmetries, and I really like that. I knew I wanted to make [Superfly] really gross and scary."

–Lead Character Designer Woodrow White

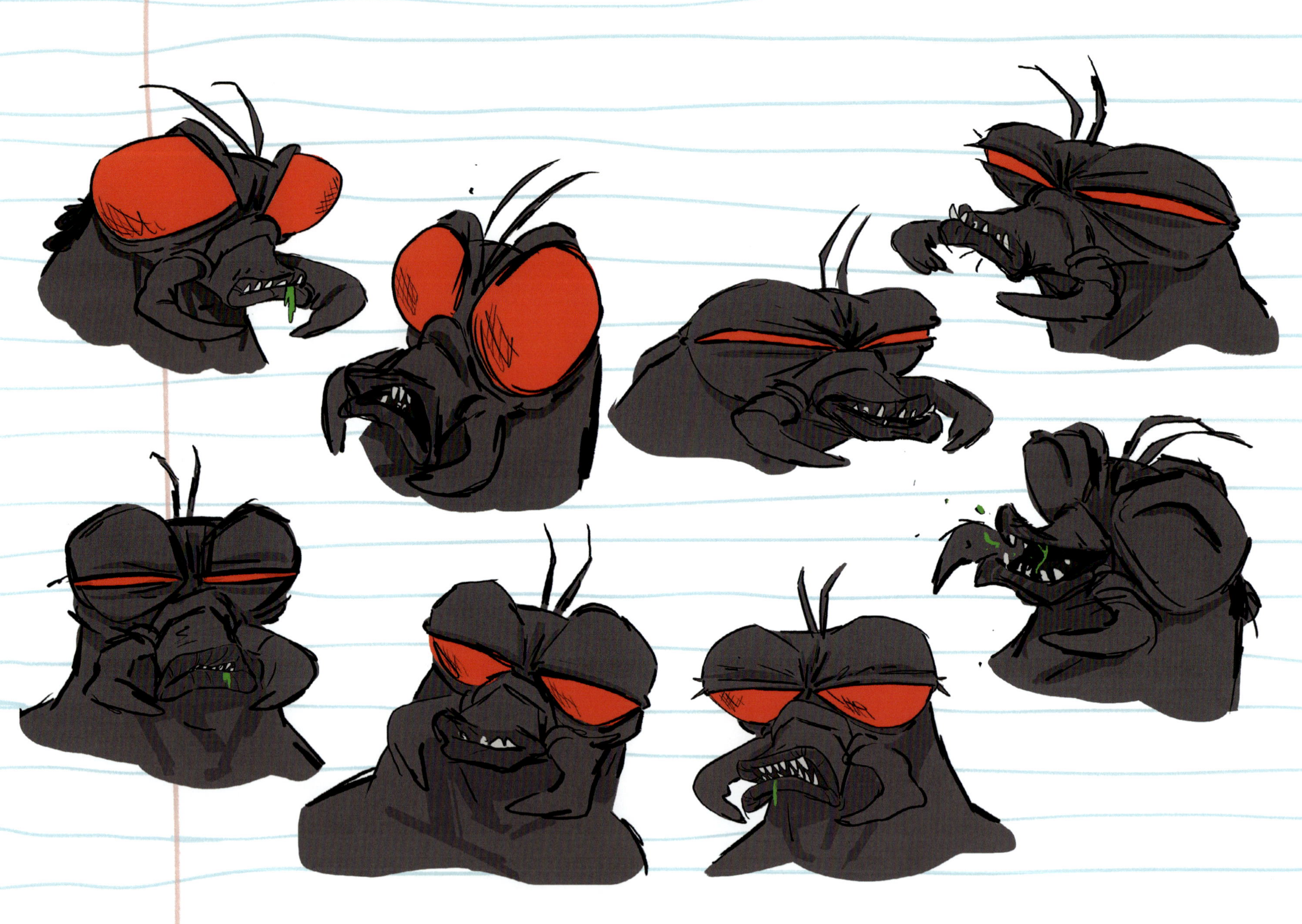

Above: Character expressions by Andrew Ross

"Superfly was one of the harder mutants to capture. Baxter Stockman used to be the villain of the movie, and it used to be that Baxter became a big mutant fly. That was his arc until we split Baxter and the mutant fly into two different characters. He took, like, 50 tries. We were going through all these different versions. Do we make him strong? Do we make him pathetic? Do we want it to look accidental? Do we want it to look more purposeful?

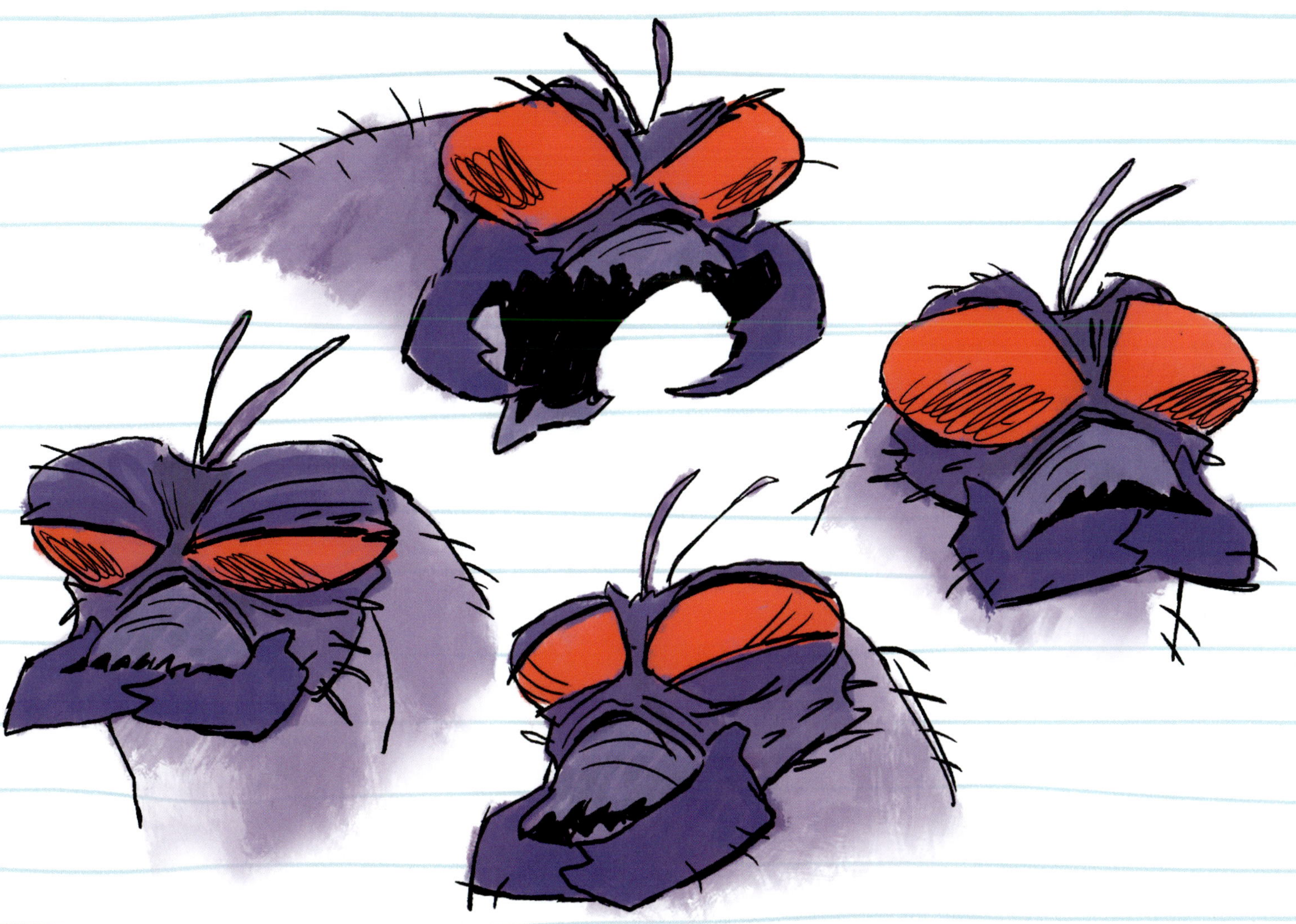

For a long time, he was kind of like this scrawny fly guy. At one point [in the scripting process], he willfully changed into a fly mutant, at another he was forcibly changed into a fly mutant. Depending on which version of the script you were reading, he was supposed to look very different in each one."

–Lead Character Designer Woodrow White

Above: Concept art by Arthur Fong

IRIDESCENT CARAPACE

flyman is covered in an reflective, iridescent carapace which reacts in a bold and vibrant way to light.

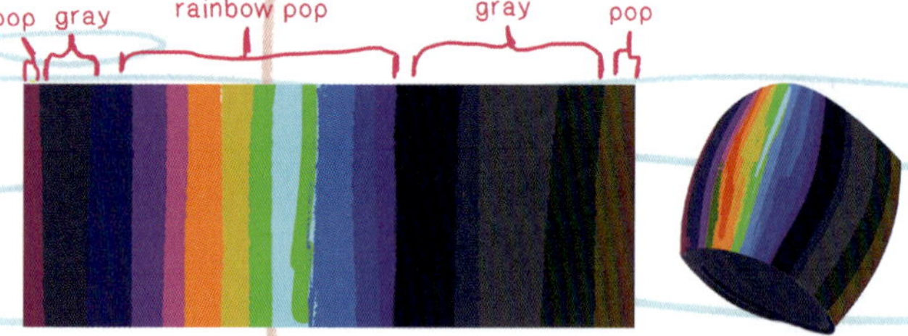

simplified model of how material reacts to light depending on angle to lightsource, (refer to flyman surfacing painting for more specific mark making and shapes)

avoid a constant rainbow strip all the way down the highlight. Reserve the maximum amount of colours and contrast for the hottest hits of light to bring variation, nuance and areas of focus to the material

Hottest values, saturation and colour variation where light is directly perpindicular to object

Slightly darker, finer pops of colour and value in less direct light

Keep the amount of values in the shadow/bounce side small and stepped to avoid too much busyness competing with the crazy rainbow strip.

"He was cool but needed a little extra something. For one of the finishing touches, I was looking at pictures of flies and said, 'Well, we should make his skin look iridescent,' and that was the cherry on top for Superfly."

–Lead Character Designer Woodrow White

Above: Concept art by Sean Sevestre
Below: Concept art by Jules Itzkoff

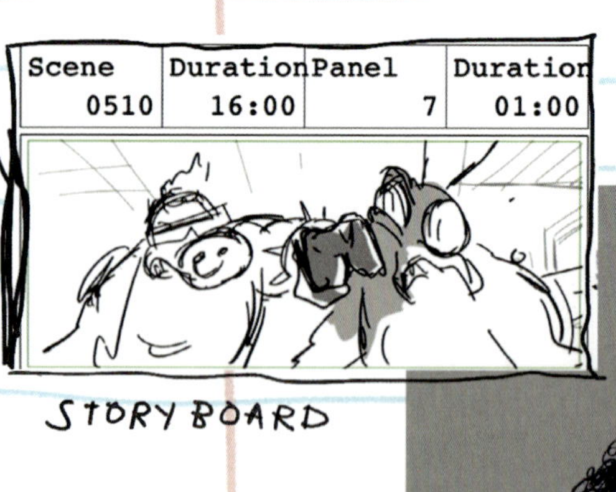

STORY BOARD

NEUTRAL

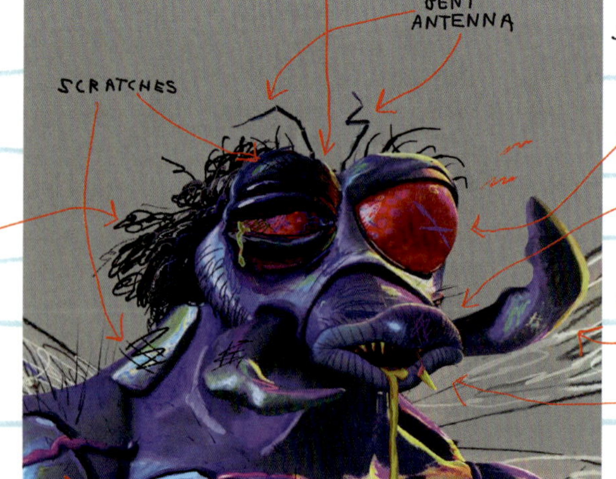

BEAT UP

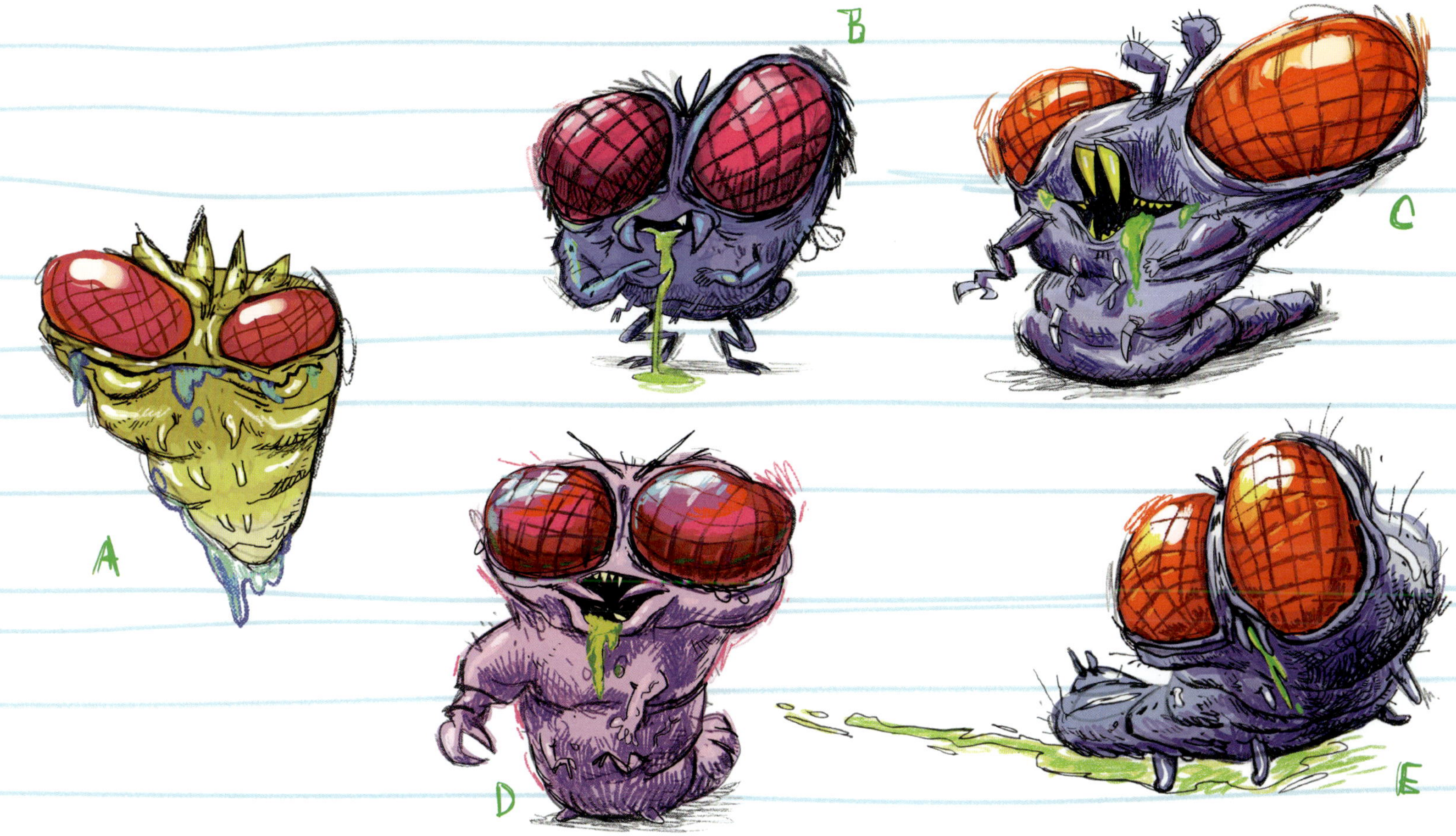

Above: Baby concept art by Dustin d'Arnault
Below: Baby character art by Sean Sevestre

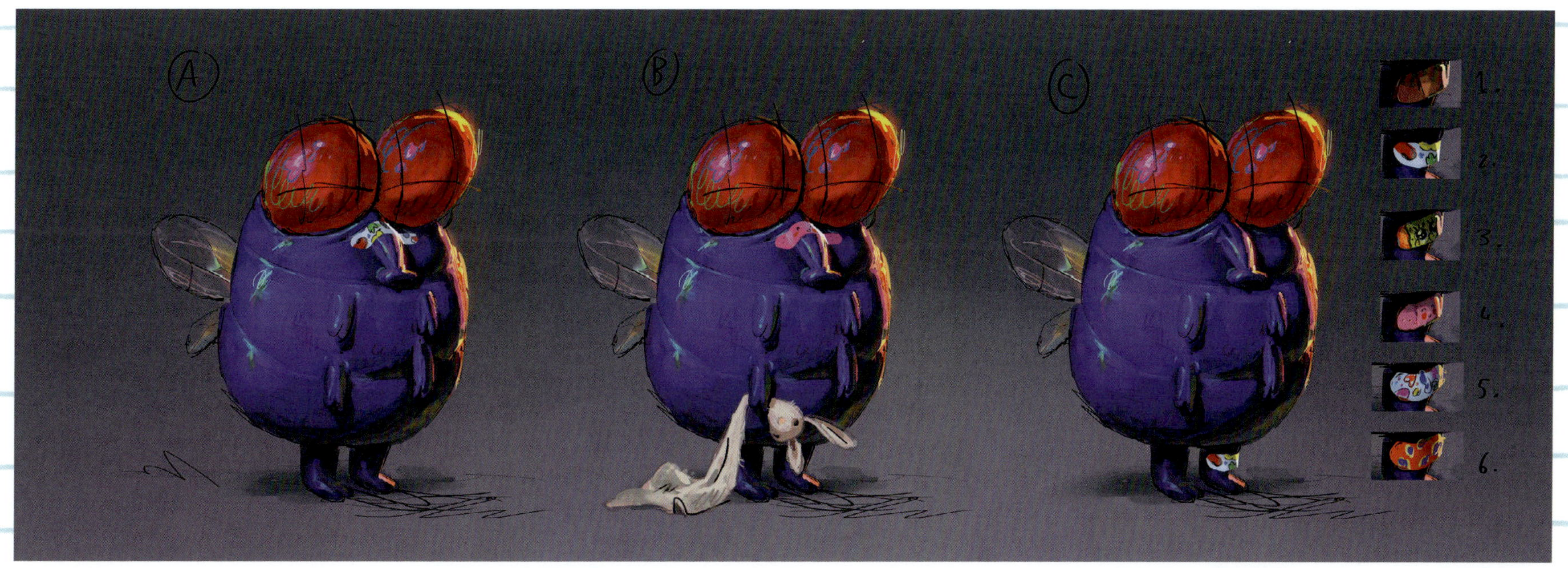

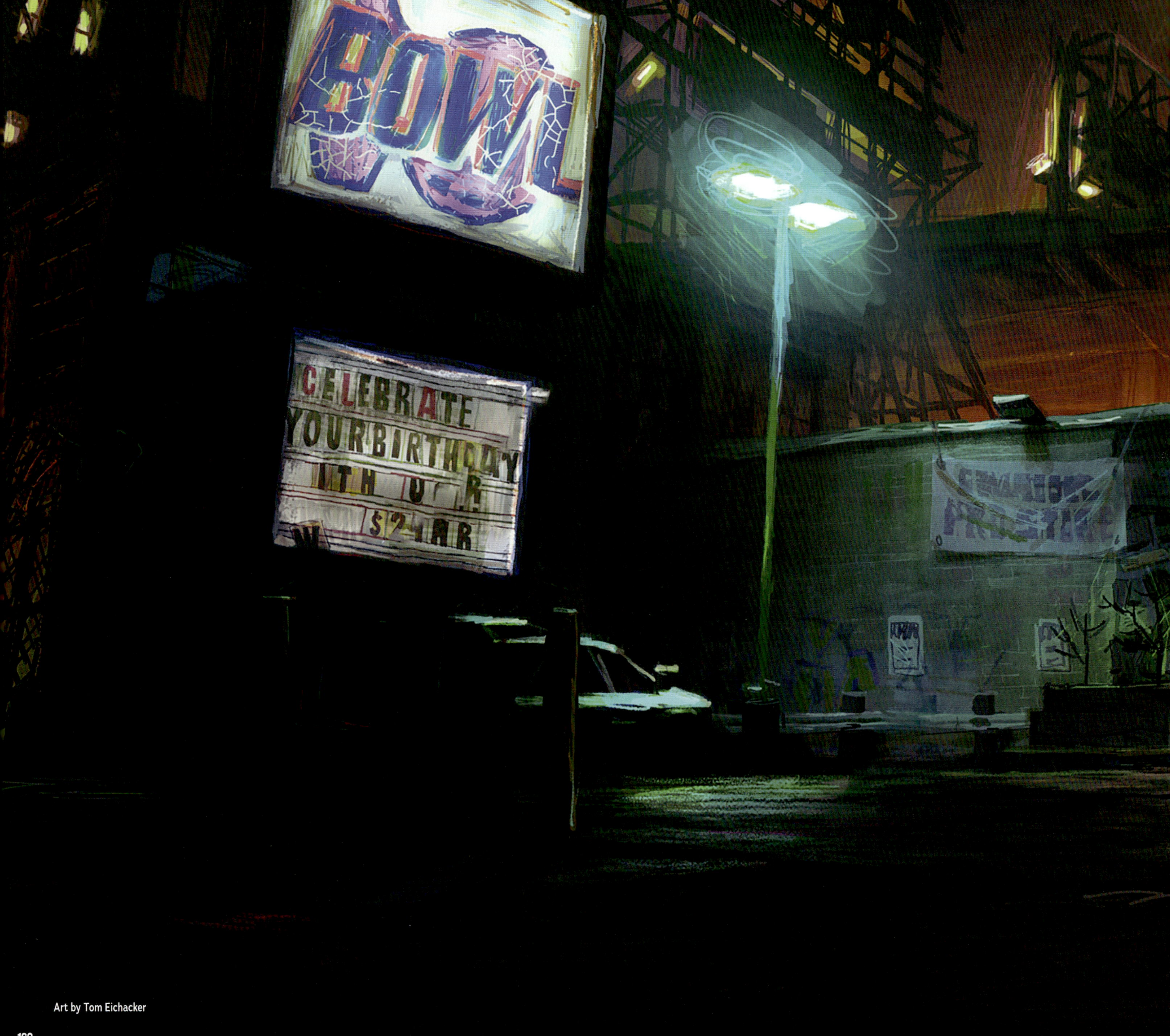

Art by Tom Eichacker

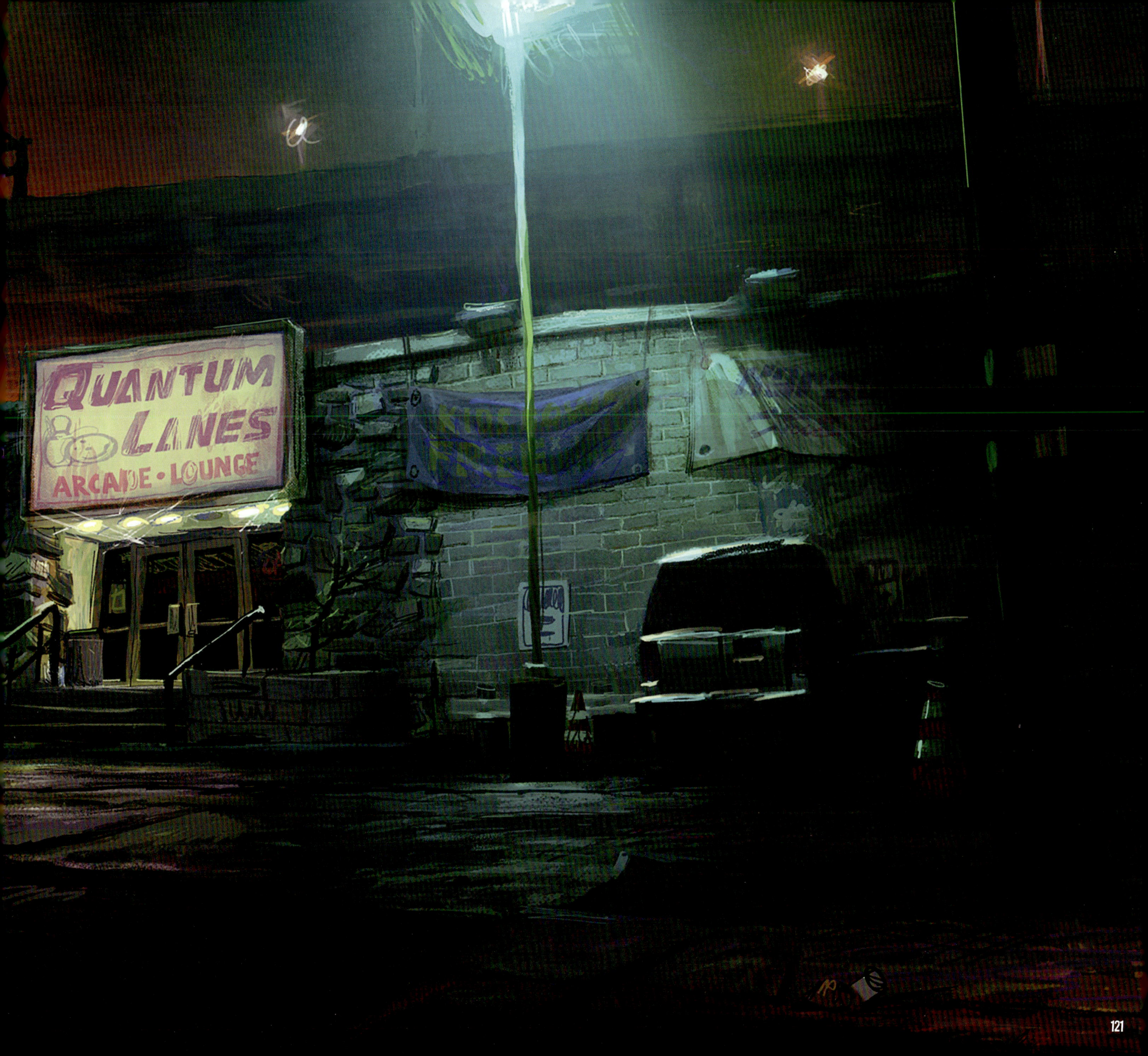
QUANTUM
LANES
ARCADE • LOUNGE

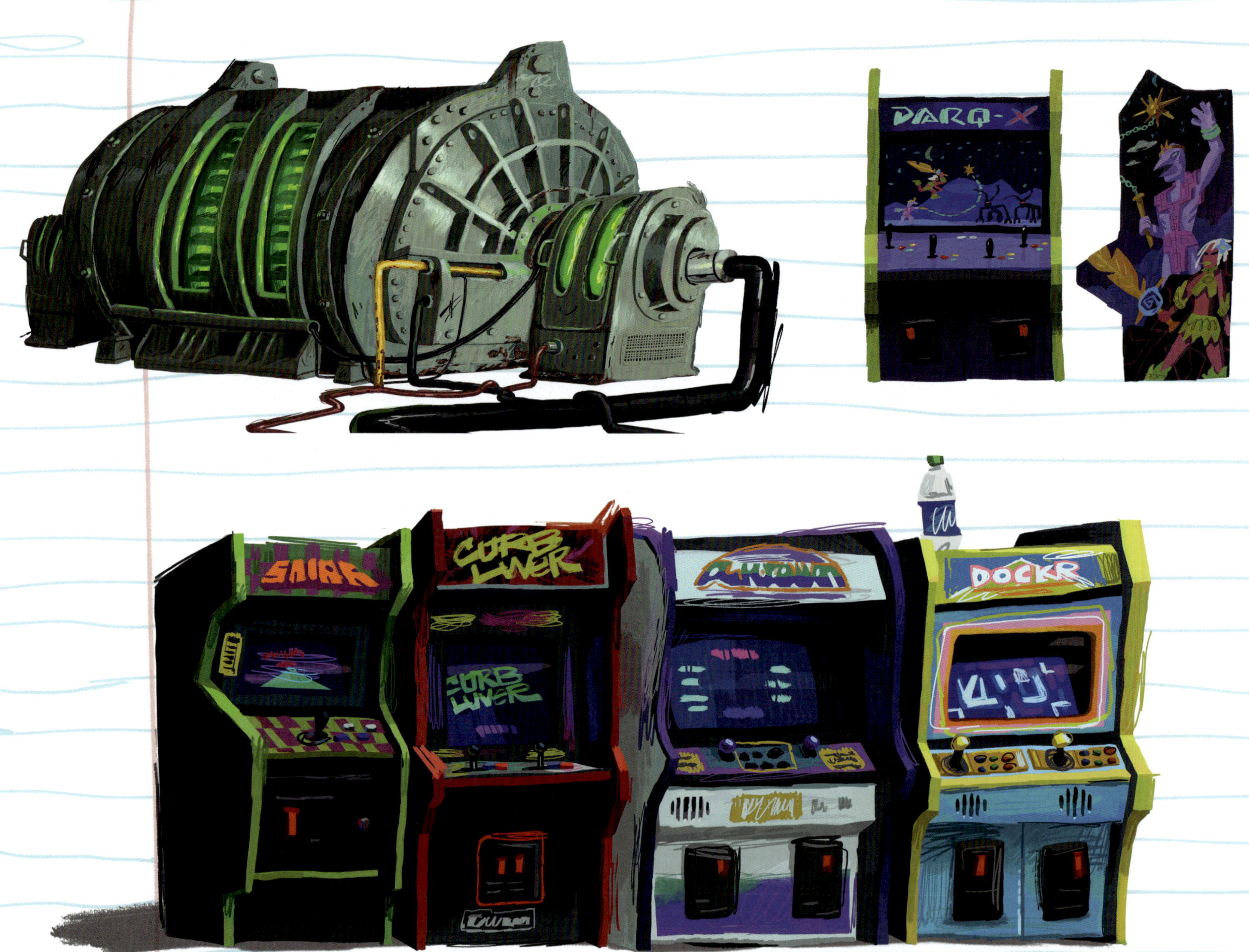

Above Left: Interior boat lab art by Jeffery Thompson
Above Right: Bowling alley arcade concept art by Garrett Lee
Below: Bowling alley arcade art by Tom Eichacker

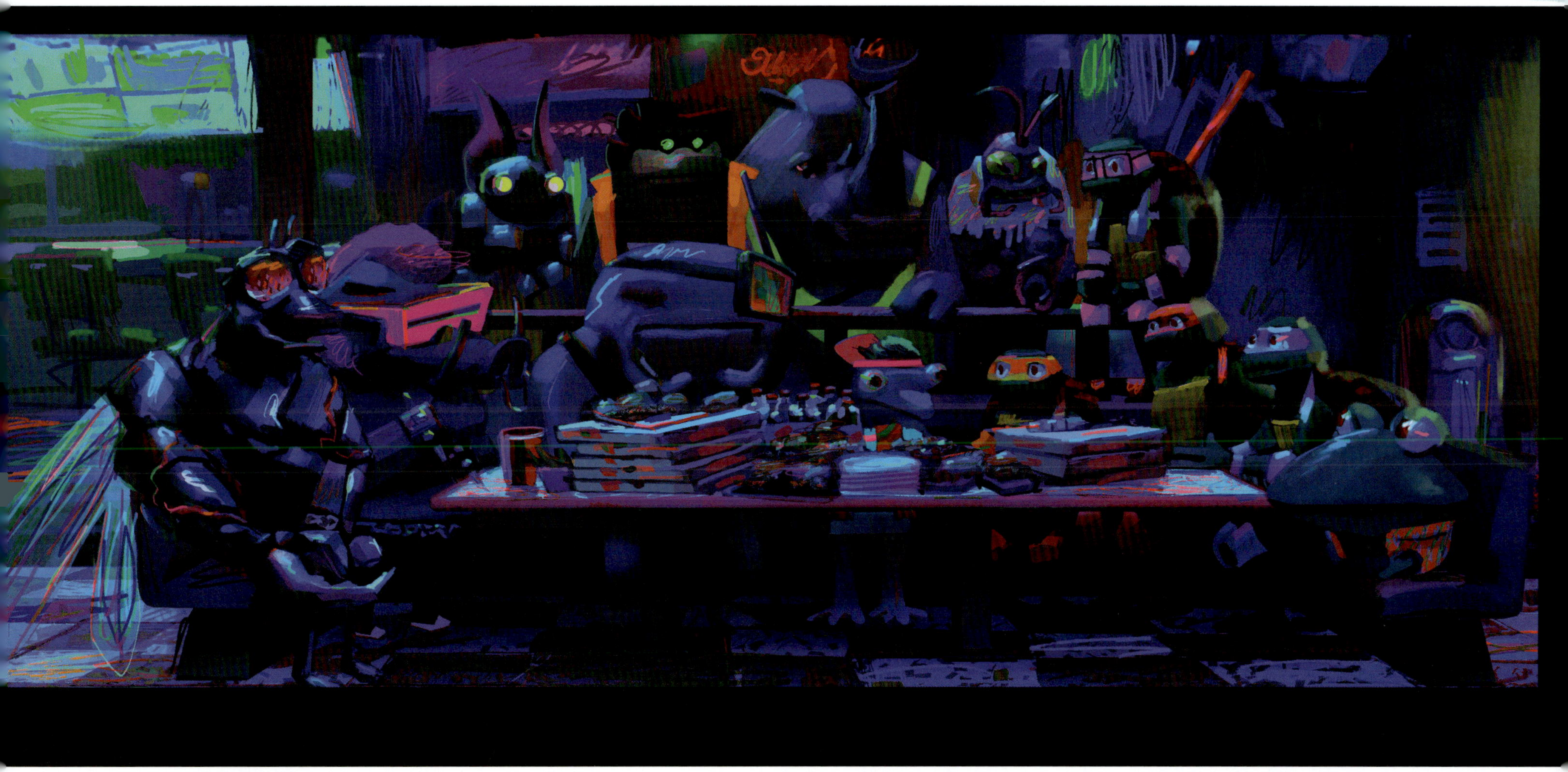

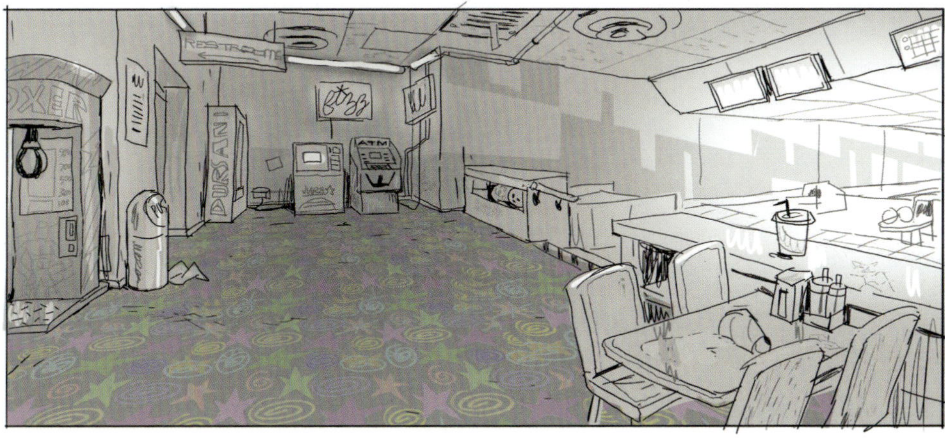

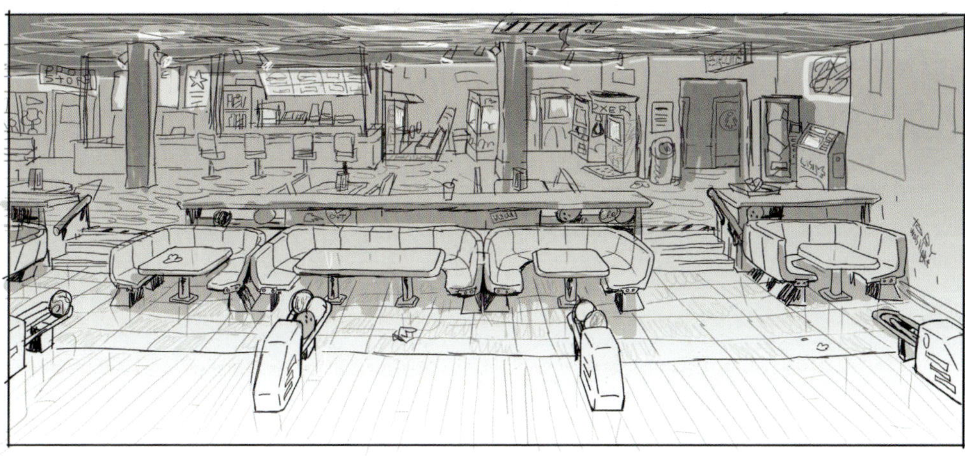

Above: Bowling alley key art by Tiffany Lam Almack
Below: Bolwing alley interior concept art by Tom Eichacker

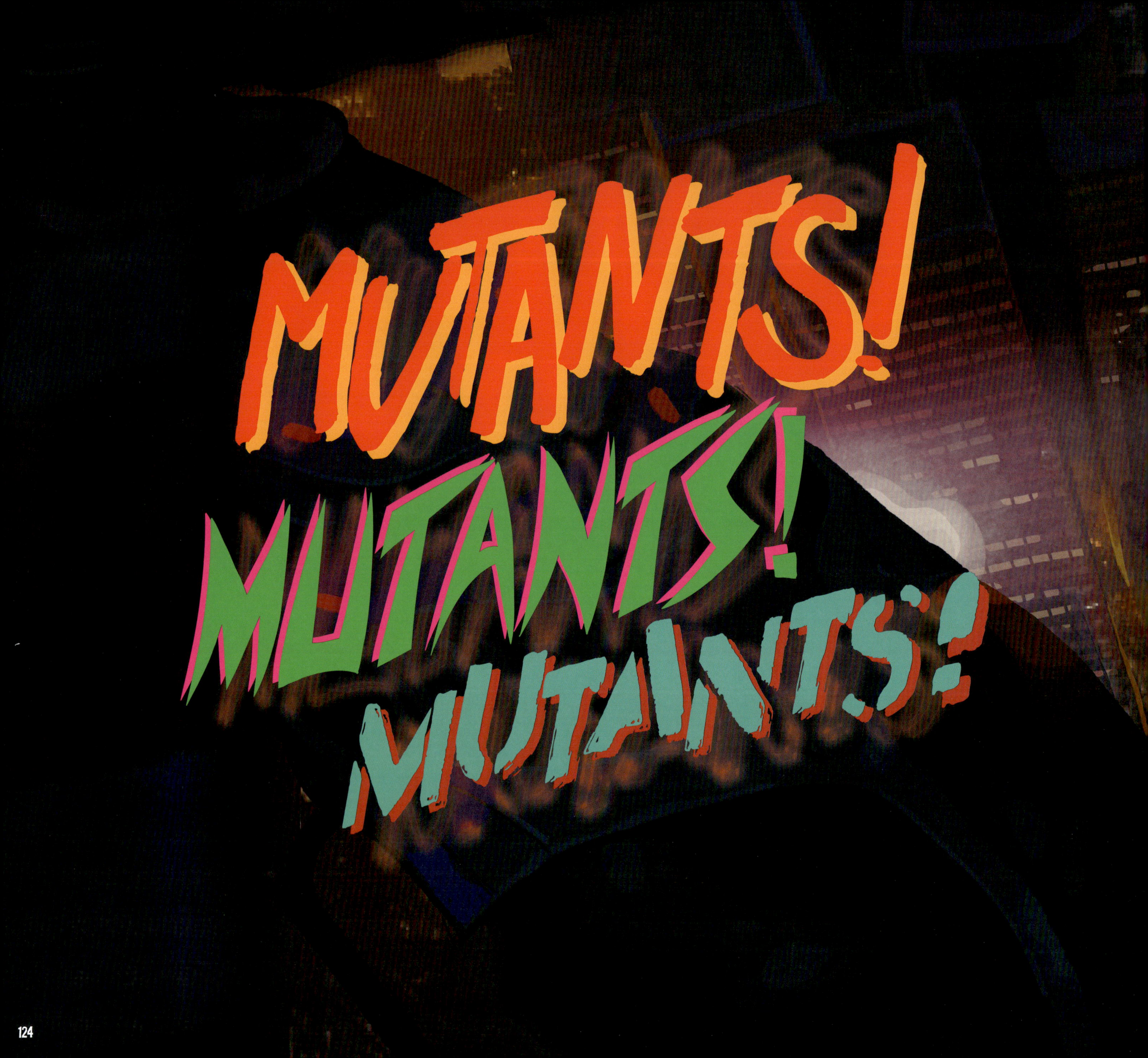
MUTANTS!
MUTANTS!
MUTANTS!

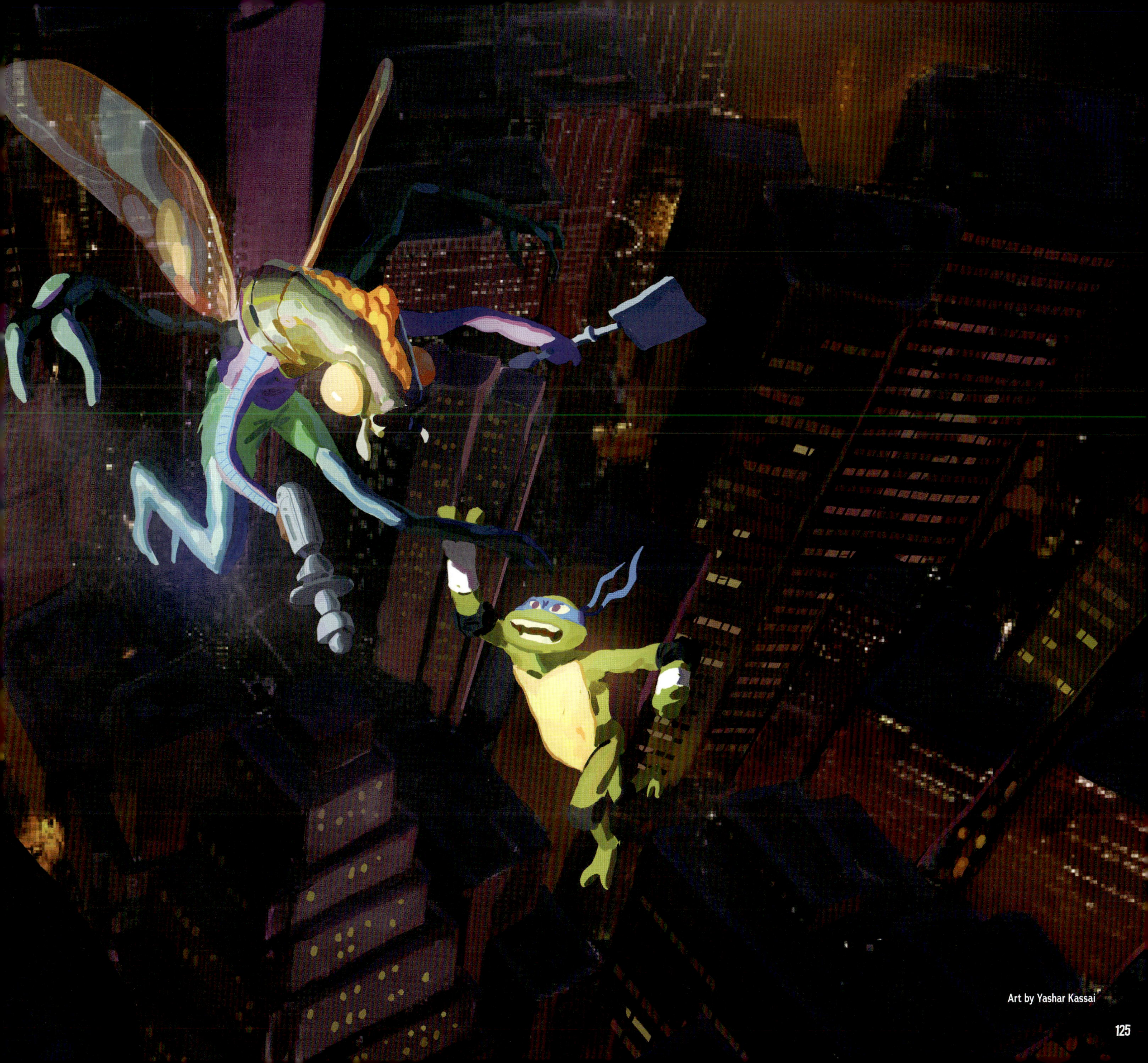

Art by Yashar Kassai

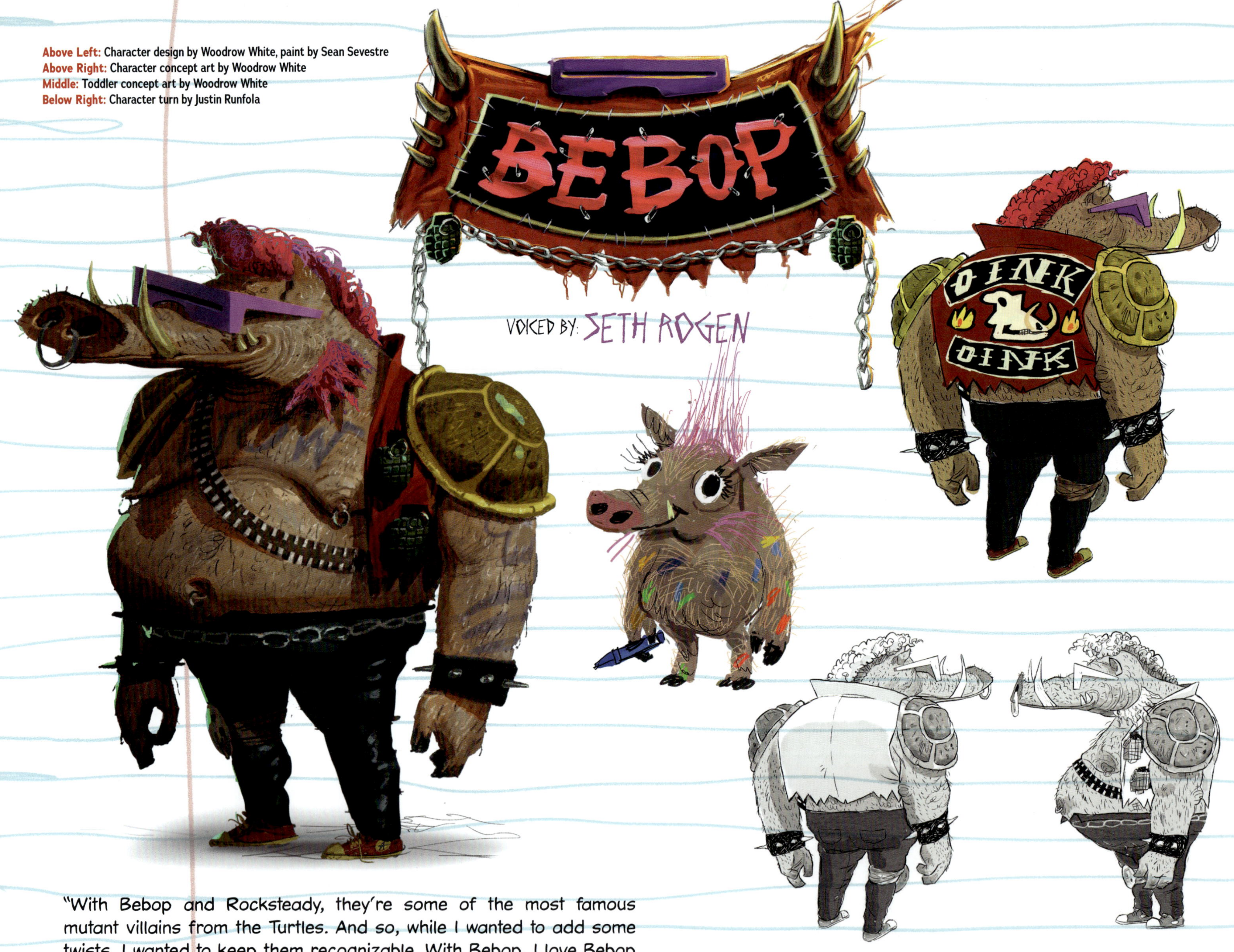

Above Left: Character design by Woodrow White, paint by Sean Sevestre
Above Right: Character concept art by Woodrow White
Middle: Toddler concept art by Woodrow White
Below Right: Character turn by Justin Runfola

"With Bebop and Rocksteady, they're some of the most famous mutant villains from the Turtles. And so, while I wanted to add some twists, I wanted to keep them recognizable. With Bebop, I love Bebop and didn't want to mess too much with him. I did want to add my own flair. I was looking at Greek pottery and the way boars are rendered in ancient Greek art. I wanted to take that sort of shape-language and apply it to Bebop. If you'll notice, he has a very long snout in this movie, and that's where it comes from.

I wanted to make Bebop a bit portly. I noticed in previous versions he'd been a number of things, like buff and skinny. I think I was adding a little inspiration from the Michael Bay movies by making him a bit tubby but with big, imposing, muscular arms with little hoof hands."

–Lead Character Designer Woodrow White

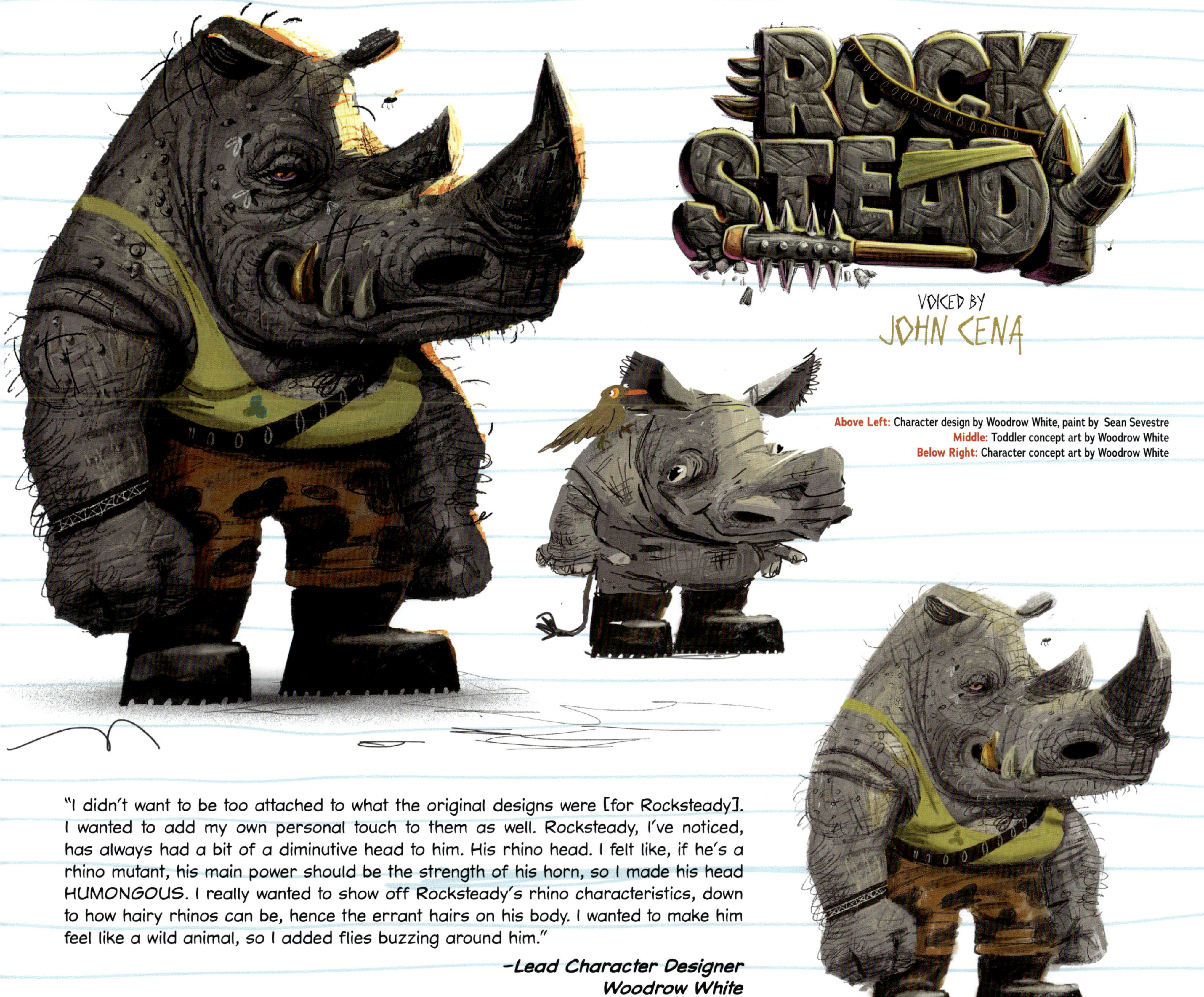

Above Left: Character design by Woodrow White, paint by Sean Sevestre
Middle: Toddler concept art by Woodrow White
Below Right: Character concept art by Woodrow White

"I didn't want to be too attached to what the original designs were [for Rocksteady]. I wanted to add my own personal touch to them as well. Rocksteady, I've noticed, has always had a bit of a diminutive head to him. His rhino head. I felt like, if he's a rhino mutant, his main power should be the strength of his horn, so I made his head HUMONGOUS. I really wanted to show off Rocksteady's rhino characteristics, down to how hairy rhinos can be, hence the errant hairs on his body. I wanted to make him feel like a wild animal, so I added flies buzzing around him."

–Lead Character Designer Woodrow White

GENGHIS FROG

VOICED BY
HANNIBAL BURESS

"Genghis Frog took a number of tries. We knew from the beginning we wanted to make him very goofy, very minuscule, a lot tinier than his earlier predecessors. I was primarily influenced by the pixie frog. I laugh whenever I see a pixie frog. I think they're really funny-looking frogs. We knew early that we wanted the Hawaiian shirt because that's hilarious."

—Lead Character Designer Woodrow White

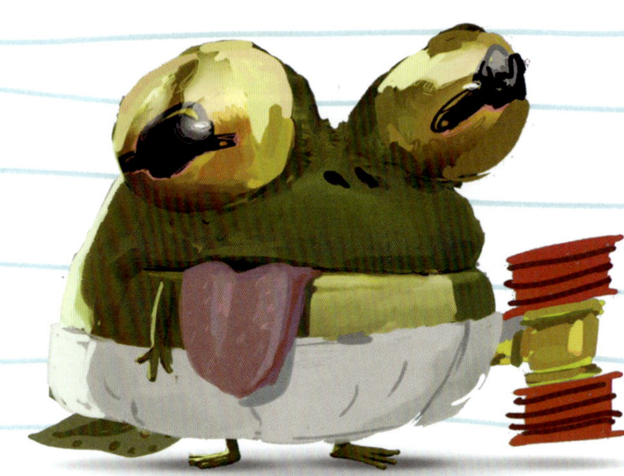

"The Genghis Frog design is more-or-less a drawing that I did. Woodrow did a pass on it but that's the only thing in the film that I drew in some form."

—Director Jeff Rowe

SPEC. 4
(eyes)

SPEC. 2
(skin)

REFERENCE FOR REFLECTION HIGHLIGHT ON EYES

LOOK OF PICTURE LINES USED TO INDICATE BUMPS ON SKIN SURFACE TO BREAK SILHOUETTE

*SKIN OVERALL SHOULD FEEL COARSE AND ROUGH, RATHER THAN WET AND GLOSSY.

Above: Toddler concept art by Yashar Kassai
Below: Character design by Jeff Rowe, paint by Alger Tam

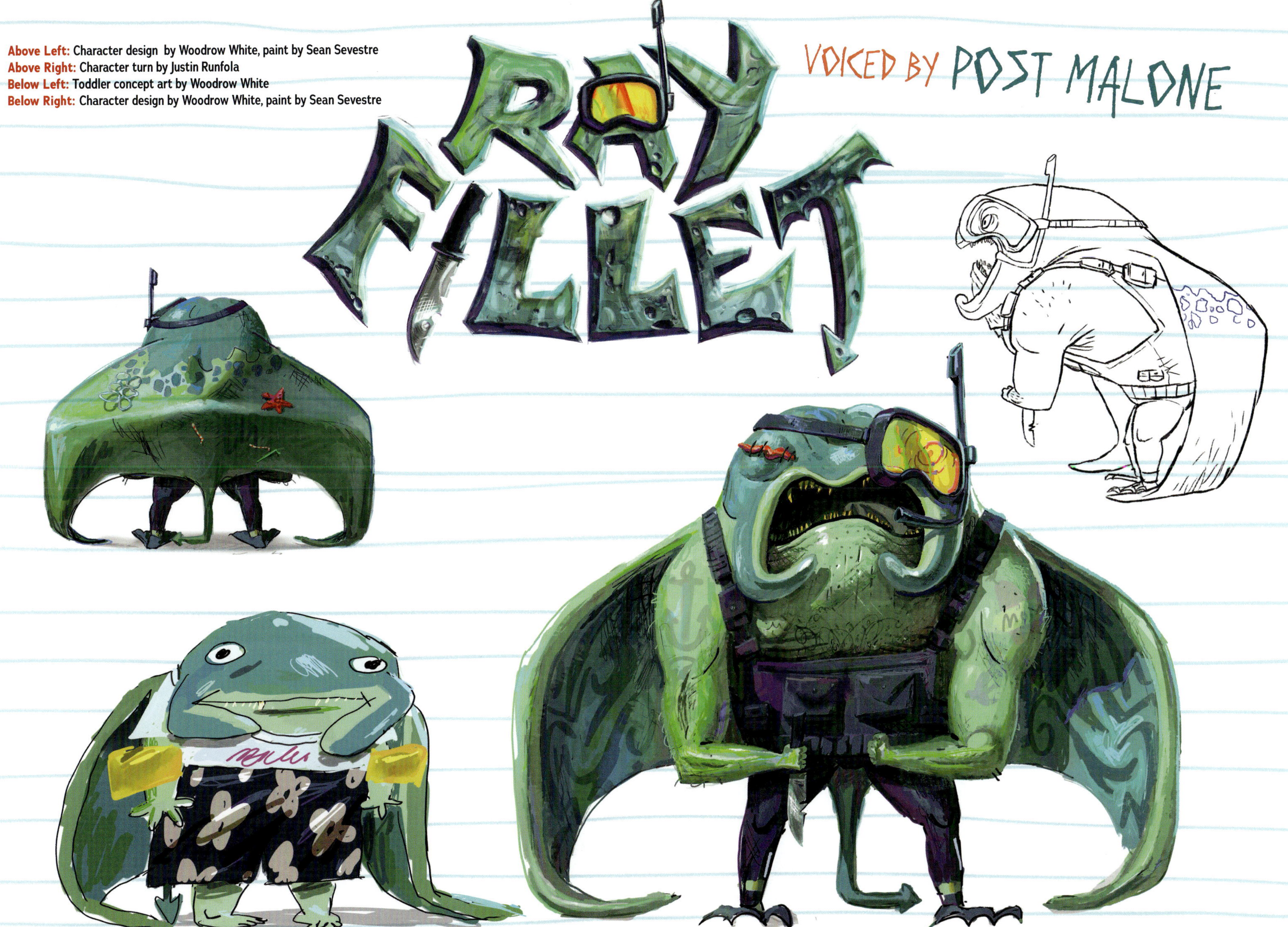

"If you look at the early toys of Ray Fillet, he looks very different. It was a huge choice on my part to scrap that completely. I wanted something that fit more of a menacing type of character. He's dressed like Superman kinda in the original cartoon. In this, I wanted to make a sorta Jean-Claude Van Damme action hero manta ray. I gave him tactical scuba gear, imagining that this guy spends a lot of time underwater, slipping under boats and submarines. He's got flippers, and he's got a combat knife. He's got an eye missing, which I liked doing. Ironically, he has a scuba mask over one eye. I wanted to use a human-sized scuba mask, but I realized there was an eye conundrum because his eyes were so far apart. So [I] just took one eye out and then strapped the one scuba eye mask over the other eye, almost like an eye patch for his remaining eye!"

–Lead Character Designer Woodrow White

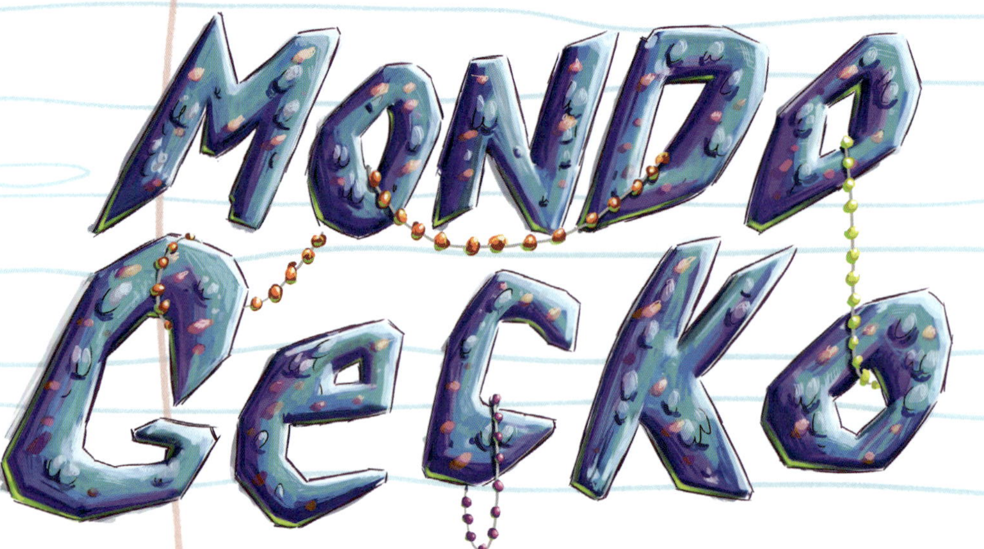

VOICED BY
PAUL RUDD

Right: Character design by Woodrow White, final paint by Sean Sevestre
Middle: Skateboard concept art by Kellan Jett
Bottom Left: Toddler concept art by Woodrow White

"Mondo Gecko happened to be my favorite mutant out of all [the ones] I've worked on. I spent one night on overtime because they told me I needed to get Mondo designed by the end of the day or else he would not have a toy. I just remember the one evening feverishly knocking out Mondo after Mondo. I finally got to one where I was looking at him and thinking about the radical skater persona, and I was listening to a lot of techno and electronic music, and I realized he should be a raver. I started looking at a lot of candy ravers for inspiration. I love rave culture, and I wanted to bring my love of rave culture into the design of one of the mutants.

He's wearing a visor with fake hair like Guy Fieri. That was inspired by some visors I saw in a gift shop in Florida. I thought those were so funny, and what if he's wearing it like a backwards baseball cap? He was always a very goofy character from the beginning, so this all fell into place. The goofier the better."

–Lead Character Designer Woodrow White

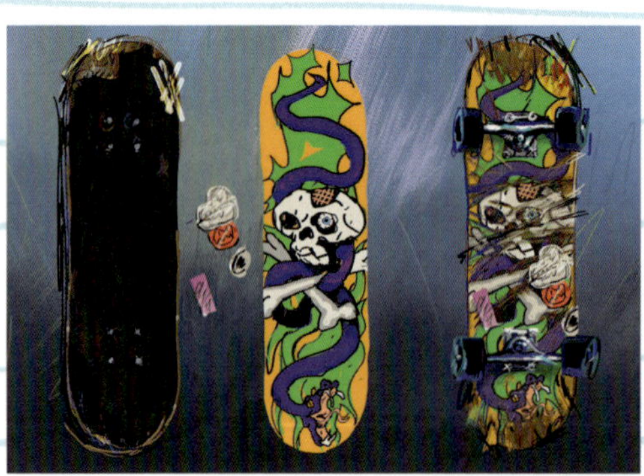

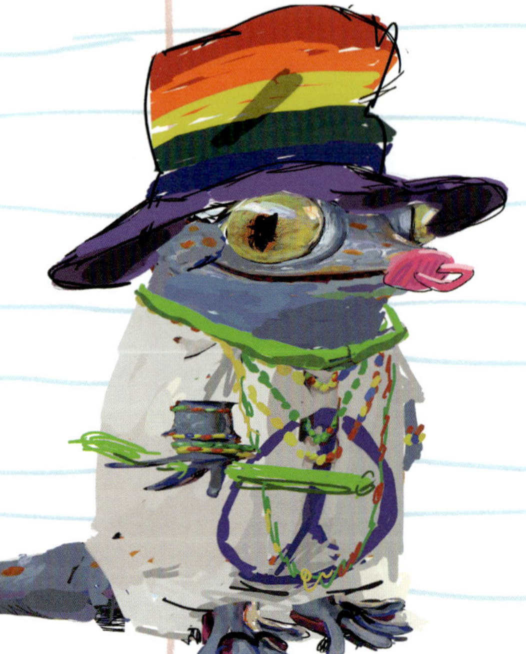

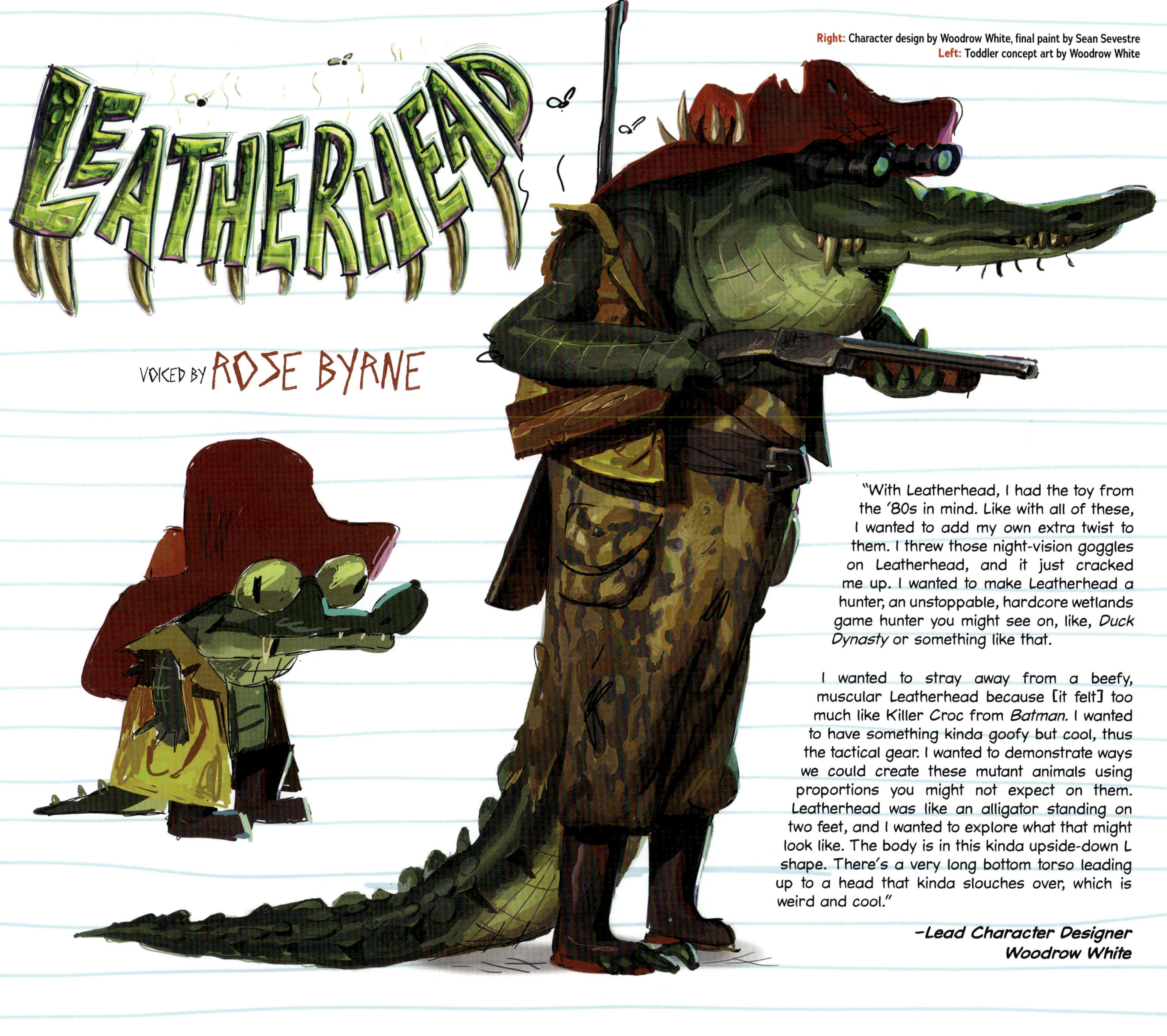

Right: Character design by Woodrow White, final paint by Sean Sevestre
Left: Toddler concept art by Woodrow White

LEATHERHEAD

VOICED BY ROSE BYRNE

"With Leatherhead, I had the toy from the '80s in mind. Like with all of these, I wanted to add my own extra twist to them. I threw those night-vision goggles on Leatherhead, and it just cracked me up. I wanted to make Leatherhead a hunter, an unstoppable, hardcore wetlands game hunter you might see on, like, *Duck Dynasty* or something like that.

I wanted to stray away from a beefy, muscular Leatherhead because [it felt] too much like Killer Croc from *Batman.* I wanted to have something kinda goofy but cool, thus the tactical gear. I wanted to demonstrate ways we could create these mutant animals using proportions you might not expect on them. Leatherhead was like an alligator standing on two feet, and I wanted to explore what that might look like. The body is in this kinda upside-down L shape. There's a very long bottom torso leading up to a head that kinda slouches over, which is weird and cool."

–Lead Character Designer Woodrow White

SCUM BUG

Above Left: Toddler concept art by Woodrow White
Above Right: Concept art by Woodrow White
Below: Character design by Woodrow White, final paint by Sean Sevestre and Tiffany Lam Almack

"I loved the original Scumbug design and wanted to bring as much of that energy into ours. We never really specify exactly what bug Scumbug is; it's kind of like a sorta mutant roach.

Jeff kept encouraging me to go as wild and preposterous as possible with Scumbug, to make Scumbug as terrifying and ugly as I could. The direction I've been wanting to hear all my life is make something as ugly and beastly as possible."

–Lead Character Designer Woodrow White

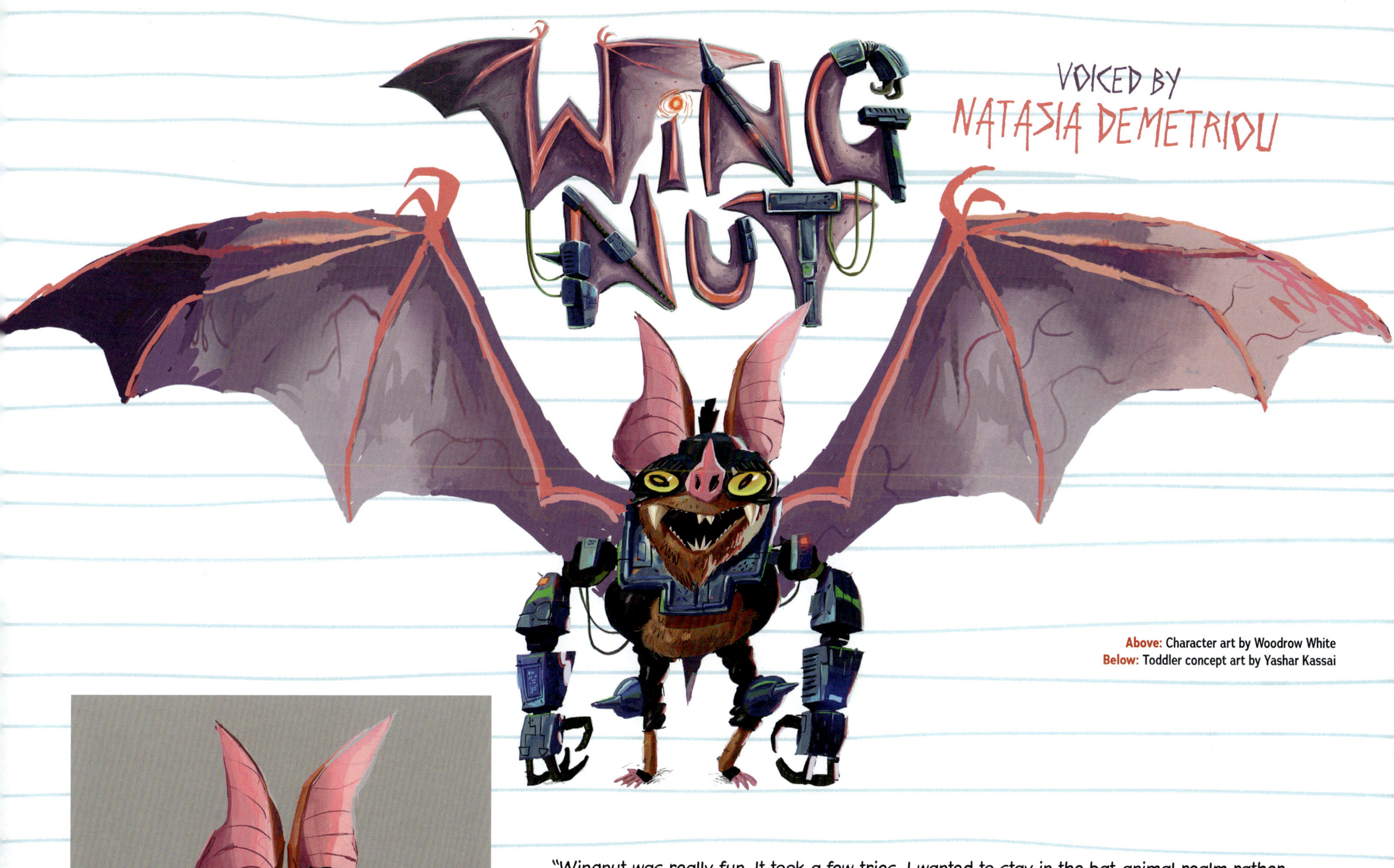

VOICED BY
NATASIA DEMETRIOU

Above: Character art by Woodrow White
Below: Toddler concept art by Yashar Kassai

"Wingnut was really fun. It took a few tries. I wanted to stay in the bat-animal realm rather than the bat-human realm. The original Wingnut has arms in addition to wings, and I wanted to take the arms out of the equation and stick with wings. I wanted the arm aspect as well but not being an organic appendage, so that's where those robotic arms came from. She is a very cybernetic mutant.

Wingnut's always had crazy gadgets attached to him or her, and I wanted to add robot arms in this version. We played a lot with adding rockets, and I had one version where the wings were augmented with machine parts, but it wasn't very readable, kind of messy. I thought the robot arms were a nice compromise where you still had the robotic aspect but it was a way more visually pleasing version of the character. It just read better."

–Lead Character Designer
Woodrow White

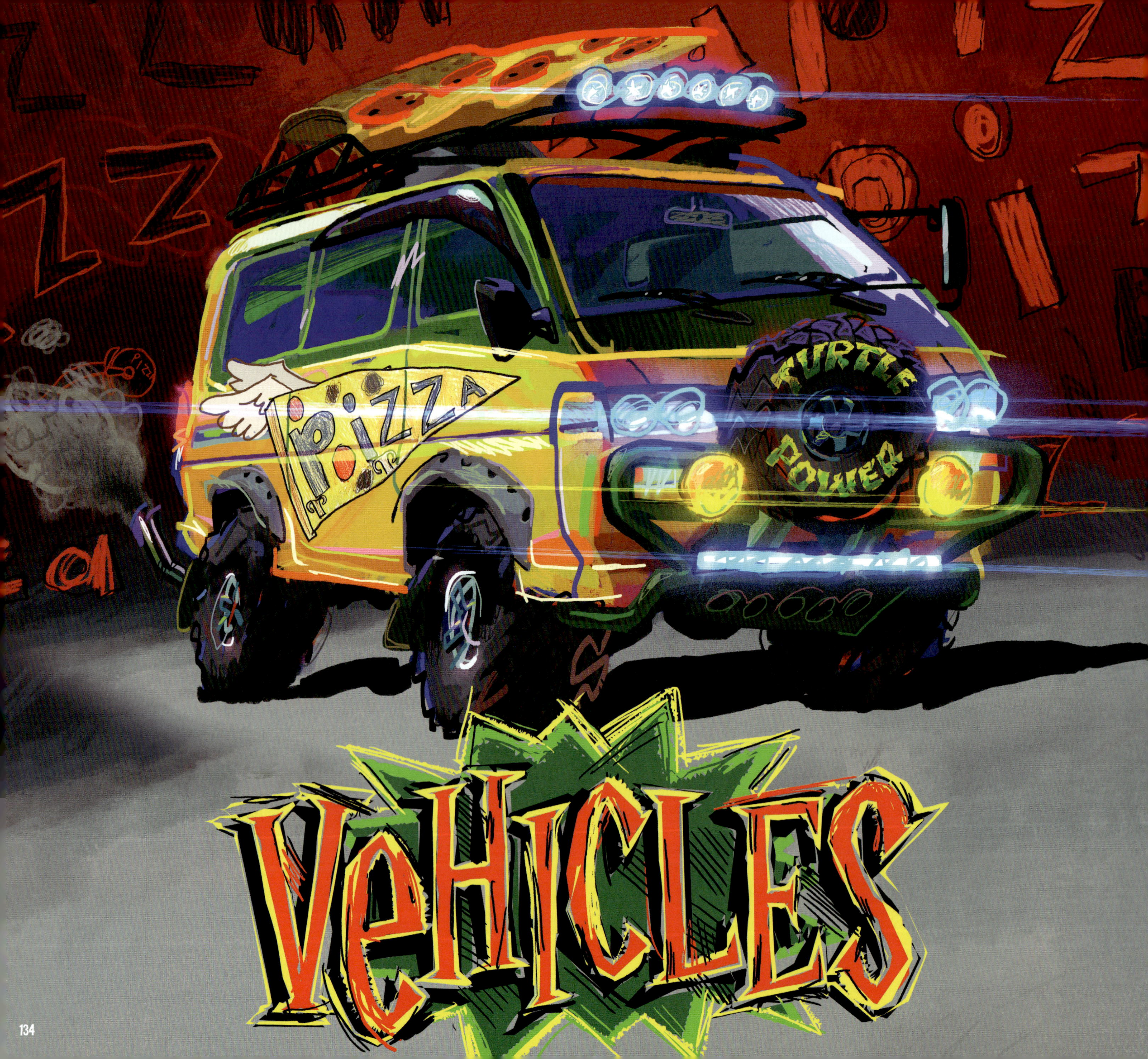
PIZZA
TURTLE POWER
VEHICLES

Opposite: Pizza van art by Arthur Fong
Above: Superfly car concept art by Arthur Fong
Below: Interior concept art by Arthur Fong

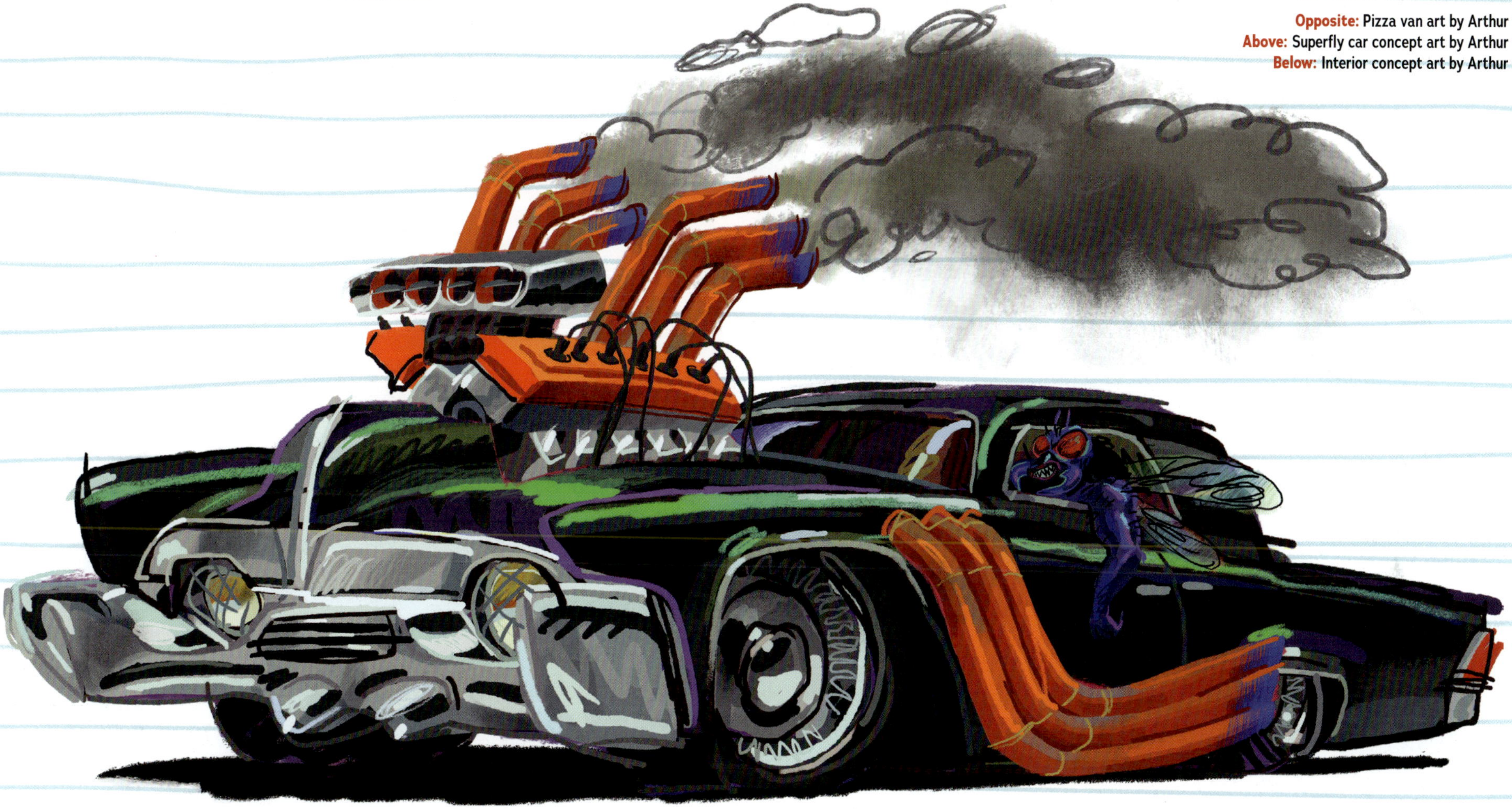

"I was born in the late '80s, and I was a big Ninja Turtles fan. So, I really thought about what kind of toy would I want if I were a kid today. I reached inside and talked to six-year-old Arthur about what mutant vehicles [he] would want. I designed these three very specific vehicles, part of it drawing from the old Playmates toys but also some integration of the things I like today. I designed Bebop's truck, Rocksteady's bike, and Superfly's lowrider car. At that time, the scene was just them meeting underneath a bridge and they'd leave, but when I showed [director] Jeff those vehicles, he lost his #&!%, and said 'I have to show this to Seth.' Seth was like, 'We gotta do something with these vehicles,' and they were inspired to rewrite the scene into a *Fast and Furious* car chase! I'm really proud of that because I [feel] that this is where the power of creation can help us. As creatives, it's our responsibility to push for better versions of ourselves, better versions of our art."

–Art Director Arthur Fong

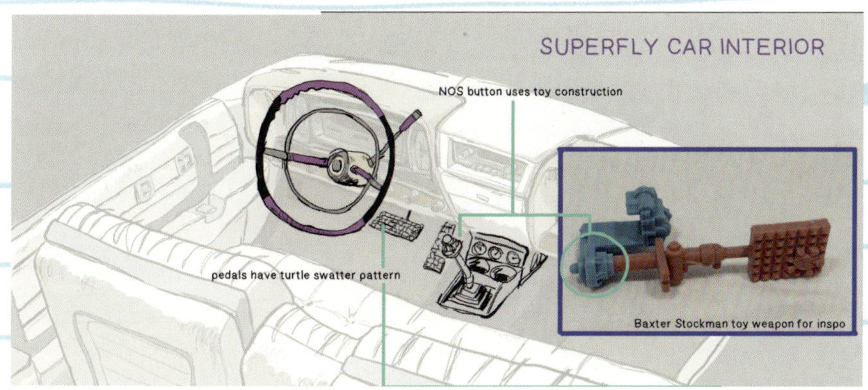

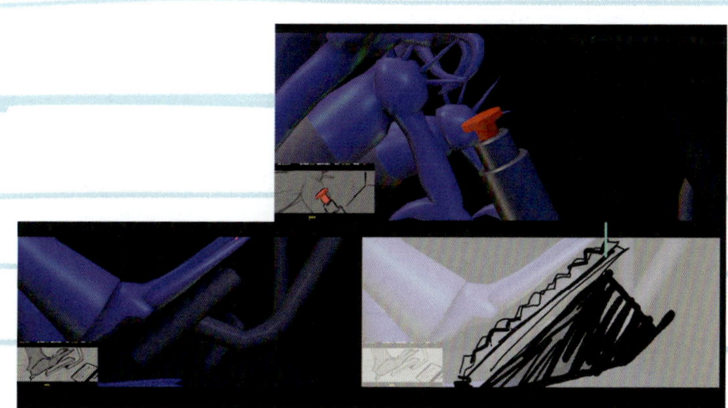

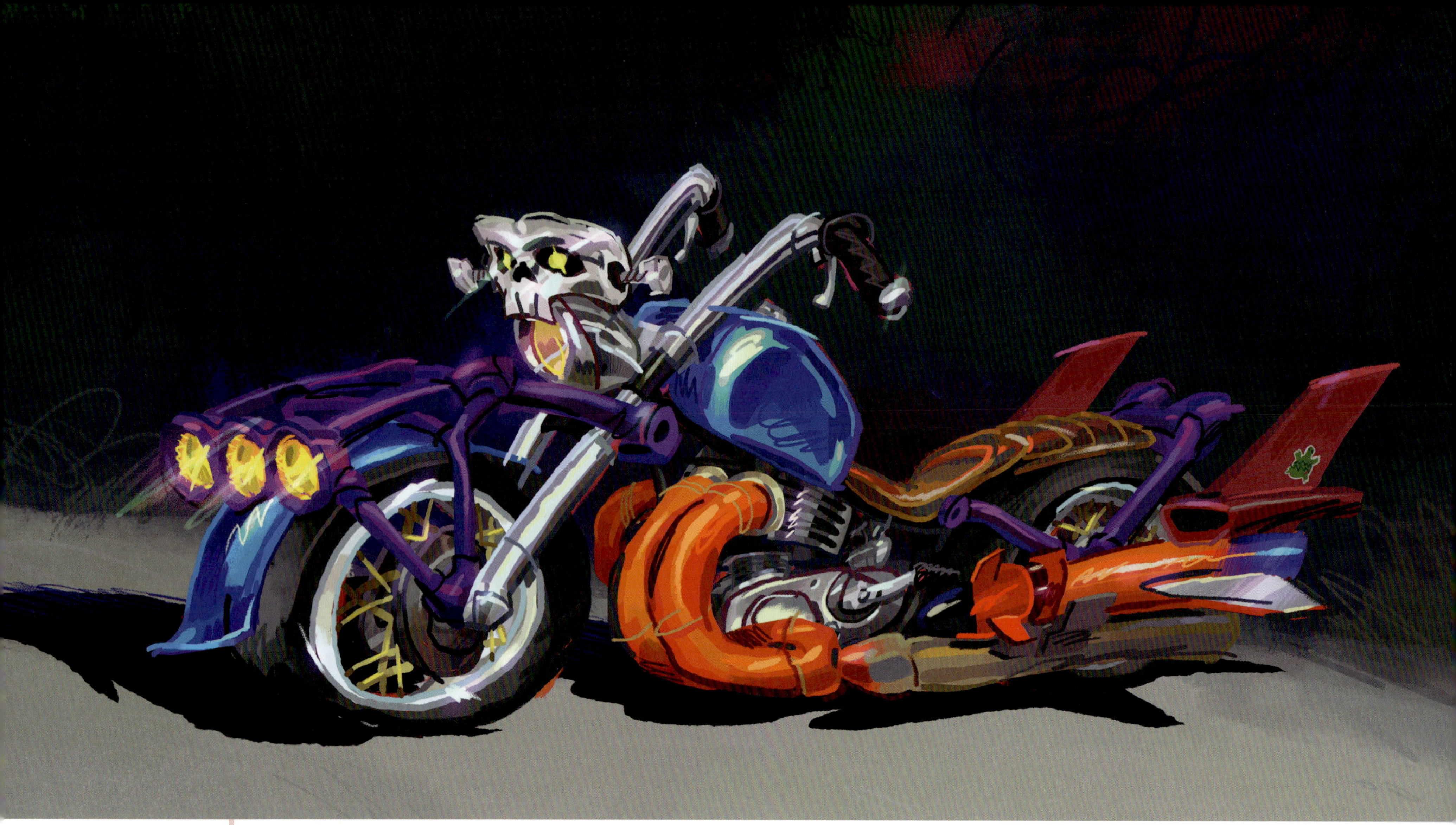

Above: Rocksteady motorcycle concept art by Arthur Fong
Below: TCRI motorcycle concept art by Kellan Jett

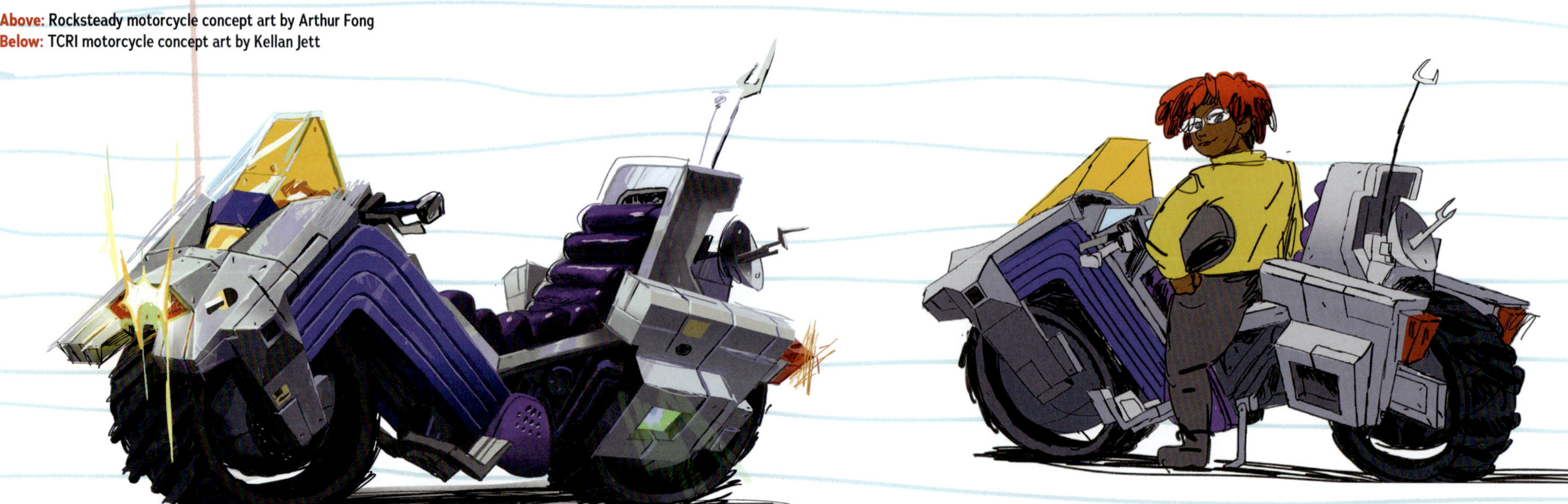

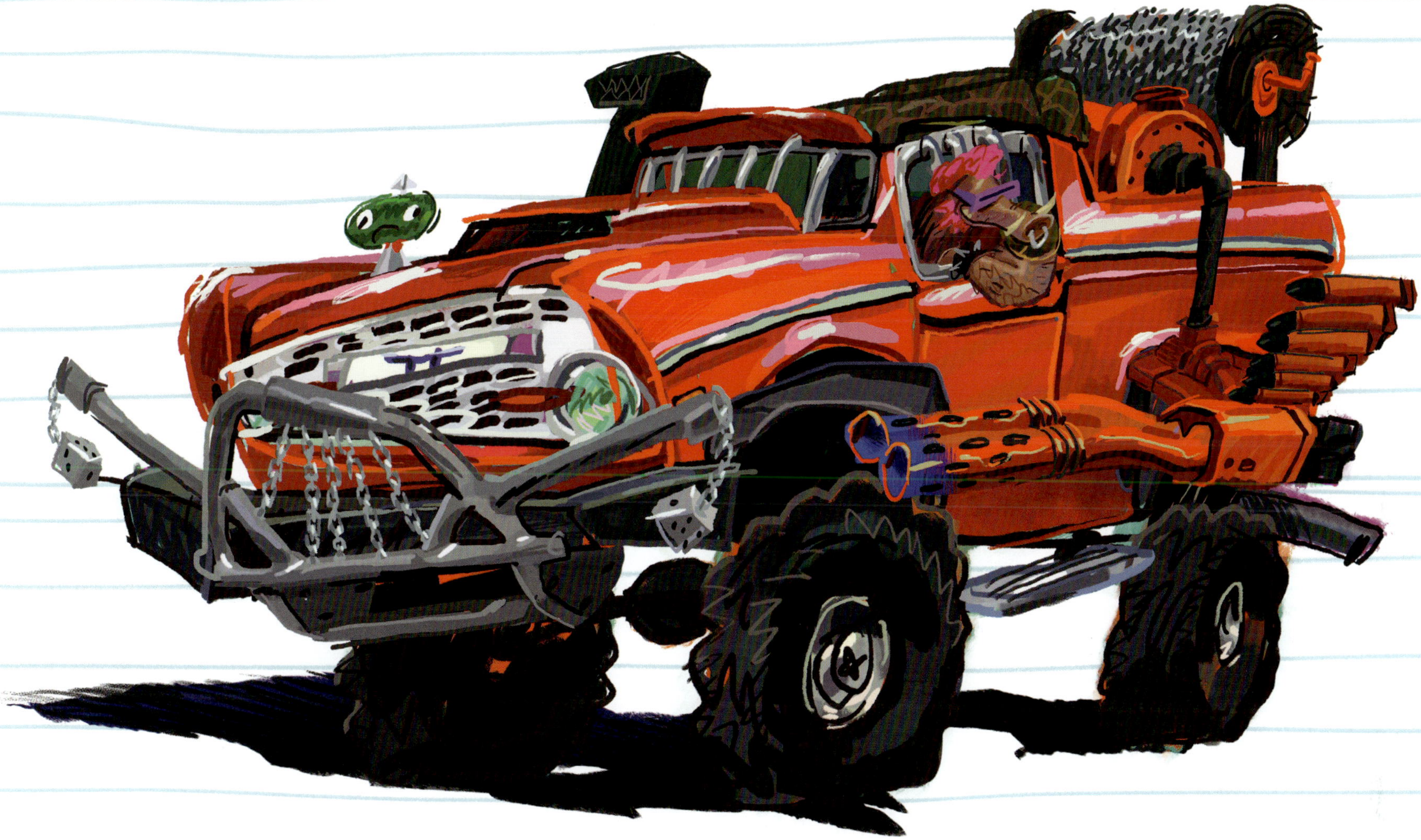

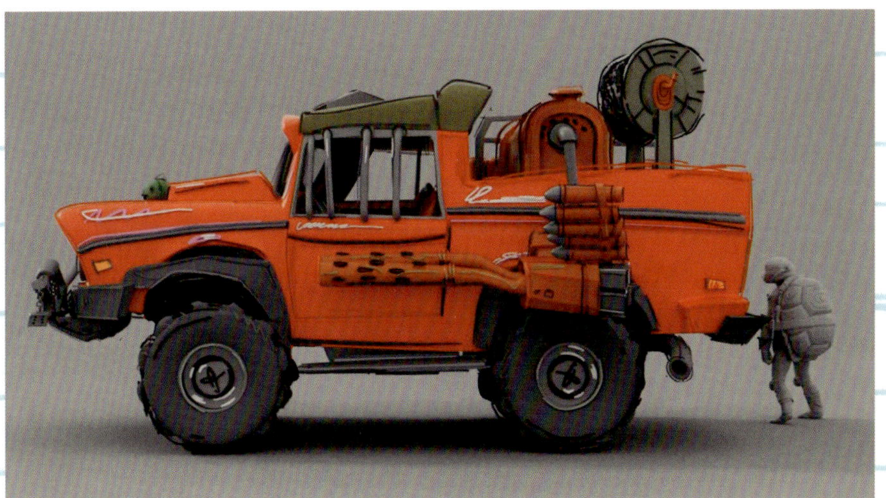

Above and Below: Bebop truck concept art by Arthur Fong

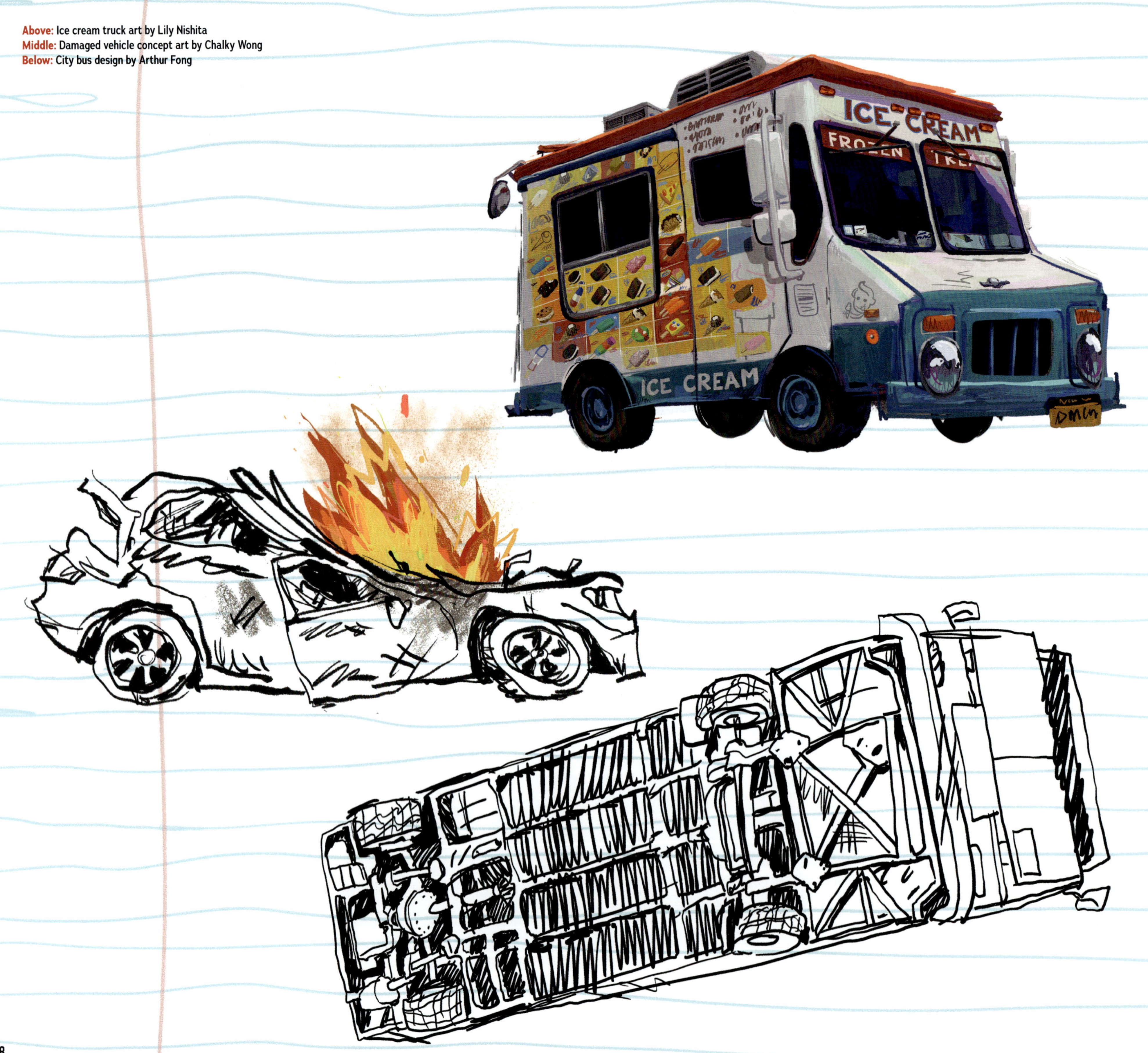

Above: Ice cream truck art by Lily Nishita
Middle: Damaged vehicle concept art by Chalky Wong
Below: City bus design by Arthur Fong

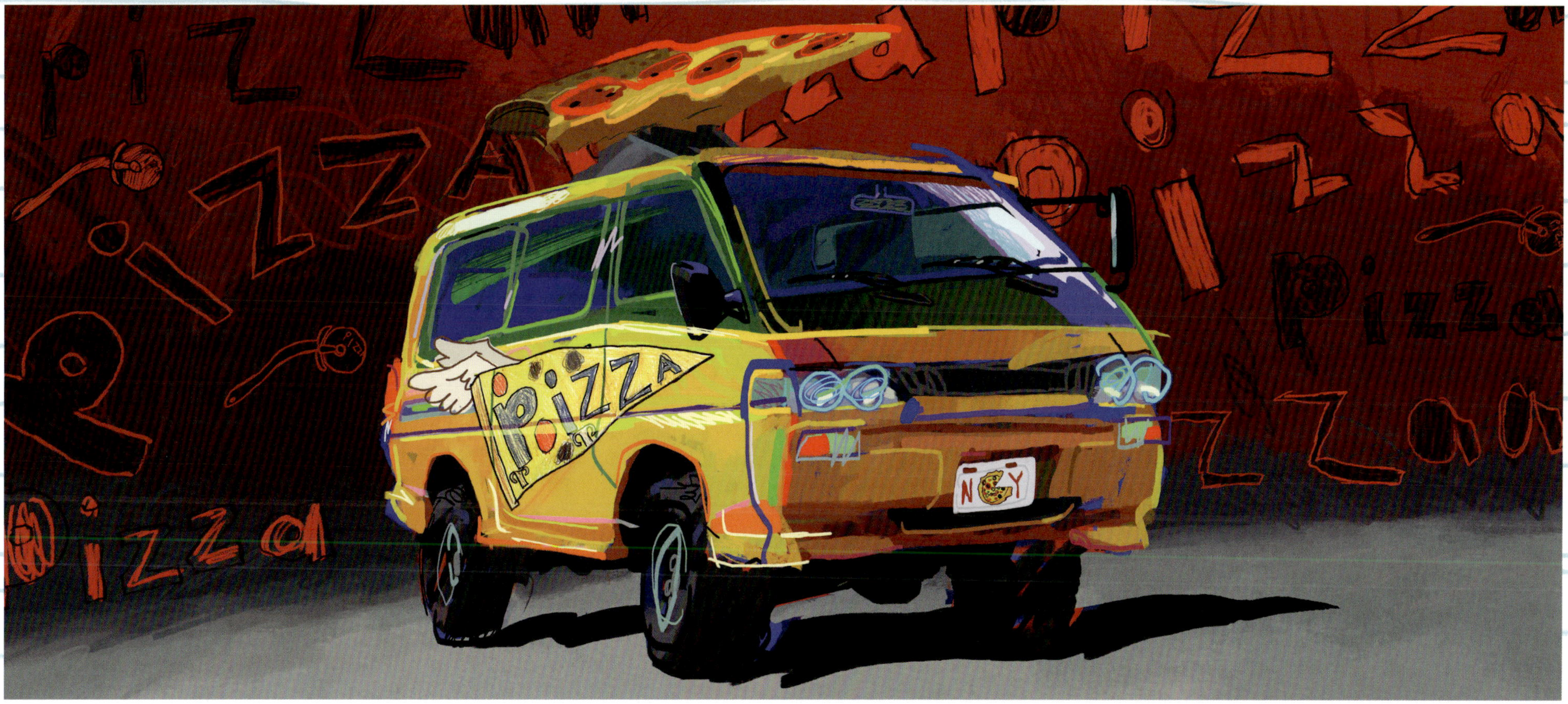

Above: Pizza van art by Arthur Fong
Below: Pizza van design sketches by Arthur Fong

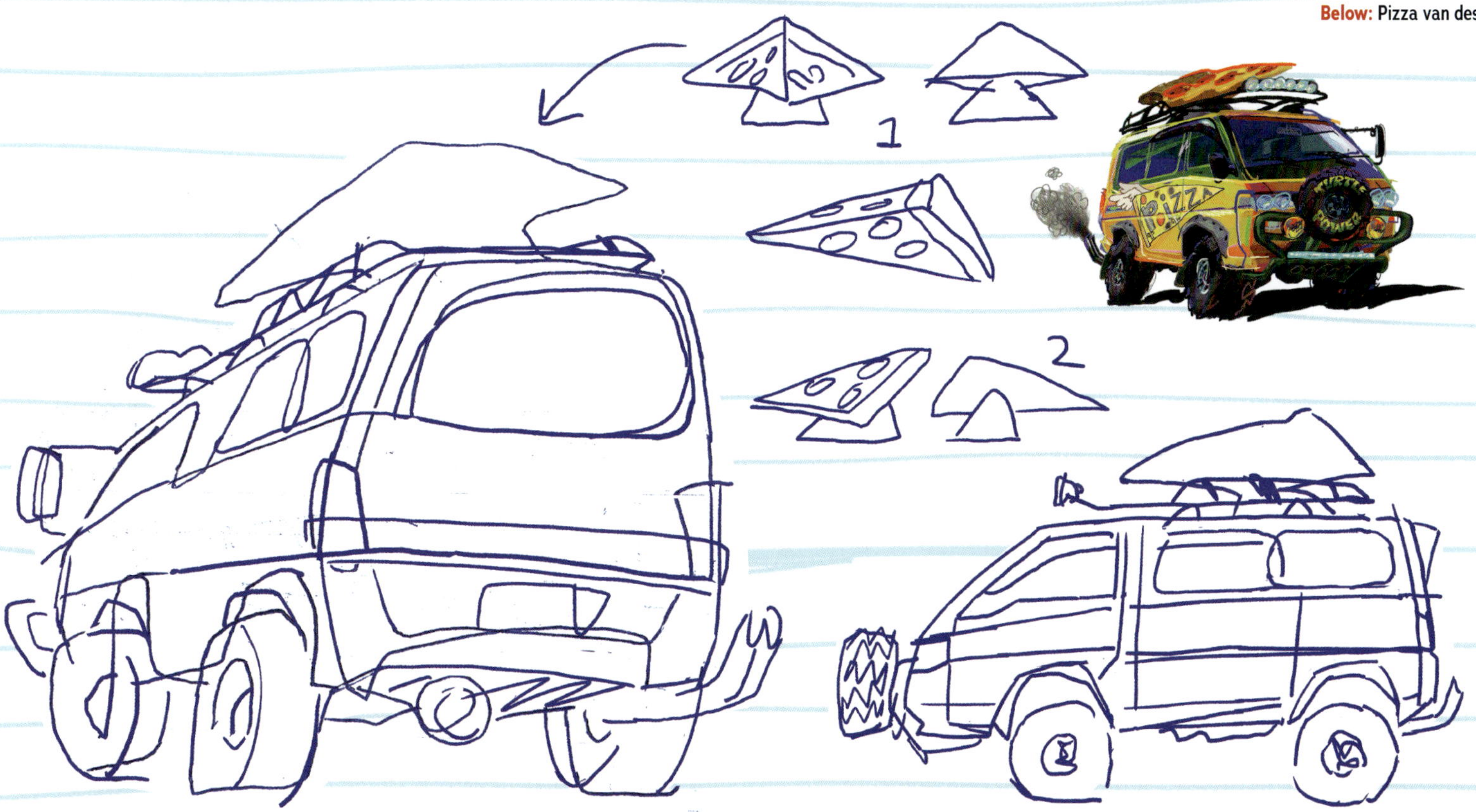

INTERVIEW WITH JEFF ROWE

Jim: As an '80s kid, it's a real thrill for me to be working on a *Teenage Mutant Ninja Turtles* art book. Could you walk me through your background, and how you came to be directing a *Turtles* feature?

Jeff: The short of it: grew up in Chicago, liked drawing, liked movies, animation seemed like a good path to combine both of them. Could not get into Cal Arts so sold all my stuff and moved to California and then went to community college for a year and then was able to get to Cal Arts. After that I worked at some odd jobs. I was an editor, I worked for a theme park design company doing concept artwork, but my first real meaningful industry job was being a writer on *Gravity Falls*. I learned so much from doing that. Alex Hirsch, the show creator, is a story genius. Everything I know about three-act structure and storytelling and delivering comedy at a regular pace and executing it at a high bar I learned from my experience on that show.

When that was wrapping, Mike Reanda was pitching *The Mitchells Vs. the Machines* at Sony and they were going to let him write it. He asked to have me on as a co-writer and then we wrote that film together. He directed it, I co-directed it. As that was winding down I started taking meetings looking for my next project. This came and I was like "they will *never* give me this job. No one has seen *Mitchells*, it's not out in theaters yet." I never thought I would get the job, I was able to get the job and it's been life changing and affirming and wonderful.

Jim: Why do you think they gave you the job?

Jeff: I think me, Seth [Rogen], and Evan [Goldberg] were on the same page about wanting it to be naturalistic first and foremost, and to feel authentic. I was like, "I want to make it authentic, and I want to make it *amazing!*" I think I just probably cared more than maybe anyone else would about making the film great. Seth and I have a similar taste in film and art and there was some feeling of, "Oh, this guy gets it. This guy gets what we're going for. I think it'll be safe in his hands."

Jim: How is *Mutant Mayhem* different from the Turtles that we've seen before, and how is it similar?

Jeff: The archetypes are there. In spirit, they're the same characters. It's still a comedic world. It's weird, we often found ourselves making strange choices. In the design of vehicles, and in the design of the TCRI world in the film, we tried to embrace a lot of what was going on in the late '80s early '90s madcap Saturday morning cartoon design sense. Instead of going the Christopher Nolan, everything-is-black-and-tactical-and-cool, we let it be weird and funny and then rendered really beautifully. The spirit is there, but it's the first time the Turtles were ever voiced by teenagers. So we had to focus on the teenage part. Teenage problems, teenage maturity, teenage approaches to problem solving. Artistically, it has a toe dipped in the '80s designs, with their skin tones and face structure and colored arm bands, but we also needed to push them to be more awkward and less muscular. They needed to feel authentically teenage.

Jim: I've spoken to Arthur–

Jeff: He's so good!

Jim: Oh, yeah, he's great. He emphasized that the team was leaning hard into the teenage side of things. Since this is for an art book, how does that sensibility influence the design choices that you make?

Jeff: This film has a completely distinct look that I have not seen in another animated feature film, inspired by actual teenage art. It comes down to things like the shape-language of the characters, the approach to backgrounds, the asymmetry in the design of everything, the kind of lack of traditional design flourishes and techniques and the kind of tricks you do to make an image pretty, we threw a lot of those out. All of that mixed with this very saturated, high-contrast, almost David Lynch like lighting or something. We just really went for it with the color and with the shadows. We didn't want to just bounce color into every dark area of the frame, we were like "let's use black and let's use brown and let's use all of the colors that we're always told not to use when making feature animation."

Jim: What about the character designs themselves?

Jeff: There was a choice to be made. Do we differentiate them, do we give them different designs, do we keep them all the same like the original series? I think we wanted to differentiate them and give them a look that somewhat matched their personalities.

All of the mutant characters and a lot of the human characters were designed by Woodrow White. He's amazing and he's had a huge influence on the look of the film. The Turtles were originally designed by this French-Canadian artist named Maxime Mary who is really great. He got them to a really good place but they were kind of really clean and slick and refined. So, then our Production Designer Yashar Kassai got in there with the liquefy tool in Photoshop and kind of pushed their proportions around and pushed Mikey's head to be more balloon shaped. We'd noodle things around until it made us laugh or until we said something like "That's funny, oh that's crazy, that doesn't look like any cartoon character I've ever seen. Let's go with that!" And then it became a process of refining that into a usable, animatable character design.

Jim: What about the character designs of the other mutants in the film? I counted fourteen mutants total which is an *awful* lot for one feature.

Jeff: Are there fourteen? Ok, so, not counting the turtles–

Jim: Well, I was counting the turtles.

Jeff: OK yeah, yeah, yeah, yeah. That makes a little more sense then. So, four turtles, Splinter, Bebop, Rocksteady, Superfly. Uh, Wingnut, Leatherhead, Genghis Frog, Mondo Gecko, Scumbug... I'm blanking.

Jim: It's not gonna be on the test.

Jeff: Ray Fillet! Fourteen.

OK, so on a lot of those Woodrow designs, he would do a drawing and then we would approve it. There was not a lot of back and forth, there was not a lot of notes. He spends, I think, a lot of time researching, thinking about it, looking at past iterations of the characters, coming up with a really strong artistic take. And then he sits down and paints it, or draws it. So, like the Bebop and Rocksteady in the movie, he did Bebop one day, he did Rocksteady the next day. We saw them and we were like "Done. Don't change a thing, put this in the movie exactly as it is. We'll find a way to break the CG pipeline to make these characters work because we love them."

Jim: Do you have a favorite mutant in the film?

Jeff: Hmmm. Well, design-wise, Ray Fillet was a big turning point for us. That design is just so cool and big. He's barely in the movie but I love him.

Jim: Usually in Turtles the fly monster is Baxter Stockman. Superfly is a pretty different interpretation of that archetype, and Baxter Stockman is also in the movie. How did that choice come about?

Jeff: In earlier versions of the story, we were using Stockman because we wanted to deal with the idea of mutation, and their origin as mutants. It is *Mutant Mayhem*, and we wanted to have all these mutants. It felt like an essential element of this story, and Baxter Stockman seemed like a good character to create that, enable that. He was our go-to there. In earlier versions of the story he was mutating and becoming a fly monster.

When we really got down to it, more so than a story about mutants, it's a story about teenagers, it's a story about being kids and growing up, and it's a story about being an outsider.

Bottom: Concept art by Maxime Mary

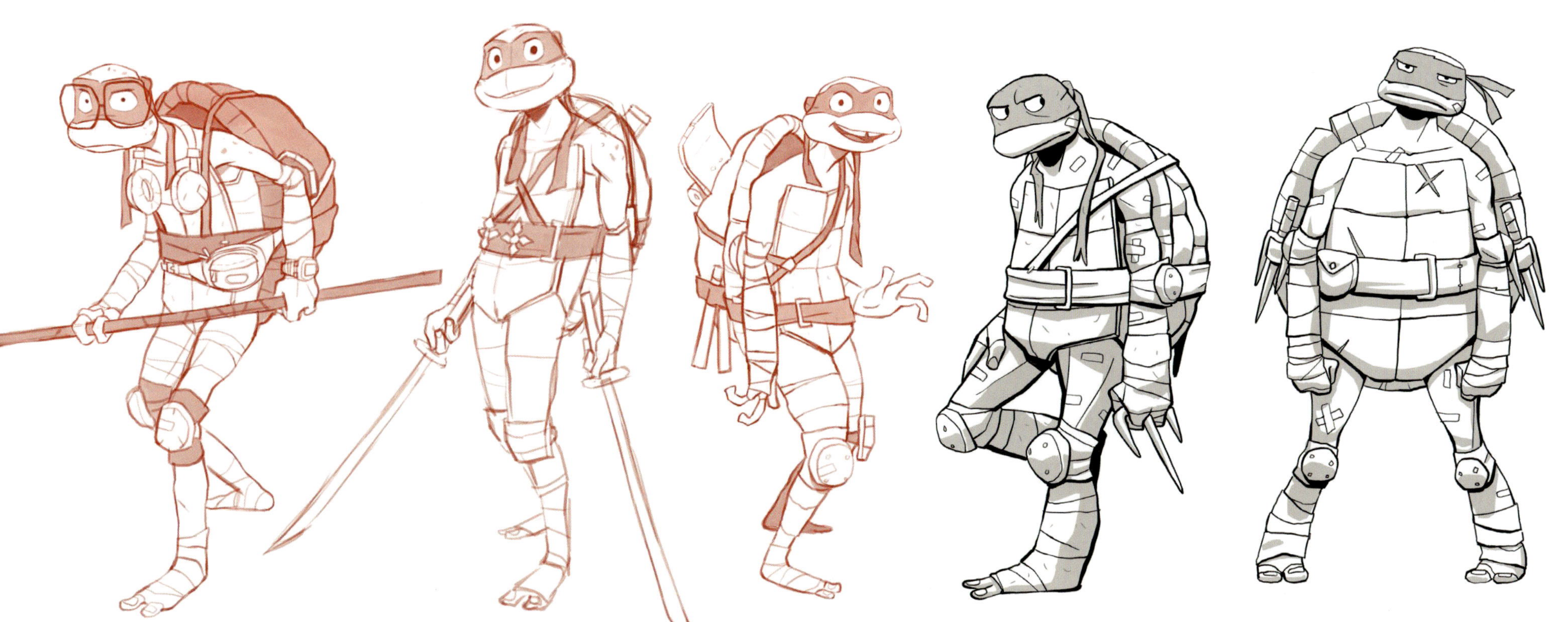

Jim: Mutant as metaphor.

Jeff: Mutant as metaphor. And it was important that the villain share a lot of those qualities with the turtles which necessitated him being a mutant too, just full on through, not a human turned into a mutant.

Superfly was born that way and had to grow up that way and had to endure the same struggles as the Turtles. He grew up on his own. He's very similar to Splinter in that way. They both raised families—It's a real Professor X/Magneto dynamic—they both have mutant families, they both did not expect to be parents, they both had traumatic events happen to them but they react to those events in completely different ways. That's the core of them. Having a villain that could echo the bad choices back to Splinter gave us a way to help Splinter grow and it clarified his relationship with the Turtles. Everything snapped into place when we made that decision. There are old designs where you'll see Superfly is wearing a Stockman sweater and it has a toy—it's even in the toy, the action figure that they made, but as a holdover from when it was Baxter Stockman.

Jim: That's a great transition to Splinter. What's your relationship like with that character?

Jeff: I'm not a martial arts guy. It was more important for me that Splinter feel like a real dad. He's a real single parent, trying his best, a little bit overwhelmed, didn't expect to be a dad, didn't know what his relationship was going to be, but he means well. He cares about his kids more than anything.

Jim: Between *Turtles* and *The Mitchells,* there are themes of family running through your work. Are you a parent?

Jeff: I am not a parent. I would say I did not have a great childhood growing up and had a complicated relationship with my parent figures. I feel like there are a lot of movies that have this sugar-coated idea of family and what that means. I was once a kid who watched movies and did not see my family in those movies and it made me feel alone. It's important to create stories that reflect to other lonely kids with complicated relationships with their parents. That's normal. That is part of the human experience and that's valid too and you're not bad for not having a great relationship with your parents.

Jim: It definitely comes across.

We've spoken about the character designs quite a lot, how about the backgrounds that they're living in? What was the design philosophy there?

Jeff: We really tried to lean into broken perspective and these lines that kind of shoot off of objects. And then creating a style for depth of field. A bunch of the artists on our team, Woodrow White, Kellan Jett, Garret Lee, Tom Eichacker, they all go and do plein air paintings together with gouache. So, every Saturday you'll find them on some corner in LA somewhere painting something. It was interesting looking at the way they paint environments and how you have depth of field in a watercolor painting and its loss of detail as you go back in frame. It's the same thing in high school drawings. You draw seven of the windows and then after you draw seven perfect rectangles you start getting lazy and they become these half circle half rectangle things. We were like, "Oh, that's how we create depth in the frame. The buildings reduce in quality the further away they get." Then we had to find a way to do that through a mix of modeling, low-rez modeling, and matte paintings.

Below: Concept art by Yashar Kassai

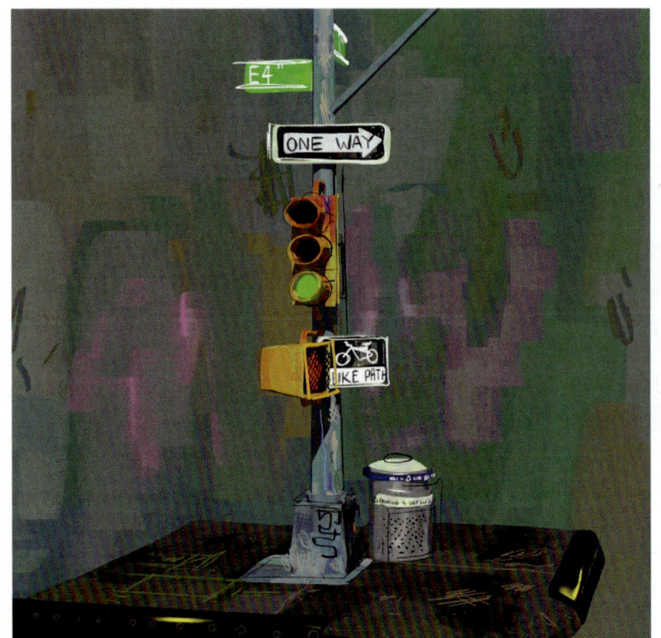

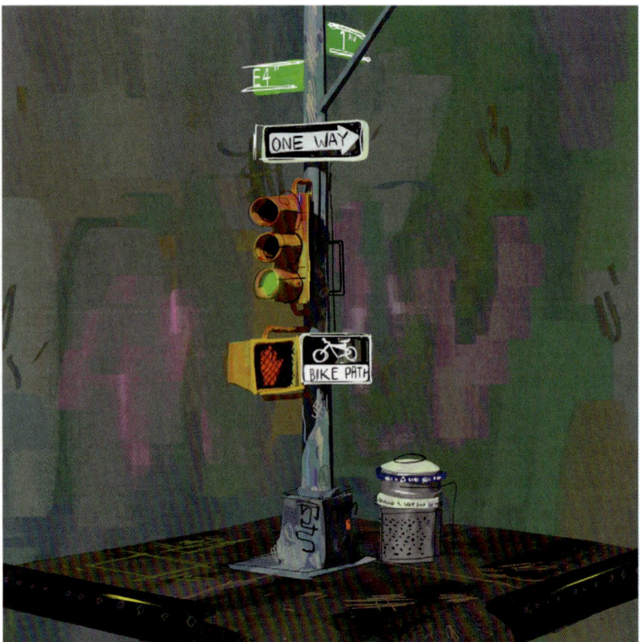

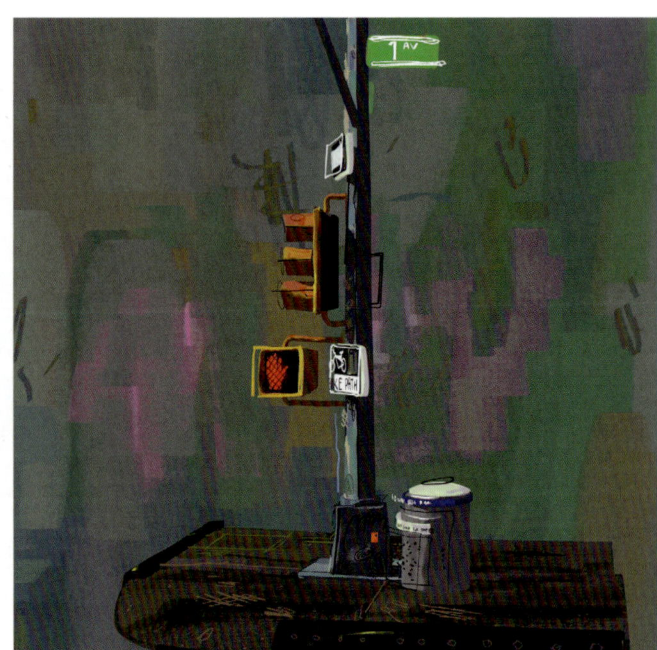

Our matte painting team, this guy Arnaud [Philippe-giraux] who's in Paris is just a brilliant matte painting genius who just embraced the style and is really carrying a lot of weight. People would be like "Oh wow that really looks like a painting. How'd you do that?" and I'd say "It *is* a painting!" We just painted the background like you would a 2D background.

Jim: What about some of the more fanciful locations? You have schools and chop shops, sure, but you also have things like the TCRI building and the sewers.

Jeff: Tiffany Lam Almack, our art director, really took the lead on the whole TCRI part of the film. We tried versions that were slick, chrome, futuristic. We tried versions that were eastern European brutalist architecture. Nothing felt as exciting to us as the original Technodrome toy from the early '90s. The whitish beige gray colors and the purples and the plastics and the weird chunky squares and shapes and the outdated sci-fi design on instrument panels. Every time we did that it felt like TMNT and not like we were trying to be cooler than the franchise inherently is.

As far as the sewers, they were hard. That's a thing you don't realize when you're a kid. It's like, it would just smell terrible, and they'd be living in human filth, and a sewer is a disgusting place. So, how do we, in a film where we prioritize naturalism and authenticity, how do we have sewers and be realistic about them and make them feel like real sewers but also without them being disgusting. A lot of that is through color and set dressing and really making it feel lived in. Everything in the sewer home is something that Splinter could have conceivably found in a pile of trash sitting outside someone's apartment and stolen and cobbled together. We tried to have him put a lot of love into the environment and make it feel as much like a home as you can with those kind of pieces.

Jim: I love the imagery of a giant kaiju battle at the end of the film with an absolutely enormous amalgam of zoo animals and marine life. How did that come about?

Jeff: We were trying to figure out "What's act three? How do we make it big?" I think I do this at some point in every three-act structure thing I've ever written or worked on where I'm like "Well, act three needs to be bigger! Is it a giant monster?" I guess I just love giant monsters. We had tossed around the idea of that being the thing and I don't think Seth and Evan were like "Yeah that's what it should be!" It was kind of just an idea out there, and I was like, "Woodrow, go just design a thing, like maybe Evan's pitch."

Backing up, at this point in the outline there was the Stockman character who cares about science, and then there was another villain character. Evan was like "Maybe the Rat King just gets a bunch of ooze and he's just doing anti-science and he's just like hosing down a bunch of zoo animals and they all like mix together into something." I was like, "That's a very funny idea. Woodrow, can you draw a giant monster formed out of every animal imaginable." So, he did that drawing and my mission became to put this in the film at all costs. This is so complex, it's so difficult, it'll be so hard to do, and that's what'll make it amazing, so we have to do it.

Jim: Honestly, it all sounds amazing. I'm really looking forward to watching the movie. I know you gotta bounce, thanks for carving out a moment to talk to me.

Jeff: Any time.

Below: Concept art by Woodrow White

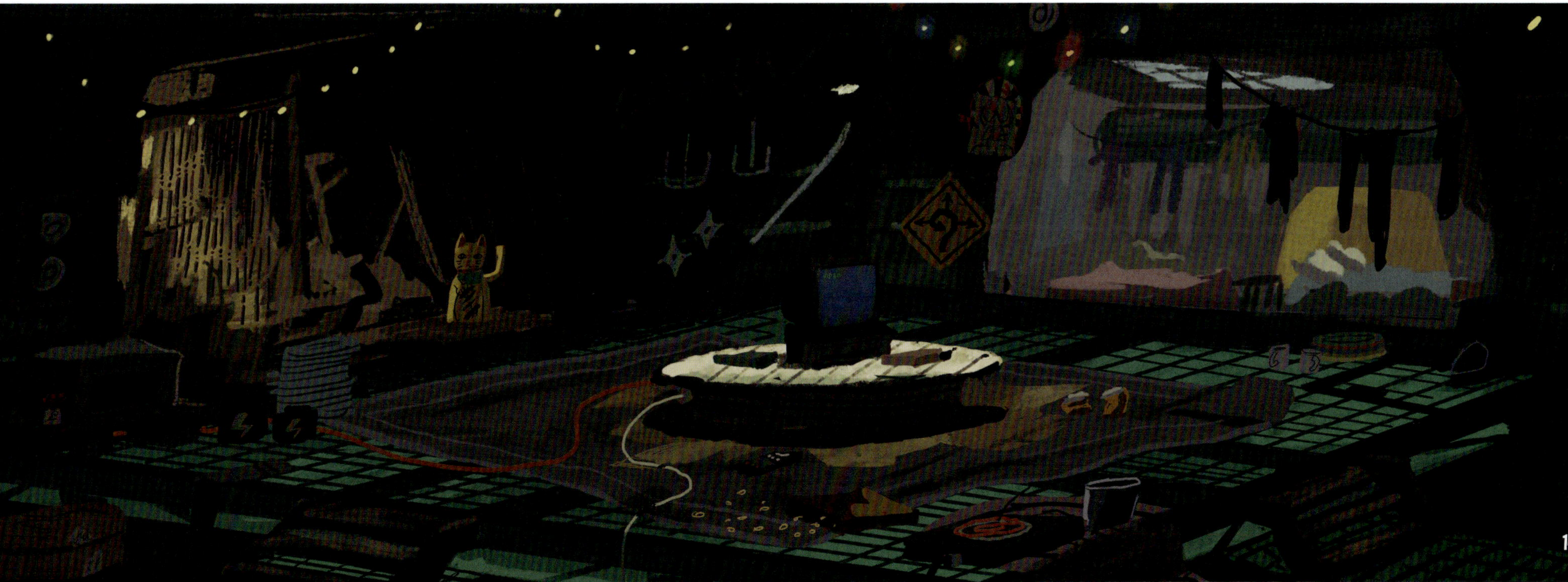

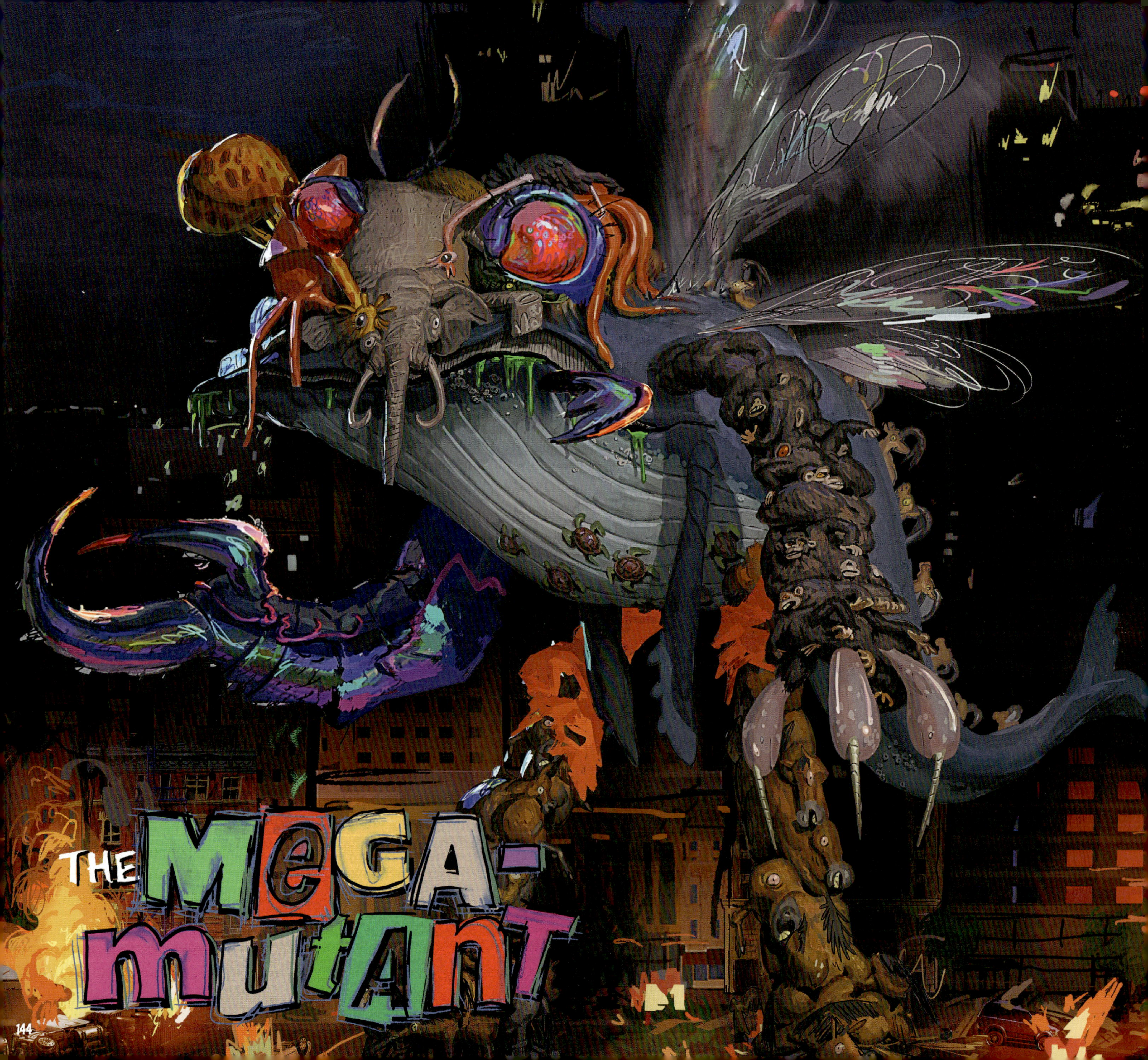
THE MEGA-
mutANT

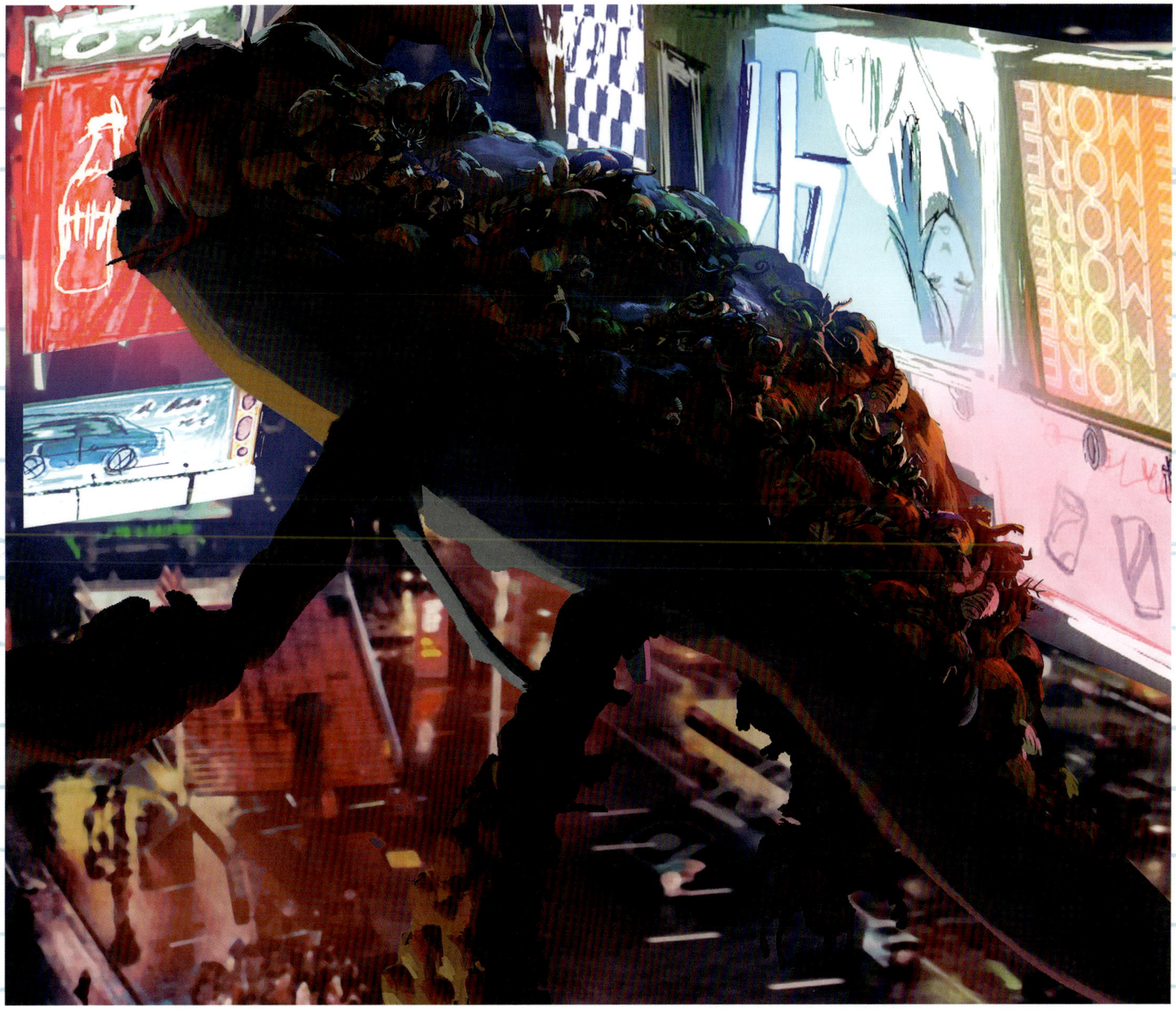

"The Megamutant has survived many drafts, and I'm so excited it has remained. Basically, it's a giant mutant that's made up of smaller animals, and that's how it was pitched to me—a giant mutant made of different animals fused together. They were like 'go have fun.'"

-Lead Character Designer Woodrow White

Above: Concept art by Yashar Kassai
Below: Early concept art by Yashar Kassai
Opposite: Character art by Yashar Kassai, Woodrow White, and Sean Sevestre
Opposite: Background art by Tiffany Lam Almack

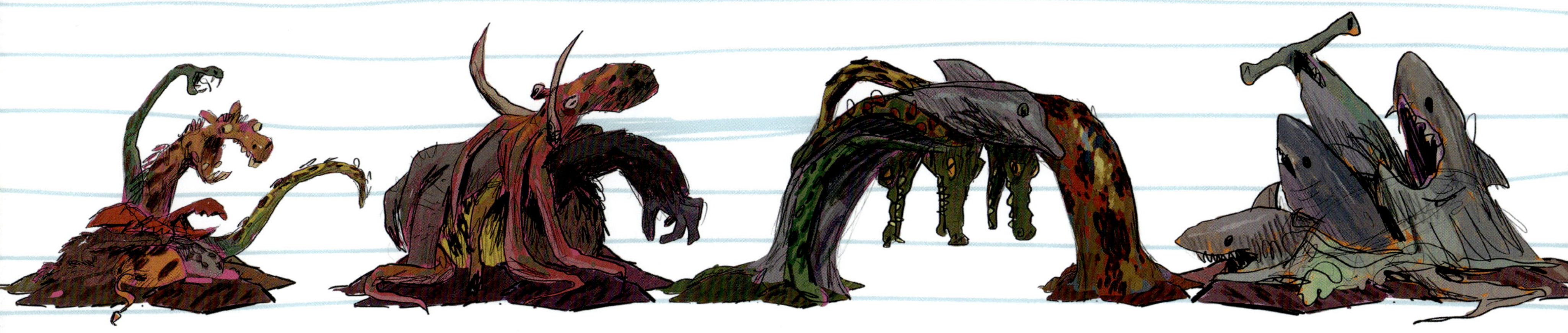

Above: Character expression by James A. Castillo, paint by Sean Sevestre
Below Left: Crustacean arm concept art by Yashar Kassai
Below Right: Mammal arm concept art by Woodrow White

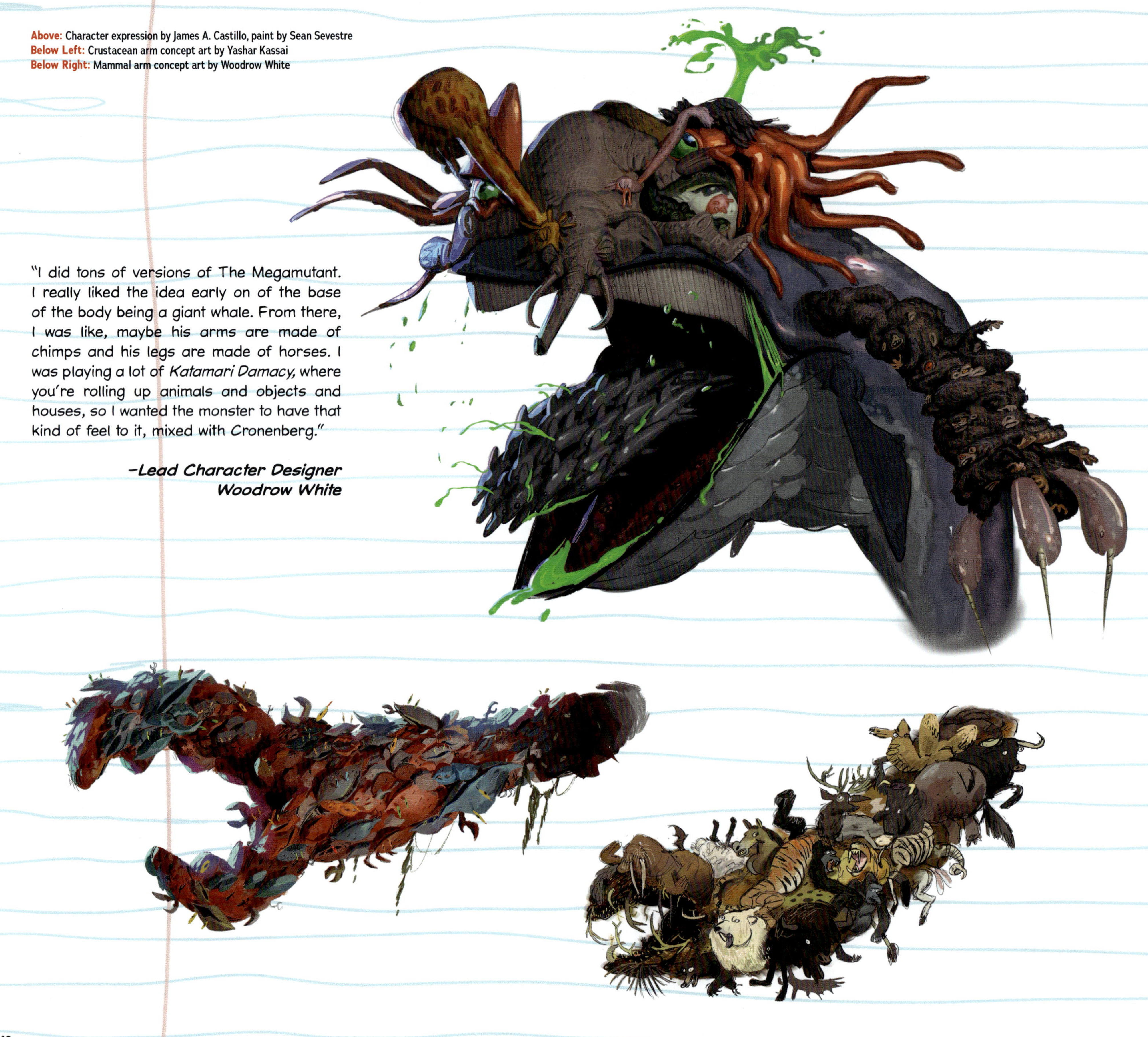

"I did tons of versions of The Megamutant. I really liked the idea early on of the base of the body being a giant whale. From there, I was like, maybe his arms are made of chimps and his legs are made of horses. I was playing a lot of *Katamari Damacy,* where you're rolling up animals and objects and houses, so I wanted the monster to have that kind of feel to it, mixed with Cronenberg."

–Lead Character Designer Woodrow White

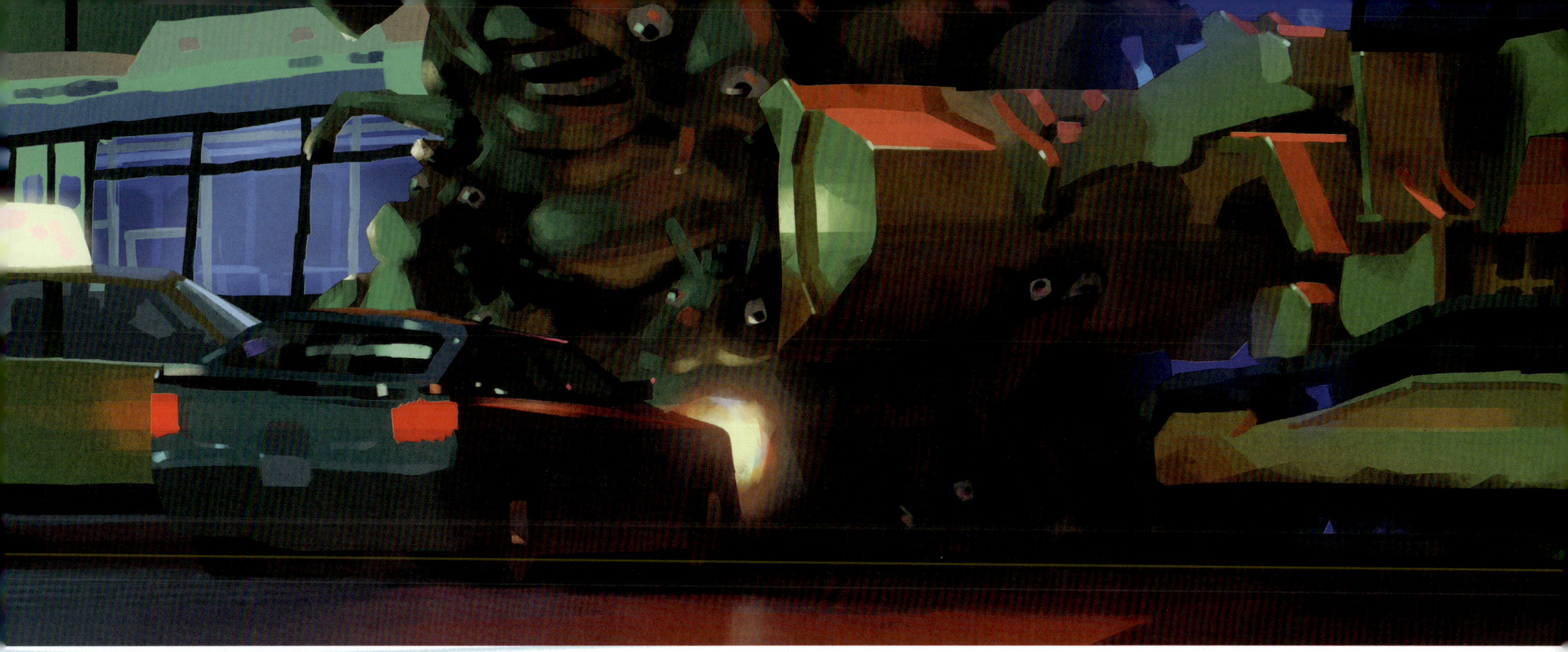

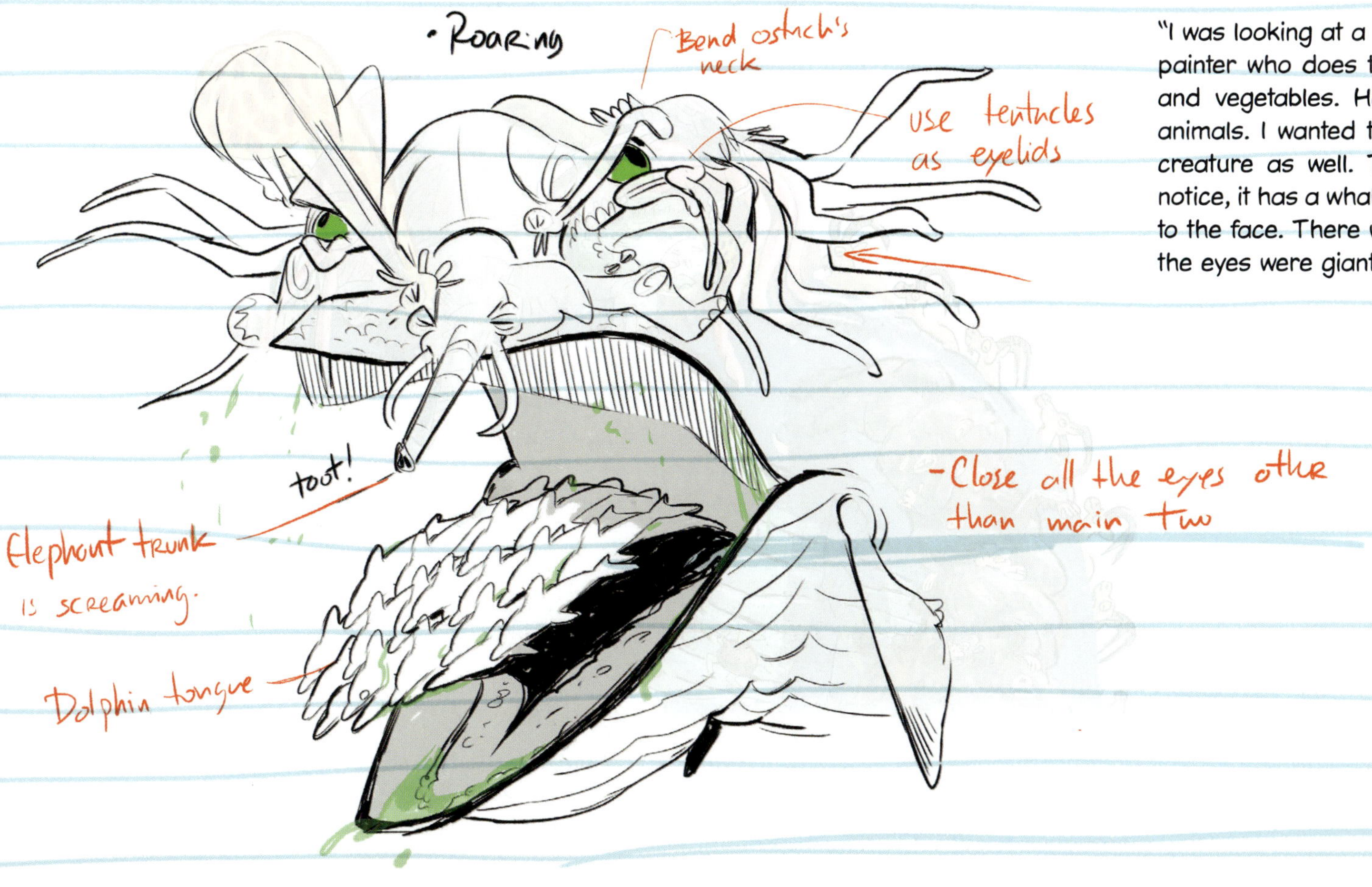

"I was looking at a lot of Giuseppe Arcimboldo. He's an Italian painter who does these portraits of faces made up of fruits and vegetables. He's done portraits of faces made up of animals. I wanted to bring a lot of Arcimboldo energy to the creature as well. That's where the face came from. If you notice, it has a whale's mouth but there are lots of components to the face. There was an eyebrow made from a giraffe neck, the eyes were giant squid eyes, and things like that."

–Lead Character Designer Woodrow White

Above: Key art by Garrett Lee
Below: Character expression art by James A. Castillo

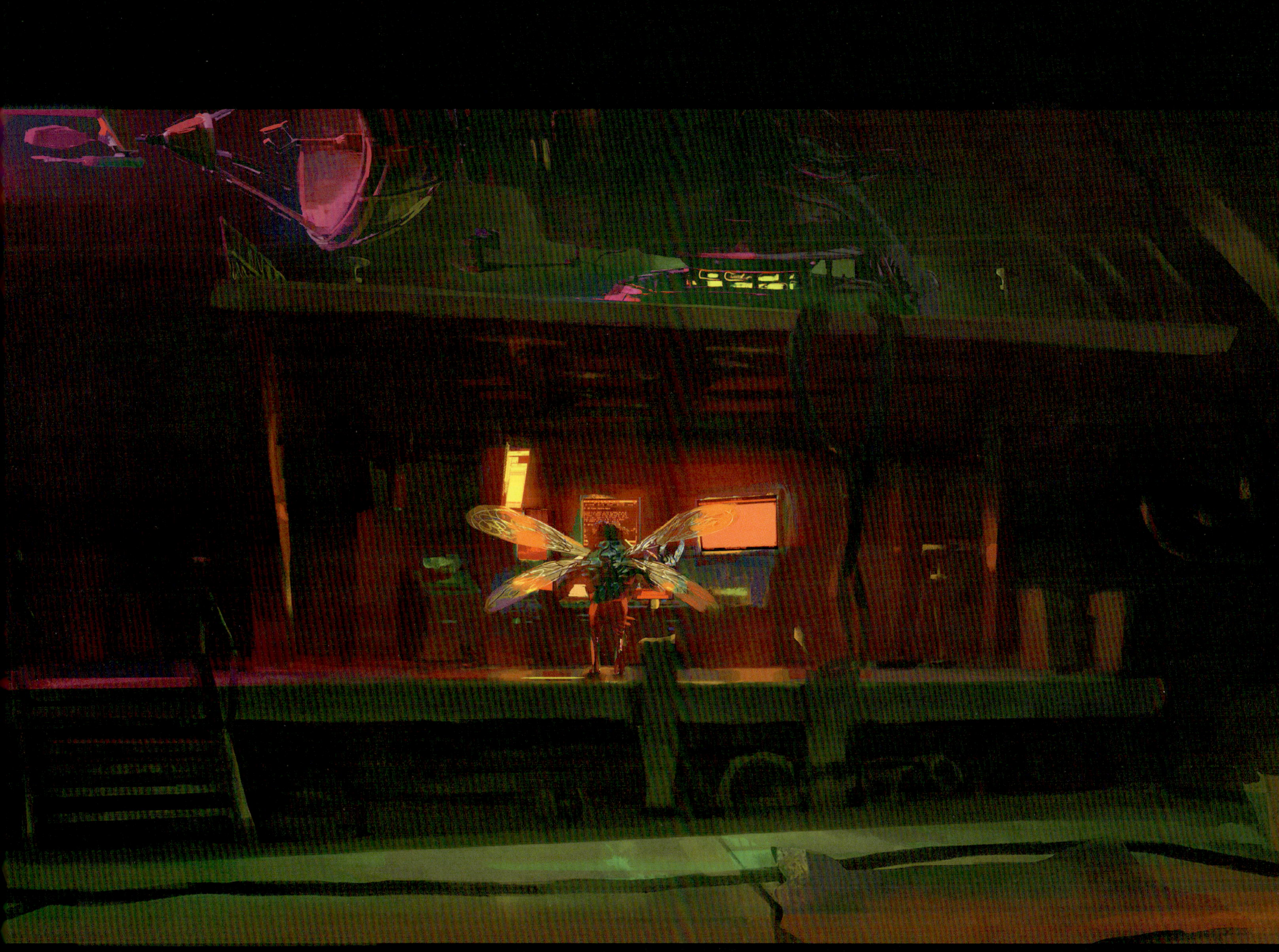

Key art by Yashar Kassai

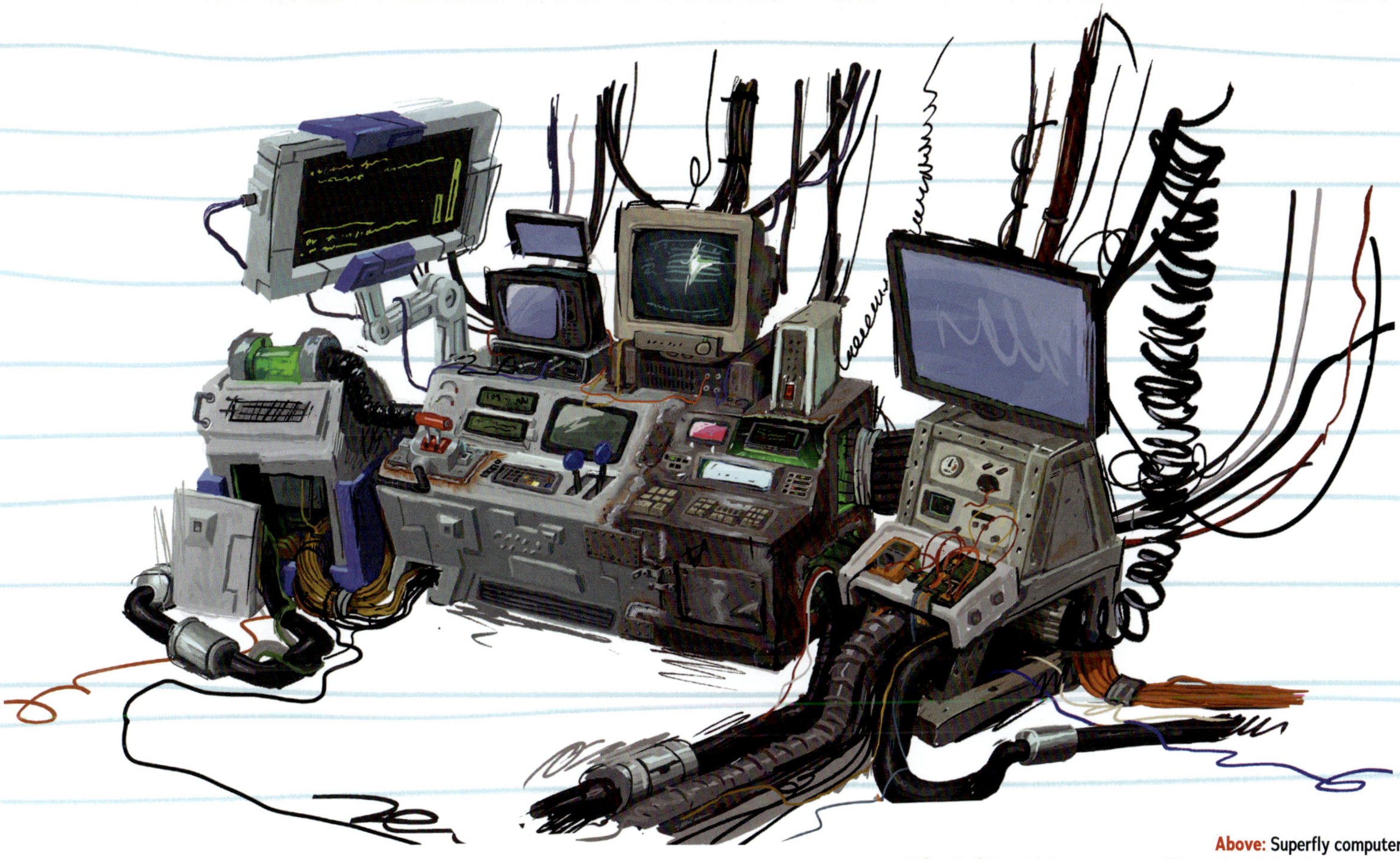

Above: Superfly computer art by Jeffrey Thompson
Below Left: Boat lab computer graphics art by Chalky Wong, motion graphics by Natan Moura
Below Right: Character art by Woodrow White and Tiffany Lam Almack.
Fun fact: this character was voiced by TMNT co-creator Kevin Eastman!

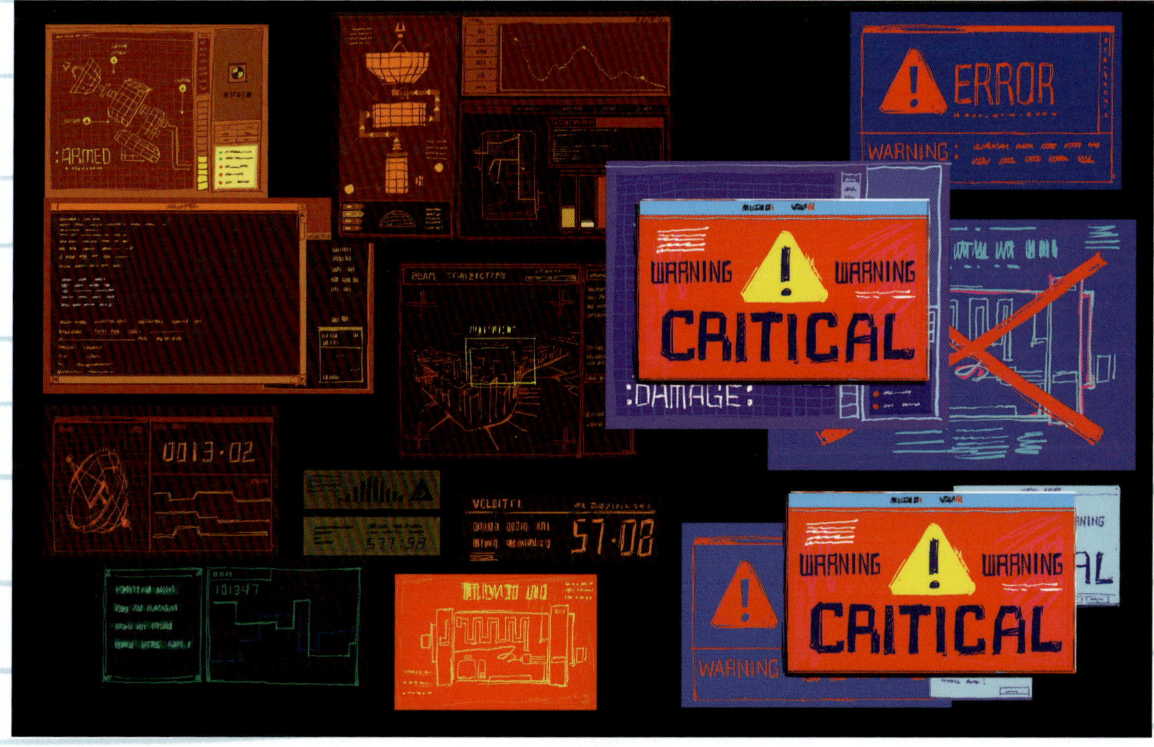

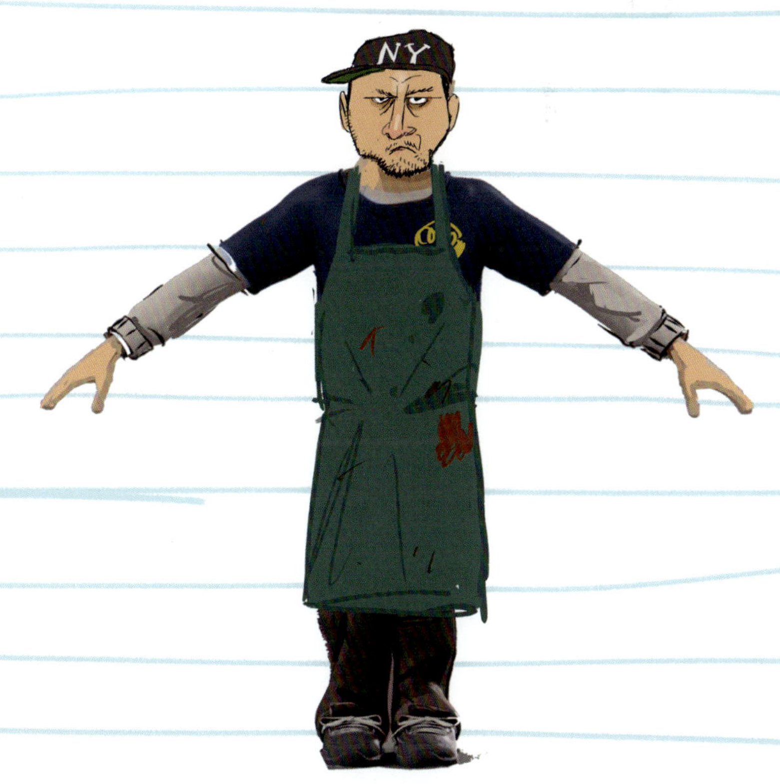

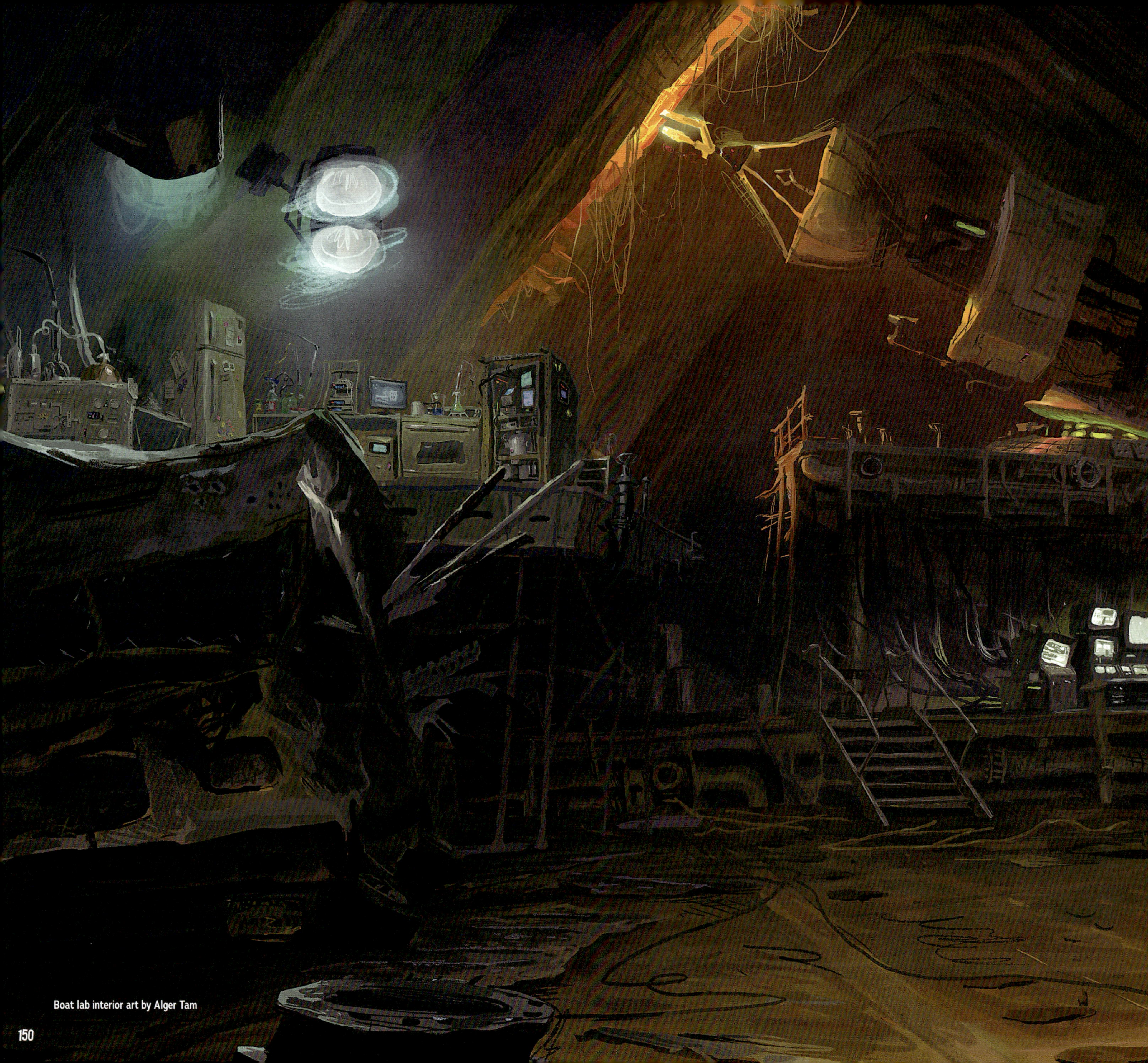

Boat lab interior art by Alger Tam

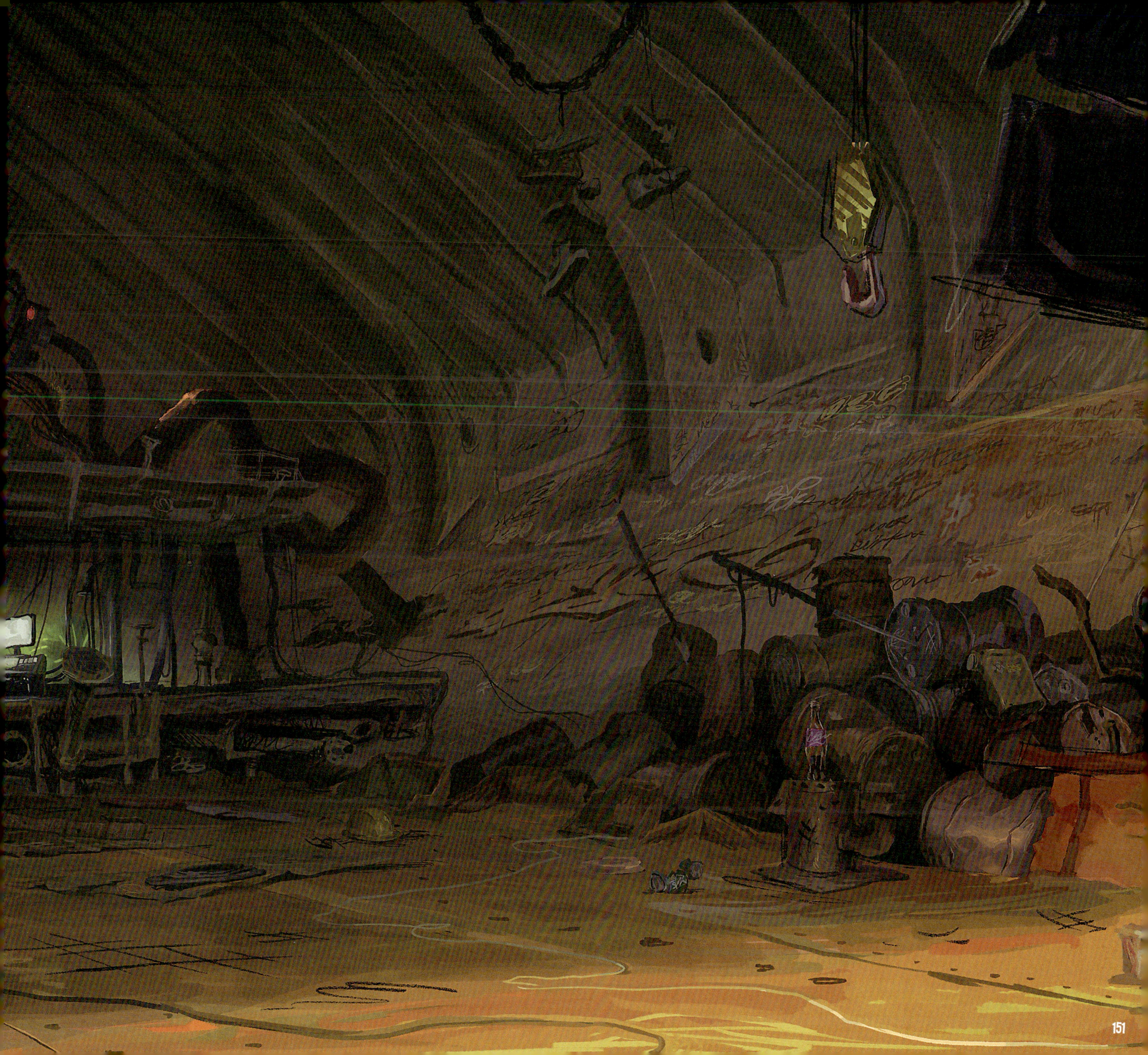

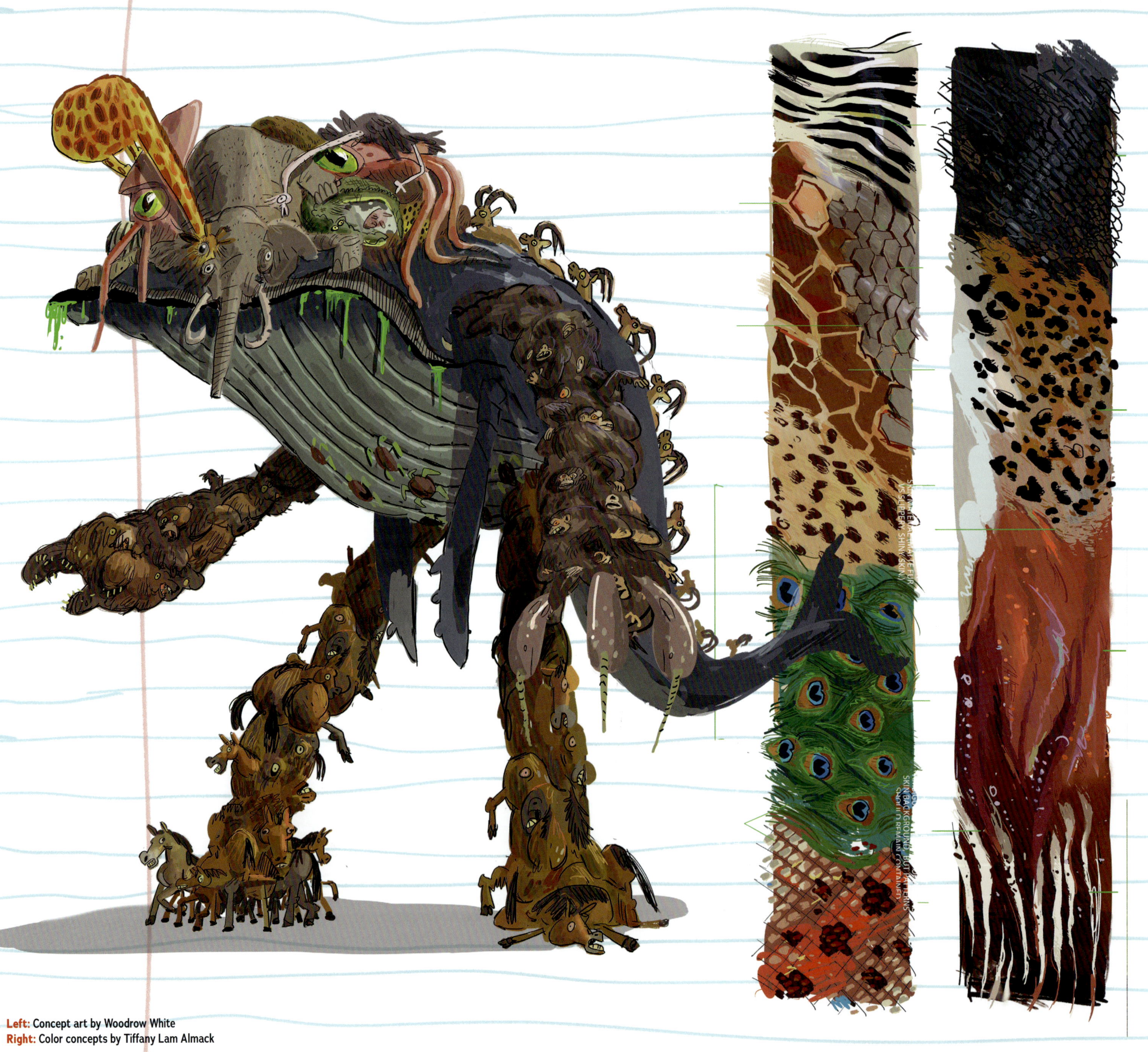

Left: Concept art by Woodrow White
Right: Color concepts by Tiffany Lam Almack

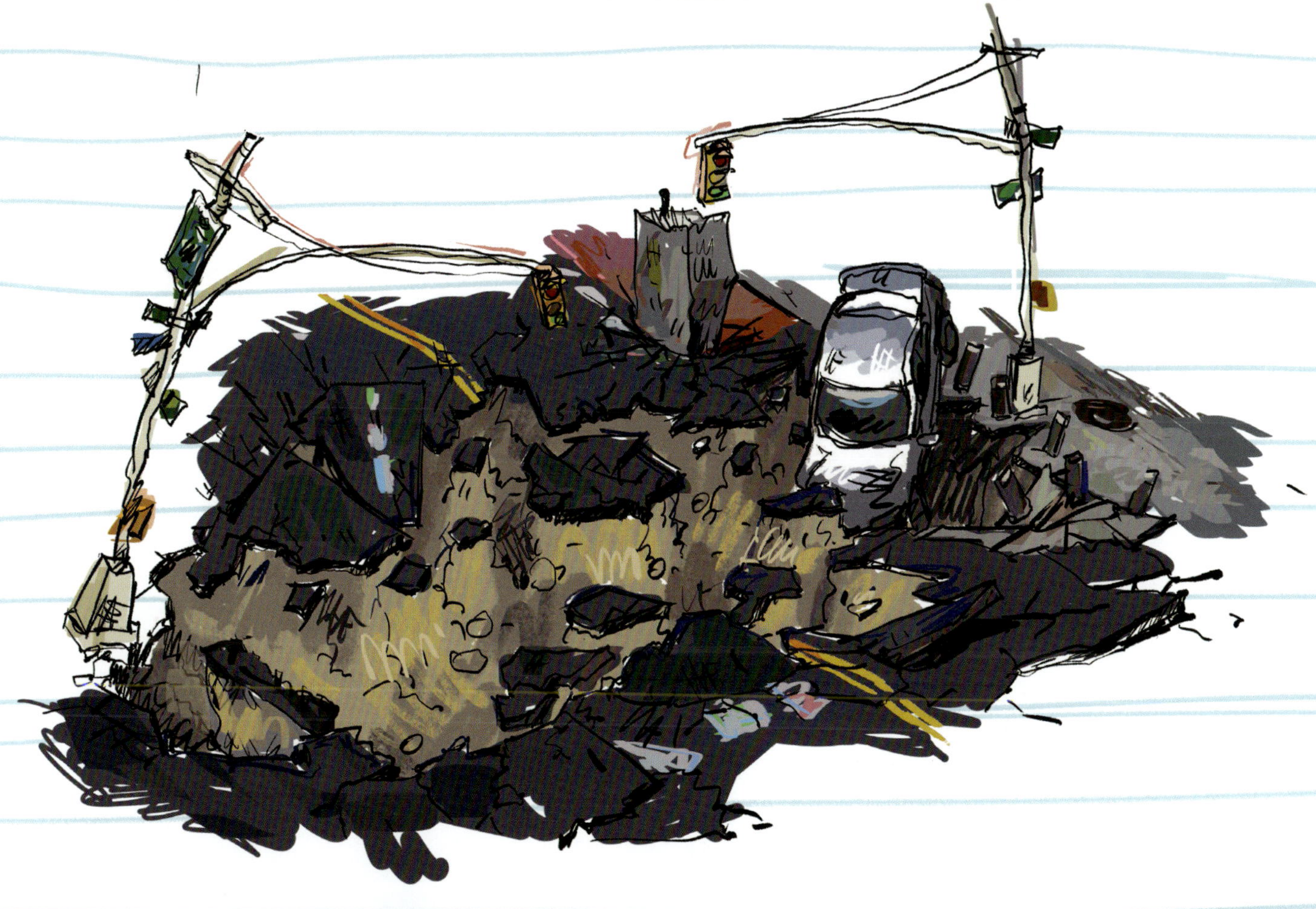

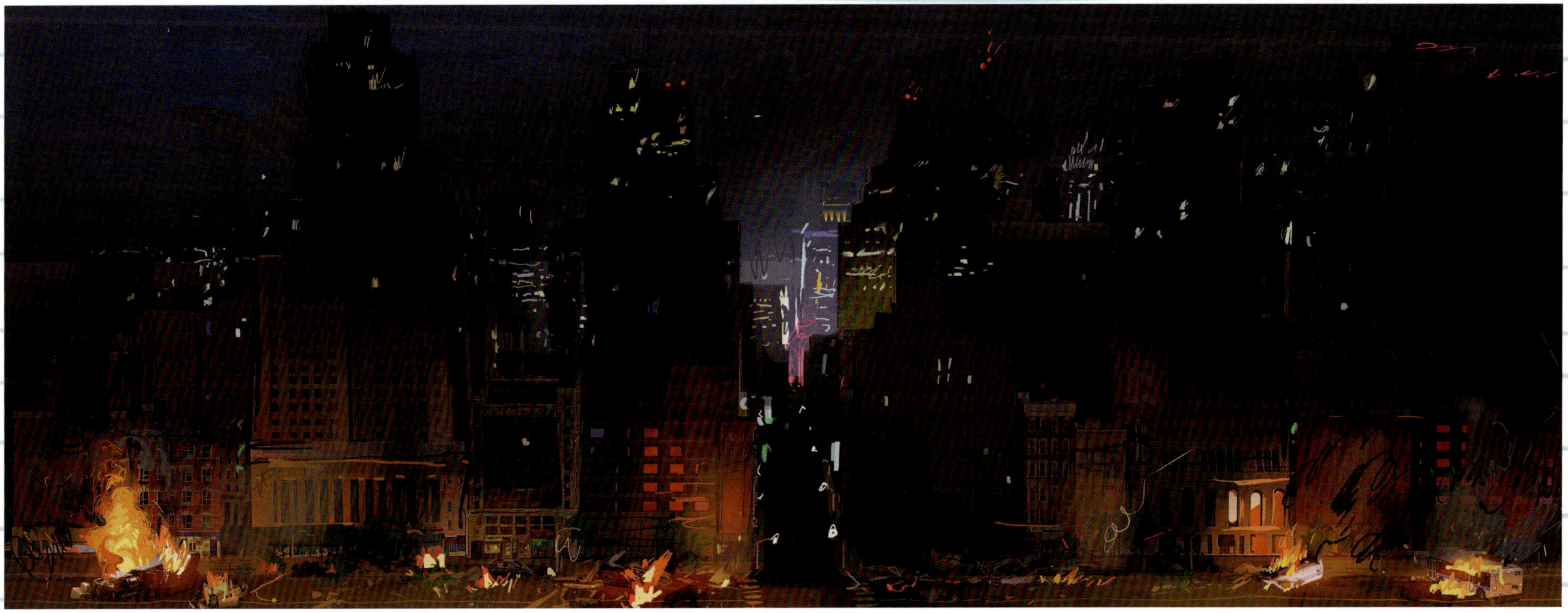

Above: Rubble art by Chalky Wong
Below: City destruction concept art by Tiffany Lam Almack

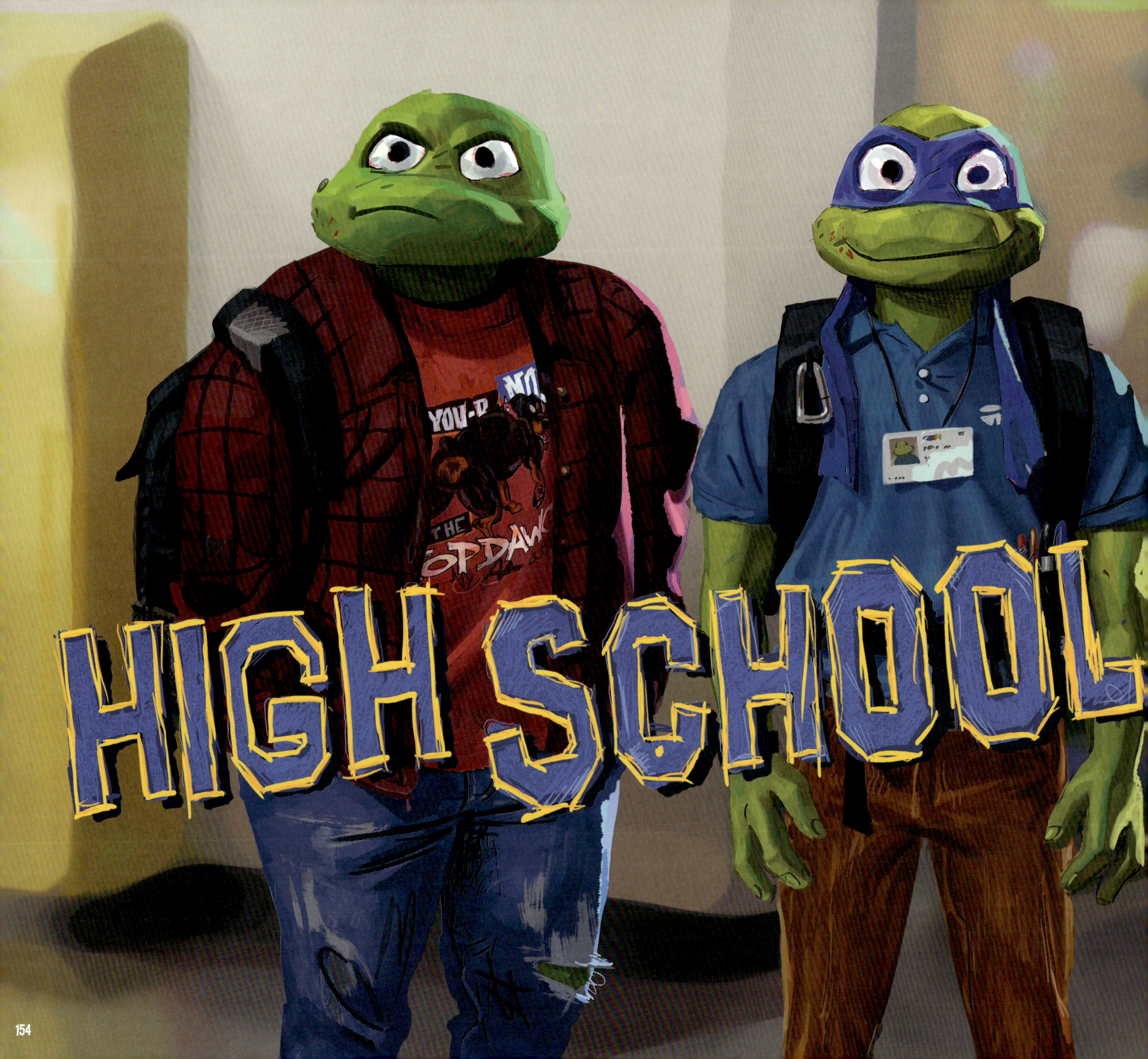
HIGH SCHOOL
YOU-R
THE

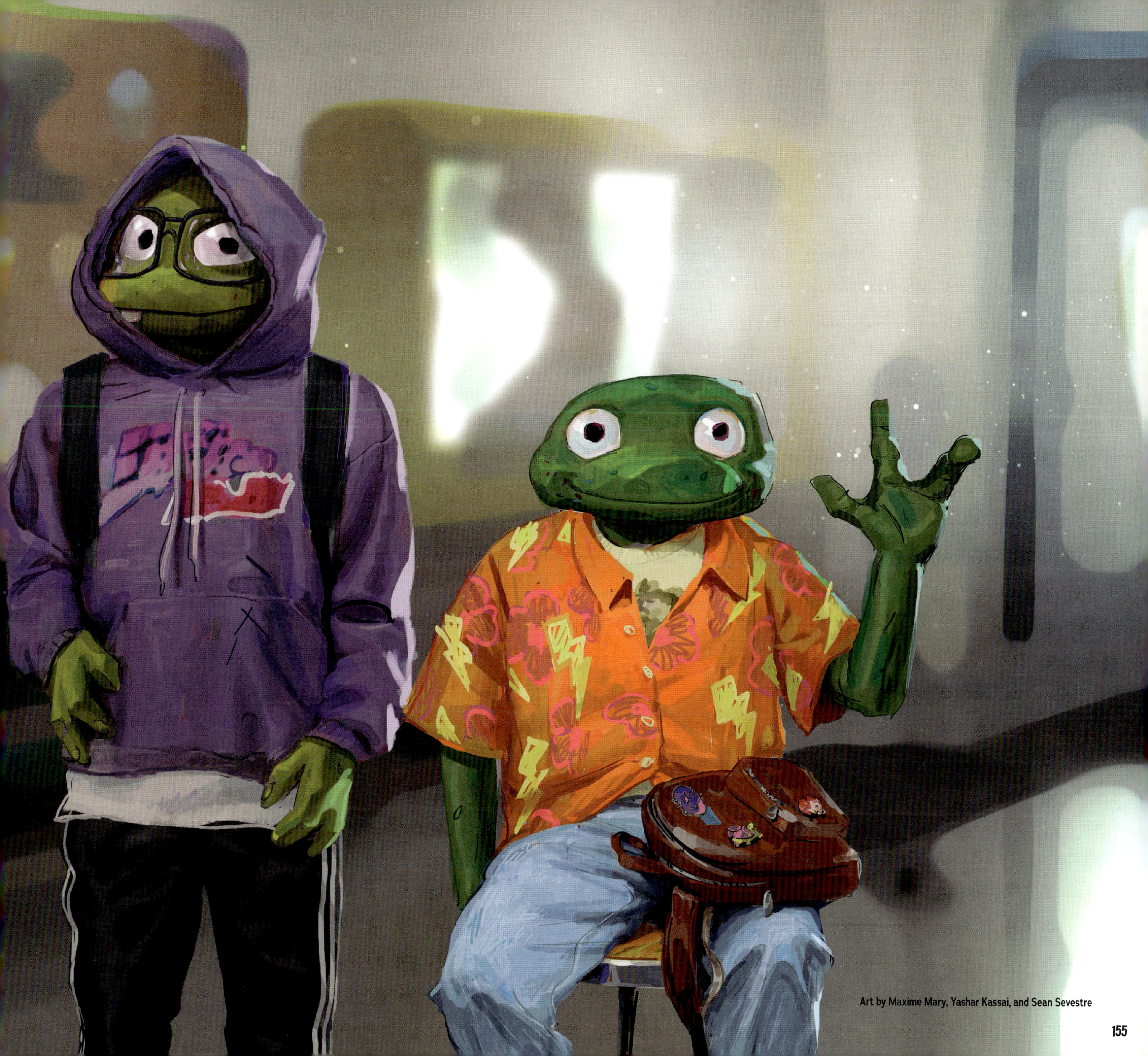

Art by Maxime Mary, Yashar Kassai, and Sean Sevestre

"High school was the whole heart of the original draft of the movie. That kinda got moved to the end of the film. They get their wish: They get to go to high school. Very early on, wanting it to be a high school movie, we were playing with the Turtles in casual street wear dressed like they were going to school versus when they're out on the streets at night as ninja.

Again, we were faithful to the color scheme, giving each of their outfits their respective colors. We really had to think about what these teenage mutant turtles would be as normal teenagers, like they want to be. They want to fit in, they want to find other people like them.

All the Turtles have different characteristics, and we had to consider what that would manifest itself as in a high school setting. So, Leo's a bit of a teacher's pet, Mikey's a class clown, Donnie's the science-nerd anime fan, Raph is, like, the jock."

—Lead Character Designer Woodrow White

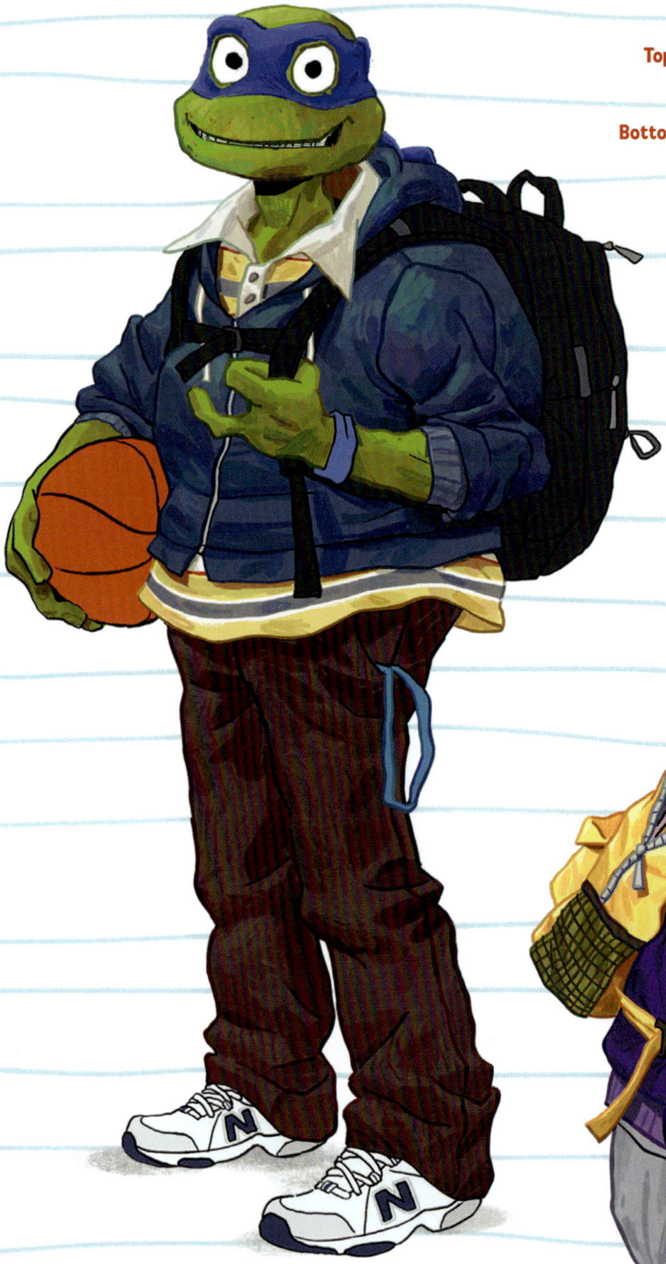

Top Middle: Leonardo student concept art by Woodrow White
Bottom Left: Leonardo student art by Arthur Fong
Bottom Left: Donatello student art by Sean Sevestre
Bottom Right: Donatello student concept art by Woodrow White

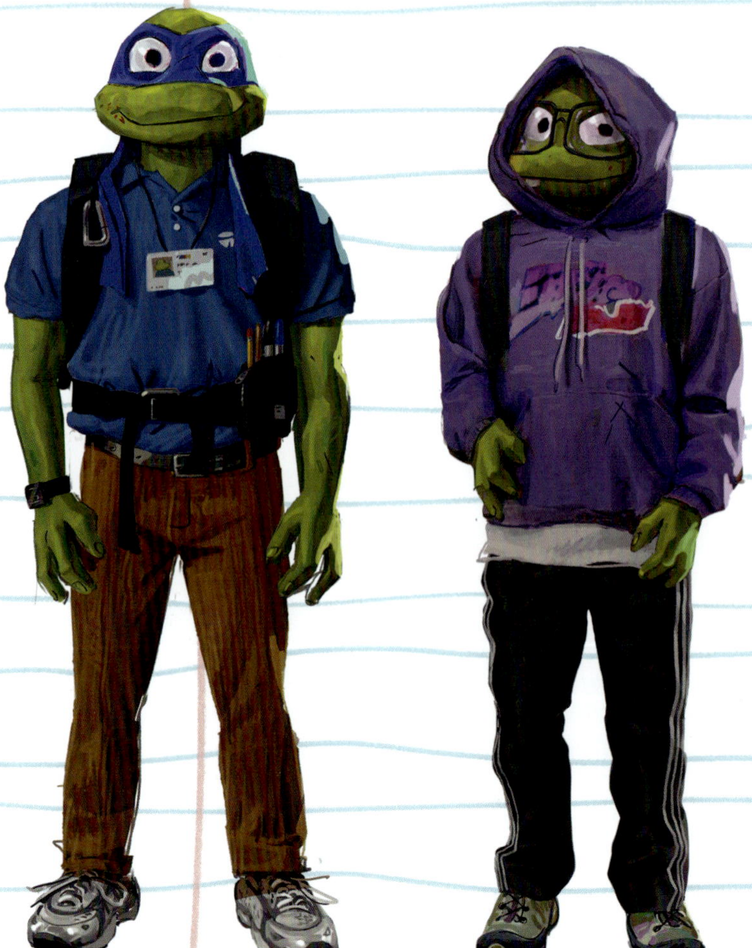

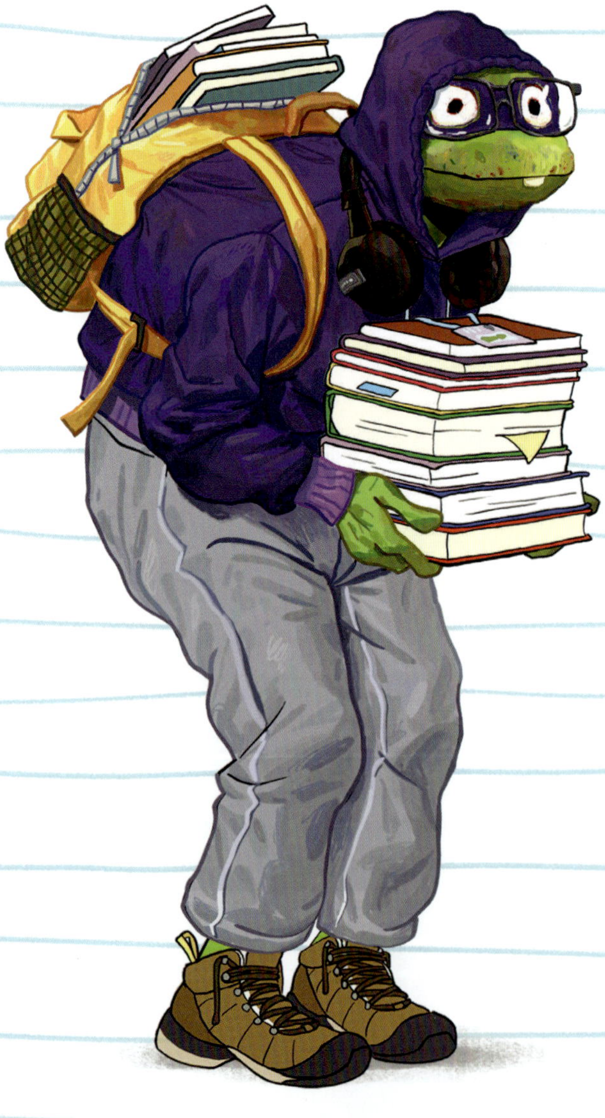

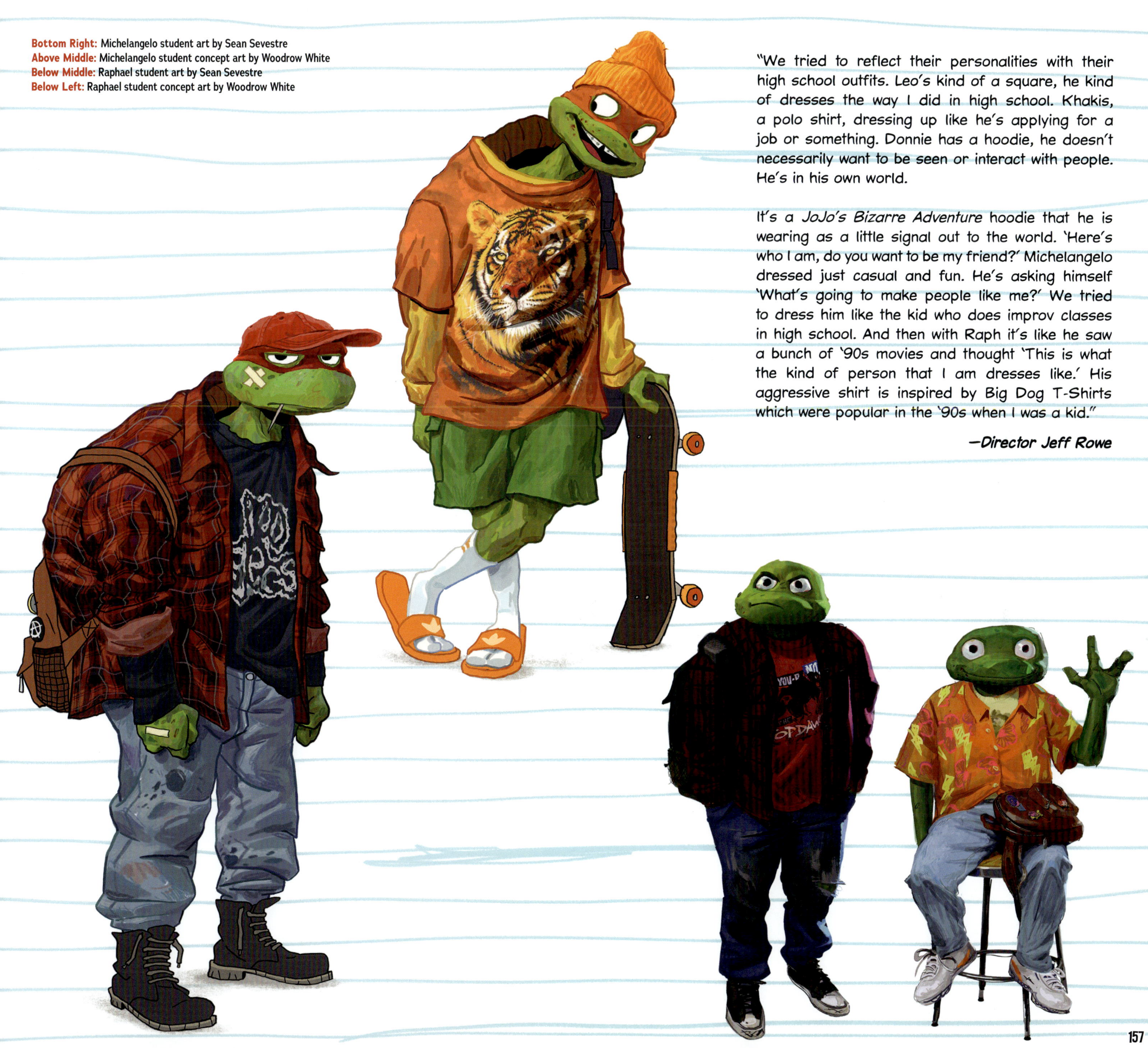

Bottom Right: Michelangelo student art by Sean Sevestre
Above Middle: Michelangelo student concept art by Woodrow White
Below Middle: Raphael student art by Sean Sevestre
Below Left: Raphael student concept art by Woodrow White

"We tried to reflect their personalities with their high school outfits. Leo's kind of a square, he kind of dresses the way I did in high school. Khakis, a polo shirt, dressing up like he's applying for a job or something. Donnie has a hoodie, he doesn't necessarily want to be seen or interact with people. He's in his own world.

It's a *JoJo's Bizarre Adventure* hoodie that he is wearing as a little signal out to the world. 'Here's who I am, do you want to be my friend?' Michelangelo dressed just casual and fun. He's asking himself 'What's going to make people like me?' We tried to dress him like the kid who does improv classes in high school. And then with Raph it's like he saw a bunch of '90s movies and thought 'This is what the kind of person that I am dresses like.' His aggressive shirt is inspired by Big Dog T-Shirts which were popular in the '90s when I was a kid."

—Director Jeff Rowe

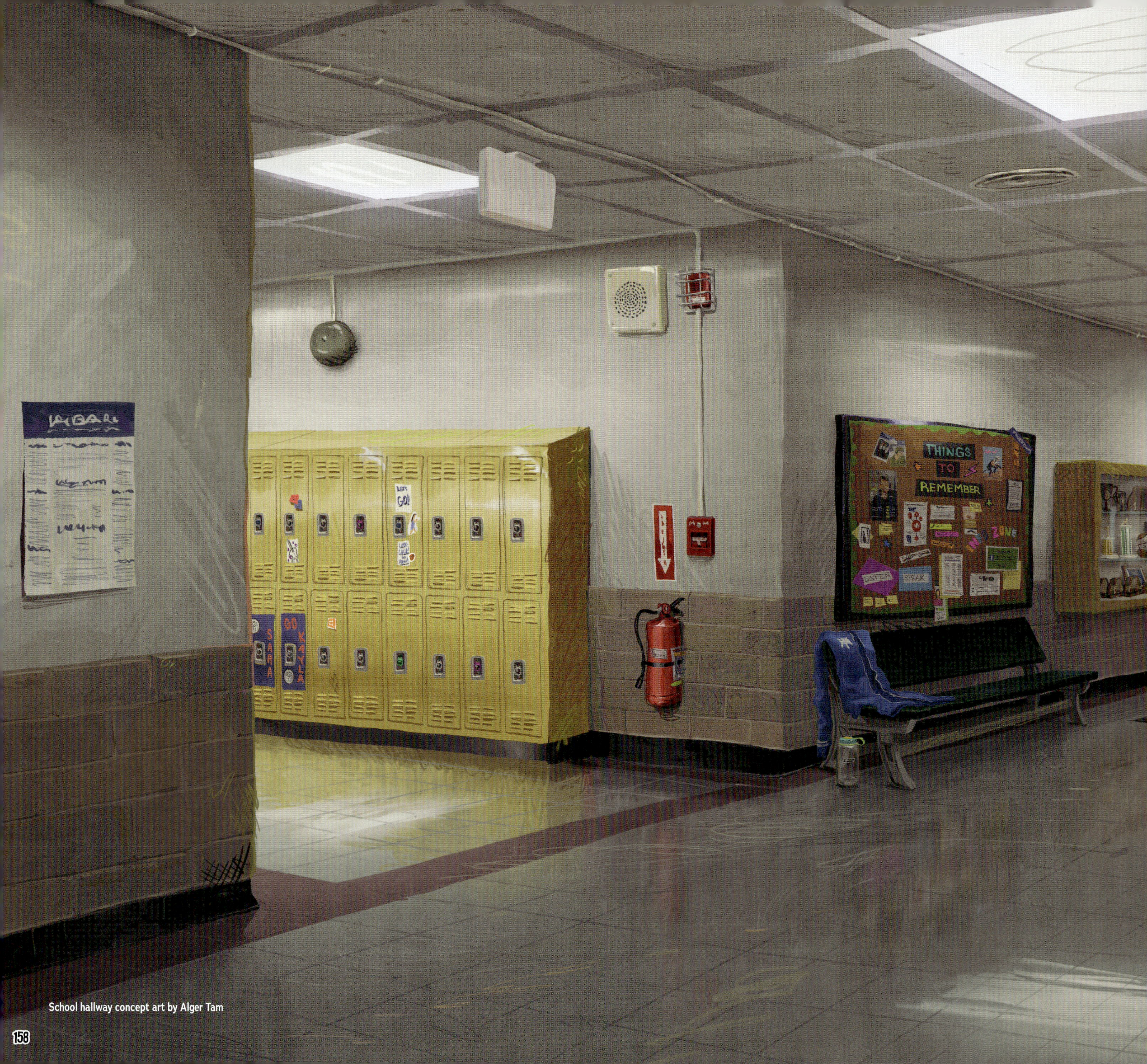

School hallway concept art by Alger Tam

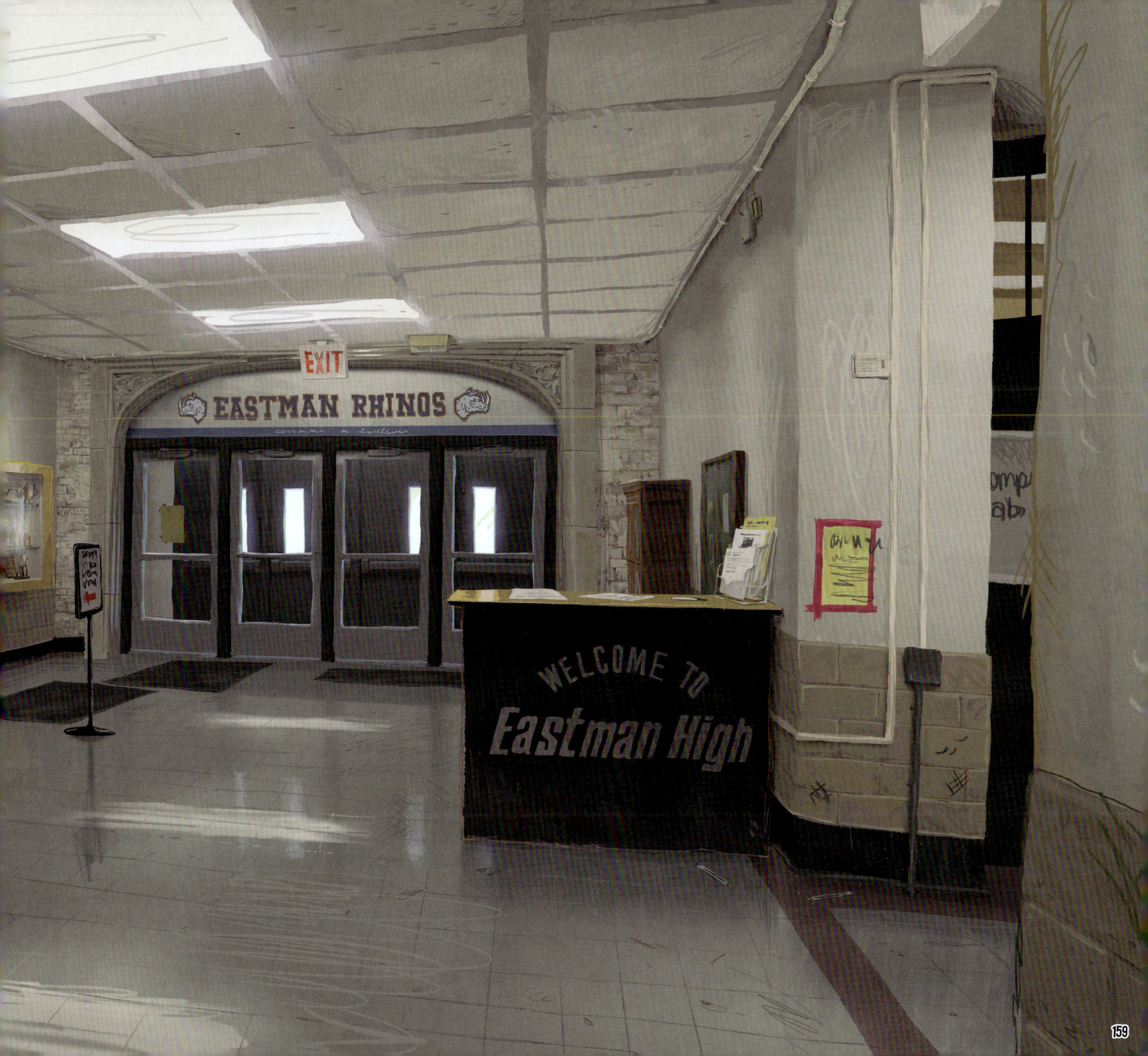
EXIT
EASTMAN RHINOS
WELCOME TO
Eastman High

Above: Students concept art by Dustin d'Arnault
Middle: Students concept art by Justin Runfola
Below: Students concept art by Woodrow White

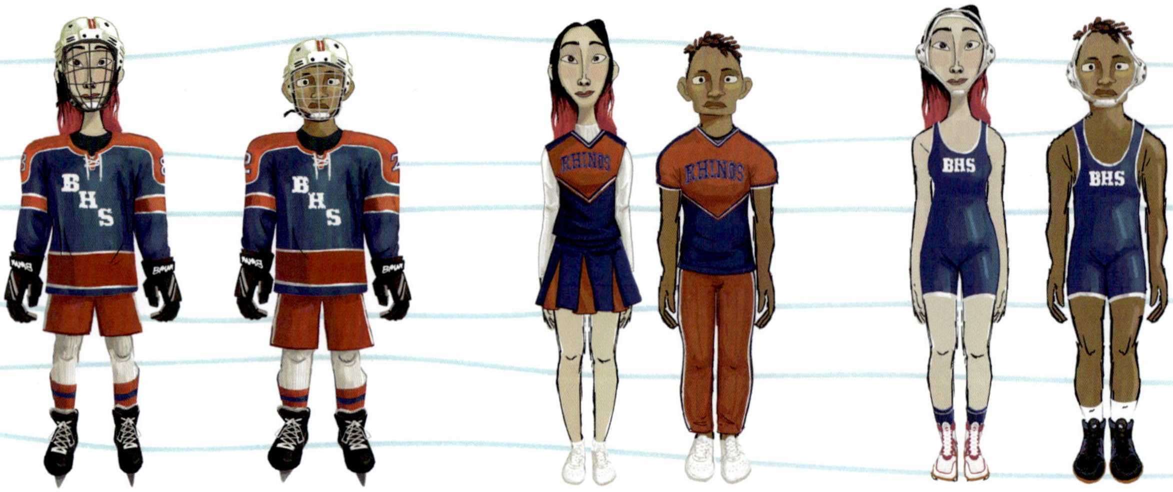

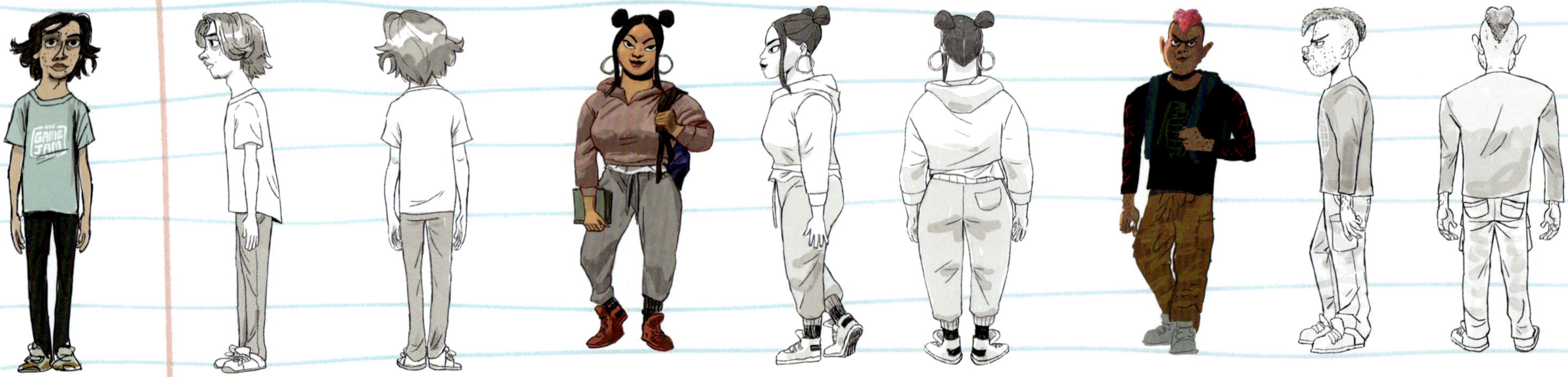

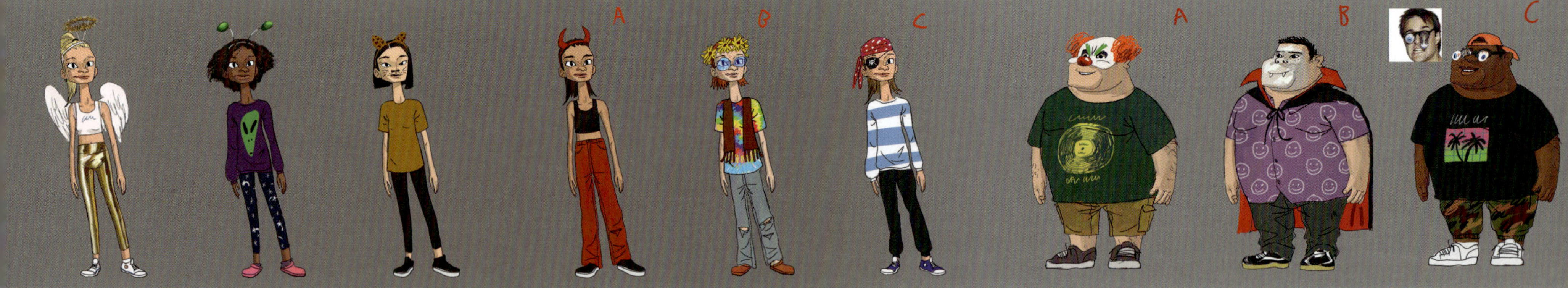

"Something that we really cared about was making sure that we made characters that everybody could say, 'Hey, I know someone exactly like that.' Independently of the aesthetics of the teen age, the process of growing up is universal. Seth Rogen said many times that this is a *Teenage Mutant Ninja Turtles* that focuses more on the teenage part than on the ninja part. Because there was a lot of attention to how the Turtles live their youth, there were a lot of expectations for all the characters that surround them. They needed to feel as developed as the Turtles. As confused, as full of potential, as conflicted as they are. Because they are the characters that the Turtles are going to become friends with, they cannot be just generic background characters. They needed to feel much more genuine."

–Character Designer James A. Castillo

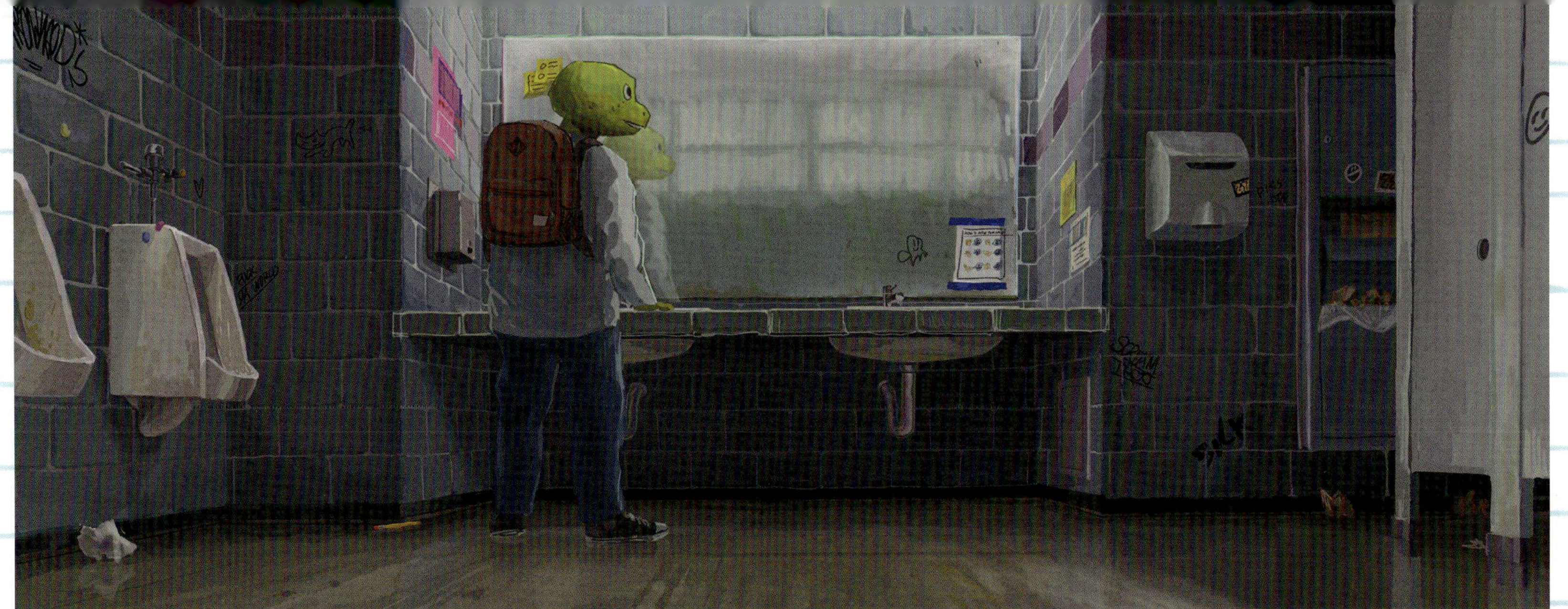

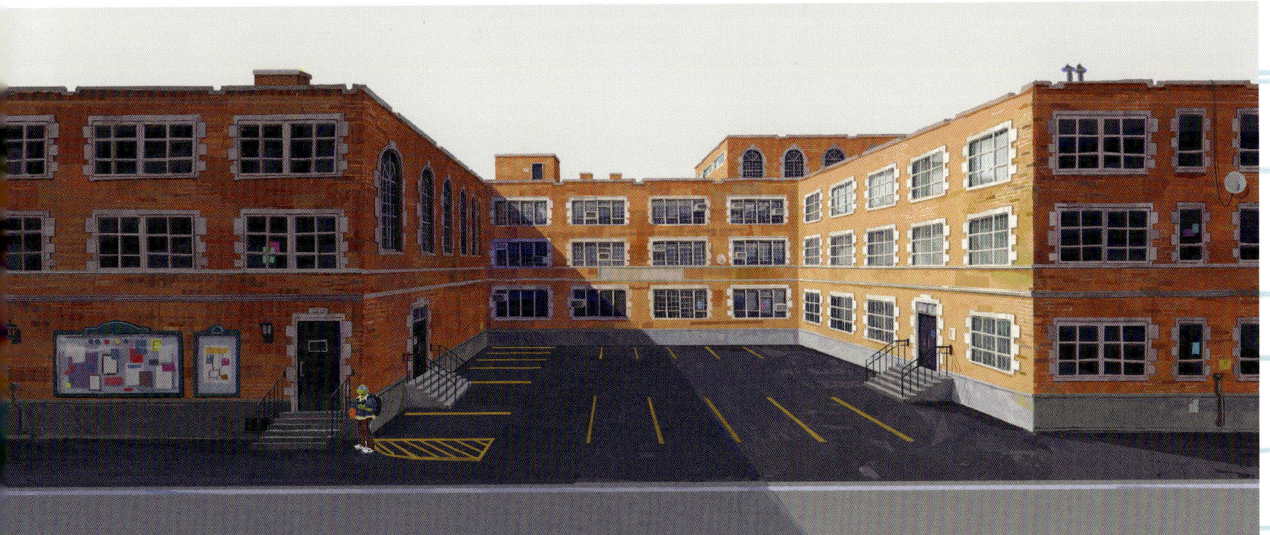

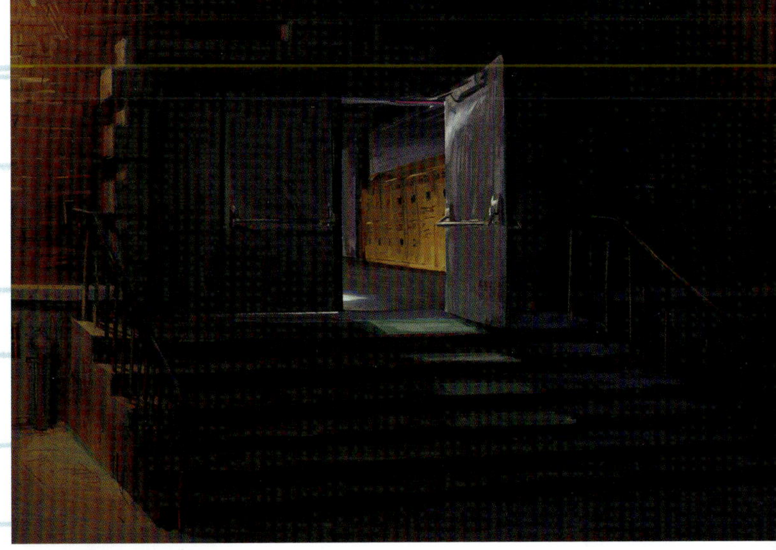

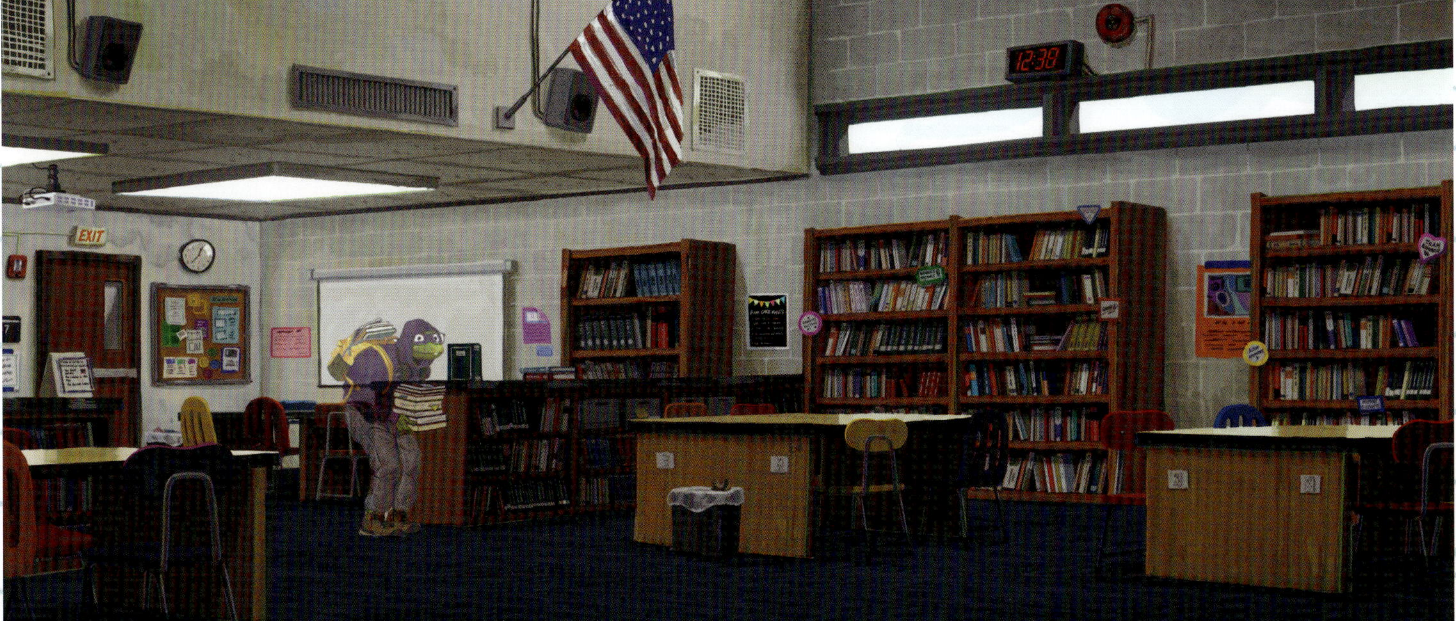

Above: School bathroom concept art by Nikita Chan
Middle Left: School exterior art by Nikita Chan
Middle Right: School exterior concept art by Lily Nishita
Below: School library concept art by Yashar Kassai

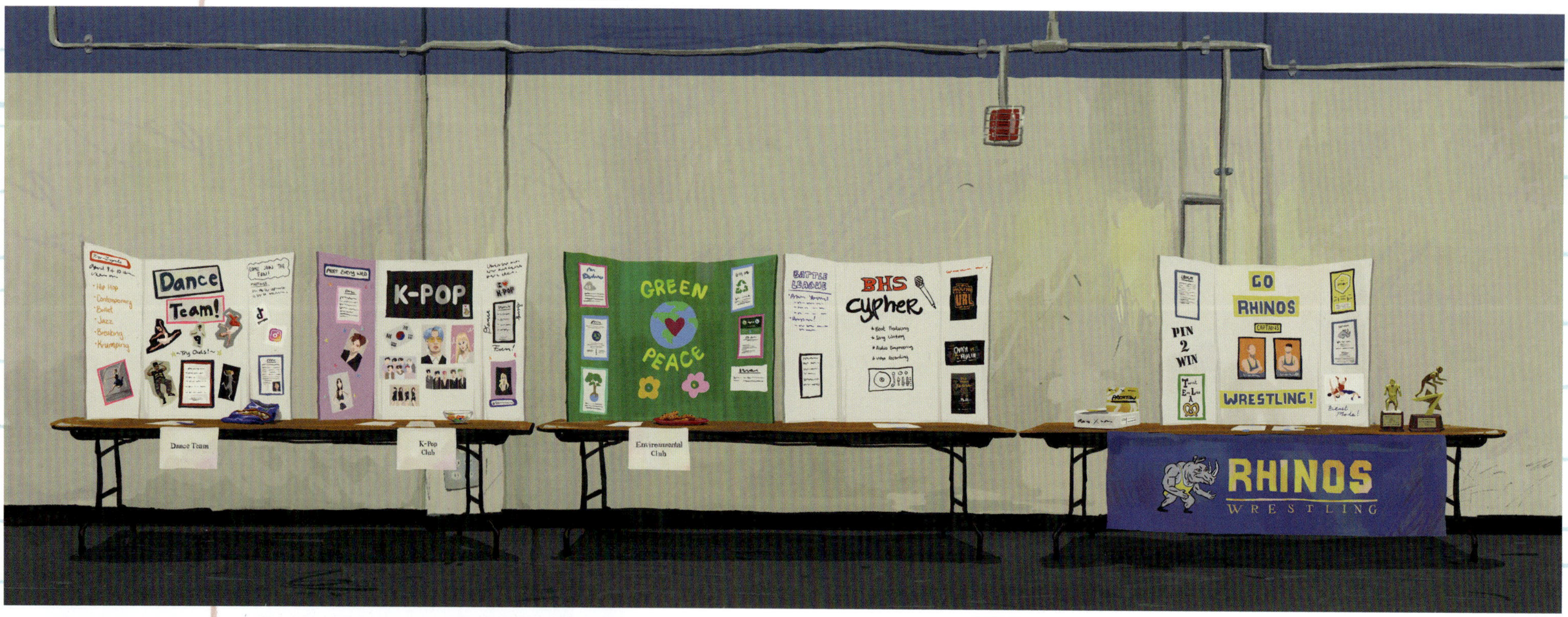

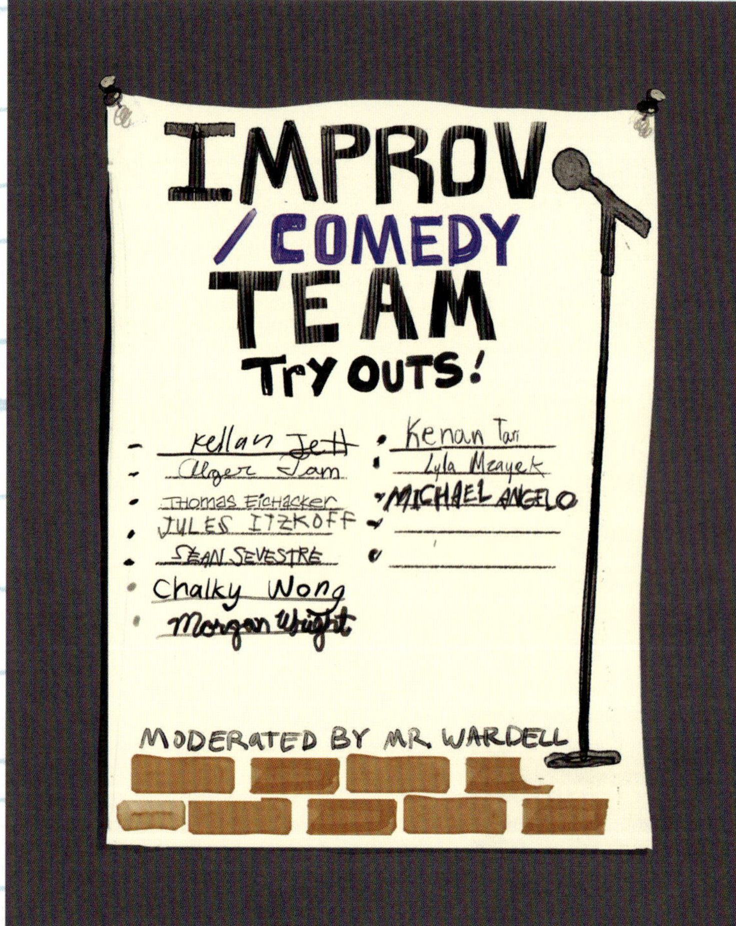

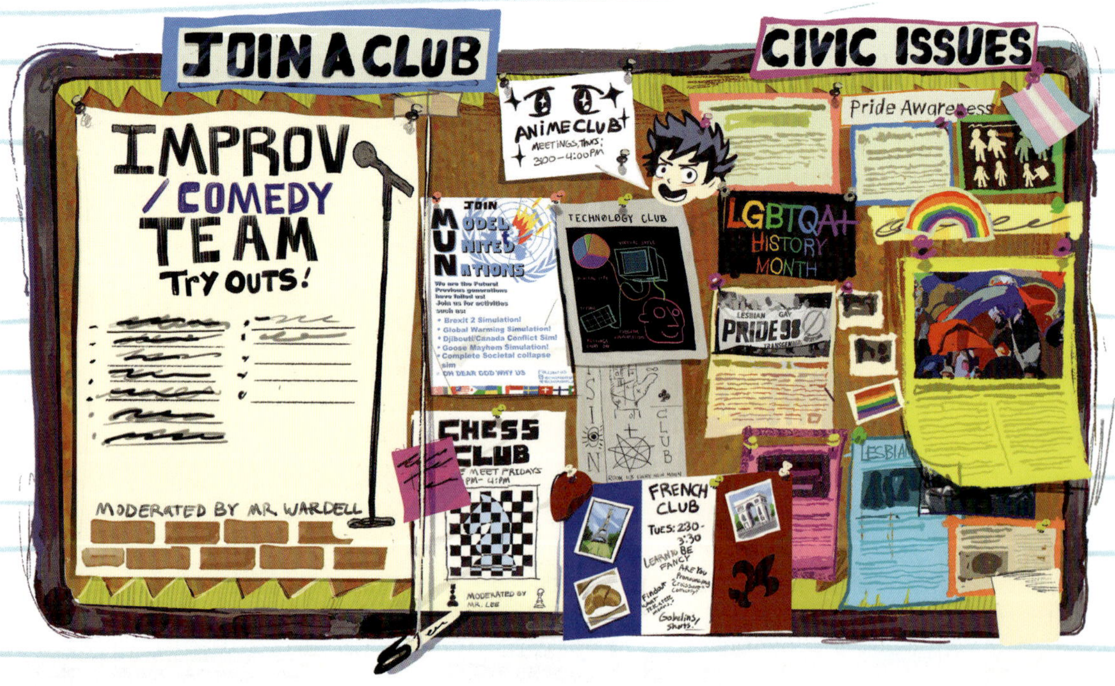

Above: School club fair concept art by Alger Tam
Below Left: School improv/comedy team try outs art by Arthur Fong
Below Right: School bulletin board art by Kellan Jett

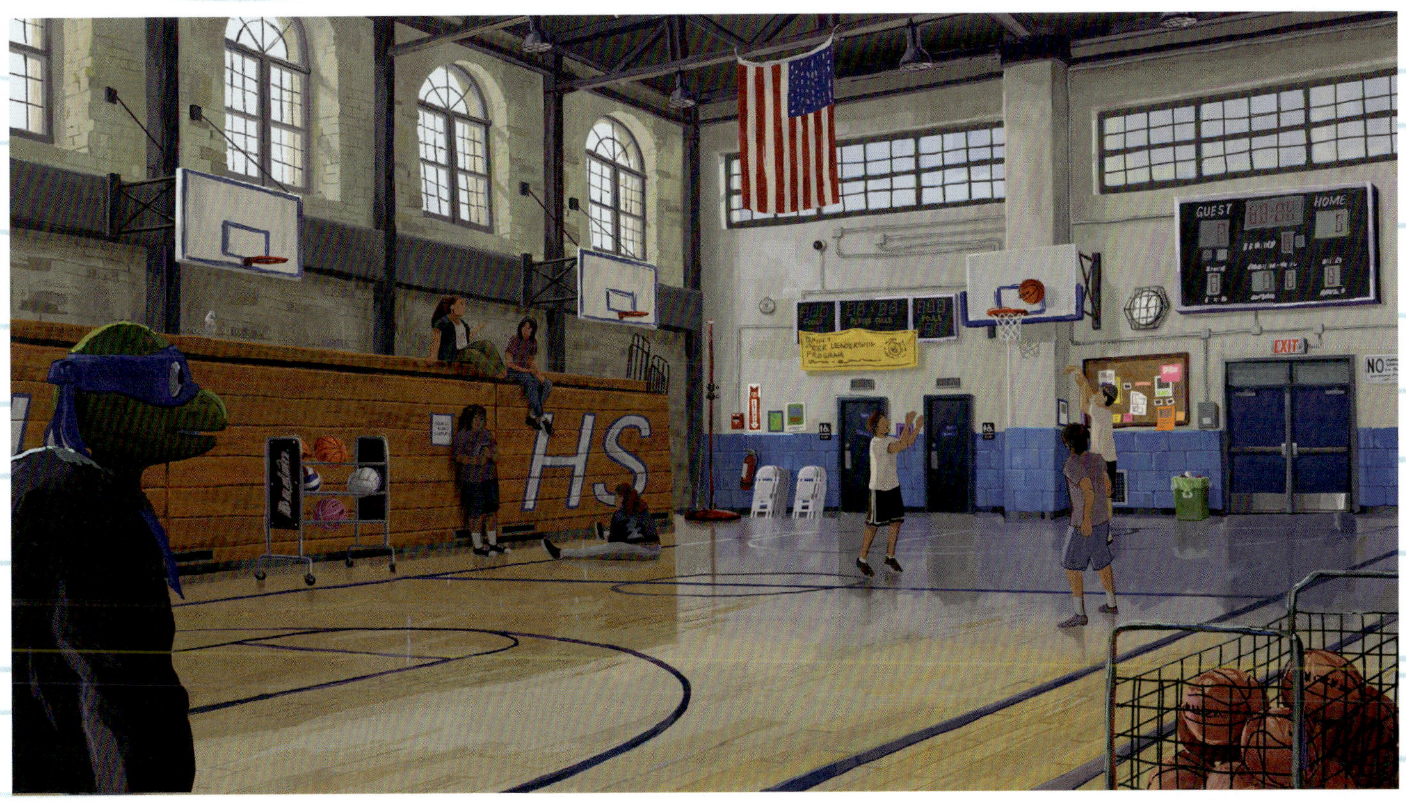

Above: School gym concept art by Nikita Chan
Below: School dance concept art by Nikita Chan

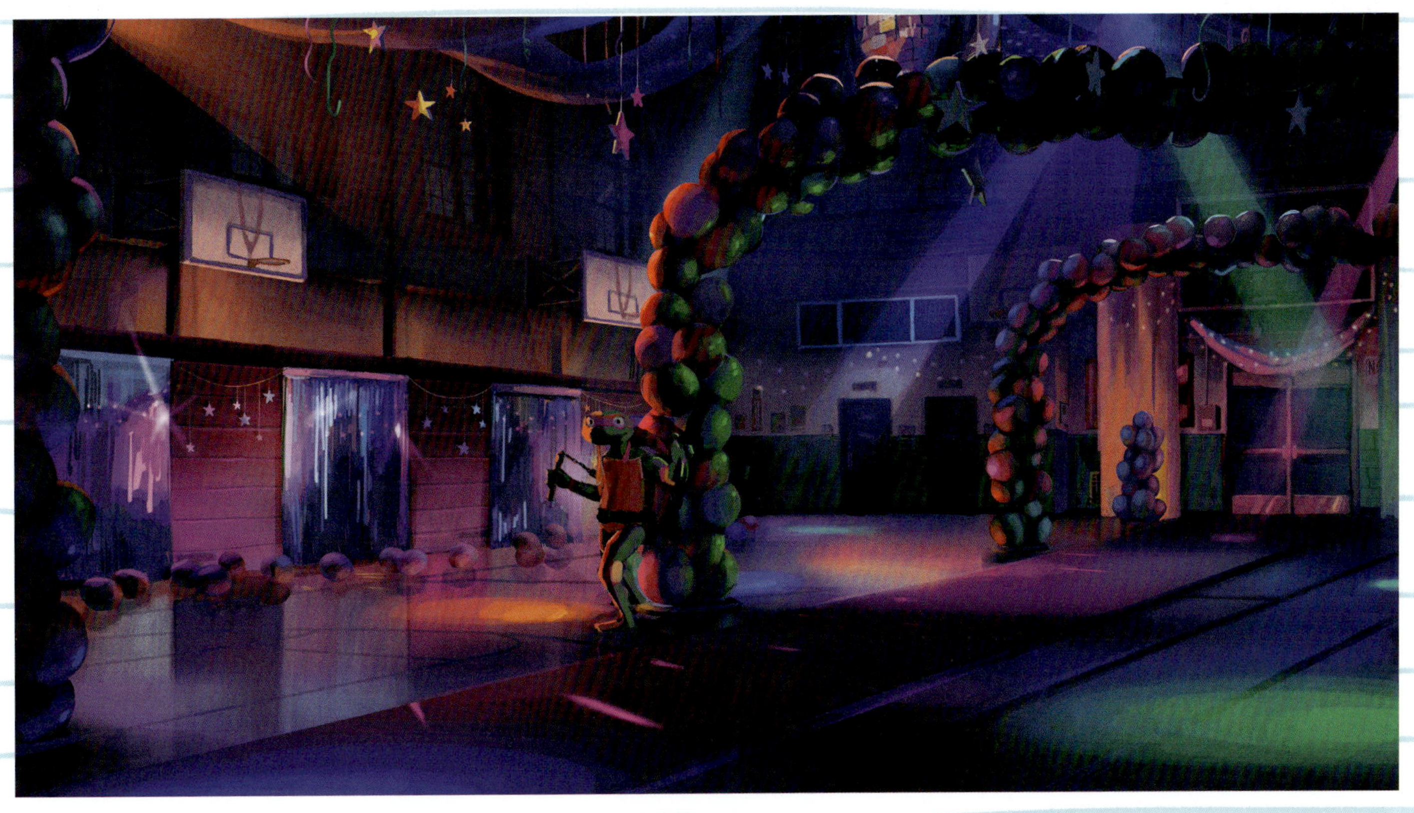

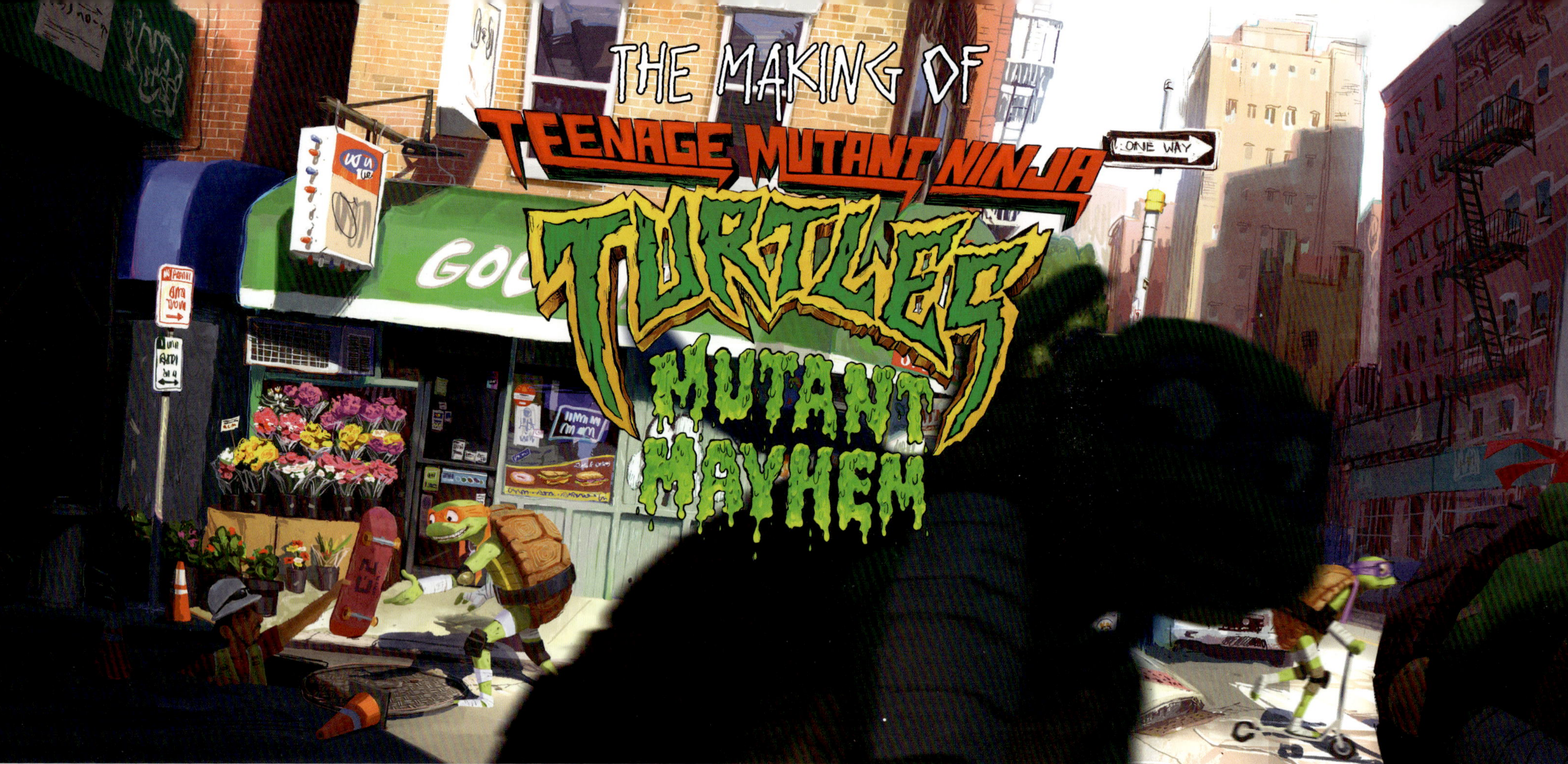

Above: Art by Kellan Jett, Alger Tam, and Yashar Kassai

FROM THE MOMENT I BEGAN WORKING ON THIS ART BOOK, I COULD TELL THERE WAS SOMETHING SPECIAL ABOUT *TEENAGE MUTANT NINJA TURTLES: MUTANT MAYHEM*.

Everyone I spoke to, and I spoke to a ton of people, was bubbling over with enthusiasm. From director Jeff Rowe to the character designers, to the head of cinematography, to the head of story, to the art directors, and way, way more, the entire production team was brimming with insight and absolutely delightful to interview. Moreover, there was a clear vision here, and everyone seemed to be on the same page about executing it.

I'm proud to get to chronicle a small fraction of its creation. For the most part, I'm going to allow the supremely talented folks to tell their stories in their own words and stay out of their way.

BY FANS FOR FANS

It's hard to overstate the sheer love for the franchise that the people working on *Mutant Mayhem* possess. Production Designer Yashar Kassai said, "I had lunchboxes, bedsheets, underwear, socks, it's the first love I could remember as a child. My parents were very generous, very willing to supply me with the Turtles goods that I wanted. Toys, especially. That was the holy grail of the franchise at the time. The endless number of characters made into toys, some of them never even present in the TV show. The show was such a good vehicle for selling toys to kids like me. I would buy ANYTHING with the Turtles name on it. Some of my fondest memories are driving to Toys 'R' Us with my mom in search of a new action figure. We'd both get genuinely excited."

Though it's not a contest, Head of Cinematography Kent Seki came to the property somewhat earlier. "I still have my copy of issue #1 of the comic book. It's all worn out, but it's the original Eastman and Laird one. I remember taking the bus when I was in middle school to the comic book shop at the Princeton Plaza in San Jose, California, walking through the comic shop, and seeing this crazy oversized comic. I thought to myself, 'Wait a minute, what's that?' I opened it up, read it, and realized it was basically a parody of Frank Miller. I remember thinking to myself, 'Oh, I'm into this!' A lot of the people on this show came from the animated version, or the Jim Henson film, or the toys, but I came to the film from the original comic."

Turtles isn't just part of their childhoods, though. It continues to inform their lives to this day. In the words of Producer Evan Goldberg, "I have a four-year-old and six-year-old boy and, I'm not exaggerating when I say this, I spend two and a half hours a day wrestling to a playlist of every *Turtles* theme song. And I am not exaggerating even one little bit. Two and a half hours every day. An hour in the morning, an hour in the afternoon, half an hour every night, of just fighting with my boys, listening on a loop. My wife cannot hear any of the theme songs ever again; she's like a shattered person forever."

Ultimately, the love that Kent, Yashar, Evan, and so many others have for the property can't help but inform the final product. In the words of Director Jeff Rowe, "*Turtles* was the first thing I ever truly loved in my life, or was a fan of. I was born in '86 so I started seeing the toys and watching the TV show probably when I was four years old. At the peak of Turtlemania, when it was impossible to find the toys from the movie, some of the best memories of my life were driving to the store with my dad and trying to find the hard-to-get movie toys like Tokka and Rahzar. Those objects, those toys, those characters meant so much to me as a kid. It was beyond just a TV show or movie. The personalities that they embodied, the fact that they were funny, the fact that they were teenagers (even though they were never played by teenagers), they seemed young and fun, and I wanted to hang out with them. And I did hang out with them in my room, alone, for many hours <laughter>. This movie sprung forth from that well of love and appreciation for the characters. We're making a modern film for modern audiences so there's a lot we had to drift away from, but the DNA is still there and we can't escape it."

PUTTING THE TEENAGE BACK IN TEENAGE MUTANT NINJA TURTLES

But what, specifically, makes *Mutant Mayhem* different from what came before? Time and again I asked the question, and time and again the answer came back the same: This is a teenage movie. "At the core of what really made this project awesome is that everyone involved is a permanent teenager," noted Evan Goldberg. "What really unlocked the art in the most exciting way was the idea that the movie was made by teenagers. So, like, the art was made by teenagers. We have Atticus Ross and Trent Reznor doing the music; they're putting it through the lens of 'We made this in our garage.' Everything we've done on this project—except for maintaining the budget, which we've been adults about—has been to look at things through the lens of a teenager."

But what exactly does it mean to have a movie "made by teenager"? As Co-Director Kyler Spears put it, "When I joined the film, there were only a few pieces of visual development art. Woodrow White had done some paintings to set the tone of the film. They had homed in on this very painterly, very sketchy, very 'drawn by a teenager' look. Yashar Kassai did a test where he modeled some city props off that design philosophy, and he offset the linework so that it looked like somehow this rendered 3D object was drawn by a 15-year-old. You could turn it 360 degrees and it was beautiful from all angles. That was it, end of discussion. We had our show style. Our vendors have done a ton of work making it so that we can have that sketchiness and imperfection, the lines on top of the 3D characters. Any time you pause the film it'll look like a piece of concept artwork, like a painting."

Below: Early Turtles concept art by Woodrow White

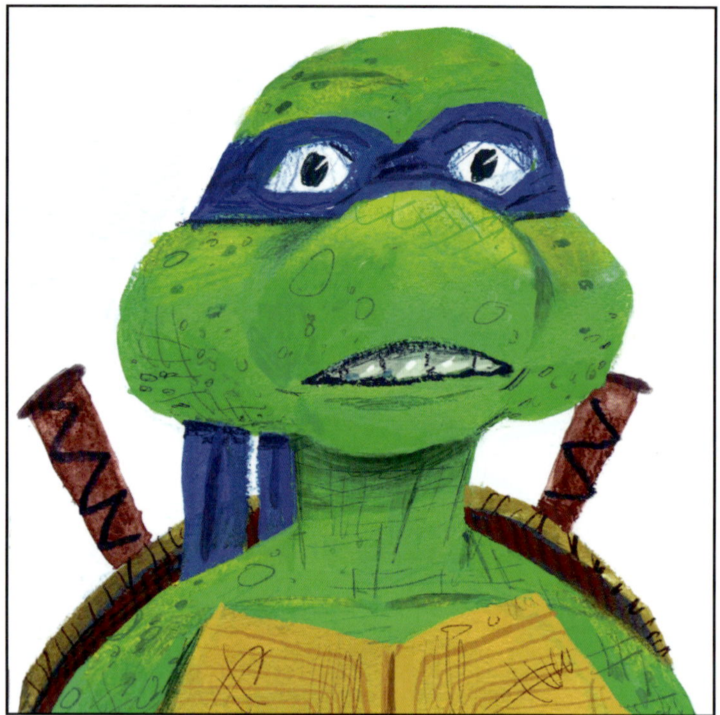

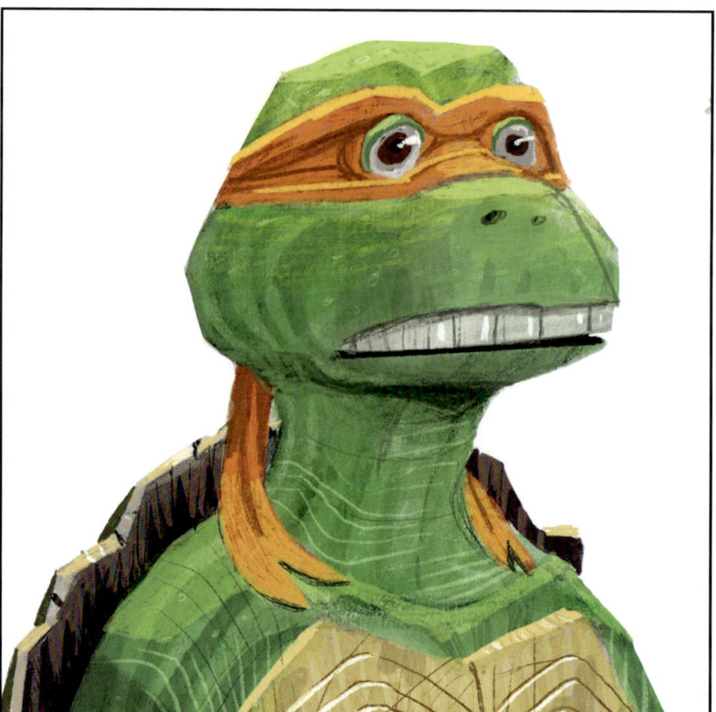

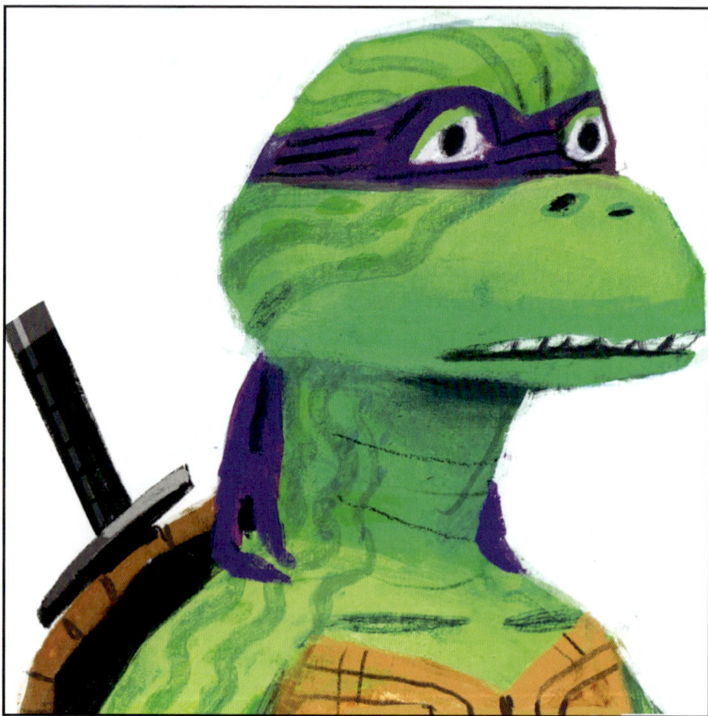

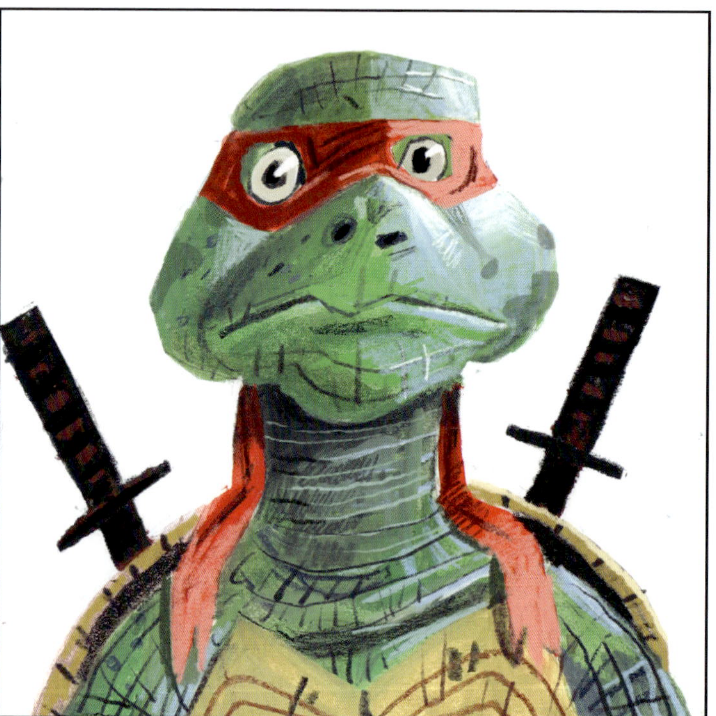

"These four early portraits were a blend of gouache paint and digital. I tried different spins on each Turtle with spots and line markings, but they felt too distracting. Looking back at these, you can see faint echoes of our shape language in the final Turtles' design. This was when I was in blue-sky territory, no path designated yet. Total shots in the dark!"

–Lead Character Designer
Woodrow White

I asked Yashar Kassai to expand on the theme, and boy howdy did he deliver. "Our director, Jeff Rowe, kept using the term 'teenage energy' in our art reviews. I really tried to be an advocate for that and so did everyone on the team. We designed things in a naive way. We drew the way a young teenager would in beginner's art class. Lines are imperfect, unstable, and timid. Beginning artists don't know why they're doing what they're doing. We really loved that. There's a charm in it because we've all drawn like that at one time. Animation isn't really touching that 'good-bad' aesthetic. We're all trained professionals, and we've been taught how to draw appealing things and paint appealing backgrounds and use appealing colors, but I think the word *appeal* can mean many different things. It was pure joy to unlearn 'good design' and draw like a 14-year-old again with the crew."

Person after person returned to this theme. Art Director Arthur Fong noted that part of his job was to remind the staff to "Forget everything you learned in art school and forget all the technique that got you to your job today. We need to start over and pretend that we're kids. *Go* back to the teenage, untrained eye, untrained way of shading. Mess things up more. Imperfection is what we're looking for on this show."

I'll let the director sum it up. "We asked, What is our touchstone? What do we want this to feel like. So we looked at high school drawings, things that we did when we were in high school, things that we found on the internet from other teenagers. There's a beautiful sincerity and intensity to the way teenagers draw. They'll really get in there, say, really shade one of the eyes, draw every eyelash, be really methodical about getting all the details in there, but then it's horribly misshapen. Your passion is betrayed by the lack of skill that you have when you're starting out drawing. You break a lot of rules. Things will be asymmetrical. Things will have weird proportions. You don't know how to draw perspective, so something like a jet fighter is kind of cheated and you see both wings at the same time even though it's a side view. We looked at a lot of those drawings and tried to break those down into their constituent parts. We asked, what are the mistakes you make when you're a teenager, and then how can we turn that into a design philosophy. And then we spent millions of dollars to make it look really, really elegant."

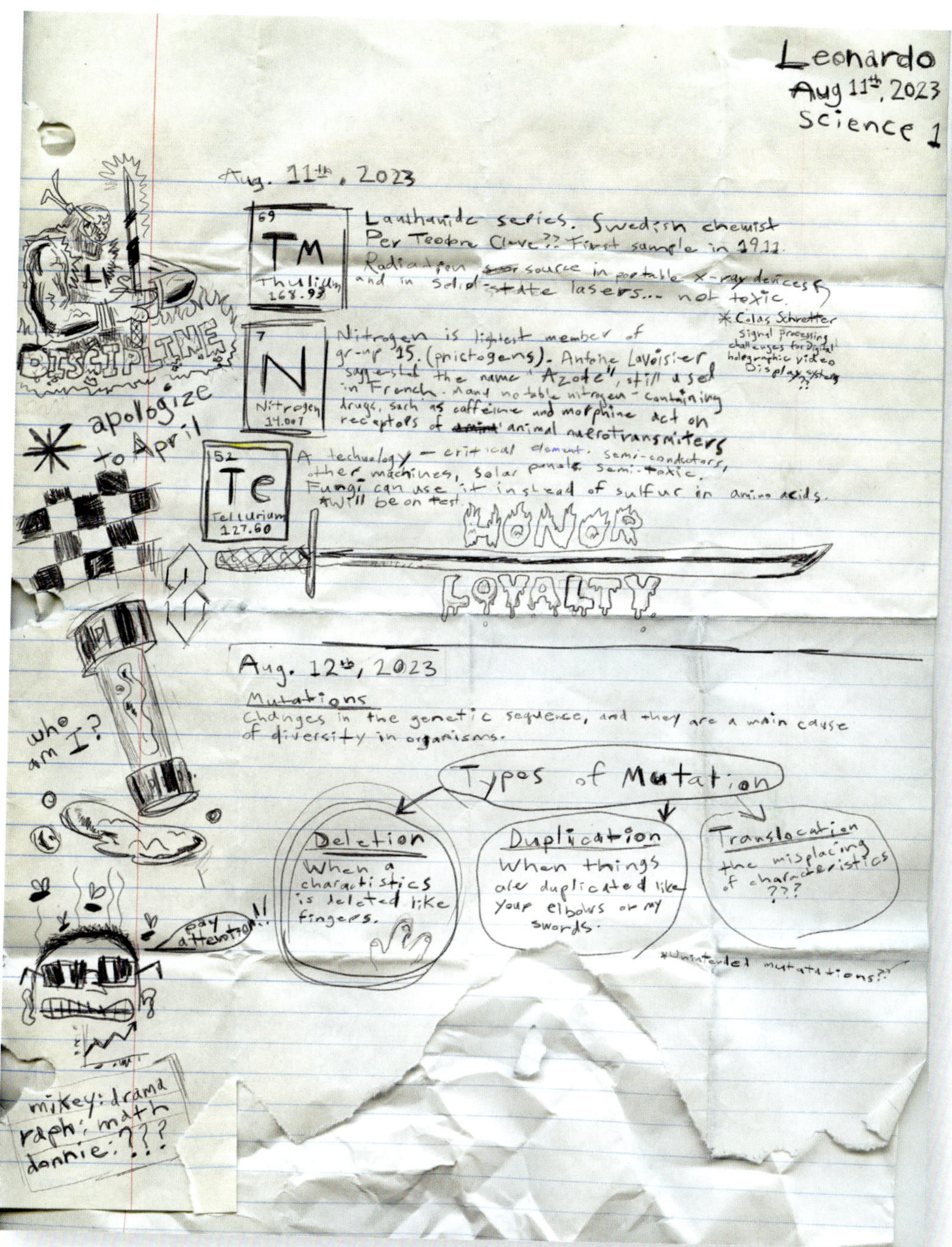

Above: Notebook page by Yashar Kassai

GIVING TEENS A VOICE

Creating a teenage movie involved more than just the visual style, however. A big component was that the Turtles should feel like authentic teens. And that meant casting actual teenagers to play the characters. Sayeth Evan Goldberg, "We very actively decided to focus more than anything on the teenage aspect. The biggest thing that we realized was that it's always been 35- to 45-year-old men doing the voices. Full-grown men. That's just crazy to us. Once we realized that, we realized art and everything aside, if we just get real kids who are actual young teenagers to voice these characters, everything will fall into place after that, and I really think it did. I think that concept is what led to art being drawn by teenagers, so to speak. Everything locked into place once we came to that conclusion."

And fall into place things did. Not only were actual teens cast to play Leo, Mikey, Donnie, and Raph but they were recorded ensemble style. And that choice unlocked everything. As Kent Seki told me, "There was a moment in the film making, sequence 380 'Watermelon Video,' the one on the rooftop with the ninja star and katana. It was initially boarded, we shot it, and then Jeff went and recorded the kids who were the actual voices, and they recorded them as an ensemble. Then we HAD to go back and reshoot it based on that recording because it was much more spontaneous. This traditional coverage of 'Oh, we go this single and then we go to that' did not fit. We had to go back in and really try to find the cinematography that matched their performance. It was an interesting place where performance really drove the camera, and the handheld really came together, and that's when we really found the movie."

Kent wasn't the only one who singled out this sequence. As Kyler Spears told it, "About six months into boarding, we finally got the boys in a room together to record, and that changed everything. From that moment on, the film was less about 'Ok, here's the script page, here's their exact lines, let's board them as they say the one thing after another.' It completely changed how we thought about boarding, how to frame the characters, how to board the interactions. Everything become more personal, down to earth. I think that really was the unlocking moment for figuring out who these characters were because we got to see them in their element being kids and interacting with each other. Not just reading lines that adults wrote but also injecting their own jokes, bouncing off of each other. That was special."

Special, indeed, but also, in the words of Evan Goldberg, a pain in the butt. "In the recording of their voices, we recorded them a lot together. It caused this wonderful, childlike energy where they're bouncing off each other. It's also something we've come to learn through this process. We realized that to actually record people in a group is pretty rare and comes with a special magic and is also a special pain in the butt for animators. We didn't really get it as we started doing it, but normally animators are used to animating one character talking while others are listening, and heroing that person for when they deliver their lines; in this, it's like four people all reacting to each other, all talking at the same time, sometimes even more. We threw them a hard thing there. They did not love that, but it made it unique."

I asked Lead Editor Greg Levitan about the unique challenges of this kind of recording. "It's amazing that we're using real teenagers for the characters of the Turtles. When we do records with them we want it to feel as realistic as possible. We bring them all in to record and they're talking over one another, just like a natural field environment would be, especially with teenagers. It's really fun and entertaining. The challenge is when we get into the post side and get into the edit. Because they're in the same room recording, there's so much overlap that we hear. What we have to do in the edit is we really fine-tune and move things. In the edit we kind of move around their dialogue, we're coming up with other ideas, we're adding a little bit more rhythm to what they've created, but we have to be very careful. It's a very challenging kind of thing we have to do in edit because we don't want to have to rerecord any lines because we really fell in love with the pace and feel of what that moment was. That was one of the most challenging things we had do, but overall, really the final product is well worth it."

I'll again give Jeff the final word. "We had to completely re-write [the film] after we started working with [the teens] and recording them ensemble, just seeing the way that they talked to each other. I think me and Seth realized that there's not a joke that we can write that will sound natural coming out of these kids, and nothing we do will be as funny as the weird stuff that they'll say on their own. It became a task of finding the film in edit, recording a lot of stuff, and then piecing together things and finding jokes instead of writing them. (We wrote a lot of jokes too of course.) I think the authenticity comes from that. It comes from their performances. We changed the way we storyboarded things too. We started editing together clips and sending them to the storyboard artists and were like 'This is what they're gonna talk like, so do the acting in the storyboard in a way that feels right for this.' The animation style, the style of performance that we went after, all of it was to support those amazing vocal performance that we were getting."

"This painting was my North Star for a while. This was the first image that Woodrow made for the film, and I was just like 'This is the movie.' These characters, the shape-language of this, the way New York looks, the amount of realism in this, the color-palate of this, the design. I was like, we have to take this and make it look like the most slick, polished thing you've ever seen. I think story-wise too, just that fish out of water sense, Donnie and Michelangelo are chatting in a very natural way, in the way you do when you walk and talk. There was a lot of personality in this that I wanted to hold on to."

—Director Jeff Rowe

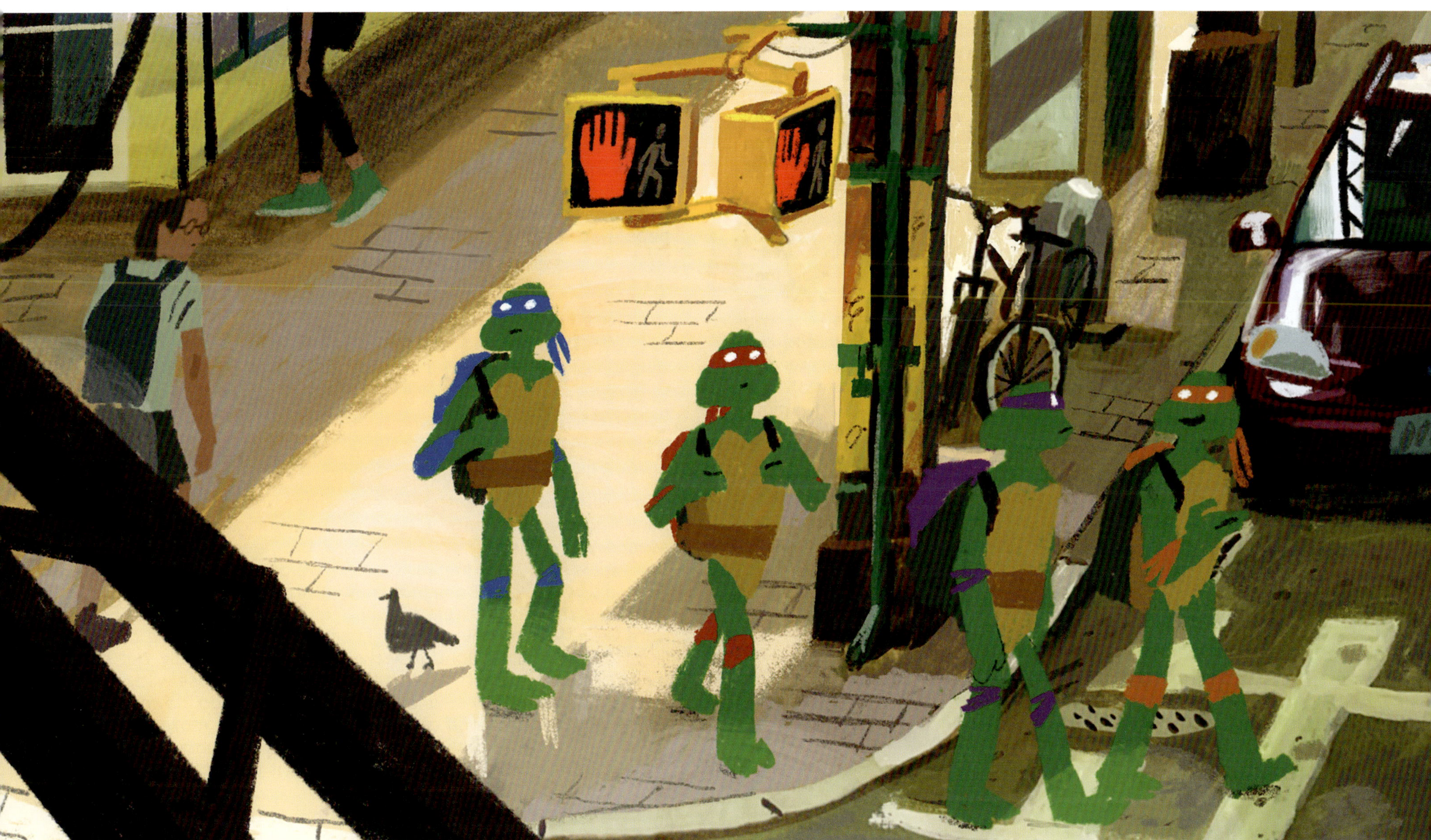

Above: Early concept art by Woodrow White

"The Turtles crossing the street was the first art I ever made for the film, back when it was just Jeff and I throwing ideas at the wall to see what would stick. Many elements have changed and stylistic choices introduced since, but that image was our first Rosetta Stone that informed the look of the film. I painted multiple scenes of just the four brothers hanging out in New York, per Jeff's instruction. Not much drama, just them casually exploring the city. I had a lot of mellow jazz in the background while painting. I was attempting to capture that same urban calmness seen in *Hey Arnold!*"

—Lead Character Designer Woodrow White

CRAZY AMBITIOUS

The idea of pursuing challenging avenues only to reap artistic dividends was a recurring one. Yashar Kassai noted that part of a production designer's job was to resolve "design conundrums." When I asked him for an example of one, he was ready to go. "Depth of field. A typical thing that happens with any good, quality camera. The subject is in focus and the background falls out of focus. Our show style is so imperfect and hand drawn that a standard camera blur didn't work. We had to create something that felt in line with the world we'd defined. The solution was making backgrounds devolve into a smudged and pencil driven mess. Developing that broke our brains a little bit."

The depth of field solution came from Art Director (Environments) Tiffany Lam Almack. "Figuring out how these buildings would look in a 3D space was initially challenging. When you look upwards, typically what you would do to give the illusion of depth is to use a blur effect. But that kind of perfect CG look didn't match our show style. Instead, we developed a system where the further the buildings got in x, y, or z space, the crazier the scribbles got. The windows on the tenth floor and up would get increasingly more abstract and more messy, breaking the silhouette. I think that really helped with the style of the movie."

Kent Seki spoke at length about the ambitious simulated camera work. "Much of what we tried to do was make the camera feel real. Even though it's an animated film that looks very painterly, we wanted the cameras to feel like actual real cameras. It was the juxtaposition of the obviously artificial, hand-created image against a camera that felt grounded in reality that created our cinematography. We'd often discuss 'How would we shoot that?' 'Oh, we would shoot that on a steady cam. It would be on a dolly track. This would be hand-held.' Even the use of whip-pans. A whip-pan is a common animated thing, you whip from one thing to another; they had to feel like a real live-action shot in-camera whip-pans." He took inspiration from *La La Land's* camera work. "You can see how the camera dips a little bit as he grabs it and operates it over. So, we built into the camera whips these little imperfections. Or if we're dollying in on a shot, we'd add a little bit of camera bounce as if the weight of the camera is effecting the boom arm. These little things, adding that imperfection, are hard to do in CG, and that's what we strove to do."

It seemed to be a moving target. As Head of Story Gabriel Lin put it, "Visually and stylistically, it's way different from anything I've ever worked on. The art team members are so talented. We'd be in meetings where we're discussing concept stuff, there'd be visual ideas for how the film could look. The next week the film might be completely different."

Character Designer James A. Castillo summed it up perfectly. "One of the things that's both beautiful and frustrating about my job, people in the art department tend to work really early on movies. We see the potential, we see the passion. Directors, producers, writers are really full-on. Then a year or two happens and the movie is made. I just saw the trailer for the first time, and I had a very genuine reaction because I have not seen anything of this movie for over a year. My reaction was probably very close to any other Turtles fan out there. I was happily surprised that something this risky and this visually appealing and interesting and ground-breaking is being pushed so high up, to compete with any other Hollywood movie. Especially because I know the people who made it, and I know that they're all the misfits, the punks, all the people who wanted to do something that was a little bit more irreverent, a little bit more fun, a little bit more grotesque. The spirit of the movie was really rebellious. Seeing the trailer makes me feel that these people were not kidding when I was talking to them a couple of years ago. They really meant it."

A FISTFUL OF MUTANTS

If *teenage* was the primary descriptor being served, surely *mutant* would be the secondary one. The movie is called *Mutant Mayhem,* after all. I asked Evan Goldberg where the name came from. "I think I came up with *Mutant Mayhem.* We originally called it *Mutant Madness* and then *The Multiverse of Madness* was announced, and then we were like, 'Dammit!' So then we pivoted to *Mutant Mayhem.* A huge part of the film is that we went through a bunch of different, iterations and then started looked at the toys from the '80s. We were like, 'Wait a minute here!' There are just incredible characters like Ray Fillet and Mondo Gecko who do not usually get put into these projects and they look nuts! They all had these wild, different, exciting, colorful looks, and so we decided to go down that path. Once we started looking at them, we realized the more mutants, the better. And then we realized the whole thing was about mutants, and it does end in literal mutant mayhem. So it just fit."

It was a truly organic process. Jeff Rowe remarked that "We started designing [the mutants] before we even had a place for them in the movie. We had Woodrow [White], who is an amazing designer and does these incredible mixed media 2D drawings of the characters that were a huge inspiration to the art team early on. Some of those came from us thinking 'Wouldn't it be cool if we had Woodrow design some of these mutants? I don't know, let's pretend we're putting Ray Fillet in the film. Woodrow, design it!' And then he would design it and we would be like 'That's the coolest design I've ever seen. I guess we have to write Ray Fillet into the movie now.' And that kind of became the process."

"The story really shifted in the writing of it," Jeff continued. "It was a very different movie for the first year and a half, two years, and then we completely pivoted. Partly to embrace a lot of the artwork that the team was doing. We would show Seth [Rogen] stuff and he would be like 'These mutant designs are so cool. I guess we should put more mutants in the movie.' And then we would rewrite the movie to put more mutants in. The design choices really informed the writing in a lot of places, which happens sometimes in animation but not always. It was exciting."

A TEAM EFFORT

Making something so genuinely exciting, ambitious, new, and unique takes many, many hands. Everyone involved was effusive with praise for, well, everyone else involved. Over and over, people pointed to Jeff Rowe as a driving force behind the film. As Evan Goldberg tells it, "The key to everything is Jeff Rowe, the director. He really is the superstar talent on this project." Indeed, many of the key creatives worked with him on *The Mitchells vs. the Machines,* which he co-directed.

Evan and his partner at Point Grey, the incomparable Seth Rogen, also received their share of praise. Greg Levitan had a quite representative response about what made this movie fun to work on. "All in all, it was very collaborative in trying to make this a very different Ninja Turtle movie. Having strong voices on the Point Grey side with Seth Rogen really helped. Jeff has been a godsend, taking this all the way through with his vision. Every department has been amazing from the art to our production team, doing records, layout, every aspect. It's really fun. Even though I wasn't a Turtles fan coming into the movie, the majority of people on this crew are, so it's really fun to feel that energy that they bring because they are true fans of the franchise. I just can't wait for this to be finished and shown. It's such a beautiful film; the look of it is fantastic. Personally, it's a nice feeling, too, because *The Mitchells vs. the Machines* didn't make it to the big screen because of the pandemic, so this'll be a nice treat in my personal journey as editor, that this movie is going to come out on the big screen."

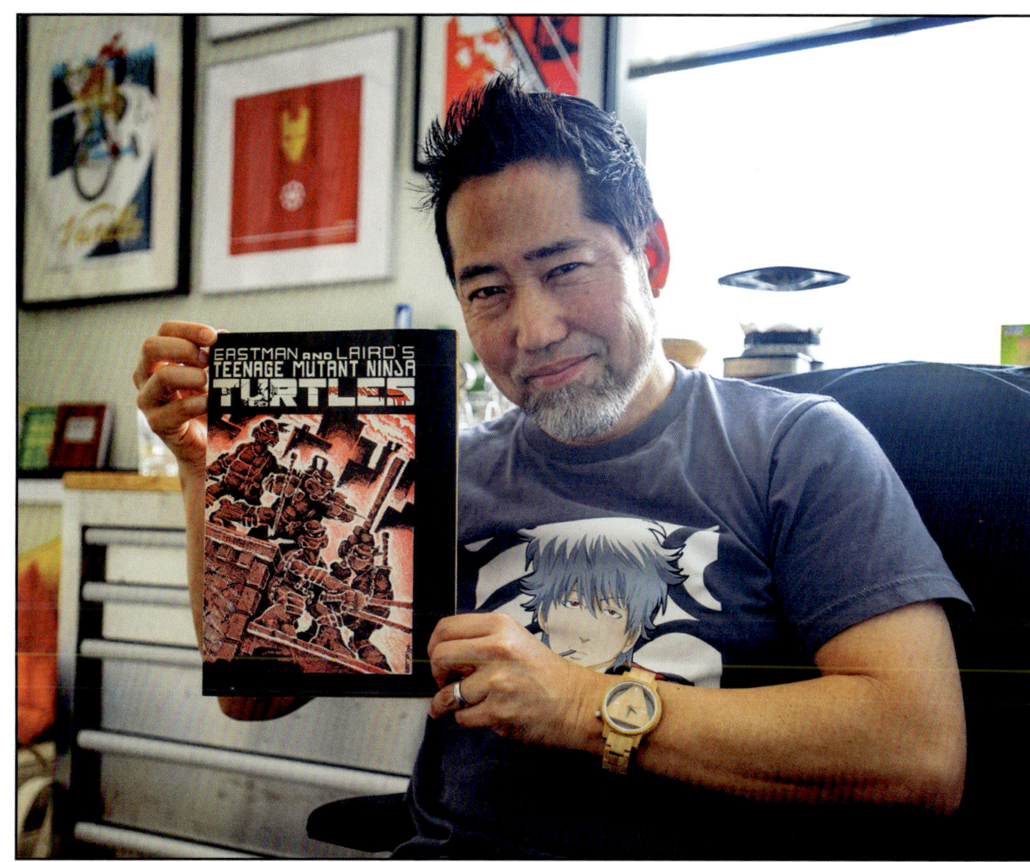

Head of Cinematography Kent Seki with his copy of *TMNT* #1.

Gabriel Lin shared similar sentiments. "The team that Jeff and Kyler managed to assemble was genuinely one of the funnest teams I've ever worked with. It's a high that I've only just recently rolled off of. Every other team is not as cool as this team, and I don't wanna go back. I hope the movie does well so we can get the team back together because it was so fun. Everyone seemed to get each other. The sense of humor was on point. One person would crack a joke of an idea and everyone else would be like, 'Yeah yeah, or, like, we could do this.' It was terrific working with everyone on this production. It's something I've not experience before."

Overall, that collaboration and level of care shows in just about every aspect of the film. I'll end with an observation from Evan Goldberg. "We just wanted to do right by the project. If I am responsible for a bad *Ninja Turtles* I will be very upset."

I don't think you need to worry, Evan.

-Jim Sorenson

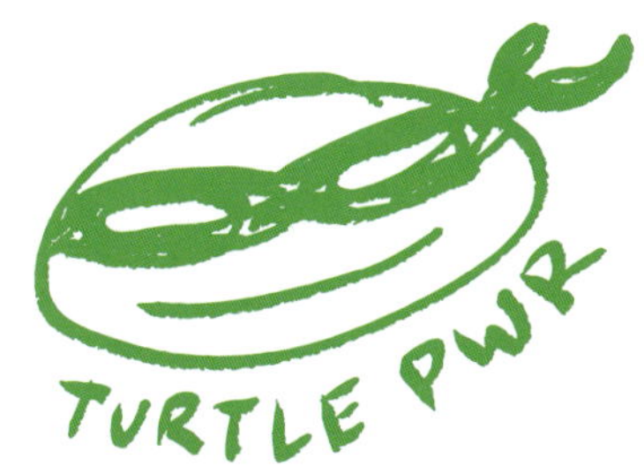

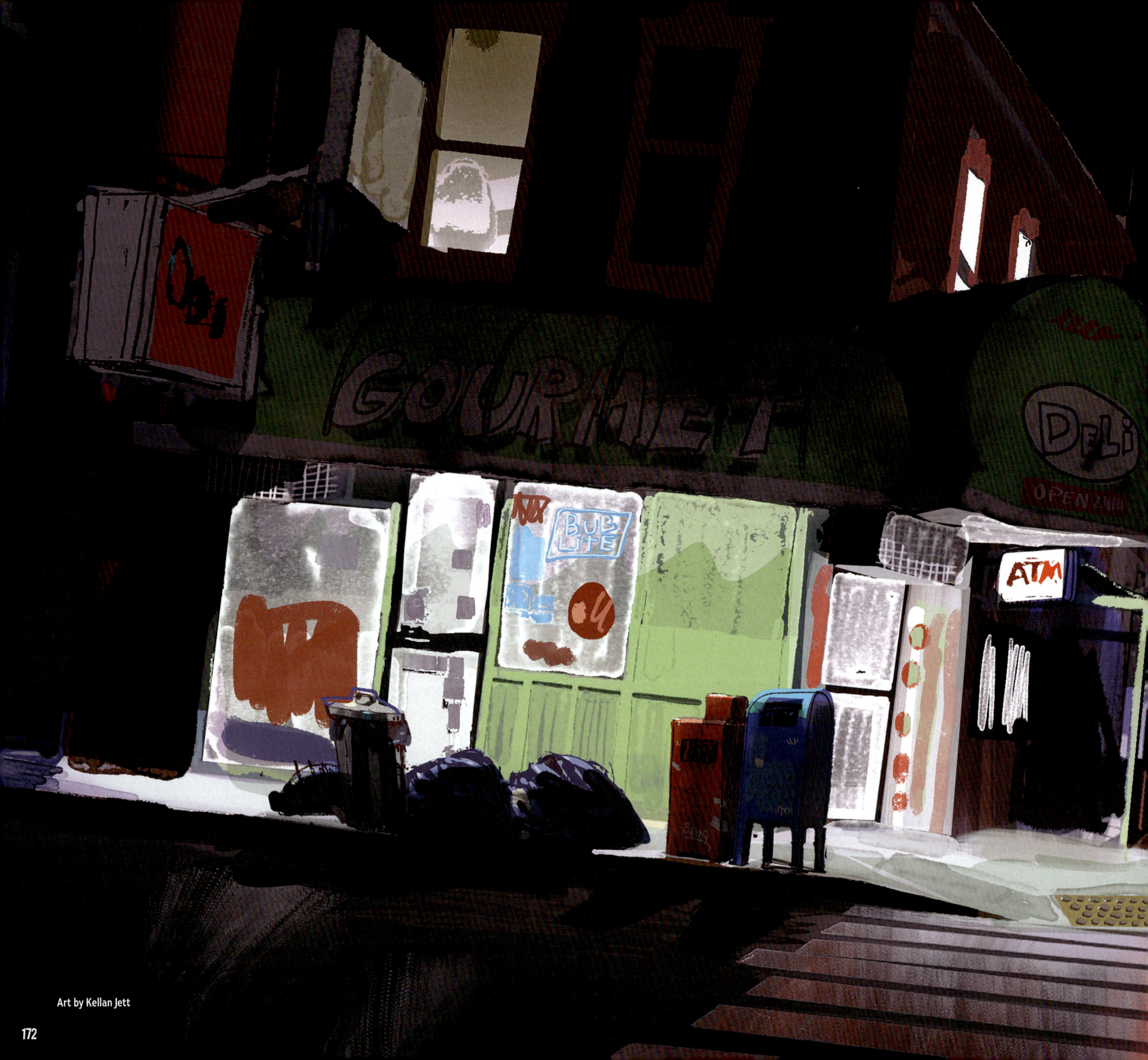

Art by Kellan Jett

ACKNOWLEDGMENTS

As a fan of TMNT for many years, pulling together *The Art of Teenage Mutant Ninja Turtles: Mutant Mayhem* has been a true joy for me. Like most things worth doing, I could never have done it alone.

I want to extend a huge thank you to everyone who worked on the film who made the time to help make this book all that it could be: Producers Seth Rogen and Evan Goldberg, Director Jeff Rowe, Co-Director Kyler Spears, Production Designer Yashar Kassai, Art Directors Arthur Fong and Tiffany Lam Almack, Visual Development Artist Lauren Airriess, Head of Cinematography/Previsualization Kent Seki, Lead Editor Greg Levitan, Head of Story Gabriel Lin, and Character Designers Woodrow White and James A. Castillo. I'd also like to thank Jeff Whitman, Jason McConnell, Lukas Williams, Christopher Zdenek, Ramsey Naito, Matthew Digiaimo Stephanie Keider, and especially Ryan Fragomeni for coordinating everything. Thank you to Peter Laird and Kevin Eastman for creating the TMNT and their continued contributions to their growing legacy.

Thanks to David Bishop for being an unofficial copy editor and sounding board, and to TMNT superfan Michele Ivey for fact-checking my brief history of the brand. I also want to extend my gratitude to my editor, Alonzo Simon, for giving me my first chance to work professionally on *Turtles* and to my wife, Ming-Li, and son, James, for putting up with my long working hours. And finally, thank you for reading all the way to the end.

–Jim Sorenson

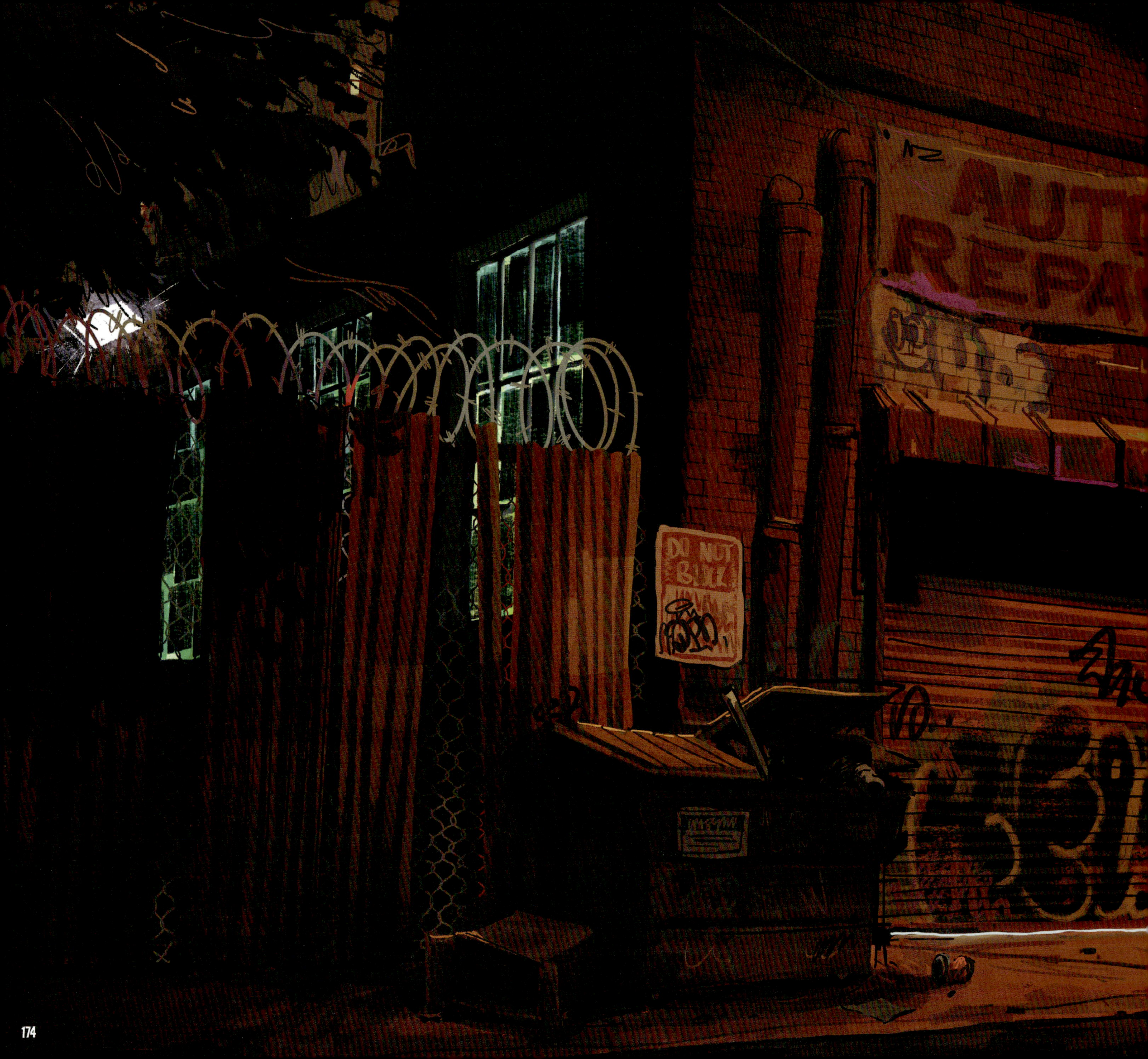

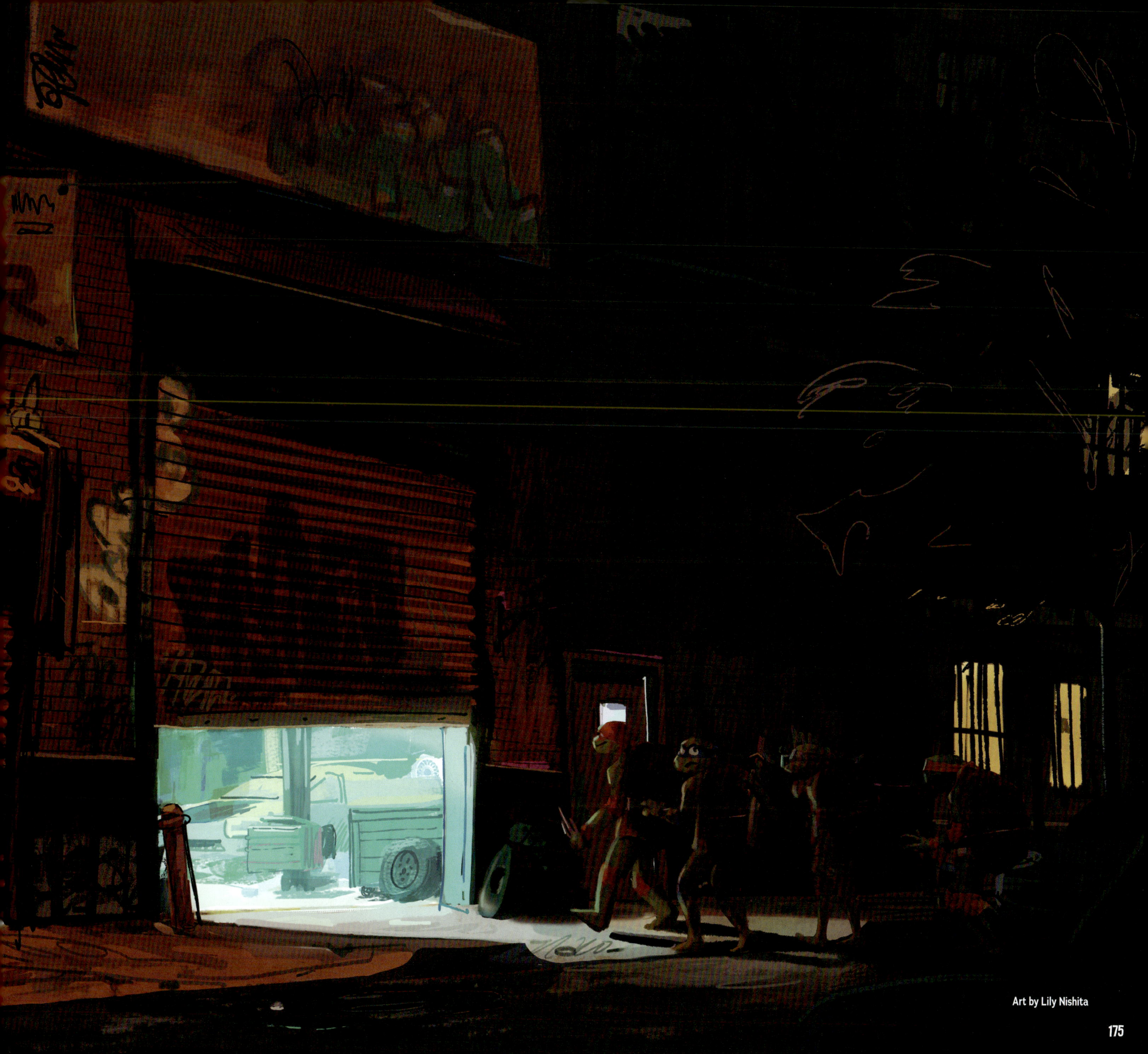

Art by Lily Nishita

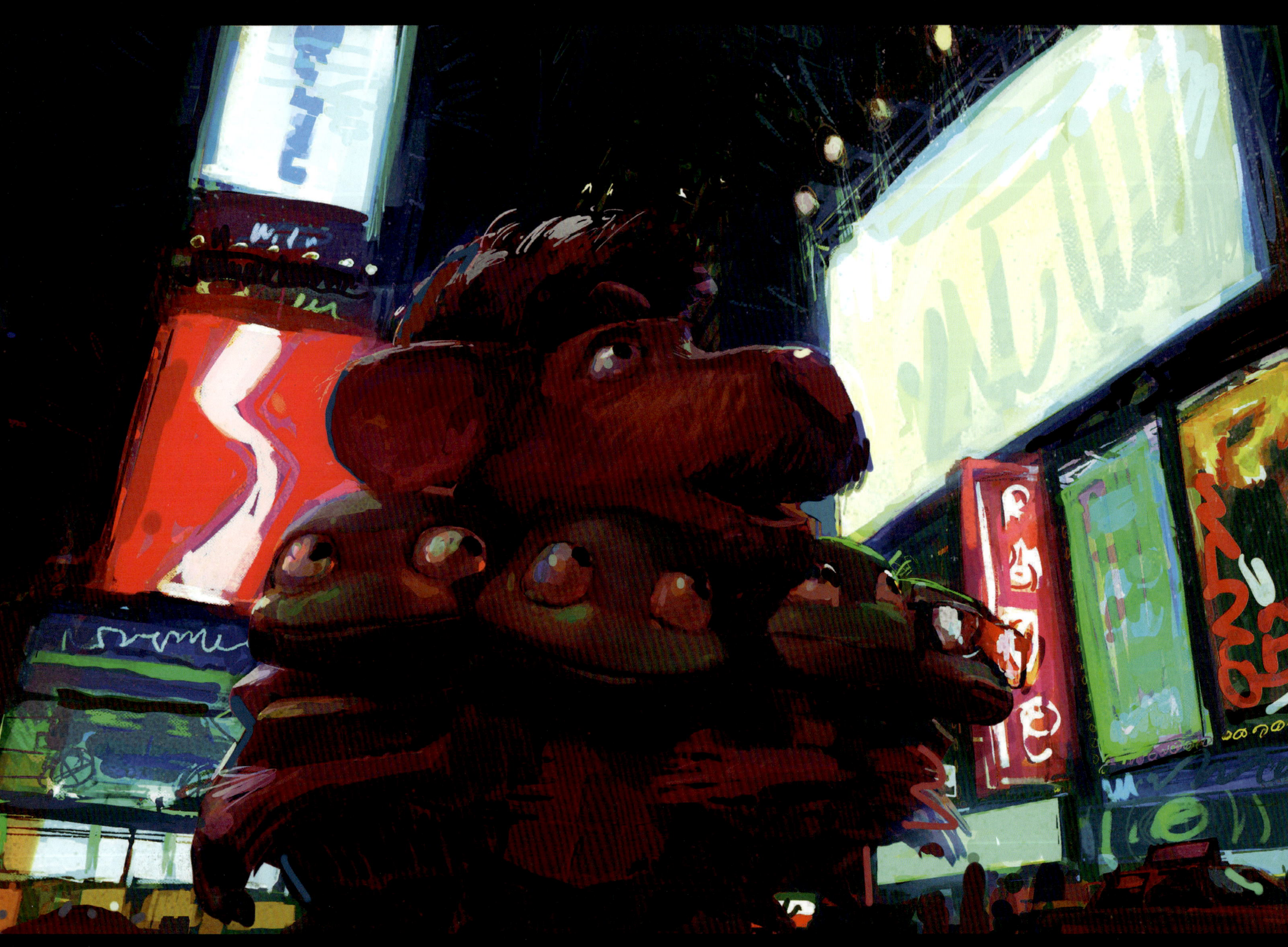

Art by David Bleich and Yashar Kassai

L
D
M

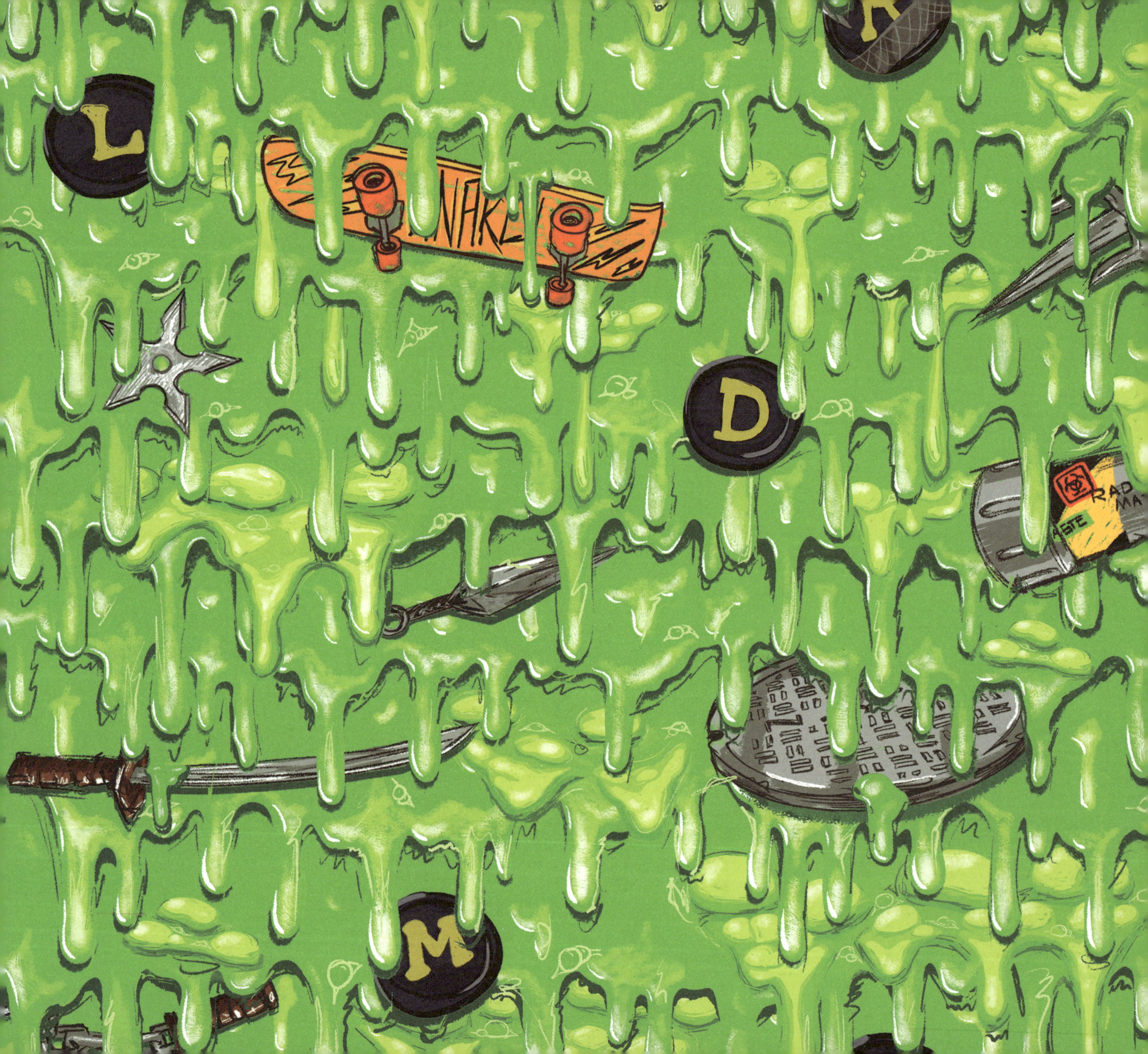
L
D
M